The Book of Jewish Prayers in English

Foreword by

Tzvee Zahavy

English translations of the Jewish prayers are based on *The Standard Prayer Book, Authorized English Translation*, Enlarged American Edition, New York, 1915, as translated by Rev. S. Singer.

PRINT EDITION

About the Author

Tzvee Zahavy received his rabbinic ordination at Yeshiva University and his PhD at Brown University. He taught as a distinguished professor at the University of Minnesota and at the Jewish Theological Seminary of America. He is the author of many books and articles on Judaism including these Kindle and print editions:

- God's Favorite Prayers
- Babylonian Talmud Tractate Hullin
- Judaism
- The Origins of Jewish Prayers
- Eleazar: Rabbi, Priest, Patriarch
- Talmud Yerushalmi Berakhot
- Rashi: The Greatest Exegete

Dedication

In loving memory of my father Rabbi Dr. Zev Zahavy, a leading rabbi of his generation, a masterful preacher and teacher and a spiritual beacon to his family, friends and congregants, and to my mother Edith Zahavy, a noted educator and a beloved wife and mother

They cherished their prayers

Contents

FOREWORD

Prayer as Visualization

In this foreword, I describe several distinct visualizations that I recognize as applicable to the Jewish prayers that follow in this book. By the term prayers, I mean the texts recited by Jews in religious ritual contexts. By the term visualizations, I mean the formation of mental visual images of a place and time, of a narrative activity or scene, or of an inner disposition. The goals of picturing these images in your mind's eye can include: (1) professed communication with God, articulation of common religious values for (2) personal satisfaction or for (3) the sake of social solidarity, or (4) attainment of altered inner emotional states or moods.

The Basis of Prayer

Jews who engage in prayer agree that they picture their acts of recitation of prayer texts as a dialogue with God. The former Chief Rabbi of the British Empire, Sir Jonathan Sacks, summed this up saying, "Prayer is the language of the soul in conversation with God. It is the most intimate gesture of the religious life, and the most transformative." See his essay introduction to the *Koren Sacks Siddur* (Jerusalem, 2009) entitled, "Understanding Jewish Prayer."

Sacks characterized the Jewish prayer book saying, "The Siddur is the choral symphony the covenantal people has sung to God across forty centuries from the days of the patriarchs until the present day." He called it a "calibrated harmony."

This depiction of prayer articulated by Sacks and many others before him is the general and foundational meta-visualization of all acts of prayer, the contextual background music in which I find the more detailed and specific visualizations that I discuss in this foreword.

Visualization Exercises

Ancient rabbis had many thoughts and prescriptions on the matters of visualizations in prayer itself. They expressed them in their own idiom through direct teachings and indirectly by formulating their rituals in certain ways.

A basic assumption in what the rabbis taught is that a person can and should use visualizations to alter his consciousness and to recite the different prayers. Starting way back in antiquity, praying Jews engaged in a series of visualization exercises three times a day.

These are some of the varied visualizations that I associate with several major Jewish prayers.

The *scribal visualization* is the state of mind you need to attain when you study texts, or when you write new materials, or when you add columns of numbers, or when you conduct inventories. It is the target kavvanah for the Shema prayer, for which many Jews sit and shade their eyes so they may concentrate on reciting the designated Torah texts.

The *priestly visualization* is the state of mind you need to attain when you comport yourself for a public ritual or pageant. It is the target kavvanah for the Amidah, where the swaying that some practice is like a marching in place. You do not want to get out of step as you move through the procession of praises, petitions and thanksgivings of the multi-part Amidah prayer.

The *mystical visualization* is the state of mind you need to attain to imagine yourself in another place, when your praying carries you off to the heavens in search of God or back in time to our momentous Israelite historical episodes. It is the target kavvanah for the many passages of the prayers which invoke the heavenly angels or recount the great miracles in our past, such as the crossing of the Red Sea and the revelation at Sinai.

The *triumphal visualization* is the state of mind you need to attain to imagine yourself victorious in a grand global historical contest. It is the target kavvanah for the Alenu which declares the ultimate triumph of the one true God at the end of time.

The *performative-mindful visualization* is the state of mind you need to attain when you perform a personal ritual act. It is the target kavvanah for the many mitzvoth that a Jew performs throughout his or her life and for the recitation of blessings. Truly, all of these enumerated visualizations are mindful in their own ways. But the performative-mindful imagination takes sharp account for the here and now, the immediate physical facts of one's present circumstances, as for example at the wedding canopy, in taking the lulav and etrog, in lighting the Hanukkah menorah, the Shabbat candles, blessing the challah and in other ritual instances.

The *compassionate-mindful visualization* is the state of mind that you seek to attain when reciting such prayers as the Tahanun, Grace after Meals or the Kol Nidre service—exercises in imagining a bond of loving-kindness with God, with oneself, and with other people.

I discuss next at greater length these visualizations that I identify with their respective prayers.

The Scribal Visualization: Shema

The Mishnah discusses how to recite the short daily prayer of three paragraphs, called the Shema. The rabbis prescribe how to act while you recite the texts and they debated the finer nuances of how one must ideate and when one may talk while engaged in the recitation:

> "At the breaks [between the paragraphs of the Shema] one may extend a greeting [to his associate] out of respect, and respond [to a greeting which was extended to him]."
> "And in the middle [of reciting a paragraph] one may extend a greeting out of fear [of a person] and respond," the words of R. Meir.
> R. Judah says, "In the middle [of reciting a paragraph] one may extend a greeting out of fear and respond out of respect.
> "At the breaks [between reciting the paragraphs] one may greet out of respect and respond to the greetings of any man." (Mishnah Berakhot 2:1)

At first glance I was satisfied to explain that this liturgical law is the rabbis' way of discussing part of a religious ritual that they called kavvanah. I concluded that this is how the ancients talked about the visualization and concentration we need to attain so as to add solemnity to a prayer ritual.

But it vexed me that they spoke about greetings when they wanted to prescribe visualization necessary for the prayer, until this happened.

While working one day at my computer, writing about Jewish prayer, my wife came in to tell me that she was going out to appointments and wanted me to know her plans for the day.

"Just a minute," I said. "I do want to hear what you are saying. Please just let me concentrate to finish writing this paragraph."

At that moment it became clear to me that when the rabbis spoke about kavvanah for reciting the Shema, they used a model of concentration that was familiar to a writer—to a person who is engaged in textual work, to a scholar sitting at his desk and trying to think through his complete thoughts.

In general terms, scribes work as follows. A writer needs to focus on composing a paragraph from beginning to end. Similarly, an accountant needs to finish scanning and calculating a column of numbers from top to bottom. A lawyer must complete the reasoning of the steps of an argument all the way through. A programmer must reach the end of writing a complex routine of computer code. All of those professions fit into the category of a reflective writing and calculating worker—which I roll up into the shorthand label "scribe."

The Priestly Visualization: Amidah

The Mishnah prescribes as follows for reciting the Amidah prayer:

> One may stand to pray only with a solemn frame of mind.
> The early pious people tarried a while before they would pray, so that they could direct their hearts to the omnipresent God.
> While one is praying, even if the king greets him, he may not respond.
> Even if a serpent is entwined around his heel, he many not interrupt his prayer. (Mishnah Berakhot 5:1)

At first glance I was satisfied to observe that this liturgical law spoke in rabbinic idiom to prescribe the correct intensity-level of the *kavvanah*—the visualization—for this prayer. Mishnah tells us that, because the Amidah is a more solemn prayer than the Shema, you need to concentrate more intensely when you recite it.

But it vexed me that the rabbis prescribed this kind of concentration and not some other. Why did they set forth these specifications regarding visualization for the person who is reciting the Amidah? And then this happened.

One day I was preparing for a lecture that I was to give about the meanings and purposes of the Amidah. I searched for a picture to put on a PowerPoint presentation, looking for a pose that illustrated the right kavvanah for this prayer. I did not want to insert an image of a man standing in prayer and wrapped around in a tallit. That seemed to be a redundant cliché that did not illuminate meaning.

I wondered what image would exhibit a person so intent and disciplined that he would not move, no matter how much distraction came into the context of his surroundings? And that is when I realized what this prayer-visualization demanded. I typed "palace guard" into Google's image search engine. I found and copied a picture of a stereotypical guard from Buckingham Palace in London, dressed in his red and black uniform and standing at attention. I inserted that graphic into my presentation.

I wanted to show the substance of the visualization—that requires a frame of mind of discipline and obedience for the recitation of the Amidah. This means that the person reciting the prayer needs to seek out a martial kind of self-possession, standing with erect posture, feet together, facing Jerusalem as specified by the rules for reciting this prayer. The person needs to bow at the proper intervals, in keeping with his martial drill.

The Mishnah instructs us that not even a coiled serpent at his heel be allowed to distract a person during his recitation of the Amidah prayer; even if a serpent is nearby, he shall not pause in his recitation. That means that through this priestly visualization he sees himself in authority, in soldierly control of his emotions and consciousness—not consequentially ecstatic or meditative in any particular way, and yet guarded against distraction.

The visualization that one must strive for in reciting the Amidah is of a certain character and nature. Like the palace guard, the person who is engaged in this prayer visualizes a military personality, intent on particularized activities. He obeys what he is commanded to obey and deliberately ignores all other noises or intrusions into his material context.

The Mystical Visualization: Kaddish

One prominent Kaddish recited in the synagogue is the mourner's Kaddish (Yatom), the one that is employed as a mourner's doxology, a praise of God. The practice of associating this prayer with a mourner first appears in the thirteenth century. The synagogue authorities endorsed the custom that mourners during the first eleven months after losing a close relative ought to rise and recite a Kaddish on their own. In the case of this Kaddish Yatom, the mourner rises in his place in the synagogue and recites the doxology at a few appointed times in the daily, Sabbath, and festival services.

The prayer is a fitting mystical visualization for the mourner who recites it. It is a mystical prayer litany of the right words of praise of God in the correct order. The mystical visualization of the Kaddish arises out of the knowledge that those lines that cite for us the adoration of God are imagined to be identical to the praises that are recited by the angels in heaven.

Reciting the Kaddish provides an appropriate vicarious association for the mourner—to stand and recite a prayer on behalf of the departed souls of the dead:

> Magnified and sanctified
> may his great name be

in the world he created by his will.
May he establish his kingdom
in your lifetime and in your days,
and in the lifetime of all the house of Israel,
swiftly and soon—and say: Amen.
May his great name be blessed forever and all time.
Blessed and praised, glorified and exalted,
raised and honored, uplifted and lauded
be the name of the Holy One, blessed be he,
beyond any blessing, song, praise and consolation
uttered in the world—and say: Amen
May there be great peace from heaven,
and life for us and for all Israel—and say: Amen.
May he who makes peace in his high places,
make peace for us and for all Israel—and say: Amen.
(Koren Siddur, p. 178)

This lilting and poetic passage does have a certain unique cadence, yet it is a standard glorification of God, adding nothing about death or dying or the deceased. I posit that this prayer is especially apropos for a mourner because reciting this heavenly angelic Aramaic praise is an epitome of a mystic's liturgy. It is a stand-in visualization by the mourner on behalf of the departed loved one. The mourner stands in place in the synagogue and recites the words.

But acting in the mode of the mystic, through the appropriate visualization of the prayer, the mourner achieves a level of mystical prayer, not just addressing God with the outpourings of personal anxiety and vexation, but imagining that he or she is standing aloft in heaven, representing the soul of her beloved departed, knocking on heaven's door to seek entry for that spirit into a secure, eternal place close to the divine light and near the warmth of God.

The visualization for mystical prayer requires that one who is addressing God from his or her pew, use the words authorized by the angels on behalf of the deceased. The visualization enables for the person who recites it to engage in an imagined ascent to heaven to plead there for the soul of the departed.

The Triumphal Visualization: Alenu

Performing on the world's center stage, the reciter of Alenu lets us know that he is a star member of the cast of the Chosen People. He is a confident monotheist who has an exciting story. As he tells it, the gods now are engaged in a continual conflict and competition. And, then, at some point in the future, there will be a final match when idolatry will lose. The victory will go to the one true God over his false competitors.

The person visualizing triumph recites the words that exhort everyone in the synagogue simultaneously with both vivid and vague visions of a cosmic struggle in heaven and on Earth. The Alenu tells us about the coming state of affairs for the Jewish people. Our destiny will be fulfilled at the end of time in a promised culmination.

This drama is proposed in the first section of the prayer:

> It is our duty to praise the Lord of all things,
> to ascribe greatness to him who formed the world in the beginning,
> since he has not made us like the nations of other lands,
> and has not placed us like other families of the earth,
> since he has not assigned unto us a portion as unto them,
> nor a lot as unto all their multitude.
> For we bend the knee and offer worship and thanks before the supreme King of kings, the Holy One, blessed be he,
> who stretched forth the heavens and laid the foundations of the earth,
> the seat of whose glory is in the heavens above,
> and the abode of whose might is in the loftiest heights.
> He is our God; there is none else: in truth he is our King; there is none besides him;
> as it is written in his Torah, "And you shall know this day, and lay it to your heart that the Lord he is God in heaven above and upon the earth beneath: there is none else." (Koren Siddur, p. 180)

Visualizing in this mode, the celebrant cheers on, urging his values on others like that of a team coach or captain in a locker room before a crucial game. However, there is an important vagary in this imagery. This is not yet a real game. In his synagogue prayers, the triumphal monotheist does not encourage and exhort his team of worshippers to go out in the street to trample the identified competing teams. The conclusion of the Aleinu prayer finally and forcefully proclaims the awaited details:

> We therefore hope in you, O Lord our God,
> that we may speedily behold the glory of your might,
> when you will remove the abominations from the earth,
> and the idols will be utterly cut off,
> when the world will be perfected under the kingdom of the Almighty,
> and all the children of flesh will call upon your name,
> when you will turn unto yourself all the wicked of the earth.
>
> Let all the inhabitants of the world perceive and know that unto you every knee must bow, every tongue must swear.
>
> Before you, O Lord our God, let them bow and fall;
> and unto your glorious name let them give honor;
> let them all accept the yoke of your kingdom,
> and do you reign over them speedily, and forever and ever.

For the kingdom is yours, and to all eternity you will reign in glory;
as it is written in your Torah, "The Lord shall reign forever and ever."

And it is said, "And the Lord shall be king over all the earth: in that day shall the Lord be One, and his name One."

The visualization that this prayer calls forth in the liturgy is of a figurative competition. It calls upon the person who recites the prayer to imagine that the ultimate showdown is near, to conjure a vision of the minutes ticking down at the close of the game. This vividly imagined visualization speaks of the end of the struggle at the end of time when the ultimate victory of the team of the one true God over the team of the false Gods is at hand.

The Performative-Mindful Visualization: Blessings

The fixed opening phrase of a berakhah, "Blessed are you O Lord, our God, King of the Universe," semantically expresses the speaker's intention to bestow good wishes upon God or to exalt God, who is referred to in the formula by three names. The person who recites a blessing learned this formula when he or she was two or three years old and hardly pondered the theological meaning or even the simple semantics of this phrase each time he or she recited it as an older child or as an adult.

I see an added purpose or function of the berakhah formula for the more mature reciter, whom I call a meditator. These recitations serve as the known cues for many instances of daily, periodic, repetitive or occasional mini-mindful meditations. These provide meaningful visualizations of pauses in the rush of one's thoughts and to the meanderings of cognitive awareness.

A meditator recites individual blessings when eating foods, performing bodily functions, witnessing meteorological events, seeing flowers, or hearing good and bad news. Liturgical variants of blessings comprise many of the synagogue texts of prayer.

Here is a summary of a small sample of many of the actions and occasions for which one recites mini-meditations, blessings in daily activities.

Blessed are You...	Purpose	Meditation
Who creates the fruit of the tree	Before eating a fruit	Mindful eating
Who creates the produce of the ground	Before eating a vegetable	Mindful eating
Who gives pleasant fragrance to fruits	Upon smelling fruits	Mindful sensing of nature
Who has withheld nothing from nature and has created in it beautiful creatures and trees for the enjoyment of human beings	Upon seeing flowering trees in their first seasonal bloom	Mindful sensing of the special beauty of nature
Who creates the fruit of the vine	Before drinking wine	Mindful drinking
Who brings forth bread from the earth	Before eating bread—a full meal	Mindful dining, for a full meal
Who commanded us to light the	After lighting the candles	Purposeful ritual, mindful of the

Sabbath/ holiday candles		passage of time
Who heals all flesh and performs wonders	After bathroom visits	Mindful of one's body and health
Whose power and might fill the world	Upon witnessing thunder or a hurricane	Mindful of disruptive events of nature
Who is good and does good	For good news	Mindful of elevating emotions
Who is the true judge	For bad news	Mindful of emotional trauma
Blessings in the synagogue	Opening or concluding paragraphs of liturgy	Mindful of the markers of the elements of prayer

There are three generally mentioned classical categories for sorting out all the blessings: (1) blessings of performance of a mitzvah (ritual acts), (2) blessings of bodily satisfaction (intake of foods, drinks, etc.) and (3) blessings of praise (liturgy).

As part performative-mindful visualization, these blessings function to demand a meditative awareness of person, body and the immediate external world. For a simple example, a person takes the blessing he or she recites upon smelling fragrant fruit, "Blessed are You, Lord our God, King of the Universe who gives pleasant fragrance to fruits" (Koren Siddur, p. 1000) as a cue to be highly aware of one's surroundings. A person takes another case, the formula spoken before eating an apple, "Blessed are You, Lord our God, King of the Universe who creates the fruit of the tree," as a cue to mindfully savor the taste and texture of foods. In both cases, visualizations of loving-kindness and compassion may accompany the awareness of the physical food.

These blessings serve as triggers. They tell the reciter to stop, to be mindful of his or her actions, to be thoughtful of what type of food is held in hand, how that food is to be regarded and classified, whether one is smelling it or eating it, and to recall what its "correct berakhah" is.

All forms of mindfulness intensify the practitioner's moments of experience and elevate ordinary events from a background of awareness to a foreground of thinking. Mindful occasions of blessings help one savor one's conscious awareness—the consistency and flavor, the origins and essences of living.

Meir, a rabbi in the Talmud in the second century, spoke of his expectation for every Jew to experience each day one hundred triggers of mindful meditation—a life punctuated daily by one hundred blessings.

To be clear, this mindful meditation through berakhot that we have described is not identical to that which Kabat-Zinn and others teach. This mindfulness is adapted to a Jewish context. In fact, through blessings, a person engages in a form of mindfulness to the second power, mindfulness squared, that is to an intensified relationship to multiple worlds, both personal and cultural.

Let me explain what Jewish-mindfulness means. When a person holds an apple in hand and recites the blessing for it, they need to know which proper berakhah to make. That means they have to relate first to that content from the Jewish cultural world, its law or halakhah. Still holding that apple in hand, they move through that relationship to look then at the fruit, to feel its heft and taste its tartness as they bite into it.

Mindful visualization exercises require that daily life not be defined only by the torrents of rushing thoughts. Mindful thinking is formed in a duplex relationship to that combination of both cultural and personal contents that are mindfully activated in a conscious mind, under its watchful control. Such visualization steers a person's thoughts and actions by meeting up with them, by making note of them, and then by becoming disentangled from those twisting currents of distractions gushing around one's life.

Blessing-meditation visualizations turn the rush of daily living into a series of discrete moments of experience, each savored fully with thanksgiving, gratitude and compassion.

The Compassionate-Mindful Visualization: Kol Nidre

The legal text of Kol Nidre that Jews recite at the outset of Yom Kippur is actually a vivid emotional liturgical visualization of meditative intent. The worshipper announces the central theme of Yom Kippur at the outset of a set of long and complex performances that will follow throughout the evening and next day.

The inaugural declaration of the centerpiece of the entire Yom Kippur liturgy creates a compassionate context for prayer. Kol Nidre is the declaration and visualization of a compassion that the liturgical practitioners will now seek for themselves. This mindset continues in the selihot, which continue as further repetitive declarations of compassion throughout the solemn Yom Kippur services.

It is not an easy task for worshippers to find this emotional outlet of compassion for themselves, along with their entire community, together on the same day at the same time in the same place. As the worshippers continue their extended visualizations of compassion, they ask God to help them attain this empathy and forgiveness. Their process extends into the viduy, the confessions of sin in which they list their shortcomings, forgive themselves and ask for forgiveness from their God.

The stoical legal declaration of Kol Nidre functions as a primary part of a warm and fervent liturgy. Worshippers say, "We release ourselves of our vows." Parishioners start with that form of proclamation because that is—in a scribal idiom—a way to say that they have compassion on themselves, they forgive themselves. Here in this collective house of gathering, they speak about themselves. They emotionally—not legally—visualize that they can annul their own wrong declarations, intentions and acts of the past and of the future.

These words in nonfigurative legal idiom are then pragmatically used as a personal meditation of compassion. This is a Jewish meditation. There is no clear abstraction to which the liturgical users appeal to formulate a definition of Jewish compassion. They inductively learn what it is from the modes in which they practice it. The people in the congregation begin this meditative analysis and perception to trigger the realization that its liturgy in this instance on Yom Kippur Eve is a long diverse set of meditative practices seeking for themselves and for their fellow Jews "rahamim" "selihah" "mehilah". The worshippers prepare to have remorse, regret and true pain because they are trapped by their shortcomings, their bad deeds, their inability to find peace. They have been disappointed, traumatized and confused by what they see around them.

They seek compassion, which is commonly defined as, "sympathetic pity and concern for the sufferings or misfortunes of others." In a process that they call "atonement" they turn this compassion inward to address their own case, to have mercy on their own souls. They perform this liturgy enmeshed in their cultural trappings, simple and ornate. The pragmatic metaphor of choice to start the engine of compassion is the conceptual legal process for the release of vows. The idiom of these most sacred prayers begins with that. Kol Nidre serves on a basic subconscious emotional level as the ordinal visualization and articulation of the Jewish meditation of compassion.

This begins the epic Jewish holiday of compassion. The worshippers employ a legal sounding idiom saying that they are releasing vows. With that visualization of Kol Nidre they are in fact starting a twenty five hour marathon of meditative compassion and forgiveness.

Visualization Circuits

The daily morning prayers in many synagogues often last no more than thirty minutes. During the short prayer services, Jews cycle through diverse visualization exercises, as we have discussed above.

With this final analogy I conclude my inquiry into the religious visualizations that I find in the major Jewish prayers. I compare the busy composite service with its rapid movements from one visualization to another to a session of training exercises.

Physical circuit-training in a gymnasium or other workout facility is a form of body conditioning or resistance training using high-intensity exercises for strength building and muscular endurance. In most circuit-training, the time between exercises is short and the trainee moves on quickly to the next exercise. In a typical exercise circuit, one completes all the prescribed exercises in the program in a short span of time.

The inner spiritual circuit-training of the prayers is a form of soul conditioning that uses high intensity exercises for visualization building and concentration endurance. In a prayer circuit, participants typically complete all the prescribed exercises in the program in a short duration. In most prayer circuit training the time between visualization events is brief. The performer moves on quickly to the next visualization event.

Jews who follow the recommended interior visualization regimens of Jewish prayer, which I have discussed above, may indeed, as Rabbi Sacks suggested, be engaged at a high level in prayer that is, "the most intimate gesture of the religious life, and the most transformative." I have proposed here that in the details of the prayers the visualizations, images and gestures of the liturgy are complex, diverse and deep in specific ways that define many important aspects of what it is to be a believing and practicing Jew.

THE BOOK OF JEWISH PRAYERS IN ENGLISH

MORNING PRAYER FOR CHILDREN

Blessed are you, O Lord our God, King of the universe, who removes sleep from my eyes, and slumber from my eyelids.

Blessed are you, O Lord our God, King of the universe, who has given us the Torah of truth, and has planted everlasting life in our midst.

Moses commanded us the Torah as an inheritance of the congregation of Jacob.

Hear, O Israel: the Lord our God, the Lord is One, Blessed be His name, whose glorious kingdom is forever and ever.

And you shall love the Lord your God with all your heart, and with all your soul, and with all your might.

And these words which I command you this day shall be upon your heart: and you shall teach them diligently unto your children, and shall talk of them when you sit in your house, and when you walk by the way, and when you lie down, and when you rise up. And you shall bind them for a sign upon your hand, and they shall be for frontlets between your eyes. And you shall write them upon the doorposts of your house and upon your gates.

O my God, guard my tongue from evil, and my lips from speaking guile.

Open my heart to your Torah, and let my soul pursue your commandments.

Let the words of my mouth and the meditation of my heart be acceptable before you, O Lord, my Rock and my Redeemer.

PRAYER ON ENTERING THE SYNAGOGUE

On entering the Synagogue say the following—

As for me, in the abundance of your loving-kindness will I come into your house: I will worship toward your holy temple in the fear of you.

Into the house of God we will walk with the throng.

How goodly are your tents, O Jacob, your dwelling places, O Israel! As for me, in the abundance of your loving-kindness will I come into your house: I will worship toward your holy temple in the fea xxx

his people by the hand of his prophet who was faithful in his house.

9. God will not alter nor change his Torah to everlasting for any other.
10. He watches and knows our secret thoughts: he beholds the end of a thing before it exists.
11. He bestows loving-kindness upon a man according to his work; he gives to the wicked evil according to his wickedness.
12. He will send our anointed at the end of days, to redeem them that wait for the end—his salvation.

13. In the abundance of his loving-kindness God will quicken the dead. Blessed forevermore be his glorious name.

He is Lord of the universe, who reigned before any creature yet was formed:
At the time when all things were made by his desire, then was his name proclaimed King.
And after all things shall have had an end, he alone, the dreaded one, shall reign;
Who was, who is, and who will be in glory.
And he is One, and there is no second to compare to him, to consort with him:
Without beginning, without end: to him belong strength and dominion.
And he is my God—my Redeemer lives—and a rock in my travail in time of distress;
And he is my banner and my refuge, the portion of my cup on the day when I call.
Into his hand I commend my spirit, when I sleep and when I wake:
And with my spirit, my body also: the Lord is with me, and I will not fear.

Blessed are you, O Lord our God, King of the universe, who has sanctified us by your commandments, and given us command concerning the washing of the hands.

Blessed are you, O Lord our God, King of the universe, who has formed man in wisdom, and created in him many orifices and vessels. It is revealed and known before the throne of your glory, that if one of these be opened, or one of these be closed, it would be impossible to exist and to stand before you. Blessed are you, O Lord, who heals all flesh and does wondrously.

Blessed are you, O Lord our God, King of the universe, who has sanctified us by your commandments, and commanded us to occupy ourselves with the words of the Torah.

Make pleasant, therefore, we beseech you, O Lord our God, the words of your Torah in our mouth and in the mouth of your people, the house of Israel, so that we with our offspring and the offspring of your people, the house of Israel, may all know your name and learn your Torah. Blessed are you, O Lord, who teaches the Torah to your people Israel.

Blessed are you, O Lord our God, King of the universe, who has chosen us from all nations and given us your Torah. Blessed are you, O Lord, who gives the Torah.

The Lord bless you, and keep you: the Lord makes his face to shine upon you, and be gracious unto you: the Lord turn his face unto you, and give you peace.

Mishnah. Treatise Peah, ch. i.

These are the things which have no fixed measure (by enactment of the Torah): the corners of the field, the first fruits, the offerings brought on appearing before the Lord at the three festivals, the practice of charity and the study of the Torah.—These are the things, the fruits of which a man enjoys in this world, while the stock remains for him for the world to come: viz., honoring father and mother, the practice of charity, timely attendance at the house of study morning and evening, hospitality to wayfarers, visiting the sick, dowering the bride, attending the dead to the grave, devotion in prayer, and making peace between man and his fellow; but the study of the Torah is equal to them all.

O my God, the soul which you gave me is pure; you did create it, you did form it, you did breathe it into me; you preserve it within me; and you will take it from me, but will restore it to me hereafter. So long as the soul is within me, I will give thanks unto you, O Lord my God and God of my fathers, Sovereign of all works, Lord of all souls! Blessed are you, O Lord, who restores souls to dead bodies.

Blessed are you, O Lord our God, King of the universe, who has given to the cock intelligence to distinguish between day and night.
Blessed are you, O Lord our God, King of the universe, who has not made me a heathen.
Blessed are you, O Lord our God, King of the universe, who has not made me a bondman.
Men say—
Blessed are you, O Lord our God, King of the universe, who has not made me a woman.
Women say—
Blessed are you, O Lord our God, King of the universe, who has made me according to your will.
Blessed are you, O Lord our God, King of the universe, who opens the eyes of the blind.
Blessed are you, O Lord our God, King of the universe, who clothes the naked.
Blessed are you, O Lord our God, King of the universe, who looses them that are bound.
Blessed are you, O Lord our God, King of the universe, who raises up them that are bowed down.
Blessed are you, O Lord our God, King of the universe, who spreads forth the earth above the waters.
Blessed are you, O Lord our God, King of the universe, who has supplied my every want.
Blessed are you, O Lord our God, King of the universe, who has made firm the steps of man.
Blessed are you, O Lord our God, King of the universe, who girds Israel with might.
Blessed are you, O Lord our God, King of the universe, who crowns Israel with glory.
Blessed are you, O Lord our God, King of the universe, who gives strength to the weary.
Blessed are you, O Lord our God, King of the universe, who removes sleep from my eyes and slumber from my eyelids.

And may it be your will, O Lord our God and God of our fathers, to make us familiar with your Torah, and to make us cleave to your commandments, O lead us not into the power of sin, or of transgression or iniquity, or of temptation, or of scorn: let not the evil inclination have sway over us: keep us far from a bad man and a bad companion: make us cleave to the good inclination and to good works: subdue our inclination so that it may submit itself to you; and let us obtain this day, and every day, grace, favor and mercy in your eyes, and in the eyes of all who behold us; and bestow loving-kindnesses upon us. Blessed are you, O Lord, who bestows loving-kindnesses upon your people Israel.

May it be your will, O Lord my God and God of my fathers, to deliver me this day, and every day, from arrogant men and from arrogance, from a bad mar., from a bad companion and from a bad neighbor, and from any mishap, and from the adversary that destroys; from a hard judgment, and from a hard opponent, whether he be a son of the covenant or be not a son or the covenant.

At all times let a man fear God as well in private as in public, acknowledge the truth, and speak the truth in his heart; and let him rise early and say:

Sovereign of all worlds! Not because of our righteous acts do we lay our supplications before you, but because of your abundant mercies. What are we? What is our life? What is our piety? What our righteousness?

What our helpfulness? What our strength? What our might? What shall we say before you, O Lord our God and God of our fathers? Are not all the mighty men as naught before you, the men of renown as though they had not been, the wise as if without knowledge, and the men of understanding as if without discernment? For most of their works are void, and the days of their lives are vanity before you, and the pre-eminence of man over the beast is naught, for all is vanity.

Nevertheless we are your people, the children of your covenant, the children of Abraham, your friend, to whom you did swear on Mount Moriah; the seed of Isaac, his only son, who was bound upon the altar the congregation of Jacob, your first barn son, whose name you did call Israel and Yeshurun by reason of the love with which you did love him, and the joy with which you did rejoice in him.

It is, therefore, our duty to thank, praise and glorify you, to bless, to sanctify and to offer praise and thanksgiving to your name. Happy are we! How goodly is our portion, and how pleasant is our lot, and how beautiful our heritage! Happy are we who, early and late, morning and evening, twice every day, declare:

Hear, O Israel: the Lord our God, the Lord is One. Blessed be His name, whose glorious kingdom is forever and ever.

You were the same ere the world was created; you have been the same since the world has been created; you are the same in this world, and you will be the same in the world to come. Sanctify your name upon them that sanctify it, yea, sanctify your name throughout your world; and through your salvation let our horn be exalted and raised on high. Blessed are you, O Lord, who sanctifies your name amongst the many,

You are the Lord our God in heaven and on earth, and in the highest heaven of heavens. Verily you are the first and you are the last, and beside you there is no God. O gather them that hope for you from the four corners of the earth. Let all the inhabitants of the world perceive and know that you are God, you alone, over all the kingdoms of the earth. You have made the heavens and the earth, the sea and all that is therein; and which among all the works of your hands, whether among those above or among those beneath, can say unto you, What do you? Our Father who are in heaven, deal kindly with us for the sake of your great name by which we are called; and fulfil unto us, O Lord our God, that which is written, At that time will I bring you in, and at that time will I gather you; for I will make you a name and a praise among all the peoples of the earth, when I bring back your captivity before your eyes, says the Lord.

Numbers xxviii. 1-8.

And the Lord spoke to Moses, saying, Command the children of Israel, and say unto them, My offerings, my food for my offerings made by fire, of a sweet savor unto me, shall you observe to offer unto me in its due season. And you shall say unto them, This is the offering made by fire which you shall offer unto the Lord; he-lambs of the first year without blemish, two day by day, for a continual burnt offering. The one lamb shall you offer in the morning, and the other lamb shall you offer at even; and the tenth part of an ephah of fine flour for a meal offering, mingled with the fourth part of an hin of beaten oil. It is a continual burnt offering, which was ordained in Mount Sinai for a sweet savor, an offering made by fire unto the Lord. And the drink offering thereof shall be the fourth part of an hin for the one lamb: in the holy place shall you pour out a drink offering of strong drink unto the Lord. And the other lamb shall you offer at even: as the meal offering of the morning, and as the drink offering thereof, you shall offer it, an offering made by fire, of a sweet savor unto the Lord.

Leviticus i. 11.

And he shall slay it on the side of the altar northward before the Lord: and Aaron's sons, the priests, shall sprinkle its blood upon the altar round about.

On Sabbath the following is added—

Numbers xxviii. 9, 10.

And on the Sabbath day two he-lambs of the first year without blemish, and two tenth parts of an ephah of fine flour for a meal offering, mingled with oil, and the drink offering thereof: this is the burnt offering of every Sabbath, beside the continual burnt offering, and the drink offering thereof.

On New Moon the following is added—

Numbers xxviii. 11-15.

And in the beginnings of your months you shall offer a burnt offering unto the Lord; two young bullocks, and one ram, seven he-lambs of the first year without blemish; and three tenth parts of an ephah of fine flour for a meal offering, mingled with oil, for each bullock; and two tenth parts of fine flour for a meal offering, mingled with oil, for the one ram; and a several tenth part of fine flour mingled with oil for a meal offering unto every lamb; for a burnt offering of a sweet savor, an offering made by fire unto the Lord. And their drink offerings shall be half a hin of wine for a bullock, and the third part of a hin for the ram, and the fourth part of a hin for a lamb: this is the burnt offering of every month throughout the months of the year. And one the-goat for a sin offering unto the Lord; it shall be offered beside the continual burnt offering, and the drink offering thereof.

Mishnah, Treatise Zebahim, ch. v.

1. Which are the places where the sacrifices were offered?—Those that were most holy were slain on the north side of the altar: the bull and the he-goat of the Day of Atonement were slain on the north side; their blood was received in a vessel of ministry on the north side, and had to be sprinkled between the staves of the ark, and towards the veil, and upon the golden altar: one of these sprinklings omitted rendered the whole ceremony invalid. The remaining blood the priest poured out at the western base of the outer altar; if, however, he did not do so, the omission did not render the ceremony invalid.

2. The bulls and he-goats which were to be wholly burnt. They were slain on the north side; their blood was received in a vessel of ministry on the north side, and had to be sprinkled towards the veil and upon the golden altar: one of these sprinklings omitted rendered the whole ceremony invalid. The remaining blood the priest poured out at the western base of the outer altar; if, however, he failed to do so, it did not render the ceremony invalid: both these and the preceding offerings were burnt in the repository of ashes.

3. The sin offerings of the congregation and of the individual.—These are the sin offerings of the congregation: the he-goats offered on the new moon and on the festivals. They were slain on the north side; their blood was received in a vessel of ministry on the north side, and of this blood four sprinklings had to be made, one upon each of the four corners of the altar. How was this done? The priest went up the ascent, passed on to the middle terrace that surrounded the altar, and came successively to the south-east, the north-east, the north-west and the south-west corners. The remaining blood he poured out at the southern base of the altar. These sacrifices might be eaten, dressed after any manner, by the males of the priesthood, within the hangings of the court, the same day and evening until midnight.

4. The burnt offering belonged to the class of the most holy. It was slain on the north side; its blood was received in a vessel of ministry on the north side; and of its blood two sprinklings had to be made (at opposite angles of the altar) so as to constitute four, (a portion of the blood thus reaching each of the four sides of the altar). This offering had also to be flayed, dismembered and totally consumed by fire.

5. The peace offerings of the congregation and the trespass offerings.—These are the trespass offerings: the trespass offerings for robbery, for profane appropriation of sanctified objects, for carnally knowing a handmaid already promised in marriage; the trespass offering of a Nazirite who has become defiled by a dead body; the trespass offering of a leper at his cleansing; the trespass offering of one who is in doubt whether he has committed an act that has to be atoned for by a sin offering. All these were slain on the north side; their blood was received in a vessel of ministry on the north side; and of their blood two sprinklings had to be made at the altar in such a manner as to constitute four. These sacrifices might be eaten, dressed after any manner, by the males of the priesthood, within the hangings of the court, the same day and evening until midnight.

6. The thank offering and the ram of the Nazirite were holy in a minor degree. They might be slain in any part of the court, of their blood two sprinklings had to be made at the altar in such a manner as to constitute four; and they might be eaten, dressed after any manner, by any person, in any part of the city, the same day and until midnight. To the portions thereof belonging to the priests the same rule 'applied as to the rest, except that the former might only be eaten by the priests, their wives, their children and their slaves.

7. The peace offerings were also holy in a minor degree. They might be slain in any part of the court; of their blood two sprinklings had to be made at the altar in such a manner as to constitute four, and they might be eaten, dressed after any manner, by any person, in any part of the city, during two days and one night. To the portions thereof belonging to the priests the same rule applied as to the rest, except that the former might only be eaten by the priests, their wives, their children and their slaves.

24

8. The first-born, the tithe of cattle and the paschal lamb were likewise holy in a minor degree. They might be slain in any part of the court; only one sprinkling of their blood had to be made; this, however, had to be done towards the base of the altar. In respect to their consumption the following differences prevailed: the first-born might be eaten only by the priests, while the tithe might be eaten by any person: both might be eaten, dressed after any manner, in any part of the city, during two days and one night. The paschal lamb might only be eaten the same evening until midnight; it might be partaken of by none but the previously appointed number of persons, and it might only be eaten roasted.

Baraita d'R. Ishmael

Rabbi Ishmael says: There are thirteen exegetical principles by which the Torah is expounded—

1. The inference from minor to major.
2. The inference from a similarity of phrases.
3. A general law may be derived by induction from different cases which, occurring in the same or in different verses, have yet some feature in common.
4. A general proposition followed by the enumeration of particulars already comprehended in the general proposition, (in which case the scope of the proposition is limited by the things specified)
5. An enumeration of particulars followed by a general proposition in which they are also comprehended, (in which case the scope of the proposition extends also to the things not specified).
6. Two general propositions, separated from each other by an enumeration of particulars, include only such things as are similar to those specified
7. An inference drawn from a general proposition complemented by a particular term, and an inference drawn from a particular term complemented by a general proposition.
8. If anything is included in a general proposition and is then made the subject of a special statement, that which is predicated of it is not to be understood as limited to itself alone, but is to be applied to the whole of the general proposition
9. If anything is included in a general proposition, and is then singled out in order to be made the subject of a special statement, similar to the general proposition, this particularization is intended, so far as its subject is concerned, to lessen and not to add to its restrictions.
10. If anything is included in a general proposition, and is then singled out in order to be made the subject of a special statement, not similar to the general proposition, this particularization is intended in some respects to lessen and in others to add to its restrictions.
11. If anything is included in a general proposition, and is then made the subject of a fresh statement (not in harmony with the former), the terms of the general proposition will not apply to it, unless the Scripture distinctly indicates that they shall apply.
12. The meaning of a passage may be deduced from its context, or from some subsequent passage.
13. Similarly, when two passages are in contradiction to each other, the explanation can be determined only when a third text is found, capable of harmonizing the two.

May it be your will, O Lord our God and God of our fathers, that the temple be speedily rebuilt in our days and grant our portion in your Torah. And there we will serve you with awe, as in the days of old, and as in ancient years.

Before putting on the Tallit, say the following—

I am here enwrapping myself in this fringed robe, in fulfilment of the command of my Creator, as it is written in the Torah, They shall make them a fringe upon the corners of their garments throughout their generations. And even as I cover myself with the Tallit in this world, so may my soul deserve to be clothed with a beauteous spiritual robe in the world to come, in the Garden of Eden. Amen.

On putting on the Tallit, say—

Blessed are you, O Lord our God, King of the universe, who has sanctified us by your commandments, and has commanded us to enwrap ourselves in the fringed garment.

How precious is your loving-kindness, O God! And the children of men take refuge under the shadow of your wings. They sate themselves with the fatness of your house; and you give them to drink of the river of your pleasures. For with you is the fountain of life: in your light do we see light. O continue your loving-kindness unto them that know you, and your righteousness to the upright in heart.

Meditation before laying the Tefillin

I am here intent upon the act of laying the Tefillin, in fulfilment of the command of my Creator, who has commanded us to lay the Tefillin, as it is written in the Torah, And you shall bind them for a sign upon your hand, and they shall be for frontlets between your eyes. Within these Tefillin are placed four sections of the Torah, that declare the absolute unity of God, and that remind us of the miracles and wonders which he wrought for us when he brought us forth from Egypt, even he who has power over the highest and the lowest to deal with them according to his will. He has commanded us to lay the Tefillin upon the hand as a memorial of his outstretched arm; opposite the heart, to indicate the duty of subjecting the longings and designs of our heart to his service, blessed be he; and upon the head over against the brain, thereby teaching that the mind, whose seat is in the brain, together with all senses and faculties, is to be subjected to his service, blessed be he. May the effect of the precept thus observed be to extend to me long life with sacred influences and holy thoughts, free from every approach, even in imagination, to sin and iniquity. May the evil inclination not mislead or entice us, but may we be led to serve the Lord as it is in our hearts to do. Amen.

On placing the Tefillah on the arm, say—

Blessed are you, O Lord our God, King of the universe, who has sanctified us by your commandments, and has commanded us to lay the Tefillin.

On placing the Tefillah on the forehead, say—

Blessed are you, O Lord our God, King of the universe, who has sanctified us by your commandments, and has given us command concerning the precept of the Tefillin.

Blessed be His name, whose glorious kingdom is forever and ever.

The retsuah strap is placed thrice round the middle finger, and the following is said—

And I will betroth you unto me forever; yea, I will betroth you unto me in righteousness, and in judgment, and in loving-kindness, and in mercy: I will even betroth you to me in faithfulness; and you shall know the Lord.

In some Congregations Psalm xxx is said here.

Blessed be he who spoke, and the world existed: blessed be he: blessed be he who was the maker of the world in the beginning: blessed be he who speaks and does: blessed be he who decrees and performs: blessed be he who has mercy upon the earth: blessed be he who has mercy upon his creatures: blessed be he who pays a good reward to them that fear him: blessed be he who lives forever, and endures to eternity: blessed be he who redeems and delivers: blessed be his name.—Blessed are you, O Lord our God, King of the universe, O God and merciful Father, praised by the mouth of your people, lauded and glorified by the tongue of your loving ones and your servants. We also will praise you, O Lord our God, with the songs of David your servant; with praises and psalms we will magnify, laud and glorify you, and we will make mention of your name, and proclaim you our King, O our God, you the only one, the life of all worlds. O King, praised and glorified be your great name forever and ever. Blessed are you, O Lord, a King extolled with praises.

1 Chron. xvi. 8-36.

O give thanks unto the Lord, call upon his name; make known his doings among the peoples. Sing unto him, sing praises unto him; tell you of all his marvelous works. Glory you in his holy name: let the heart of them rejoice that seek the Lord. Search you for the Lord and his strength; seek you his face evermore. Remember his marvelous works that he has done: his wonders, and the judgments of his mouth; O you seed of Israel, his servant, you children of Jacob, his chosen ones. He is the Lord our God: his judgments are in all the earth. Remember his covenant forever, the word which he commanded to a thousand generations; (the covenant) which he made with Abraham, and his oath unto Isaac; and confirmed the same unto Jacob for a statute, to Israel for an everlasting covenant: saying, Unto you will I give the land of Canaan, as the lot of your inheritance: when you were but a few men in number; yea, few, and sojourners in it; and they went about from nation to nation, and from one kingdom to another people. He suffered no man to oppress them; yea, he rebuked kings for their sakes; (saying), Touch not my anointed ones, and do my prophets no harm. Sing unto the Lord, all the earth; proclaim his salvation from day to day. Recount his glory among the nations, his marvels among all the peoples. For great is the Lord, and exceedingly to be praised: he is to be feared above all gods. For all the gods of the peoples are things of naught; but the Lord made the heavens. Grandeur and majesty are before him: strength and gladness are in his place. Give unto the Lord, you families of the peoples, give unto the Lord glory and strength. Give unto the Lord the glory due unto his name: take an offering, and come before him: worship the Lord in the beauty of holiness. Tremble before him all the earth; the world also is set firm, that it cannot be moved. Let the heavens rejoice, and let the earth be glad; and let them say among the nations, The Lord reigns. Let the sea roar, and the fullness thereof; let the plain exult, and all that is therein. Then shall the trees of the forest exult before the Lord, for he comes to judge the earth. O give thanks unto the Lord; for he is good: for his loving-kindness endures forever. And say ye, Save us, O God of our salvation, and gather us and deliver us from the nations, to give thanks unto your holy name, and to triumph in your praise. Blessed be the Lord, the God of Israel, from everlasting even to everlasting. And all the people said, Amen, and praised the Lord.

Exalt you the Lord our God, and worship at his footstool; holy is he. Exalt you the Lord our God, aim worship at his holy mount; for the Lord our God is holy. And he, being merciful, forgives iniquity, and destroys not: yea, many a time he turns his anger away, and does not stir up all his wrath. Withhold not you your tender mercies from me, O Lord: let your loving-kindness and your truth continually preserve me. Remember, O Lord, your tender mercies and your loving-kindnesses; for they have been ever of old. Ascribe you strength unto God: his majesty is over Israel, and his strength is in the skies. O God, you are to be feared out of your holy places: the God of Israel he gives strength and power unto his people. Blessed be God. O God of vengeance, Lord, O God of vengeance, shine forth. Lift up yourself, you judge of the earth: render to the proud their desert. Salvation belongs unto the Lord: your blessing be upon your people. (Selah.) The Lord of hosts is with us; the God of Jacob is our stronghold. (Selah.) O Lord of hosts, happy is the man that trusts in you. Save, Lord: may the King answer us on the day when we call. Save your people, and bless your inheritance: feed them, and carry them forever Our soul waits for the Lord: he is our help and our shield. For our heart shall rejoice in him, because we have trusted in his holy name. Let your loving-kindness, O Lord, be upon us, according as we have hoped for you. Show us your loving-kindness, O Lord, and grant us your salvation. Rise up for our help and set us free for your loving-kindness' sake. I am the Lord your God, who brought you up out of the land of Egypt: open wide your mouth and I will fill it. Happy is the people, that is in such a case: happy is the people, whose God is the Lord. And as for me, I have trusted in your loving-kindness; my heart shall be glad in your salvation: I will sing unto the Lord, because he has dealt bountifully with me.

The following Psalm is omitted on Sabbaths, Holydays, the day before Passover, the Intermediate days of Passover, and on the day before the Day of Atonement.

Psalm c.

A Psalm of Thanksgiving. Shout for joy unto the Lord, all you lands. Serve the Lord with joy: come before him with exulting. Know you that the Lord he is God: he has made us, and we are his, his people and the sheep of his pasture. Enter into his gates with thanksgiving, and into his courts with praise: give thanks unto him, bless his name. For the Lord is good; his loving-kindness is everlasting; and his faithfulness from generation to generation.

On Weekdays continue "Let the glory," etc.

On Sabbaths and Holydays, and on Hoshana Rabba, the following Psalms are said:

Psalm xix.

For the Chief Musician. A Psalm of David. The heavens recount the glory of God, and the firmament declares his handiwork. Day unto day pours forth speech, and night unto night proclaims knowledge. There is no speech nor language; their voice cannot be heard. Their sound is gone out through all the earth, and their words to the end of the world; in them has he set a tent for the sun. And he is as a bridegroom coming out of his chamber, and rejoices as a strong man to run his course. His going forth is from the end of the heaven, and his circuit unto the ends of it: and there is nothing hid from his heat.— The Torah of the Lord is perfect, restoring the soul: the testimony of the Lord is faithful, making wise the simple. The precepts of the Lord are right, rejoicing the heart: the commandment of the Lord is pure, enlightening the eyes. The fear of the Lord is clean, enduring forever; the judgments of the Lord are truthful, righteous altogether. More to be desired are they than gold, yea, than much fine gold; sweeter also than honey and the droppings of the honeycomb. Moreover by them is your servant warned: in keeping them there is great reward. Who can discern his errors? Clear you me from hidden faults. Keep back your servant also from presumptuous sins; let them not have dominion over me: then shall I be blameless, and I shall be clear from great transgression. Let the words of my mouth and the meditation of my heart be acceptable before you, O Lord, my Rock and my Redeemer.

Psalm xxxiv.

A Psalm of David; when he changed his behavior before Abimelech, who drove him away, and he departed.

I will bless the Lord at all times: his praise shall continually be in my mouth.
My soul shall make her boast in the Lord: the meek shall hear and rejoice.
O magnify the Lord with me, and let us exalt his name together.
I sought the Lord, and he answered me, and delivered me from all my fears.
They looked unto him, and shone with joy: and their faces shall not be confounded.
This sufferer cried, and the Lord heard him, and saved him out of all his troubles.
The angel of the Lord encamps round about them that fear him, and delivers them.
O taste and see that the Lord is good: happy is the man that takes refuge in him.
O fear the Lord, you his holy ones: for there is no want to them that fear him.
Young lions do lack, and suffer hunger: but they that seek the Lord shall not want any good.
Come, you children, hearken unto me: I will teach you the fear of the Lord.
What man is he that delights in life, and loves many days that he may see good?
Keep your tongue from evil and your lips from speaking guile.
Depart from evil and do good; seek peace and pursue it.
The eyes of the Lord are towards the righteous, and his ears are towards their cry.
The face of the Lord is against them that do evil, to cut off the remembrance of them from the earth.
(The righteous) cry, and the Lord hearkens, and delivers them out of all their troubles.
The Lord is nigh unto them that are of a broken heart, and saves such as are of a contrite spirit.
Many are the evil fortunes of the righteous: but the Lord delivers him out of them all.
He keeps all his bones: not one of them is broken.
Evil shall slay the wicked; and they that hate the righteous shall be condemned.
The Lord sets free the soul of his servants; and none that take refuge in him shall be condemned.

Psalm xc.

A Prayer of Moses, the man of God. O Lord, you have been a dwelling place unto us in all generations. Before the mountains were brought forth, or ever you gave birth to the earth and the world, even from everlasting to everlasting you are God. You turn man back to dust, and say, Return, you children of men. For a thousand years in your sight are but as yesterday when it is past, and as a watch in the night. You carry them away as with a flood; they are in a sleep: in the morning they are like grass which sprouts afresh. In the morning it blooms and sprouts afresh; in the evening it is cut down, and withers. For we are consumed by your anger, and in your wrath are we confounded. You have set our iniquities before you, our secret sins in the light of your countenance. For all our days have passed away in your wrath, we bring our years to an end like a sound. The days of our years are threescore years and ten, or even by reason of strength fourscore years; yet is their pride but travail and nothingness; for it is soon gone by, and we fly away. Who knows the power of your anger, and your wrath according to the fear that is due unto you? So teach us to number our days, that we may get us a heart of wisdom. Return, O Lord; how long?—and repent you concerning your servants. O satisfy us in the morning with your loving-kindness; that we may exult and rejoice all our days. Make us rejoice according to the days wherein you have afflicted us, the years wherein we have seen evil. Let your work be made manifest unto your servants, and your majesty upon their children.

And let the pleasantness of the Lord our God be upon us; and establish you the work of our hands upon us; yea, the work of our hands establish you it.

Psalm xci.

He that dwells in the shelter of the Most High abides under the shadow of the Almighty. I say of the Lord, He is my refuge and my fortress; my God, in whom I trust.—For he shall deliver you from the snare of the fowler, and from the noisome pestilence. He shall cover you with his pinions, and under his wings shall you take refuge: his truth shall be a shield and a buckler. You shall not be afraid of the terror by night, nor of the arrow that flies by day; of the pestilence that walks in darkness, nor of the plague that ravages at noon day. A thousand may fall at your side, and ten thousand at your right hand; it shall not come nigh unto you. Only with your eyes shall you look on, and see the retribution of the wicked.—For you, O Lord, are my refuge.—You have made the Most High your dwelling place; there shall no evil befall you, neither shall any scourge come nigh your tent. For he shall give his angels charge over you, to keep you in all your ways. They shall bear you upon their hands, lest you strike your foot against a stone. You shall tread upon the lion and the adder; upon the young lion and the serpent shall you trample.— Because he has set his love upon me, therefore will I deliver him: I will set him on high, because he knows my name. When he calls upon me, I will answer him; I will be with him in trouble: I will deliver him and honor him. With length of days will I satisfy him, and will let him see my salvation.

Repeat the last verse.

Psalm cxxxv.

Praise you the Lord. Praise you the name of the Lord; praise him, O you servants of the Lord: you that stand in the house of the Lord, in the courts of the house of our God. Praise you the Lord; for the Lord is good: sing praises unto his name; for it is pleasant. For the Lord has chosen Jacob unto himself, and

Israel for his peculiar treasure. For I know that the Lord is great, and that our Lord is above all gods. Whatsoever the Lord pleases, that does he, in heaven and in earth, in the seas and in all deeps. He causes vapors to ascend from the ends of the earth; he makes lightnings for the rain; he brings forth the wind out of his treasuries. It is he who smote the firstborn of Egypt, both of man and beast. He sent signs and wonders into the midst of you, O Egypt, upon Pharaoh, and upon all his servants. It is he who smote great nations, and slew mighty kings; Sihon king of the Amorites, and Og king of Bashan, and all the kingdoms of Canaan: and gave their land for a heritage, a heritage unto Israel his people. Your name, O Lord, endures forever; your memorial, O Lord, throughout all generations. For the Lord shall judge his people, and repent himself concerning his servants.

The idols of the nations are silver and gold, the work of men's hands. They have mouths, but they speak not; eyes have they, but they see not; they have ears, but they hear not; neither is there any breath in their mouths. They that make them shall become like unto them; yea, every one that trusts in them. O house of Israel, bless you the Lord: O house of Aaron, bless you the Lord: O house of Levi, bless you the Lord: you that fear the Lord, bless you the Lord. Blessed be the Lord out of Zion, who dwells at Jerusalem. Praise you the Lord.

Psalm cxxxvi.

O give thanks unto the Lord; for he is good: for his loving-kindness endures forever.

O give thanks unto the God of gods: for his loving-kindness endures forever.

O give thanks unto the Lord of lords: for his loving-kindness endures forever.

To him who alone does great marvels: for his loving-kindness endures forever.

To him that by understanding made the heavens: for his loving-kindness endures forever.

To him that spread forth the earth above the waters: for his loving-kindness endures forever.

To him that made great lights: for his loving kindness endures forever.

The sun to rule by day: for his loving-kindness endures forever.

The moon and stars to rule by night: for his loving-kindness endures forever.

To him that smote the Egyptians in their first born: for his loving-kindness endures forever.

And brought out Israel from among them: for his loving-kindness endures forever.

With a strong hand, and with a stretched out arm: for his loving-kindness endures forever.

To him who parted the Red Sea in sunder: for his loving-kindness endures forever.

And made Israel to pass through the midst of it: for his loving-kindness endures forever.

But overthrew Pharaoh and his host in the Red Sea: for his loving-kindness endures forever.

To him who led his people through the wilderness: for his loving-kindness endures forever.

To him who smote great kings; for his loving-kindness endures forever.

And slew mighty kings: for his loving-kindness endures forever.

Sihon king of the Amorites: for his loving-kindness endures forever.

And Og king of Bashan: for his loving-kindness endures forever.

And gave their land for a heritage: for his loving-kindness endures forever.

Even a heritage under Israel his servant: for his loving-kindness endures forever.

Who remembered us in our low estate: for his loving-kindness endures forever.

And has released us from our adversaries: for his loving-kindness endures forever.

He gives food to all flesh: for his loving-kindness endures forever.
O give thanks unto the God of heaven: for his loving-kindness endures forever.

Psalm xxxiii.

Exult in the Lord, O you righteous: praise is seemly for the upright. Give thanks unto the Lord with the lyre; sing praises unto him with the harp of ten strings. Sing unto him a new song; play skilfully with shouts of joy. For the word of the Lord is right; and all his work is done in faithfulness. He loves righteousness and justice: the earth is full of the loving-kindness of the Lord. By the word of the Lord the heavens were made; and all the host of them by the breath of his mouth. He gathers the waters of the sea together as a heap: he lays up the floods in store-houses. Let all the earth fear the Lord: let all the inhabitants of the world stand in awe of him. For he spoke, and it was; he commanded, and it stood fast. The Lord has frustrated the design of the nations; he has foiled the thoughts of the peoples. The counsel of the Lord stands fast forever, the thoughts of his heart to all generations. Happy is the nation whose god is the Lord; the people whom he has chosen for his own inheritance. The Lord looks down from heaven; he beholds all the sons of men; from the place of his habitation he gazes upon all the inhabitants of the earth; he that fashions the hearts of them all, that gives heed to all their works. A king is not saved by greatness of power: a mighty man is not delivered by greatness of strength. A horse is a vain thing for safety: neither shall he rescue any by his great power. Behold the eye of the Lord is upon them that fear him, upon them that hope for his loving-kindness to deliver their soul from death, and to keep them alive in famine. Our soul waits for the Lord: he is our help and our shield. For our heart shall rejoice in him, because we have trusted in his holy name. Let your loving-kindness, O Lord, be upon us, according as we have hoped for you.

Psalm xcii.

A Psalm, a Song for the Sabbath Day. It is a good thing to give thanks unto the Lord, and to sing praises unto your name, O Most High: to declare your loving-kindness in the morning, and your faithfulness every night, with an instrument of ten strings and with a harp, with thoughtful music upon the lyre. For you, O Lord, have made me rejoice through your work: I will exult in the work of your hands. How great are your works, O Lord: your thoughts are very deep. A brutish man knows it not, neither does a fool understand this: when the wicked sprang up as the grass, and all the workers of iniquity flourished, it was that they might be destroyed forever. But you, O Lord, are on high forevermore. For, lo, your enemies, O Lord, for, lo, your enemies shall perish; all the workers of iniquity shall be scattered. But my horn have you exalted, like that of the wild-ox: I am anointed with fresh oil. My eye also has seen my desire on my enemies; my ears have heard my desire of them that rose up against me, doers of evil. The righteous shall spring up like a palm-tree; he shall grow tall like a cedar in Lebanon. Planted in the house of the Lord, they shall blossom in the courts of our God. They shall still shoot forth in old age; they shall be full of sap and green: to declare that the Lord is upright: he is my rock, and there is no unrighteousness in him.

Psalm xciii.

The Lord reigns; he has robed him in majesty; the Lord has robed him, yea, he has girded himself with strength: the world also is set firm, that it cannot be moved. Your throne is set firm from of old: you are from everlasting. The streams have lifted up, O Lord, the streams have lifted tip their voice; the streams lift up their roaring. Than the voices of many waters, mighty waters, breakers of the sea, more mighty is the Lord on high. Your testimonies are very faithful: holiness becomes your house, O Lord, forevermore.

On Weekdays continue here from above.

Let the glory of the Lord endure forever; let the Lord rejoice in his works. Let the name of the Lord be blessed from this time forth and forevermore. From the rising of the sun unto the going down thereof the Lord's name is to be praised. The Lord is high above all nations, and his glory above the heavens. Your name, O Lord, endures forever; your memorial, O Lord, throughout all generations. The Lord has established his throne in the heavens; and his kingdom rules over all. Let the heavens rejoice, and let the earth be glad; and let them say among the nations, The Lord reigns. The Lord reigns; the Lord has reigned; the Lord shall reign forever and ever. The Lord is King forever and ever; the nations are perished out of his land. The Lord has frustrated the design of the nations; he has foiled the thoughts of the peoples. Many are the thoughts in a man's heart; but the counsel of the Lord, that shall stand. The counsel of the Lord stands fast forever, the thoughts of his heart to all generations. For he spoke, and it was; he commanded, and it stood fast. For the Lord has chosen Zion; he has desired it for his habitation. For the Lord has chosen Jacob unto himself, Israel for his peculiar treasure. For the Lord will not cast off his people, neither will he forsake his inheritance. And he, being merciful, forgives iniquity, and destroys not: yea, many a time he turns his anger away, and does not stir up all his wrath. Save, Lord: may the King answer us on the day when we call.

Happy are they that dwell in your house: they will be ever praising you. (Selah.)
Happy is the people that is in such a case: happy is the people, whose God is the Lord.
Psalm cxlv. A Psalm of Praise: of David.
I will extol you, my God, O King; and I will bless your name forever and ever.
Every day will I bless you; and I will praise your name forever and ever.
Great is the Lord, and exceedingly to be praised: and his greatness is unsearchable.
One generation shall laud your works to another, and shall declare your mighty acts.
On the majestic glory of your splendor, and on your marvelous deeds, will I meditate.
And men shall speak of the might of your awful acts; and I will recount your greatness.
They shall pour forth the fame of your great goodness and shall exult in your righteousness.
The Lord is gracious and merciful; slow to anger and of great loving-kindness.
The Lord is good to all; and his tender mercies are over all his works.
All your works shall give thanks unto you, O Lord; and your loving ones shall bless you.
They shall speak of the glory of your kingdom, and talk of your power.
To make known to the sons of men his mighty acts, and the majestic glory of his kingdom.
Your kingdom is an everlasting kingdom, and your dominion endures throughout all generations.
The Lord upholds all that fall, and raises up all those that are bowed down.
The eyes of all wait upon you; and you give them their food in due season.
You open your hand, and satisfy every living thing with favor.

The Lord is righteous in all his ways, and loving in all his works.

The Lord is nigh unto all them that call upon him. To all that call upon him in truth.

He will fulfil the desire of them that fear him; he also will hear their cry and will save them.

The Lord guards all them that love him; but all the wicked will he destroy.

My mouth shall speak of the praise of the Lord; and let all flesh bless his holy name forever and ever.

But we will bless the Lord from this time forth and forevermore. Praise you the Lord.

Psalm cxlvi.

Praise you the Lord. Praise the Lord, O my soul: I will praise the Lord, while I live; I will sing praises unto my God while I have my being. Put not your trust in princes, in a son of man, in whom there is no help, When his breath goes forth, he returns to his earth; in that very day his designs perish. Happy is he that has the God of Jacob for his help, whose hope is in the Lord, his God: who made heaven and earth, the sea, and all that is therein; who keeps truth forever; who executes judgment for the oppressed; who gives food to the hungry: the Lord looses the prisoners; the Lord opens the eyes of the blind; the Lord raises up them that are bowed down; the Lord loves the righteous; the Lord guards the strangers; he upholds the fatherless and widow; but the way of the wicked he makes crooked. The Lord shall reign forever, your God, O Zion, unto all generations. Praise you the Lord.

Psalm cxlvii.

Praise you the Lord; for it is good to sing praises unto our God; for it is pleasant, and praise is seemly. The Lord does build up Jerusalem; he gathers together the outcasts of Israel. He heals the broken in heart, and binds up their wounds. He counts the number of the stars; he calls them all by their names. Great is our Lord, and mighty in power; his understanding is infinite. The Lord upholds the meek; he abases the wicked to the ground. Sing unto the Lord with thanksgiving; sing praises upon the lyre unto our God: who covers the heaven with clouds, who prepares rain for the earth, who makes grass to sprout upon the mountains; who gives to the beast its food, and to the young ravens which cry. He delights not in the strength of the horse. He takes no pleasure in the vigor of a man. The Lord takes pleasure in them that fear him, in them that hope for his loving-kindness. Extol the Lord, O Jerusalem; praise your God, O Zion. For he has strengthened the bars of your gates; he has blessed your children within you. He makes peace in your borders; he satisfies you with the fat of wheat. He sends out his commandment to the earth; his word runs very swiftly. He gives snow like wool; he scatters hoar frost like ashes. He casts forth his ice like morsels: who can stand before his cold? He sends out his word, and melts them: he causes his wind to blow, and the waters flow. He declares his words unto Jacob, his statutes and his judgments unto Israel. He has not dealt so with any nation: and as for his judgments, they do not know them. Praise you the Lord.

Psalm cxlviii.

Praise you the Lord. Praise you the Lord from the heavens: praise him in the heights. Praise you him, all his angels; praise you him, all his host. Praise you him, sun and moon: praise him, all you stars of light. Praise him, you heavens of heavens, and you waters that are above the heavens. Let them praise the name of the Lord: for he commanded, and they were created. He has established them forever and ever: he gave a decree which none shall transgress. Praise the Lord from the earth, you sea-monsters and all deeps: fire and hail, snow and smoke; stormy wind, fulfilling his word: mountains and all hills; fruit trees and all cedars: wild beasts and all cattle; creeping things and winged birds: kings of the earth and all peoples; princes and all judges of the earth: both young men and maidens; old men and children: let them praise the name of the Lord; for his name alone is exalted: his majesty is above the earth and heaven. And he has lifted up a horn for his people, to the praise of all his loving ones: even of the children of Israel, the people near unto him: praise you the Lord.

Psalm cxlix.

Praise you the Lord. Sing unto the Lord a new song; his praise in the assembly of those that love him. Let Israel rejoice in his Maker: let the children of Zion be glad in their King. Let them praise his name with the dance: let them sing praises unto him with the timbrel and lyre. For the Lord takes pleasure in his people: he adorns the meek with salvation. Let those that love him triumph in glory: let them exult upon their beds. High praises of God are in their throat, and a two-edged sword in their hand; to execute vengeance upon the nations, and punishments upon the peoples: to bind their kings with chains, and their nobles with fetters of iron; to execute upon them the judgment written: this is an honor for all his loving ones. Praise you the Lord.

Psalm cl.

Praise you the Lord. Praise God in his sanctuary: praise him in the firmament of his power. Praise him for his mighty acts: praise him according to his abundant greatness. Praise him with the blast of the horn: praise him with the harp and the lyre. Praise him with the timbrel and dance: praise him with stringed instruments and the pipe. Praise him with the clear-toned cymbals; praise him with the loud-sounding cymbals. Let everything that has breath praise the Lord: praise you the Lord.

The last verse is repeated.

Blessed he the Lord forevermore. Amen, and Amen. Blessed be the Lord out of Zion, who dwells in Jerusalem. Praise you the Lord. Blessed be the Lord God, the God of Israel, who alone does wondrous things: and blessed be his glorious name forever; and let the whole earth be filled with his glory. Amen, and Amen.

The following to "worship you," is said standing.

1 Chron. xxix. 10-13.

And David blessed the Lord in the presence of all the congregation: and David said, Blessed are you, O Lord, the God of Israel our father, from everlasting to everlasting. Yours, O Lord, is the greatness, and the power, and the glory, and the victory, and the majesty: for all that is in the heaven and in the earth is yours; Yours, O Lord, is the kingdom, and the supremacy as head over all. Riches and honor come of you, and you rule over all; and in your hand are might and power; and in your hand it is to make great, and to give strength unto all. Now, therefore, our God, we give thanks unto you, and praise your glorious name.

Nehemiah ix. 6-11.

You are the Lord, even you alone; you have made the heavens, the heaven of heavens, and all their host, the earth and all things that are thereon, the seas and all that is in them, and you give life to them all; and the host of heaven worship you. You are the Lord the God, who did choose Abram, and brought him forth out of Ur of the Chaldees, and gave him the name of Abraham: and found his heart faithful before you:

And you made a covenant with him to give the land of the Canaanite, the Hittite, the Amorite, and the Perizzite, and the Jebusite, and the Girgashite, even to give it unto his seed, and has performed your words; for you are righteous. And you saw the affliction of our fathers in Egypt, and heard their cry by the Red Sea; and showed signs and wonders upon Pharaoh, and on all his servants, and on all the people of his land; for you knew that they dealt arrogantly against them; and did make you a name, as it is this day. And you did divide the sea before them, so that they went through the midst of the sea on the dry land; and their pursuers you did cast into the depths, as a stone into the mighty waters.

Exod. xiv. 30-xv. 18.

Thus the Lord saved Israel that day out of the hand of the Egyptians; and Israel saw the Egyptians dead upon the sea shore. And Israel saw the great power which the Lord put forth against the Egyptians, and the people feared the Lord: and they believed in the Lord, and in Moses his servant.

Then sang Moses and the children of Israel this song unto the Lord, and spoke, saying: I will sing unto the Lord, for he has been highly exalted: the horse and his rider has he thrown into the sea. The Lord is my strength and song, and he is become my salvation: this is my God, and I will glorify him; my father's God, and I will exalt him. The Lord is a man of war: the Lord is his name. Pharaoh's chariots and his host has he cast into the sea: and his chosen captains are sunk in the Red Sea. The floods cover them: they went down into the depths like a stone. Your right hand, O Lord, that is glorious in power, your right hand, O Lord, dashes in pieces the enemy. And in the greatness of your majesty you overthrow them that rise up against you: you send forth your wrath, it consumes them as stubble. And with the blast of your nostrils the waters were piled up, the streams stood upright as a heap; the floods were congealed in the heart of the sea. The enemy said, I will pursue, I will overtake, I will divide the spoil: my lust shall be satisfied upon them; I will draw my sword, my hand shall destroy them. You did blow with your wind, the sea covered them: they sank as lead in the mighty waters. Who is like unto you, O Lord, amongst the mighty ones: who is like unto you, glorious in holiness, revered in praises, doing marvels? You stretched out your right hand, the earth swallowed them. You in your loving-kindness have led the people which you have redeemed: you have guided them in your strength to your holy habitation. The peoples have heard it; they tremble: pangs have taken hold of the inhabitants of Philistia. Then were the dukes of Edom confounded; the mighty men of Moab, trembling takes hold of them: all the inhabitants of Canaan are melted away. Terror and dread falls upon them: by the greatness of your arm they are as still as a stone; till your people pass over, O Lord, till the people pass over, which you have acquired. You will bring them in, and plan them in the mountain of your inheritance, the place, O Lord, which you have made for you to dwell in, the sanctuary, O Lord, which your hands have established. The Lord shall reign forever and ever. The Lord shall reign forever and ever.

For the kingdom is the Lord's: and he is ruler over the nations. And saviors shall come up on mount Zion to judge the mount of Esau; and the kingdom shall be the Lord's. And the Lord shall be King over all the earth: in that day shall the Lord be One, and his name One. And in your Torah it is written, saying, Hear, O Israel: the Lord our God, the Lord is One.

On Sabbaths and Holydays continue here "The breath," etc.

Praised be your name forever, O our King, the great and holy God and King, in heaven and on earth; for unto you, O Lord our God, and God of our fathers, song and praise are becoming, hymn and psalm, strength and dominion, victory, greatness and might, renown and glory, holiness and sovereignty, blessings and thanksgivings from henceforth even forever. Blessed are you, O Lord, God and King, great in praises, God of thanksgivings, Lord of wonders, who make choice of song and psalm, O King and God, the life of all worlds.

Reader.—Magnified and sanctified be his great name in the world which he has created according to his will. May he establish his kingdom during your life and during your days, and during the life of all the house of Israel, even speedily and at a near time, and say ye, Amen.

Cong. and Reader.—Let his great name be blessed forever and to all eternity.

Reader.—Blessed, praised and glorified, exalted, extolled and honored, magnified and lauded be the name of the Holy One, blessed be he; though he be high above all the blessings and hymns, praises and consolations, which are uttered in the world; and say ye, Amen.

Congregation in an undertone. Blessed, praised, glorified, exalted and extolled be the name of the supreme King of kings, the Holy One, blessed be he, who is the first and the last, and beside him there is no God. Extol you him that rides upon the heavens by his name Yah, and rejoice before him. His name is exalted above all blessing and praise. Blessed be His name, whose glorious kingdom is forever and ever. Let the name of the Lord be blessed from this time forth and forevermore.

Reader.—Bless you the Lord who is to be blessed.

Cong. and Reader.—Blessed is the Lord who is to be blessed forever and ever.

Blessed are you, O Lord our God, King of the universe, who forms light and creates darkness, who makes peace and creates all things:

Who in mercy give light to the earth and to them that dwell thereon and in your goodness renews the creation every day continually. How manifold are your works, O Lord! In wisdom have you made them all: the earth is full of your possessions. O King, who alone was exalted from aforetime, praised, glorified and extolled from days of old; O everlasting God, in your abundant mercies, have mercy upon us, Lord of our strength, Rock of our stronghold. Shield of our salvation, you Stronghold of ours!

The blessed God, great in knowledge, prepared and formed the rays of the sun: it was a boon he produced as a glory to his name: he set the luminaries round about his strength. The chiefs of his hosts are holy beings that exalt the Almighty, and continually declare the glory of God and his holiness. Be you blessed, O Lord our God, for the excellence of your handiwork, and for the bright luminaries which you have made: they shall glorify you forever.

Be you blessed, O our Rock, our King and Redeemer, Creator of holy beings, praised be your name forever, O our King; Creator of ministering spirits, all of whom stand in the heights of the universe, and proclaim with awe in unison aloud the words of the living God and everlasting King. All of them are beloved, pure and mighty; and all of them in dread and awe do the will of their Master; and all of them open their mouths in holiness and purity, with song and psalm, while they bless and praise, glorify and reverence, sanctify and ascribe sovereignty to—

The name of the Divine King, the great, mighty and dreaded One, holy is he; and they all take upon themselves the yoke of the kingdom of heaven one from the other, and give sanction to one another to hallow their Creator: in tranquil joy of spirit, with pure speech and holy melody they all respond in unison, and exclaim with awe:

Holy, holy, holy is the Lord of hosts: the whole earth is full of his glory.

And the Ophanim and the holy Chayoth with a noise of great rushing, upraising themselves towards the Seraphim, thus over against them offer praise and say:

Blessed be the glory of the Lord from his place.

To the blessed God they offer pleasant melodies; to the King, the living and ever-enduring God, they utter hymns and make their praises heard; for he alone performs mighty deeds, and makes new things; he is the Lord of battles; he sows righteousness, causes salvation to spring forth, creates remedies, and is revered in praises. He is the Lord of wonders, who in his goodness renews the creation every day continually; as it is said, (O give thanks) to him that makes great lights, for his loving-kindness endures forever. O cause a new light to shine upon Zion, and may we all be worthy soon to enjoy its brightness. Blessed are you, O Lord, Creator of the luminaries.

With abounding love have you loved us, O Lord our God, with great and exceeding pity have you pitied us. O our Father, our King, for our fathers' sake, who trusted in you, and whom you did teach the statutes of life, be also gracious unto us and teach us. O our Father, merciful Father, ever compassionate, have mercy upon us; O put it into our hearts to understand and to discern, to mark, learn and teach, to heed, to do and to fulfil in love all the words of instruction in your Torah. Enlighten our eyes in your Torah, and let our hearts cleave to your commandments, and unite our hearts to love and fear your name, so that we be never put to shame. Because we have trusted in your holy, great and revered name, we shall rejoice and he glad in your salvation. O bring us in peace from the four corners of the earth, and make us go upright to our land; for you are a God who works salvation. You have chosen us from all peoples and tongues, and has brought us near unto your great name forever in faithfulness, that we might in love give thanks unto you and proclaim your unity. Blessed are you, O Lord, who has chosen your people Israel in love.

When Prayers are not said with the Congregation, add—

God, faithful King!

Deut. vi. 4-9.

Hear, O Israel: the Lord our God, the Lord is One.

Blessed be His name, whose glorious kingdom is forever and ever.

And you shall love the Lord your God with all your heart, and with all your soul, and with all your might. And these words, which. I command you this day, shall be upon your heart: and you shall teach them diligently unto your children, and shall talk of them when you sit-test in your house, and when you walk by the way, and when you lie down, and when you rise up. And you shall bind them for a sign upon your hand, and they shall be for frontlets between your eyes. And you shall write them upon the door posts of your house, and upon your gates.

Deut. xi. 13-21.

And it shall come to pass, if you shall hearken diligently unto my commandments which I command you this day, to love the Lord your God, and to serve him with all your heart and. with all your soul, that I will give the rain of your land in its season, the former rain and the latter rain, that you may gather in your corn, and your wine, and your oil. And I will give grass in your field for your cattle, and you shall eat and be satisfied. Take heed to yourselves, lest your heart be deceived, and you turn aside, and serve other gods, and worship them; and the anger of the Lord be kindled against you, and he shut up the heaven, that there be no rain, and that the land yield not her fruit; and you perish quickly from off the good land which the Lord gives you. Therefore shall you lay up these my words in your heart and in your soul; and you shall bind them for a sign upon your hand, and they shall be for frontlets between your eyes. And you shall teach them your children, talking of them when you sit in your house, and when you walk by the way, and when you lie down, and when you rise up. And you shall write them upon the door posts of your house, and upon your gates: that your days may be multiplied, and the days of your children, upon the land which the Lord swore to your fathers to give them, as the days of the heavens above the earth.

Numbers xv. 37-41.

And the Lord spoke to Moses, saying, Speak unto the children of Israel, and bid them that they make them a fringe upon the corners of their garments throughout their generations, and that they put upon the fringe of each corner a cord of blue: and it shall be unto you for a fringe, that you may look upon it, and remember all the commandments of the Lord, and do them; and that you go not about after your own heart and your own eyes, after which you use to go astray: that you may remember and do all my commandments, and be holy unto your God. I am the Lord your God, who brought you out of the land of Egypt, to be your God: I am the Lord your God.

True and firm, established and enduring, right and faithful, beloved and precious, desirable and pleasant, revered and mighty, well-ordered and acceptable, good and beautiful is this your word unto us forever and ever. It is true, the God of the universe is our King, the Rock of Jacob, the Shield of our salvation: throughout all generations he endures and his name endures; his throne is established, and his kingdom and his faithfulness endure forever. His words also live and endure; they are faithful and desirable forever and to all eternity, as for our fathers so also for us, our children, our generations, and for all the generations of the seed of Israel his servants.

For the first and for the last ages your word is good and endures forever and ever; it is true and trustworthy, a statute which shall not pass away. True it is that you are indeed the Lord our God, and the God of our fathers, our King, our fathers' King, our Redeemer, the Redeemer of our fathers, our Maker, the Rock of our salvation; our Deliverer and Rescuer from everlasting, such is your name; there is no God beside you.

You have been the help of our fathers from of old, a Shield and Savior to their children after them in every generation: in the heights of the universe is your habitation, and your judgments and your righteousness reach to the furthest ends of the earth. Happy is the man who hearkens unto your commandments, and lays up your Torah and your word in his heart. True it is that you are indeed the Lord of your people, and a mighty King to plead their cause. True it is that you are indeed the first and you are the last, and beside you we have no King, Redeemer and Savior. From Egypt you did redeem us, O Lord our God, and from the house of bondmen you did deliver us; all their first born you did slay, but your first-born you did redeem; you did divide the Red Sea, and drown the proud; but you made the beloved to pass through, while the waters covered their adversaries, not one of whom was left. Wherefore the beloved praised and extolled God, and offered hymns, songs, praises, blessings and thanksgivings to the King and God, who lives and endures; who is high and exalted, great and revered; who brings low the haughty, and raises up the lowly, leads forth the prisoners, delivers the meek, helps the poor, and answers his people when they cry unto him; even praises to the Most High God, blessed is he, and ever to be blessed. Moses and the children of Israel sang a song unto you with great joy, saying, all of them,

Who is like unto you, O Lord, among the might ones? Who is like unto you, glorious in holiness revered in praises, doing marvels?

With a new song the redeemed people offered praise unto your name at the sea shore: they all gave thanks in unison, and proclaimed your sovereignty, and said,

The Lord shall reign forever and ever.

O Rock of Israel, arise to the help of Israel, and deliver, according to your promise, Judah and Israel. Our Redeemer, the Lord of hosts is his name, the Holy One of Israel. Blessed are you, O Lord, who has redeemed Israel.

The following prayer (Amidah) to "as in ancient years," is to be said standing.

O Lord, open you my lips, and my mouth shall declare your praise.

Blessed are you, O Lord our God and God of our fathers, God of Abraham, God of Isaac, and God of Jacob, the great, mighty and revered God, the most high God, who bestows loving-kindnesses, and possesses all things; who remembers the pious deeds of the patriarchs, and in love will bring a redeemer to their children's children for your name's sake.

During the Ten Days of Penitence say—

Remember us unto life, O King, who delights in life, and inscribe us in the book of life, for your own sake, O living God.

O King, Helper, Savior and Shield. Blessed are you, O Lord, the Shield of Abraham.

You, O Lord, are mighty forever, you quicken the dead, you are mighty to save,

From the Eighth Day of Solemn Assembly until the First Day of Passover say—

You cause the wind to blow and the rain to fall

You sustain the living with loving-kindness, quicken the dead with great mercy, support the falling, heal the sick, loosest the bound, and keeps your faith to them that sleep in the dust. Who is like unto you, Lord of mighty acts, and who resembles you, O King, who kills and quickens, and causes salvation to spring forth?

During the Ten Days of Penitence say—

Who is like unto you, Father of mercy, who in mercy remembers your creatures unto life?

Yea, faithful are you to quicken the dead. Blessed are you, O Lord, who quickens the dead.

You are holy, and your name is holy, and holy beings praise you daily. (Selah.) Blessed are you, O Lord, the holy God.

During the Ten Days of Penitence conclude the blessing thus—
the holy King.

When the Reader repeats the Amidah, the following is said, to "holy God."

Reader.—We will sanctify your name in the world even as they sanctify it in the highest heavens, as it is written by the hand of your prophet:

And they called one unto the other and said,

Cong.—Holy, holy, holy is the Lord of hosts: the whole earth is full of his glory.

Reader.—Those over against them say, Blessed-

Cong.—Blessed be the glory of the Lord from his place.

Reader.—And in your Holy Words it is written, saying,

Cong.—The Lord shall reign forever, your God, O Zion, unto all generations. Praise you the Lord.

Reader.—Unto all generations we will declare your greatness, and to all eternity we will proclaim your holiness, and your praise, O our God, shall not depart from our mouth forever, for you are a great and holy God and King. Blessed are you, O Lord, the holy God.

During the Ten Days of Penitence conclude the Blessing thus:
the holy King.

You favor man with knowledge, and teach mortals understanding. O favor us with knowledge, understanding and discernment from you. Blessed are you, O Lord, gracious Giver of knowledge.

Cause us to return, O our Father, unto your Torah; draw us near, O our King, unto your service, and bring us back in perfect repentance unto your presence. Blessed are you, O Lord, who delights in repentance.

Forgive us, O our Father, for we have sinned; pardon us, O our King, for we have transgressed;

On Fast Days Selichoth are inserted here.

For you do pardon and forgive. Blessed are you, O Lord, who are gracious, and do abundantly forgive.

Look upon our affliction and plead our cause, and redeem us speedily for your name's sake; for you are a mighty Redeemer. Blessed are you, O Lord, the Redeemer of Israel.

On Fast Days the Reader here says "Answer us," etc., and concludes thus—

Blessed are you, O Lord, who answers in time of trouble.

Heal us, O Lord, and we shall be healed; save us and we shall be saved; for you are our praise. Vouchsafe a perfect healing to all our wounds; for you, almighty King, are a faithful and merciful Physician. Blessed are you, O Lord, who heals the sick of your people Israel.

Bless this year unto us, O Lord our God, together with every kind of the produce thereof, for our welfare; give a blessing

During the Winter Season substitute for the last sentence:
Give dew and rain for a blessing upon the face of the earth.

upon the face of the earth. O satisfy us with your goodness, and bless our year like other good years. Blessed are you, O Lord, who blesses the years.

Sound the great horn for our freedom; lift up the ensign to gather our exiles, and gather us from the four corners of the earth. Blessed are you, O Lord, who gathers the banished ones of your people Israel.

Restore our judges as at the first, and our counsellors as at the beginning; remove from us grief and suffering; reign you over us, O Lord, you alone, in loving-kindness and tender mercy, and justify us in judgment. Blessed are you, O Lord, the King who loves righteousness and judgment.

During the Ten Days of Penitence conclude the blessing thus—
the King of Judgment.

And for slanderers let there be no hope, and let all wickedness perish as in a moment; let all your enemies be speedily cut off, and the dominion of arrogance do you uproot and crush, cast down and humble speedily in our days. Blessed are you, O Lord, who breaks the enemies and humblest the arrogant.

Towards the righteous and the pious, towards the elders of your people the house of Israel, towards the remnant of their scribes, towards the proselytes of righteousness, and towards us also may your tender mercies be stirred, O Lord our God; grant a good reward unto all who faithfully trust in your name; set our portion with them forever, so that we may not be put to shame; for we have trusted in you. Blessed are you, O Lord, the stay and trust of the righteous.

And to Jerusalem, your city, return in mercy, and dwell therein as you have spoken; rebuild it soon in our days as an everlasting building, and speedily set up therein the throne of David. Blessed are you, O Lord, who rebuilds Jerusalem.

Speedily cause the offspring of David, your servant, to flourish, and let his horn be exalted by your salvation, because we wait for your salvation all the day. Blessed are you, O Lord, who causes the horn of salvation to flourish.

Hear our voice, O Lord our God; spare us and have mercy upon us, and accept our prayer in mercy and favor; for you are a God who hearkens unto prayers and supplications: from your presence, O our King, turn us not empty away; for you hearken in mercy to the prayer of your people Israel. Blessed are you, O Lord, who hearkens unto prayer.

Accept, O Lord our God, your people Israel and their prayer; restore the service to the oracle of your house; receive in love and favor both the fire-offerings of Israel and their prayer; and may the service of your people Israel be ever acceptable unto you.

On New Moon and the Intermediate Days of Passover and Sukkot the following is added—

Our God and God of our fathers! May our remembrance rise, come and be accepted before you, with the remembrance of our fathers, of Messiah the son of David your servant, of Jerusalem your holy city, and of all your people the house of Israel, bringing deliverance and well-being, grace, loving-kindness and mercy, life and peace on this day of

On Passover—
the Feast of Unleavened Bread.
On New Moon say—

the New Moon.

On Sukkot—

the Feast of Sukkot.

Remember us, O Lord our God, thereon for our well-being; be mindful of us for blessing, and save us unto life: by your promise of salvation and mercy, spare us and be gracious unto us; have mercy upon us and save us; for our eyes are bent upon you, because you are a gracious and merciful God and King.

And let our eyes behold your return in mercy to Zion. Blessed are you, O Lord, who restores your divine presence unto Zion.

We give thanks unto you, for you are the Lord our God and the God of our fathers forever and ever; you are the Rock of our lives, the Shield of our salvation through every generation. We will give thanks unto you and declare your praise for our lives which are committed unto your hand, and for our souls which are in your charge, and for your miracles, which are daily with us, and for your wonders and your benefits, which are wrought at all times, evening, morn and noon. O you who are all-good, whose mercies fail not; you, merciful Being, whose loving-kindnesses never cease, we have ever hoped in you.

Congregation in an undertone

We give thanks unto you, for you are the Lord our God and the God of our fathers, the God of all flesh, our Creator and the Creator of all things in the beginning. Blessings and thanksgivings be to your great and holy name, because you have kept us in life and has preserved us: so may you continue to keep us in life and to preserve us. O gather our exiles to your holy courts to observe your statutes, to do your will, and to serve you with a perfect heart; seeing that we give thanks unto you. Blessed be the God to whom thanksgivings are due.

On Chanukah and Purim the following is added—

We thank you also for the miracles, for the redemption, for the mighty deeds and saving acts, wrought by you, as well as for the wars which you did wage for our fathers in days of old, at this season.

On Chanukah.

In the days of the Hasmonean, Mattathias son of Yohanan, the High Priest, and his sons, when the iniquitous power of Greece rose up against your people Israel to make them forgetful of your Torah, and to force them to transgress the statutes of your will, then did you in your abundant mercy rise up for them in the time of their trouble; you did plead their cause, you did judge their suit, you did avenge their wrong; you delivered the strong into the hands of the weak, the many into the hands of the few, the impure into the hands of the pure, the wicked into the hands of the righteous, and the arrogant into the hands of them that occupied themselves with your Torah: for yourself you did make a great and holy name in your world, and for your people Israel you did work a great deliverance and redemption as at this day. And thereupon your children came into the oracle of your house, cleansed your temple, purified your sanctuary, kindled lights in your holy courts, and appointed these eight days of Chanukah in order to give thanks and praises unto your great name.

On Purim.

In the days of Mordecai and Esther, in Shushan the capital, when the wicked Haman rose up against them, and sought to destroy, to slay and make to perish all the Jews, both young and old, little children and women, on one day, on the thirteenth day of the twelfth month, which is the month Adar, and to take the spoil of them for a prey,—then did you in your abundant mercy bring his counsel to naught, did frustrate his design, and return his recompense upon his own head; and they hanged him and his sons upon the gallows.

For all these things your name, O our King, shall be continually blessed and exalted forever and ever.

During the Ten Days of Penitence say—
O inscribe all the children of your covenant for a happy life.

And everything that lives shall give thanks unto you forever, and shall praise your name in truth, O God, our salvation and our help. Blessed are you, O Lord, whose name is All-good, and unto whom it is becoming to give thanks.

At the repetition of the Amidah by the Reader, the following is introduced—

Our God and God of our fathers, bless us with the three-fold blessing of your Torah written by the hand of Moses your servant, which was spoken by Aaron and his sons, the priests, your holy people, as it is said, The Lord bless you, and keep you: the Lord make his face to shine upon you, and be gracious unto you: the Lord turn his face unto you, and give you peace.

Grant peace, welfare, blessing, grace, loving kindness and mercy unto us and unto all Israel, your people. Bless us, O our Father, even all of us together, with the light of your countenance for by the light of your countenance you have given us, O Lord our God, the Torah of life, loving-kindness and righteousness, blessing, mercy, life and peace; and may it be good in your sight to bless your people Israel at all times and in every hour with your peace.

During the Ten Days of Penitence say—
In the book of life, blessing, peace and good sustenance may we be remembered and inscribed before you, we and all your people the house of Israel, for a happy life and for peace. Blessed are you, O Lord, who makes peace.

Blessed are you, O Lord, who blesses your people Israel with peace.

O my God! guard my tongue from evil and my lips from speaking guile; and to such as curse me let my soul be dumb, yea, let my soul be unto all as the dust. Open my heart to your Torah, and let my soul pursue your commandments. If any design evil against me, speedily make their counsel of none effect, and frustrate their designs. Do it for the sake of your name, do it for the sake of your right hand, do it for the sake of your holiness, and do it for the sake of your Torah. In order that your beloved ones may be delivered, O save with your right hand, and answer me. Let the words of my mouth and the meditation of my heart be acceptable before you, O Lord, my Rock and my Redeemer. He who makes peace in his high places, may he make peace for us and for all Israel, and say ye, Amen.

May it be your will, O Lord our God and God of our fathers, that the temple be speedily rebuilt in our days, and grant our portion in your Torah. And there we will serve you with awe, as in the days of old, and as in ancient years. Then shall the offering of Judah and Jerusalem be pleasant unto the Lord, as in the days of old, and as in ancient years.

In illness, or when time is lacking, the following shortened form of the Amidah may be said—

"O Lord," to "holy God."

Give us understanding, O Lord our God, to know your ways; circumcise our hearts to fear you, and forgive us so that we may be redeemed. Keep us far from sorrow; satiate us on the pastures of your land, and gather our scattered ones from the four corners of the earth. Let them that go astray be judged according to your will, and wave your hand over the wicked. Let the righteous rejoice in the rebuilding of your city, and in the establishment of your temple, and in the flourishing of the horn of David your servant, and in the clear-shining light of the son of Jesse, your anointed. Even before we call, do you answer. Blessed are you, O Lord, who hearkens unto prayer.

Continue—

"Accept," to "ancient years."

On New Moon, the Intermediate Days of Passover and Sukkot, and on the Feast of Dedication, say "Hallel."

During the Ten Days of Penitence, except on the Sabbath, the following to "and save us", is said.

Our Father, our King, we have sinned before you.
Our Father, our King, we have no king but you.
Our Father, our King, deal with us for the sake of your name.
Our Father, our King, let a happy year begin for us.
Our Father, our King, nullify all evil decrees against us.
Our Father, our King, nullify the designs of those that hate us.
Our Father, our King, make the counsel of our enemies of none effect.
Our Father, our King, rid us of every oppressor and adversary.
Our Father, our King, close the mouths of our adversaries and accusers.
Our Father, our King, of pestilence and the sword, of famine, captivity and destruction, rid the children of your covenant.
Our Father, our King, withhold the plague from your inheritance.
Our Father, our King, forgive and pardon all our iniquities.
Our Father, our King, blot out our transgressions, and make them pass away from before your eyes.
Our Father, our King, erase in your abundant mercies all the records of our guilt.
Our Father, our King, bring us back in perfect repentance unto you.

Our Father, our King, send a perfect healing to the sick of your people.

Our Father, our King, rend the evil judgment decreed against us.

Our Father, our King, let your remembrance of us be for good.

Our Father, our King, inscribe us in the book of happy life.

Our Father, our King, inscribe us in the book of redemption and salvation.

Our Father, our King, inscribe us in the book of maintenance and sustenance.

Our Father, our King, inscribe us in the book of merit.

Our Father, our King, inscribe us in the book of forgiveness and pardon.

Our Father, our King, let salvation soon spring forth for us.

Our Father, our King, exalt the horn of Israel, your people.

Our Father, our King, exalt the horn of your anointed.

Our Father, our King, fill our hands with your blessings.

Our Father, our King, fill our storehouses with plenty.

Our Father, our King, hear our voice, spare us, and have mercy upon us.

Our Father, our King, receive our prayer in mercy and in favor.

Our Father, our King, open the gates of heaven unto our prayer.

Our Father, our King, we pray you, turn us not back empty from your presence.

Our Father, our King, remember that we are but dust.

Our Father; our King, let this hour be an hour of mercy and a time of favor with you.

Our Father, our King, have compassion upon us and upon our children and our infants.

Our Father, our King, do this for the sake of them that were slain for your holy name.

Our Father, our King, do it for the sake of them that were slaughtered for your Unity.

Our Father, our King, do it for the sake of them that went through fire and water for the sanctification of your name.

Our Father, our King, avenge before our eyes your blood of your servants that has been shed.

Our Father, our King, do it for your sake, if not for ours.

Our Father, our King, do it for your sake, and save us.

Our Father, our King, do it for the sake of your abundant mercies.

Our Father, our King, do it for the sake of your great, mighty and revered name by which we are called.

Our Father, our King, be gracious unto us and answer us, for we have no good works of our own; deal with us in charity and kindness, and save us.

On Mondays and Thursdays the following is said to "the Lord is One." On other Week Days continue, "And David said," etc. Both these Prayers are omitted on New Moon, during the whole month of Nisan, on the thirty-third day of Counting the Omer, from the first day of Sivan until the second day after Pentecost, on the 9th and 15th of Ab, on the day before New Year, from the day before the Fast of Atonement until the second day after Sukkot, on the Feast of Dedication, on the 15th of Shebat, on the two days of Purim, and on the two days of Purim Katon, the 14th and 15th of Adar Rishon. These prayers are also omitted in the house of a mourner during the week of mourning, and at the celebration of a circumcision.

And he, being merciful, forgives iniquity and destroys not: yea, many a time he turns his anger away and cloth not stir up all his wrath. Withhold not you your tender mercies from us, O Lord: let your loving-kindness and your truth continually preserve us. Save us, O Lord our God, and gather us from amongst the nations, to give thanks unto your holy name, and to triumph in your praise. If you should mark iniquities, O Lord, who could stand? But there is forgiveness with you, that you may be feared. Not according to our sins will you deal with us, nor requite us according to our iniquities. If our iniquities testify against us, work you, O Lord, for your name's sake. Remember, O Lord, your tender mercies and your loving-kindnesses; for they have been ever of old. May the Lord answer us in the day of trouble, the name of the God of Jacob set us up on high. Save, Lord: may the King answer us on the day when we call. Our Father, our King, be gracious unto us and answer us, for we have no good works of our own; deal with us in charity for your name's sake. Our Lord, our God, hearken to the voice of our supplications, and remember unto us the covenant of our fathers, and save us for your name's sake. And now, O Lord our God, that has brought your people forth out of the land of Egypt with a mighty hand, and have made you a name as at this day; we have sinned, we have done wickedly. O Lord, according to all your righteous acts, let your anger and your fury, I pray you, be turned away from your city Jerusalem, your holy mountain; because for our sins and for the iniquities of our fathers, Jerusalem and your people are become a reproach to all that are round about us. Now therefore, hearken, O our God, unto the prayer of your servant and to his supplications, and cause your face to shine upon your sanctuary that is desolate, for the Lord's sake.

Incline your ear, O my God, and hear; open your eyes, and behold our desolations, and the city which is called by your name: for we do not lay our supplications before you because of our righteous acts, but because of your abundant mercies. O Lord, hear; O Lord forgive; O Lord, hearken and do; defer not; for your own sake, O my God, because your city and your people are called by your name. O our Father, merciful Father, show us a sign for good, and gather our scattered ones from the four corners of the earth. Let all the nations perceive and know that you are the Lord our God. And now, O Lord, you are our Father; we are the clay, and you are our potter, yea, we are all the work of your hand. Save us for your name's sake, our Rock, our King, and our Redeemer. Spare your people, O Lord, and give not your inheritance over to reproach, that the nations should make a by-word of them. Wherefore should they say among the peoples, Where is their God? We know that we have sinned, and there is none to stand up in our behalf; let your great name stand for our defense in time of trouble. We know that we have no good works of our own; deal with us in charity for your name's sake. As a father has mercy upon his children, so, O Lord, have mercy upon us, and save us for your name's sake. Have pity upon your people; have mercy upon your inheritance; spare, we pray you, according to the abundance of your tender mercies; be gracious unto us and answer us, for charity is yours, O Lord; you do wondrous things at all times.

Look, we beseech you, and speedily have mercy upon your people for your name's sake in your abundant mercies. O Lord our God, spare and be merciful; save the sheep of your pasture; let not wrath rule over us, for our eyes are bent upon you; save us for your name's sake. Have mercy upon us for the sake of your covenant; look, and answer us in time of trouble, for salvation is yours, O Lord. Our hope is in you, O God of forgiveness. We beseech you, forgive, O good and forgiving God, for you are a gracious and merciful God and King.

We beseech you, O gracious and merciful King, remember and give heed to the Covenant between the Pieces (with Abraham), and let the binding (upon the altar) of (Isaac) an only son appear before you, to the welfare of Israel. Our Father, our King, be gracious unto us and answer us, for we are called by your great name. You who does wondrous things at all times, deal with us according to your loving-kindness. O gracious and merciful Being, look, and answer us in time of trouble, for salvation is yours, O Lord. Our Father, our King, our Refuge, deal not with us according to the evil of our doings; remember, O Lord, your tender mercies and your loving-kindnesses; save us according to your abundant goodness, and have pity upon us, we beseech you, for we have no other God beside you, our Rock. Forsake us not, O Lord our God, be not far from us; for our soul is shrunken by reason of the sword and captivity and pestilence and plague, and of every trouble and sorrow. Deliver us, for we hope in you; put us not to shame, O Lord our God; make your countenance to shine upon us; remember unto us the covenant of our fathers, and save us for your name's sake. Look upon our troubles, and hear the voice of our prayer, for you hear the prayer of every mouth.

Merciful and gracious God! Have mercy upon us and upon all your works, for there is none like unto you, O Lord our God. We beseech you, forgive our transgressions, O our Father, our King, our Rock and our Redeemer, O living and everlasting God, mighty in strength, loving and good to all your works; for you are the Lord our God. O God, who are slow to anger and full of mercy, deal with us according to the abundance of your tender mercies, and save us for your name's sake. Hear our prayer, O our King, and deliver us from the hand of our enemies; hear our prayer, O our King, and deliver us from all trouble and sorrow. You are our Father, our King, and we are called by your name; desert us not. Forsake us not, our Father, and cast us not off, O our Creator, and forget us not, O our Maker, for you are a gracious and merciful God and King.

There is none gracious and merciful like you, O Lord our God; there is none like you, O God, slow to anger and abounding in loving-kindness and truth. Save us in your abundant mercies; from fierceness and rage deliver us. Remember your servants, Abraham, Isaac and Jacob; look not unto our stubbornness and our wickedness and our sin. Turn from your fierce anger, and repent of the evil against your people. Remove from us the stroke of death, for you are merciful, for such is your way— showing loving-kindness freely throughout all generations. Spare your people, O Lord, and deliver us from your wrath, and remove from us the stroke of the plague, and harsh decrees, for you are the Guardian of Israel. Unto you, O Lord, belongs righteousness, but unto us confusion of face. How may we complain? What can we say, what can we speak, or how can we justify ourselves? We will search our ways and try them, and turn again to you; for your right hand is stretched out to receive the penitent. Save, we beseech you, O Lord; we beseech you, O Lord, send prosperity. We beseech you, O Lord, answer us on the day when we call. For you, O Lord, we wait; for you, O Lord, we hope; in you, O Lord, we trust; be not silent, nor let us be oppressed; for the nations say, Their hope is lost. Let every knee and all that is lofty bow down to you alone.

O you, who opens your hand to repentance, to receive transgressors and sinners—our soul is sore vexed through the greatness of our grief; forget us not forever; arise and save us, for we trust in you. Our Father, our King, though we be without righteousness and good deeds, remember unto us the covenant of our fathers, and the testimony we bear every day that the Lord is One. Look upon our affliction, for many are our grief and the sorrows of our heart. Have pity upon us, O Lord, in the land of our captivity, and pour not out your wrath upon us, for we are your people, the children of your covenant. O God, look upon our sunken glory among the nations, and the abomination in which we are held as of utter defilement. How long shall your strength remain in captivity, and your glory in the hand of the foe? Arouse your might and your zeal against your enemies, that they may be put to shame and broken down in their might. O let not our travail seem little in your sight. Let your tender mercies speedily come to meet us in the day of our trouble; and if not for our sake, do it for your own sake, and destroy not the remembrance of our remnant; but be gracious unto a people, who in constant love proclaim the unity of your name twice every day, saying, Hear, O Israel: the Lord our God, the Lord is One.

And David said unto Gad, I am troubled exceedingly; let us fall, I pray you, into the hand of the Lord, for his mercies are many; but let me not fall into the hand of man.

O you who are merciful and gracious, I have sinned before you. O Lord, full of mercy, have mercy upon me and receive my supplications.

Psalm vi.

O Lord, rebuke me not in your anger: neither chasten me in your hot displeasure. Be gracious unto me, O Lord; for I am withered away: O Lord, heal me; for my bones are troubled. My soul also is sore troubled: and you, O Lord, how long? Return, O Lord, deliver my soul: save me for your loving-kindness' sake. For in death there is no remembrance of you: in the grave who shall give you thanks? I am weary with my groaning; every night I make my bed to swim; I melt away my couch with my tears. My eye wastes away because of grief it waxes old because of all my adversaries. Depart from me, all you workers of iniquity; for the Lord has heard the voice of my weeping. The Lord has heard my supplication; the Lord will receive my prayer. All my enemies shall be ashamed and sore troubled: they shall turn back, they shall be ashamed suddenly.

On Monday and Thursday Mornings the following is added. On other Weekdays, and in the Afternoon Service, continue "O Guardian of Israel."

Reader and Cong.—O Lord God of Israel, turn from your fierce wrath, and repent of the evil against your people.

Cong.—Look from heaven and see how we have become a scorn and a derision among the nations; we are accounted as sheep brought to the slaughter, to be slain and destroyed, or to be smitten and reproached.

Cong. and Reader.—Yet, despite all this, we have not forgotten your name: we beseech you, forget us not.

Cong.—Strangers say, There is no hope or expectancy for you. Be gracious unto a people that trust in your name. O you who are most pure, bring our salvation near. We are weary, and no rest is granted us. Let your tender mercies subdue your anger from us.

Cong. and Reader.—We beseech you, turn from your wrath, and have mercy upon the treasured people whom you have chosen.

Cong.—O Lord, spare us in your tender mercies, and give us not into the hands of the cruel. Wherefore should the nations say, Where now is their God? For your own sake deal kindly with us, and delay not.

Cong. and Reader.—We beseech you, turn from your wrath, and have mercy upon the treasured people whom you have chosen.

Cong.—Hear our voice, and be gracious, and forsake us not in the hand of our enemies to blot out our name; remember what you have sworn to our fathers, I will multiply your seed as the stars of heaven— and now we are left a few out of many.

Cong. and Reader.—Yet, despite all this, we have not forgotten your name: we beseech you, forget us not.

Cong.—Help us, O God of our salvation, for the sake of the glory of your name; and deliver us, and pardon our sins for your name's sake.

Cong. and Reader.—O Lord God of Israel, turn from your fierce wrath, and repent of the evil against your people.

O Guardian of Israel, guard the remnant of Israel, and suffer not Israel to perish, who say, Hear O Israel.

O Guardian of an only nation, guard the remnant of an only nation, and suffer not an only nation to perish, who proclaim the unity of your name, saying, The Lord our God, the Lord is One.

O Guardian of a holy nation, guard the remnant of a holy nation, and suffer not a holy nation to perish, who thrice repeat the three-fold sanctification unto the Holy One.

O You who are propitiated by prayers for mercy, and are conciliated by supplications, be you propitious and reconciled to an afflicted generation; for there is none that helps.

Our Father, our King, be gracious unto us, and answer us, for we have no good works of our own; deal with us in charity and loving-kindness, and save us.

As for us, we know not what to do; but our eyes are upon you. Remember, O Lord, your tender mercies and your loving-kindnesses; for they have been ever of old. Let your loving-kindness, O Lord, be upon us, according as we have waited for you. Remember not against us the iniquities of our ancestors: let your tender mercies speedily come to meet us; for we are brought very low. Be gracious unto us, O Lord, be gracious unto us; for we are sated to the full with contempt. In wrath remember to be merciful. For he knows our frame; he remembers that we are dust. Help us, O God of our salvation, for the sake of the glory of your name; and deliver us, and pardon our sins, for your name's sake.

Reader.—Magnified and sanctified be his great name in the world which he has created according to his will. May he establish his kingdom during your life and during your days, and during the life of all the house of Israel, even speedily and at a near time, and say ye, Amen.

Cong. and Reader.—Let his great name be blessed forever and to all eternity.

Reader.—Blessed, praised and glorified, exalted, extolled and honored, magnified and lauded be the name of the Holy One, blessed be he; though he be high above all the blessings and hymns, praises and consolations, which are uttered in the world; and say ye, Amen.

On Mondays and Thursdays the following two paragraphs are added. They are, however, omitted on the following days—New Moon, the day before Passover, the Fast of Ab, the day before the Fast of Atonement, during the Feast of Dedication, the two days of Purim, and of Purim Katon, the 14th and 15th of Adar Rishon.

O God, slow to anger and abounding in loving-kindness and truth, rebuke us not in your anger. Have pity upon your people, O Lord, and save us from all evil. We have sinned against you, O Lord: forgive, we beseech you, according to the abundance of your tender mercies, O God.

O God, slow to anger and abounding in loving-kindness and truth, hide not your face from us. Have pity upon Israel, your people, and deliver us from all evil. We have sinned against you, O Lord; forgive, we beseech you, according to the abundance of your tender mercies, O God.

ORDER OF READING THE TORAH

The following to "as of old," forms part of the Service when Prayers are said with a Congregation on Mondays and Thursdays, and also, with the exception of "May it be the will," etc., to "Amen," on Sabbath Afternoons, New Moon, the Intermediate Days of Passover and Sukkot, and on Fast Days (Mornings and Afternoons).

The ark is opened.

Reader and Cong.—And it came to pass, when the ark set forward, that Moses said, Rise up, O Lord, and your enemies shall be scattered, and they that hate you shall flee before you. For out of Zion shall go forth the Torah, and the word of the Lord from Jerusalem.

Blessed be he who in his holiness gave the Torah to his people Israel.

The Reader takes the Scroll of the Torah, and says—

Magnify the Lord with me, and let us exalt his name together.

Reader and Cong.—Yours, O Lord, is the greatness, and the power, and the glory, and the victory, and the majesty: for all that is in the heaven and in the earth is yours; Yours, O Lord, is the kingdom, and the supremacy as head over all. Exalt you the Lord our God, and worship at his footstool: holy is he. Exalt you the Lord our God, and worship at his holy mount; for the Lord our God is holy.

May the Father of mercy have mercy upon a people that have been borne by him. May he remember the covenant with the patriarchs, deliver our souls from evil hours, check the evil inclination in them that have been carried by him, grant us of his grace an everlasting deliverance, and in the attribute of his goodness fulfil our desires by salvation and mercy.

The Scroll of the Torah is placed upon the desk. The Reader unrolls it, and says the following—

And may his kingdom be soon revealed and made visible unto us, and may he be gracious unto our remnant and unto the remnant of his people, the house of Israel, granting them grace, kindness, mercy and favor; and let us say, Amen. Ascribe, all of you, greatness unto our God, and render honor to the Torah.

Here the Reader names the Person who is to be called to the Reading of the Torah.

Blessed be he, who in his holiness gave the Torah unto his people Israel. The Torah of the Lord is perfect, restoring the soul: the testimony of the Lord is faithful, making wise the simple. The precepts of the Lord are right, rejoicing the heart: the commandment of the Lord is pure, enlightening the eyes. The Lord will give strength unto his people: the Lord will bless his people with peace. As for God, his way is perfect: the word of the Lord is tried: he is a shield unto all them that trust in him.

Cong. and Reader.—And you that cleave unto the Lord your God are alive every one of you this day.

Those who are called to the Reading of the Torah say the following Blessing—

Bless you the Lord who is to be blessed.

Cong.—Blessed be the Lord, who is to be blessed forever and ever.

The Response of the Congregation is repeated and the Blessing continued—

Blessed are you, O Lord our God, King of the universe, who has chosen us from all peoples, and has given us your Torah. Blessed are you, O Lord, who gives the Torah.

After the Reading of a Section of the Torah, the following Blessing is said—

Blessed are you, O Lord our God, King of the universe, who has given us the Torah of truth, and has planted everlasting life in our midst. Blessed are you, O Lord, who gives the Torah.

Persons who have been in peril of their lives, during journeys by sea or land, in captivity or sickness, upon their deliverance or recovery say the following, after the conclusion of the last Blessing—

Blessed are you, O Lord our God, King of the universe, who vouchsafes benefits unto the undeserving, who has also vouchsafed all good unto me.

The Congregation responds—

He who has vouchsafed all good unto you, may he vouchsafe all good unto you forever.

After the Reading of the Torah, the Scroll is held up, and the Congregation say the following:-

And this is the Torah which Moses set before the children of Israel, according to the commandment of the Lord by the hand of Moses. It is a tree of life to them that grasp it, and of them that uphold it every one is rendered happy. Its ways are ways of pleasantness, and all its paths are peace. Length of days is in its right hand; in its left hand are riches and honor. It pleased the Lord, for his righteousness' sake, to magnify the Torah and to make it honorable.

On those Mondays and Thursdays when the Prayers are said, the Reader adds the following, previous to the Scroll of the Torah being returned to the Ark—

May it be the will of our Father who is in heaven to establish the Temple, the house of our life, and to restore his divine presence in our midst, speedily in our days; and let us say, Amen.

May it be the will of our Father who is in heaven to have mercy upon us and upon our remnant, and to keep destruction and the plague from us and from all his people, the house of Israel; and let us say, Amen.

May it be the will of our Father who is in heaven to preserve among us the wise men of Israel; them, their wives, their sons and daughters, their disciples and the disciples of their disciples in all the places of their habitation; and let us say, Amen.

May it be the will of our Father who is in heaven that good tidings of salvation and comfort may be heard and published, and that he may gather our banished ones from the four corners of the earth; and let us say, Amen.

As for our brethren, the whole house of Israel, such of them as are given over to trouble or captivity, whether they abide on the sea or on the dry land,—may the All-present have mercy upon them, and bring them forth from trouble to enlargement, from darkness to light, and from subjection to redemption, now speedily and at a near time; and let us say, Amen.

On returning the Scroll of the Torah to the Ark, the Reader says—

Let them praise the name of the Lord; for his name alone is exalted:

Congregation.—His majesty is above the earth and heaven; and he has lifted up a horn for h, people, to the praise of all his loving ones, even of the children of Israel, the people near unto him. Praise you the Lord.

Psalm xxiv.

A Psalm of David: The earth is the Lord's and the fullness thereof; the world, and they that dwell therein. For it is he that has founded it upon the seas, and established it upon the floods. Who may ascend the mountain of the Lord? And who may stand in his holy place? He that has clean hands and a pure heart; who has not set his desire upon vanity, and has not sworn deceitfully. He shall receive a blessing from the Lord, and righteousness from the God of his salvation. This is the generation of them that seek after him, that seek your face, (O God of) Jacob! (Selah.) Lift up your heads, O you gates; and be you lifted up, you everlasting doors, that the King of glory may come in. Who, then, is the King of glory? The Lord strong and mighty. The Lord mighty in battle. Lift up your heads, O you gates; yea, lift them up, you everlasting doors, that the King of glory may come in. Who, then, is the King of glory? The Lord of hosts, he is the King of glory. (Selah.)

While the Scroll of the Torah is being placed in the Ark, the following to "as of old" is said—

And when it rested, he said, Return, O Lord, unto the ten thousands of the thousands of Israel. Arise, O Lord, unto your resting place; you, and the ark of your strength. Let your priests be clothed with righteousness; and let your loving ones shout for joy. For the sake of David your servant, turn not away the face of your anointed. For I give you good doctrine; forsake you not my Torah. It is a tree of life to them that grasp it, and of them that uphold it every one is rendered happy. Its ways are ways of pleasantness, and all its paths are peace. Turn you us unto you, O Lord, and we shall return: renew our days as of old.

Happy are they that dwell in your house: they will be ever praising you. (Selah.)
Happy is the people that is in such a case: happy is the people, whose God is the Lord.
Psalm cxlv. A Psalm of Praise: of David
I will extol you, my God, O King; and I will bless your name forever and ever.
Every day will I bless you; and I will praise your name forever and ever.
Great is the Lord, and exceedingly to be praised: and his greatness is unsearchable.
One generation shall laud your works to another, and shall declare your mighty acts.
On the majestic glory of your grandeur, and on your marvelous deeds, will I meditate.
And men shall speak of the might of your awful acts; and I will recount your greatness.
They shall pour forth the fame of your great goodness, and shall exult in your righteousness.
The Lord is gracious and merciful; slow to anger and of great loving-kindness.
The Lord is good to all; and his tender mercies are over all his works.
All your works shall give thanks unto you, O Lord; and your loving ones shall bless you.
They shall speak of the glory of your kingdom, and talk of your power.
To make known to the sons of men his mighty acts, and the majestic glory of his kingdom.
Your kingdom is an everlasting kingdom, and your dominion endures throughout all generations.
The Lord upholds all that fall, and raises up all those that are bowed down.
The eyes of all wait upon you; and you gives them their food in due season.
You opens your hand, and satisfies every living thing with favor.
The Lord is righteous in all his ways, and loving in all his works.
The Lord is nigh unto all them that call upon him to all that call upon him in truth.
He will fulfil the desire of them that fear him: he also will hear their cry, and will save them.

The Lord guards all them that love him; but all the wicked will he destroy.
My mouth shall speak of the praise of the Lord; and let all flesh bless his holy name forever and ever.
But we will bless the Lord from this time forth and forever more. Praise you the Lord.

On the following days Psalm xx is omitted: New Moon, the day before Passover, on the Fast of Ab, the day before the Fast of Atonement, during the Feast of Dedication, on Purim and Purim Katan.

Psalm xx.

For the Chief Musician. A Psalm of David. The Lord answer you in the day of trouble; the name of the God of Jacob set you up on high; send you help from the sanctuary, and uphold you out of Zion; remember all your offerings, and accept your burnt sacrifice (Selah); grant you your heart's desire, and fulfil all your purpose. We will exult in your salvation, and in the name of our God we will set up our banners: the Lord fulfil all your petitions. Now know I that the Lord saves his anointed; he will answer him from his holy heaven with the mighty saving acts of his right hand. Some trust in chariots and some in horses: but we will make mention of the name of the Lord our God. They are bowed down and fallen: but we are risen and stand upright. Save, Lord: may the King answer us on the day when we call.

And a redeemer shall come to Zion and to them that turn from transgression in Jacob, says the Lord. And as for me, this is my covenant with them, says the Lord: my spirit that is upon you, and my words which I have put in your mouth, shall not depart out of your mouth, nor out of the mouth of your seed, nor out of the mouth of your seed's seed, says the Lord, from henceforth and forever.

But you are holy, O you that dwells amid the praises of Israel. And one cried unto another, and said, Holy, holy, holy is the Lord of hosts: the whole earth is full of his glory. And they receive sanction the one from the other, and say, Holy in the highest heavens, the place of his divine abode; holy upon earth, the work of his might; holy forever and to all eternity is the Lord of hosts; the whole earth is full of the radiance of his glory. Then a wind lifted me up, and I heard behind me the voice of a great rushing (saying), Blessed be the glory of the Lord from his place. Then a wind lifted me up, and I heard behind me the voice of a great rushing, of those who uttered praises, and said, Blessed be the glory of the Lord from the region of his divine abode. The Lord shall reign forever and ever. The kingdom of the Lord endures forever and to all eternity. O Lord, the God of Abraham, of Isaac and of Israel, our fathers, keep this forever in the imagination of the thoughts of the heart of your people, and direct their heart unto you. And he, being merciful, forgives iniquity and destroys not: yea, many a time he turns his anger away, and does not stir up all his wrath. For you, O Lord, are good and forgiving, and abounding in loving-kindness to all them that call upon you. Your righteousness is an everlasting righteousness, and your Torah is truth. You will show truth to Jacob and loving-kindness to Abraham, according as you have sworn unto our fathers from the days of old. Blessed be the Lord day by day; if one burdens us, God is our salvation. (Selah.) The Lord of hosts is with us; the God of Jacob is our stronghold. (Selah.) O Lord of hosts, happy is the man that trusts in you. Save, Lord: may the King answer us on the day when we call. Messed is our God, who has created us for his glory, and has separated us from them that go astray, and has given us the Torah of truth and planted everlasting life in our midst. May he open our heart unto his Torah, and place his love and fear within our hearts, that we may do his will and serve him with a perfect heart, that we may not labor in vain, nor bring forth for confusion. May it be your will, O Lord our God and God of our fathers that we may keep your statutes in this world, and be worthy to live to witness and inherit happiness and blessing in the days of the Messiah and in the life of the world to come. To the end that my glory may sing praise unto you, and not be silent: O Lord my God, I will give thanks unto you forever. Blessed is the man that trusts in the Lord, and whose trust the Lord is. Trust you in the Lord forever; for in Yah the Lord is an everlasting rock

And they that know your name will put their trust in you; for you have not forsaken them that seek you, Lord. It pleased the Lord, for his righteousness' sake, to magnify the Torah and to make it honorable.

On the days when the Additional Service is said, the Reader here says Half Kaddish, to "in the world; and say ye, Amen"; on other days, the whole Kaddish, as follows—

And now, I pray you, let the power of the Lord be great, according as you have spoken. Remember, O Lord, your tender mercies and your loving-kindness; for they have been ever of old.

Reader.—Magnified and sanctified be his great name in the world which he has created according to his will. May he establish his kingdom during your life and during your days, and during the life of all the house of Israel, even speedily and at a near time, and say ye, Amen.

Cong. and Reader.—Let his great name be blessed forever and to all eternity.

Reader.—Blessed, praised and glorified, exalted, extolled and honored, magnified and lauded be the name of the Holy One, blessed be he; though he be high above all the blessings and hymns, praises and consolations, which are uttered in the world; and say ye, Amen.

Cong.—Accept our prayer in mercy and in favor.

Reader.—May the prayers and supplications of all Israel be accepted by their Father who is in heaven; and say ye, Amen.

Cong.—Let the name of the Lord be blessed from this time forth and forevermore.

Reader.—May there be abundant peace from heaven, and life for us and for all Israel; and say ye, Amen.

Cong.—My help is from the Lord, who made heaven and earth.

Reader.—He who makes peace in his high places, may he make peace for us and for all Israel; and say ye, Amen.

It is our duty to praise the Lord of all things, to ascribe greatness to him who formed the world in the beginning, since he has not made us like the nations of other lands, and has not placed us like other families of the earth, since he has not assigned unto us a portion as unto them, nor a lot as unto all their multitude. For we bend the knee and offer worship and thanks before the supreme King of kings, the Holy One, blessed be he, who stretched forth the heavens and laid the foundations of the earth, the seat of whose glory is in the heavens above, and the abode of whose might is in the loftiest heights. He is our

God; there is none else an truth he is our King; there is none besides him; as it is written in his Torah, And you shall know this day, and lay it to your heart, that the Lord he is God in heaven above and upon the earth beneath: there is none else.

We therefore hope in you, O Lord our God, that we may speedily behold the glory of your might, when you will remove the abominations from the earth, and the idols will be utterly cut off, when the world will be perfected under the kingdom of the Almighty, and all the children of flesh will call upon your name, when you will turn unto yourself all the wicked of the earth. Let all the inhabitants of the world perceive and know that unto you every knee must bow, every tongue must swear. Before you, O Lord our God, let them bow and fall; and unto your glorious name let them give honor; let them all accept the yoke of your kingdom, and do you reign over them speedily, and forever and ever. For the kingdom is yours, and to all eternity you will reign in glory; as it is written in your Torah, the Lord shall reign forever and ever. And it is said, And the Lord shall be king over all the earth: in that day shall the Lord be One, and his name One.

The following Prayer for a Sick Person may be introduced—

May it be your will, O Lord our God, and God of our fathers, speedily to send a perfect healing from heaven, a healing of soul and body unto the sick . . . among the other sick of Israel.

On the Fast of the Ninth of Ab the following is added at the Afternoon Service—

Comfort, O Lord our God, the mourners of Zion, and the mourners of Jerusalem, and the city that is in mourning, laid waste, despised and desolate; in mourning for that she is childless, laid waste as to her dwellings, despised in the downfall of her glory, and desolate through the loss of her inhabitants: she sits with her head covered like a barren woman who has not borne. Legions have devoured her; worshippers of strange gods have possessed her: they have put your people Israel to the sword, and in willfulness have slain the loving ones of the Most High. Therefore let Zion weep bitterly, and Jerusalem give forth her voice. O my heart, my heart! how it grieves for the slain! My bowels, my bowels! how they yearn for the slain! For you, O Lord, did consume her with fire; and with fire you will in future restore her, as it is said, As for me, I will be unto her, says the Lord, a wall of fire round about, and I will be a glory in the midst of her. Blessed are you, O Lord, who comforts Zion and rebuilds Jerusalem.

"Speedily," etc.

On Fast Days the Congregation here says the following—

Answer us, O Lord, answer us on this day of the fast of our humiliation, for we are in great trouble. Turn not to our wickedness; conceal not your face from us, and hide not yourself from our supplication. Be near, we entreat you, unto our cry; let your loving-kindness be a comfort to us; even before we call unto you answer us, according as it is said, And it shall come to pass that, before they call, I will answer; while they are yet speaking, I will hear; for you, O Lord, are he who answers in time of trouble, who delivers and rescues in all times of trouble and distress; for you hearkens, etc.

At the Conclusion Service on the Day of Atonement, "seal us" is substituted for "inscribe us" in this and the following sentences.

THE MOURNER'S KADDISH

And now, I pray you, let the power of the Lord be great, according as you have spoken. Remember, O Lord, your tender mercies and your loving-kindnesses; for they have been ever of old.

Mourner.—Magnified and sanctified be his great name in the world which he has created according to his will. May he establish his kingdom during your life and during your days, and during the life of all the house of Israel, even speedily and at a near time, and say ye, Amen.

Cong. and Mourner.—Let his great name be blessed forever and to all eternity.

Mourner.—Blessed, praised and glorified, exalted, extolled and honored, magnified and lauded be the name of the Holy One, blessed be he; though he be high above all the blessings and hymns, praises and consolations, which are uttered in the world; and say ye, Amen.

Cong.—Let the name of the Lord be blessed from this time forth and forevermore.

Mourner.—May there be abundant peace from heaven, and life for us and for all Israel; and say ye, Amen.

Cong.—My help is from the Lord, who made heaven and earth.

Mourner.—He who makes peace in his high places, may he make peace for us and for all Israel; and say ye, Amen.

THE WEEKDAY PSALMS

Psalm for the First Day of the Week.

This is the First Day of the Week on which the Levites in the Temple used to say—
Psalm xxiv.

A Psalm of David: The earth is the Lord's, and the fullness thereof; the world, and they that dwell therein. For it is he that has founded it upon the seas, and established it upon the floods. Who may ascend the mountain of the Lord? And who may stand in his holy place? He that has clean hands and a pure heart; who has not set his desire upon vanity, and has not sworn deceitfully. He shall receive a blessing from the Lord, and righteousness from the God of his salvation. This is the generation of them that seek after him, that seek your face, (O God of) Jacob! (Selah.) Lift up your heads, O you gates; and be you lifted up, you everlasting doors, that the King of glory may come in. Who, then, is the King of glory? The Lord strong and mighty, the Lord mighty in battle. Lift up your heads, O you gates; yea, lift them up, you everlasting doors, that the King of glory may come in. Who, then, is the King of glory? The Lord of hosts, he is the King of glory. (Selah.)

Psalm for the Second Day of the Week.

This is the Second Day of the Week on which the Levites in the Temple used to say—
(Psalm xlviii.)

A Song; a Psalm of the Sons of Korah. Great is the Lord, and highly to be praised, in the city of our God, in his holy mountain. Beautiful in elevation, the joy of the whole earth is mount Zion,—at the sides of the north,—the city of the great king. God has made himself known in her palaces as a stronghold. For, lo, the kings met each other, they passed on together. They saw it; then were they amazed; they were confounded, they hasted away. Trembling took hold of them there; pangs as of a woman in travail. With an east wind you did break the ships of Tarshish. As we have heard, so have we seen in the city of the Lord of hosts, in the city of our God: God will establish it forever. (Selah.) We thought of your loving-kindness, O God, in the midst of your temple. As is your name, O God, so is your renown unto the ends of the earth; your right hand is full of righteousness. Let mount Zion rejoice, let the daughters of Judah be glad, because of your judgments. Compass you Zion and go round about her: count the towers thereof. Mark you well her rampart, traverse her palaces; that you may tell a later generation, that this God is our God forever and ever: he will be our guide even unto death.

Psalm for the Third Day of the Week.

This is the Third Day of the Week, on which the Levites in the Temple used to say—
(Psalm lxxxii.)

A Psalm of Asaph. God stands in the congregation of the mighty; he judges among the judges. How long will you judge unjustly, and respect the persons of the wicked? (Selah.) Judge the lowly and fatherless: do justice to the afflicted and destitute. Rescue the lowly and needy: deliver them out of the hand of the wicked. They know not, neither do they understand; they walk about in darkness: all the foundations of the earth are moved. I said, you are gods, and all of you sons of the Most High. Nevertheless you shall die like men, and fall like one of the princes. Arise, O God, judge the earth: for you shall possess all the nations.

Psalm for the Fourth Day of the Week.

This is the Fourth Day of the Week, on which the Levites in the Temple used to say—
(Psalm xciv.)

O God of vengeance, Lord, O God of vengeance, shine forth. Lift up yourself, you judge of the earth: render to the proud their desert. Lord, how long shall the wicked, how long shall the wicked triumph? They prate, they speak arrogantly: all the workers of iniquity are boastful. They crush your people, O Lord, and afflict your heritage. They slay the widow and the stranger, and murder the fatherless. And they say, The Lord will not see, neither will the God of Jacob give heed. Give heed, you brutish among the people: and you fools, when will you be wise? He that planted the ear, shall he not hear? He that formed the eye, shall he not see? He that chastens the nations, shall not he punish, even he that teaches man knowledge? The Lord knows the thoughts of men, that they are vanity. Happy is the man whom you chastens, O Lord, and teaches out of your Torah; that you may give him rest from the days of evil, until the pit be dug for the wicked. For the Lord will not cast off his people, neither will he forsake his inheritance. For judgment shall return unto righteousness: and all the upright in heart shall follow it. Who will rise up for me against the evil-doers, who will stand up for me against the workers of iniquity? Unless the Lord had been my help, my soul had soon dwelt in silence. When I say, My foot slips, your loving-kindness, O Lord, holds me up. In the multitude of my thoughts within me, your comforts delight my soul. Hath the tribunal of destruction fellowship with you, which frames mischief by statute? They gather themselves together against the soul of the righteous, and condemn the innocent blood. But the Lord is become my stronghold; and my God the rock of my refuge. And he brings back upon them their own iniquity, and for their evil shall cut them off; the Lord our God shall cut them off.

O come, let us exult before the Lord: let us shout for joy to the rock of our salvation.

Psalm for the Fifth Day of the Week.

This is the Fifth Day of the Week, on which the Levites in the Temple used to say—
(Psalm lxxxi.)

To the Chief Musician. Set to the Gittith. A Psalm of Asaph. Exult aloud unto God our strength: shout for joy unto the God of Jacob. Raise the song, and strike the timbrel, the pleasant lyre with the harp. Blow the horn on the new moon, at the beginning of the month, for our day of festival. For it is a statute of Israel, a decree of the God of Jacob. He appointed it in Joseph for a testimony, when he went forth over the land of Egypt: where I heard a language that I knew not. I removed his shoulder from the burden: his hands were freed from the basket. You called in trouble and I delivered you; I answered you in the secret place of thunder, I proved you at the waters of Meribah. (Selah.) Hear, O my people, and I will testify against you: O Israel, if you will hearken unto me. There shall be no strange god in you; neither shall you worship any foreign god. I am the Lord your God, who brought you out of the land of Egypt: open wide your mouth, and I will fill it. But my people hearkened not to my voice; and Israel was not willing towards me. So I let them go in the stubbornness of their heart, that they might walk in their own counsels. O that my people would hearken unto me, that Israel would walk in my ways. I would soon subdue their enemies, and turn my hand against their adversaries. The haters of the Lord should submit themselves unto him; so that their time might endure forever. He would feed them also with the fat of wheat: and with honey out of the rock would I satisfy you.

Psalm for the Sixth Day of the Week.

This is the Sixth Day of the Week, on which the Levites in the Temple used to say—
Psalm xciii.

The Lord reigns; he has robed him in majesty; the Lord has robed him, yea, he has girded himself with strength: the world also is set firm, that it cannot be moved. Your throne is set firm from of old: you are from everlasting. The streams have lifted up, O Lord, the streams have lifted up their voice; the streams lift up their roaring. Than the voices of many waters, mighty waters, breakers of the sea, more mighty is the Lord on high. Your testimonies are very faithful: holiness becomes your house, O Lord, forevermore.

On the days when Tachanun is said, the following is added after the Psalm of the day—

Psalm lxxxiii.

A Song: A Psalm of Asaph. O God, keep not you silence: hold not your peace, and be not still, O God. For, lo, your enemies make a tumult: and they that hate you have lifted up the head. They take crafty counsel against your people, and consult together against your hidden ones. They have said, Come and let us cut them off from being a nation; that the name of Israel may be remembered no more. For they have consulted together with one consent; against you do they make a covenant. The tents of Edom and the Ishmaelites; Moab and the Hagarenes; Gebal, and Ammon, and Amalek; Philistia with the inhabitants of Tyre: Assyria also is joined with them; they have been an arm of help to the children of Lot. (Selah.) Do you unto them as unto Midian; as to Sisera, as to Jabin, at the brook Kishon. They were destroyed at Endor; they became as dung for the earth. Make their nobles like Oreb and Zeeb; yea, all their princes like Zebah and Zalmunna: who said, Let us take to ourselves in possession the habitations of God. O my God, make them like the whirling dust, as stubble before the wind; as the fire that burns the forest, and as the flame that sets the mountains on fire: so pursue them with your storm, and confound them with your hurricane. Fill their faces with confusion; that they may seek your name, O Lord. Let them be ashamed and confounded tor ever; yea, let them be abashed and perish. That they may know that you, of whom alone the name is the Lord, are Most High over all the earth

On New Moon, Psalm civ is read.

From the beginning of the Month of Elul until Hoshana Rabba, the following Psalm is read every Morning and Evening—

Psalm xxvii.

A Psalm of David. The Lord is my light and my salvation; whom shall I fear? The Lord is the stronghold of my life; of whom shall I be afraid? When evil-doers drew nigh against me to eat up my flesh, even my adversaries and my foes, they stumbled and fell. Though a host should encamp against me, my heart would not fear; though war should rise against me, even then would I be confident. One thing have I asked of the Lord, that will I seek after: that I may dwell in the house of the Lord all the days of my life, to behold the pleasantness of the Lord, and to inquire in his temple. For in the day of trouble he will hide me in his pavilion: in the shelter of his tabernacle will be conceal me; he will lift me up upon a rock. And now shall my head be lifted up above my enemies round about me; and I will offer in his tabernacle sacrifices of joyful shouting; I will sing, yea, I will sing praises unto the Lord. Hear, O Lord, when I cry with my voice; have pity upon me, and answer me. My heart says unto you, (since you have said), Seek you my face, your face, Lord will I seek. Hide not your face from me; thrust not your servant away in anger: you have been my help; cast me not off, neither forsake me, O God of my salvation. For nay father and my mother have forsaken me, but the Lord will take me up. Teach me your way, O Lord; and lead me on an even path, because of them that lie in wait for me Give me not up to the will of my adversaries: for false witnesses have risen up against me, and such as breathe out violence. (I should despair), unless I believed to see the goodness of the Lord in the land of the living. Wait for the Lord; be strong and let your heart take courage; yea, wait you for the Lord.

In some Congregations the following Psalm is said daily before "Blessed be he," etc.

Psalm xxx.

A Psalm; a Song at the Dedication of the House; a Psalm of David. I will extol you, O Lord; for you have drawn me up, and have not made my foes to rejoice over me. O Lord, my God, I cried unto you, and you did heal me. O Lord, you brought up my soul from the grave; you have kept me alive, that I should not go down to the pit. Sing praise unto the Lord, O you his loving ones, and give thanks to his holy name. For his anger is but for a moment; his favor is for a lifetime: weeping may tarry for the night, but joy comes in the morning. As for me, I said in my prosperity I shall never be moved. You, Lord, of your favor had made my mountain to stand strong; you did hide your face; I was confounded. I cried unto you, O Lord; and unto the Lord I made supplication: What profit is there in my blood if I go down to the pit? Can the dust give thanks to you? Can it declare your truth? Hear, O Lord, and be gracious unto me; Lord, be you my helper. You have turned for me my mourning into dancing; you have loosed my sackcloth, and girded me with gladness: to the end that my glory may sing praise to you, and not be silent: O Lord my God, I will give thanks unto you forever.

THE KADDISH DERABBANAN

Kaddish to be said after reading Lessons from the Works of the Rabbis—

Reader.—Magnified and sanctified be his great name In the world which he has created according to his will. May he establish his kingdom during your life and during your days, and during the life of all the house of Israel, even speedily and at a near time, and say ye, Amen.

Cong. and Reader.—Let his great name be blessed forever and to all eternity.

Reader.—Blessed, praised and glorified, exalted, extolled and honored; magnified and lauded be the name of the Holy One, blessed be he; though he be high above all the blessings and hymns, praises and consolations, which are uttered in the world; and say ye, Amen.

Unto Israel, and unto the Rabbis, and unto their disciples, and unto all the disciples of their disciples, and unto all who engage in the study of the Torah, in this or in any other place, unto them and unto you be abundant peace, grace, loving-kindness, mercy, long life, ample sustenance and salvation from the Father who is in heaven, and say ye, Amen.

Cong.—Let the name of the Lord be blessed from this time forth and forevermore.

Reader.—May there be abundant peace from heaven, and a happy life for us and for all Israel; and say ye, Amen.

Cong.—My help is from the Lord, who made heaven and earth.

Reader.—He who makes peace in his high places, may he in his mercy make peace for us and for all Israel; and say ye, Amen.

PRAYER FOR SUSTENANCE.

My help is from the Lord, who made heaven and earth. Cast your burden upon the Lord, and he shall sustain you. Mark the perfect man, and behold the upright; for the latter end of that man is peace. Trust in the Lord, and do good; dwell in the land, and feed upon faithfulness. Behold, God is my salvation; I will trust and will not be afraid: for Yah the Lord is my strength and song, and he is become my salvation.—O Sovereign of the universe, in your holy words it is written, saying, He that trusts in the Lord, loving-kindness shall compass him, about; and it is written, And you give life to them all. O Lord God of truth, vouchsafe blessing and prosperity upon all the work of my hands, for I trust in you that you will so bless me through my occupation and calling, that I may be enabled to support myself and the members of my household with ease and not with pain, by lawful and not by forbidden means, unto life and peace. In me also let the scripture be fulfilled, Cast your burden upon the Lord, and he shall sustain you. Amen!

THE TEN COMMANDMENTS.
Exodus xx. 1-17.

And God spoke all these words, saying.

1. I am the Lord your God, who brought you out of the land of Egypt, out of the house of bondage.

2. You shall have no other gods before me. You shall not make unto you a graven image; nor the form of anything that is in heaven above, or that is in the earth beneath, or that is in the water under the earth; you shall not bow down yourself unto them, nor serve them: for I the Lord your God am a jealous God, visiting the iniquity of the fathers upon the children, upon the third and upon the fourth generation, unto them that hate me: and showing loving-kindness to the thousandth generation, unto them that love me and keep my commandments.

3. You shall not take the name of the Lord your God in vain; for the Lord will not hold him guiltless that takes his name in vain.

4. Remember the Sabbath day to keep it holy. Six days shall you labor, and do all your work: but the seventh day is a Sabbath unto the Lord your God: in it you shall not do any work, you, nor your son, nor your daughter, your manservant, nor your maidservant, nor your cattle, nor your stranger that is within your gates: for in six days the Lord made heaven and earth, the sea and all that is therein, and rested on the seventh day: wherefore the Lord blessed the Sabbath day and hallowed it.

5. Honor your father and your mother: that your days may be long upon the land which the Lord your God gives you.

6. You shall not murder.

7. You shall not commit adultery.

8. You shall not steal.

9. You shall not bear false witness against your neighbor.

10. You shall not covet your neighbor s house, you shall not covet your neighbor's wife, nor his manservant nor his maidservant, nor his ox, nor his ass, nor any thing that is your neighbor's.

THIRTEEN PRINCIPLES OF THE FAITH

1. I believe with perfect faith that the Creator, blessed be his name, is the Author and Guide of everything that has been created, and that he alone has made, does make, and will make all things.

2. I believe with perfect faith that the Creator, blessed be his name, is a Unity, and that there is no unity in any manner like unto his, and that he alone is our God, who was, is, and will be.

3. I believe with perfect faith that the Creator, blessed be his name, is not a body, and that he is free from all the accidents of matter, and that he has not any form whatsoever.

4. I believe with perfect faith that the Creator, blessed be his name, is the first and the last.

5. I believe with perfect faith that to the Creator, blessed be his name, and to him alone, it is right to pray, and that it is not right to pray to any being besides him.

6. I believe with perfect faith that all the words of the prophets are true.

7. I believe with perfect faith that the prophecy of Moses our teacher, peace be unto him, was true, and that he was the chief of the prophets, both of those that preceded and of those that followed him.

8. I believe with perfect faith that the whole Torah, now in our possession, is the same that was given to Moses our teacher, peace be unto him.

9. I believe with perfect faith that this Torah will not be changed, and that there will never be any other law from the Creator, blessed be his name.

10. I believe with perfect faith that the Creator, blessed be his name, knows every deed of the children of men, and all their thoughts, as it is said, It is he that fashions the hearts of them all, that gives heed to all their deeds.

11. I believe with perfect faith that the Creator, blessed be his name, rewards those that keep his commandments, and punishes those that transgress them.

12. I believe with perfect faith in the coming of the Messiah, and, though he tarry, I will wait daily for his coming.

13. I believe with perfect faith that there will be a resurrection of the dead at the time when it shall please the Creator, blessed be his name, and exalted be the remembrance of him forever and ever.

For your salvation I hope, O Lord! I hope, O Lord, for your salvation! O Lord, for your salvation I hope!

AFTERNOON SERVICE FOR WEEKDAYS.

Happy are they that dwell in your house: they will be ever praising you. (Selah.)

Happy is the people, that is in such a case: happy is the people, whose God is the Lord.

Psalm cxlv. A Psalm of Praise: of David.

I will extol you, my God, O King; and I will bless your name forever and ever.

Every day will I bless you; and I will praise your name forever and ever.

Great is the Lord, and exceedingly to be praised: and his greatness is unsearchable.

One generation shall laud your works to another, and shall declare your mighty acts.

On the majestic glory of your splendor, and on your marvelous deeds, will I meditate.

And men shall speak of the might of your awful acts; and I will recount your greatness.

They shall pour forth the fame of your great goodness, and shall exult in your righteousness.

The Lord is gracious and merciful; slow to anger and of great loving-kindness.

The Lord is good to all; and his tender mercies are over all his works.

All your works shall give thanks unto you, O Lord; and your loving ones shall bless you.

They shall speak of the glory of your kingdom, and talk of your power.

To make known to the sons of men his mighty acts, and the majestic glory of his kingdom.

Your kingdom is an everlasting kingdom, and your dominion endures throughout all generations.

The Lord upholds all that fall, and raises up all those that are bowed down.

The eyes of all wait upon you; and you give them their food in due season.

You open your hand, and satisfy every living thing with favor.

The Lord is righteous in all his ways, and loving in all his works.

The Lord is nigh unto all them that call upon him, to all that call upon him in truth.

He will fulfil the desire of them that fear him; he also will hear their cry, and will save them.

The Lord guards all them that love him; but all the wicked will he destroy.

My mouth shall speak of the praise of the Lord; and let all flesh bless his holy name forever and ever.

But we will bless the Lord from this time forth and forevermore. Praise you the Lord.

Reader.—Magnified and sanctified be his great name in the world which he has created according to his will. May he establish his kingdom during your life and during your days, and during the life of all the house of Israel, even speedily and at a near time, and say ye, Amen.

Cong. and Reader.—Let his great name be blessed forever and to all eternity.

Reader.—Blessed, praised and glorified, exalted, extolled and honored, magnified and lauded be the name of the Holy One, blessed be he; though he be high above all the blessings and hymns, praises and consolations, which are uttered in the world; and say ye, Amen.

On Fast Days the Scroll of the Torah is taken from the Ark, and the portion of the Torah beginning Vy'chal is read.

The following prayer (Amidah) to "as in ancient years," is to be said standing.

O Lord, open you my lips, and my mouth shall declare your praise.

Blessed are you, O Lord our God and God of our fathers, God of Abraham, God of Isaac, and God of Jacob, the great, mighty and revered God, the most high God, who bestows loving-kindnesses, and possesses all things; who remembers the pious deeds of the patriarchs, and in love will bring a redeemer to their children's children for your name's sake.

During the Ten Days of Penitence say—

Remember us unto life, O King, who delights in life, and inscribe us in the book of life, for your own sake, O living God.

O King, Helper, Savior and Shield. Blessed are you, O Lord, the Shield of Abraham.

You, O Lord, are mighty forever, you quicken the dead, you are mighty to save.

From the Eighth Day of Solemn Assembly until the First Day of Passover say—

You cause the wind to blow and the rain to fall.

You sustain the living with loving-kindness, quicken the dead with great mercy, support the falling, heal the sick, loose the bound, and keep your faith to them that sleep in the dust. Who is like unto you, Lord of mighty acts, and who resembles you, O King, who kills and quickens, and causes salvation to spring forth?

During the Ten Days of Penitence say—

Who is like unto you, Father of mercy, who in mercy remembers your creatures unto life?

Yea, faithful are you to quicken the dead. Blessed are you, O Lord, who quickens the dead.

You are holy, and your name is holy, and holy beings praise you daily. (Selah.) Blessed are you, O Lord, the holy God.

During the Ten Days of Penitence conclude the blessing thus—
the holy King.

When the Reader repeats the Amidah, the following is said, to "holy God."

Reader.—Those over against them say, Blessed—

Cong.—Blessed he the glory of the Lord from his place.

Reader.—And in your Holy Words it is written, saying,

Cong.—The Lord shall reign forever, your God, O Zion, unto all generations. Praise you the Lord.

Reader.—Unto all generations we will declare your greatness, and to all eternity we will proclaim your holiness, and your praise, O our God, shall not depart from our mouth forever, for you are a great and holy God and King. Blessed are you, O Lord, the holy God.

During the Ten Days of Penitence conclude the blessing thus—
the holy King.

You favor man with knowledge, and teach mortals understanding. O favor us with knowledge, understanding and discernment from you. Blessed are you, O Lord, gracious Giver of knowledge.

Cause us to return, O our Father, unto your Torah; draw us near, O our King, unto your service, and bring us back in perfect repentance unto your presence. Blessed are you, O Lord, who delights in repentance.

Forgive us, O our Father, for we have sinned; pardon us, O our King, for we have transgressed;

(On Fast Days Selichoth are inserted here.)

For you do pardon and forgive. Blessed are you, O Lord, who are gracious, and dost abundantly forgive.

Look upon our affliction and plead our cause, and redeem us speedily for your name's sake; for you are a mighty Redeemer. Blessed are you, O Lord, the Redeemer of Israel.

On Fast Days the Reader here says "Answer us," etc., and concludes thus—

Blessed are you, O Lord, who answers in time of trouble.

Heal us, O Lord, and we shall be healed; save us and we shall be saved; for you are our praise. Vouchsafe a perfect healing to all our wounds; for you, almighty King, are a faithful and merciful Physician. Blessed are you, O Lord, who heals the sick of your people Israel.

Bless this year unto us, O Lord our God, together with every kind of the produce thereof, for our welfare; give a blessing

During the Winter Season substitute for the last sentence:
Give dew and rain for a blessing upon the face of the earth.

upon the face of the earth. O satisfy us with your goodness, and bless our year like other good years. Blessed are you, O Lord, who blesses the years.

Sound the great horn for our freedom; lift up the ensign to gather our exiles, and gather us from the four corners of the earth. Blessed are you, O Lord, who gathers the banished ones of your people Israel.

Restore our judges as at the first, and our counsellors as at the beginning; remove from us grief and suffering; reign you over us, O Lord, you alone, in loving-kindness and tender mercy, and justify us in judgment. Blessed are you, O Lord, the King who loves righteousness and judgment.

During the Ten Days of Penitence conclude the blessing thus—
the King of Judgment.

And for slanderers let there be no hope, and let all wickedness perish as in a moment; let all your enemies be speedily cut off, and the dominion of arrogance do you uproot and crush, cast down and humble speedily in our days. Blessed are you, O Lord, who breaks the enemies and humbles the arrogant.

Towards the righteous and the pious, towards the elders of your people the house of Israel, towards the remnant of their scribes, towards the proselytes of righteousness, and towards us also may your tender mercies be stirred, O Lord our God; grant a good reward unto all who faithfully trust in your name; set our portion with them forever, so that we may not be put to shame; for we have trusted in you. Blessed are you, O Lord, the stay and trust of the righteous.

And to Jerusalem, your city, return in mercy, and dwell therein as you have spoken; rebuild it soon in our days as an everlasting building, and speedily set up therein the throne of David. Blessed are you, O Lord, who rebuilds Jerusalem.

Speedily cause the offspring of David, your servant, to flourish, and let his horn be exalted by your salvation, because we wait for your salvation all the day. Blessed are you, O Lord, who causes the horn of salvation to flourish.

Hear our voice, O Lord our God; spare us and have mercy upon us, and accept our prayer tin mercy and favor; for you are a God who hearkens unto prayers and supplications: from your presence, O our King, turn us not empty away; for you hearken in mercy to the prayer of your people Israel. Blessed are you, O Lord, who hearkens unto prayer.

Accept, O Lord our God, your people Israel and their prayer; restore the service to the oracle of your house; receive in love and favor both the fire-offerings of Israel and their prayer; and may the service of your people Israel be ever acceptable unto you.

On New Moon and the Intermediate Days of Passover and Sukkot the following is added—

Our God and God of our fathers! May our remembrance rise, come and be accepted before you, with the remembrance of our fathers, of Messiah the son or David your servant, of Jerusalem your holy city, and of all your people the house of Israel, bringing deliverance and well-being, grace, loving-kindness and mercy, life and peace on this day of

On New Moon say—
the New Moon.
On Passover—
the Feast of Unleavened Bread.
On Sukkot—
the Feast of Sukkot.

Remember us, O Lord our God, thereon for our wellbeing; be mindful of us for blessing, and save us unto life: by your promise of salvation and mercy, spare us and be gracious unto us; have mercy upon us and save us; for our eyes are bent upon you, because you are a gracious and merciful God and King.

And let our eyes behold your return in mercy to Zion. Blessed are you, O Lord, who restores your divine presence unto Zion.

We give thanks unto you, for you are the Lord our God and the God of our fathers forever and ever; you are the Rock of our lives, the Shield of our salvation through every generation. We will give thanks unto you and declare your praise for our lives which are committed unto your hand, and for our souls which are in your charge, and for your miracles, which are daily with us, and for your wonders and your benefits, which are wrought at all times, evening, morn and noon. O you who are all-good, whose mercies fail not; you, merciful Being, whose loving-kindnesses never cease, we have ever hoped in you.

Congregation in an undertone—

We give thanks unto you, for you are the Lord our God and the God of our fathers, the God of all flesh, our Creator and the Creator of all things in the beginning. Blessings and thanksgivings be to your great and holy name, because you have kept us in life and has preserved us: so may you continue to keep us in life and to preserve us. O gather our exiles to your holy courts to observe your statutes, to do your will, and to serve you with a perfect heart; seeing that we give thanks unto you Blessed be the God to whom thanksgivings are due.

On Chanukah and Purim say—
We thank you, etc.,

For all these things your name, O our King, shall be continually blessed and exalted forever and ever.

During the Ten Days of Penitence say—
O inscribe all the children of your covenant for a happy life.

And everything that lives shall give thanks unto you forever, and shall praise your name in truth, O God, our salvation and our help. Blessed are you, O Lord, whose name is All-good, and unto whom it is becoming to give thanks.

Grant abundant peace unto Israel your people forever; for you are the sovereign Lord of all peace; and may it be good in your sight to bless your people Israel at all times and in every hour with your peace

During the Ten Days of Penitence say—

In the book of life, blessing, peace and good sustenance may we be remembered and inscribed before you, we and all your people the house of Israel, for a happy life and for peace. Blessed are you, O Lord, who makes peace.

Blessed are you, O Lord, who blesses your, people Israel with peace.

O my God! guard my tongue from evil and my lips from speaking guile; and to such as curse me let my soul be dumb, yea, let my soul be unto all as the dust. Open my heart to your Torah, and let my soul pursue your commandments. If any design evil against me, speedily make their counsel of none effect, and frustrate their designs. Do it for the sake of your name, do it for the sake of your right hand, do it for the sake of your holiness do it for the sake of your Torah. In order that your beloved ones may be delivered, O save with your right hand, and answer me. Let the words of my mouth and the meditation of my heart be acceptable before you, O Lord, my Rock and my Redeemer. He who makes peace in his high places, may he make peace for us and for all Israel, and say ye, Amen.

May it be your will, O Lord our God and God of our fathers, that the temple be speedily rebuilt in our days, and grant our portion in your Torah. And there we will serve you with awe, as in the days of old, and as in ancient years. Then shall the offering of Judah and Jerusalem be pleasant unto the Lord, as in the days of old, and as in ancient years.

During the Ten Days of Penitence, Friday excepted, say Our Father, Our King. Then say the following; but if Tachanun is omitted, the Reader, immediately after the Amidah, says the whole Kaddish.

And David said unto Gad, I am troubled exceedingly; let us fall, I pray you, into the hand of the Lord, for his mercies are many; but let me not fall into the hand of man.

O you who are merciful and gracious, I have sinned before you. O Lord, full of mercy, have mercy upon me and receive my supplications.

Psalm vi.

O Lord, rebuke me not in your anger: neither chasten me in your hot displeasure. Be gracious unto me, O Lord; for I am withered away: O Lord, heal me; for my bones are troubled. My soul also is sore troubled: and you, O Lord, how long? Return, O Lord, deliver my soul: save me for your loving-kindness' sake. For in death there is no remembrance of you: in the grave who shall give you thanks? I am weary with my groaning; every night I make my bed to swim; I melt away my couch with my tears. My eye wastes away because of grief; it waxes old because of all my adversaries. Depart from me, all you workers of iniquity; for the Lord has heard the voice of my weeping. The Lord has heard my supplication; the Lord will receive my prayer. All my enemies shall be ashamed and sore troubled: they shall turn back, they shall be ashamed suddenly.

O Guardian of Israel, guard the remnant of Israel, and suffer not Israel to perish, who say, Hear, O Israel.

O Guardian of an only nation, guard the remnant of an only nation, and suffer not an only nation to perish, who proclaim the unity of your name, saying, The Lord our God, the Lord is One.

O Guardian of a holy nation, guard the remnant of a holy nation, and suffer not a holy nation to perish, who thrice repeat the three-fold sanctification unto the Holy One.

O You who are propitiated by prayers for mercy, and are conciliated by supplications, be you propitious and reconciled to an afflicted generation; for there is none that helps.

Our Father, our King, be gracious unto us and answer us, for we have no good works of our own; deal with us in charity and loving-kindness, and save us.

As for us, we know not what to do; but our eyes are upon you. Remember, O Lord, your tender mercies and your loving-kindnesses; for they have been ever of old. Let your loving-kindness, O Lord, be upon us, according as we have waited for you. Remember not against us the iniquities of our ancestors: let your tender mercies speedily come to meet us; for we are brought very low. Be gracious unto us, O Lord, be gracious unto us; for we are sated to the full with contempt. In wrath remember to be merciful. For he knows our frame; he remembers that we are dust. Help us, O God of our salvation, for the sake of the glory of your name; and deliver us, and pardon our sins, for your name's sake.

Reader.—Magnified and sanctified be his great name in the world which he has created according to his will. May he establish his kingdom during your life and during your days, and during the life of all the house of Israel, even speedily and at a near time, and say ye, Amen.

Cong. and Reader.—Let his great name be blessed forever and to all eternity.

Reader.—Blessed, praised and glorified, exalted, extolled and honored, magnified and lauded be the name of the Holy One blessed be he: though he be high above all the blessings and hymns praises and consolations, which are uttered in the world; and say ye, Amen.

Cong.—Accept our prayer in mercy and in favor.

Reader.—May the prayers and supplications of all Israel be accepted by their Father who is in heaven; and say ye, Amen.

Cong.—Let the name of the Lord be blessed from this time forth and forevermore.

Reader.—May there be abundant peace from heaven, and life for us and for all Israel; and say ye, Amen.

Cong.—My help is from the Lord, who made heaven and earth.

Reader.—He who makes peace in his high places, may ne make peace for us and for all Israel; and say ye, Amen.

It is our duty to praise the Lord of all things, to ascribe greatness to him who formed the world in the beginning, since he has not made us like the nations of other lands, and has not placed us like other families of the earth, since he has not assigned unto us a portion as unto them, nor a lot as unto all their multitude. For we bend the knee and offer worship and thanks before the supreme King of kings, the Holy One, blessed be he, who stretched forth the heavens and laid the foundations of the earth, the seat of whose glory is in the heavens above, and the abode of whose might is in the loftiest heights. He is our God; there is none else: in truth he is our King; there is none besides him; as it is written in his Torah, And you shall know this day, and lay it to your heart, that the Lord he is God in heaven above and upon the earth beneath: there is none else.

We therefore hope in you, O Lord our God, that we may speedily behold the glory of your might, when you will remove the abominations from the earth, and the idols will be utterly cut off, when the world will be perfected under the kingdom of the Almighty, and all the children of flesh will call upon your name, when you will turn unto yourself all the wicked of the earth. Let all the inhabitants of the world perceive and know that unto you every knee must bow, every tongue must swear. Before you, O Lord our God, let them bow and fall; and unto your glorious name let them give honor; let them all accept the yoke of your kingdom, and do you reign over them speedily, and forever and ever. For the kingdom is yours, and to all eternity you will reign in glory; as it is written in your Torah, The Lord shall reign forever and ever. And it is said, And the Lord shall be king over all the earth: in that day shall the Lord be One, and his name One.

The following Kaddish is said by a Mourner.

Mourner.—Magnified and sanctified be his great name in the world which he has created according to his will. May he establish his kingdom during your life and during your days, and during the life of all the house of Israel, even speedily and at a near time, and say ye, Amen.

Cong. and Mourner.—Let his great name be blessed forever and to all eternity.

Mourner.—Blessed, praised and glorified, exalted, extolled and honored, magnified and lauded be the name of the Holy One, blessed be he; though he be high above all the blessings and hymns, praises and consolations, which are uttered in the world; and say ye, Amen.

Cong.—Let the name of the Lord be blessed from this time forth and forevermore.

Mourner.—May there be abundant peace from heaven, and life for us and for all Israel; and say ye, Amen.

Cong.—My help is from the Lord, who made heaven and earth.

Mourner.—He who makes peace in his high places, may he make peace for us and for all Israel; and say ye, Amen.

Reader.—We will sanctify your name in the world even as they sanctify it in "the highest heavens, as it is written by the hand of your prophet:

And they called one unto the other and said,

Cong.—Holy, holy, holy is the Lord of hosts: the whole earth is full of his glory.

The following Prayer for a Sick Person may be introduced here—

May it be your will, O Lord our God, and God of our fathers, speedily to send a perfect healing from heaven, a healing of soul and body unto the sick . . . among the other sick of Israel.

On the Fast of the Ninth of Ab the following is added—

Comfort, O Lord our God, the mourners of Zion, and the mourners of Jerusalem, and the city that is in mourning, laid waste, despised and desolate; in mourning for that she is childless, laid waste as to her dwellings, despised in the downfall of her glory, and desolate through the loss of her inhabitants: she sits with her head covered like a barren woman who has not borne. Legions have devoured her; worshippers of strange gods have possessed her: they have put your people Israel to the sword, and in willfulness have slain the loving ones of the Most High. Therefore let Zion weep bitterly, and Jerusalem give forth her voice. O my heart, my heart! how it grieves for the slain! My bowels, my bowels! how they yearn for the slain! For you, O Lord, did consume her with fire; and with fire you will in future restore her, as it is said, As for me, I will be unto her, says the Lord, a wall of fire round about, and I will be a glory in the midst of her. Blessed are you, O Lord, who comforts Zion and rebuilds Jerusalem.

"Speedily," etc.

On Fast Days the Congregation says the following—

Answer us, O Lord, answer us on this day of the fast of our humiliation, for we are in great trouble. Turn not to our wickedness; conceal not your face from us, and hide not yourself from our supplication. Be near, we entreat you, unto our cry; let your loving-kindness be a comfort to us; even before we call unto you answer us, according as it is said, And it shall come to pass that, before they call, I will answer; while they are yet speaking, I will hear; for you, O Lord, are he who answers in time of trouble, who delivers and rescues in all times of trouble and distress.

EVENING SERVICE FOR WEEKDAYS AND THE TERMINATION OF THE SABBATH

On Weekdays, if the Evening Service is read after nightfall, commence here. At the termination of the Sabbath say Psalms cxliv and lxvii; then continue, "And he being merciful." On Weekdays, if the Evening Service is read before nightfall, commence, "And he being merciful."

Psalm cxxxiv.

A Song of Degrees.—Behold, bless you the Lord, all you servants of the Lord, who stand in the house of the Lord in the night seasons. Lift up your hands towards the sanctuary, and bless you the Lord. The Lord bless you out of Zion; even he that made heaven and earth.

The Lord of hosts is with us; the God of Jacob is our stronghold. (Selah.)

To be said three times.

O Lord of hosts, happy is the man that trusts in you.

To be said three times.

Save, Lord: may the King answer us on the day when we call.

To be said three times.

Reader.—Magnified and sanctified be his great name in the world which he has created according to his will. May he establish his kingdom during your life and during your days,. and during the life of all the house of Israel, even speedily and at a near time, and say ye, Amen.

Cong. and Reader.—Let his great name be blessed forever and to all eternity.

Reader.—Blessed, praised and glorified, exalted, extolled and honored, magnified and lauded be the name of the Holy One, blessed be he; though he be high above all the blessings and hymns, praises and consolations, which are uttered in the world; and say ye, Amen.

And he being merciful, forgives iniquity, and destroys not: yea, many a time he turns his anger away, and does not stir up all his wrath. Save, Lord may the King answer us on the day when we cal!.

Congregation in an undertone.

Blessed, praised, glorified, exalted and extolled be the name of the supreme King of kings, the Holy One, blessed be he, who is the first and the last, and beside him there is no God. Extol you him that rides upon the heavens by his name Yah, and rejoice before him. His name is exalted above all blessing and praise. Blessed be His name, whose glorious kingdom is forever and ever. Let the name of the Lord be blessed from this time forth and forevermore.

Reader.—Bless you the Lord who is to be blessed.

Cong. and Reader.—Blessed is the Lord who is to be blessed forever and ever.

Blessed are you, O. Lord our God, King of the universe, who at your word brings on the evening twilight, with wisdom opens the gates of the heavens, and with understanding changes times and varies the seasons, and arranges the stars in their watches in the sky, according to your will. You create day and night; you roll away the light from before the darkness, and the darkness from before the light; you make the day to pass and the night to approach, and divide the day from the night, the Lord of hosts is your name; a God living and enduring continually, may you reign over us forever and ever. Blessed are you, O Lord, who brings on the evening twilight.

With everlasting love you have loved the house of Israel, your people; a Torah and commandments, statutes and judgments have you taught us. Therefore, O Lord our God, when we lie down and when we rise up we will meditate on your statutes: yea, we will rejoice in the words of your Torah and in your commandments forever; for they are our life and the length of our days, and we will meditate on them day and night. And may you never take away your love from us. Blessed are you, O Lord, who loves your people Israel.

When Prayers are not said with the Congregation, add—

God, faithful King!

Deut. vi. 4-9.

Hear, O Israel: the Lord our God, the Lord is One.

Blessed be His name, whose glorious kingdom is forever and ever.

And you shall love the Lord your God with all your heart and with all your soul, and with all your might. And these words, which I command you this day, shall be upon your heart: and you shall teach them diligently unto your children, and shall talk of them when you sit in your house, and when you walk by the way, and when you lie down, and when you rise up. And you shall bind them for a sign upon your hand, and they shall be for frontlets between your eyes. And you shall write them upon the door posts of your house, and upon your gates.

Deut. xi. 13-21.

And it shall come to pass, if you shall hearken. diligently unto my commandments, which T command you this day, to love the Lord your God, and to serve him with all your heart and with all your soul, that I will give the rain of your land in its season, the former rain and the latter rain, that you may gather in your corn, and your wine, and your oil. And I will give grass in your field for your cattle, and you shall eat and be satisfied. Take heed to yourselves, lest your heart be deceived, and you turn aside, and serve other gods, and worship them; and the anger of the Lord be kindled against you, and he shut up the heaven, that there be no rain, and that the land yield not her fruit; and you perish quickly from off the good land which the Lord gives you. Therefore shall you lay up these my words in your heart and in your soul; and you shall bind them for a sign upon your hand, and they shall be for frontlets between your eyes. And you shall teach them your children, talking of them when you sit in your house, and when you walk by the way, and when you lie down, and when you rise up. And you shall write them upon the door posts of your house, and upon your gates: that your days may be multiplied, and the days of your children, upon the land which the Lord swore unto your fathers to give them, as the days of the heavens above the earth.

Numbers xv. 37-41.

And the Lord spoke to Moses, saying, Speak unto the children of Israel, and bid theirs that they make them a fringe upon the corners of their garments, throughout their generations, and that they put upon the fringe of each corner a cord of blue: and it shall be unto you for a fringe, that you may look upon it, and remember all the commandments of the Lord, and do them; and that you go not about after your own heart and your own eyes, after which you use to go astray: that you may remember and do all my commandments, and be holy unto your God. I am the Lord your God, who brought you out of the land of Egypt, to be your God: I am the Lord your God.

True and trustworthy is all this, and it is established with us that he is the Lord our God, and there is none beside him, and that We, Israel, are his people. It is he who redeemed us from the hand of kings, even our King, who delivered us from the grasp of all the terrible ones; the God, who on our behalf dealt out punishment to our adversaries, and requited all the enemies of our soul; who does great things past finding out, yea, and wonders without number; who holds our soul in life, and has not suffered our feet to be moved; who made us tread upon the high places of our enemies, and exalted our horn over all them that hated us; who wrought for us miracles and vengeance upon Pharaoh, signs and wonders in the land of the children of Ham; who in his wrath smote all the first-born of Egypt, and brought forth his people Israel from among them to everlasting freedom; who made his children pass between the divisions of the Red Sea, hilt sank their pursuers and their enemies in the depths. Then his children beheld his might. They praised and gave thanks unto his name and willingly accepted his sovereignty. Moses and the children of Israel sang a song unto you with great joy, saying, all of them,

Who is like unto you, O Lord, among the mighty ones? Who is like unto you, glorious in holiness, revered in praises, doing wonders?

Your children beheld your sovereign power, as you did cleave the sea before Moses: they exclaimed, This is my God! and said, The Lord shall reign forever and ever.

And it is said, For the Lord has delivered Jacob, and redeemed him from the hand of him that was stronger than he. Blessed are you, O Lord, who has redeemed Israel.

Cause us, O Lord our God, to lie down in peace, and raise us up, O our King, unto life. Spread over us the tabernacle of your peace; direct us right through your own good counsel; save us for your name's sake; be you a shield about us; remove from us every enemy, pestilence, sword, famine and sorrow; remove also the adversary from before us and from behind us. O shelter us beneath the shadow of your wings; for you, O God, are our Guardian and our Deliverer; yea, you, O God, are a gracious and merciful King; and guard our going out and our coming in unto life and unto peace from this time forth and forevermore. Blessed are you, O Lord, who guards your people Israel forever.

Blessed be the Lord forevermore. Amen and Amen. Blessed be the Lord out of Zion, who dwells in Jerusalem. Praise you the Lord. Blessed be the Lord God, the God of Israel, who alone does wondrous things: and blessed be his glorious name forever; and let the whole earth be filled with his glory. Amen and Amen. Let the glory of the Lord endure forever; let the Lord rejoice in his works. Let the name of the Lord be blessed from this time forth and forevermore. For the Lord will not forsake his people for his great name's sake; because it has pleased him to make you a people unto himself. And when all the people saw it, they fell on their faces: and they said, The Lord, he is God; the Lord, he is God. And the Lord shall be King over all the earth: in that day shall the Lord be One, and his name One. Let your loving-kindness, O Lord, be upon us, according as we have hoped for you. Save us, O God of our salvation, and gather us and deliver us from the nations, to give thanks unto your holy name, and to triumph in your praise. All nations whom you have made shall come and worship before you, O Lord; and they shall glorify your name: for you are great and do marvelous things; you are God alone. But we are your people and the sheep of your pasture; we will give thanks unto you forever: we will recount your praise to all generations.

Blessed be the Lord by day; blessed be the Lord by night; blessed be the Lord when we lie down; blessed be the Lord when we rise up. For in your hand are the souls of the living and the dead, as it is said, In his hand is the soul of every living thing, and the spirit of all human flesh. Into your hand I commend my spirit; you have redeemed me, O Lord God of truth. Our God who are in heaven, assert the unity of your name, and establish your kingdom continually, and reign over us forever and ever.

May our eyes behold, our hearts rejoice, and our souls be glad in your true salvation, when it shall be said unto Zion, your God reigns. The Lord reigns; the Lord has reigned; the Lord shall reign forever and ever: for the kingdom is yours, and to everlasting you will reign in glory; for we have no king but you. Blessed are you, O Lord, the King, who constantly in his glory will reign over us and over all his works forever and ever.

Reader.—Magnified and sanctified be his great name in the world which he has created according to his will. May he establish his kingdom during your life and during your days, and during the life of all the house of Israel, even speedily and at a near time, and say ye, Amen.

Cong. and Reader.—Let his great name be blessed forever and to all eternity.

Reader.—Blessed, praised and glorified, exalted, extolled and honored, magnified and lauded be the name of the Holy One, blessed be he; though he be high above all the blessings and hymns, praises and consolations, which are uttered in the world; and say ye, Amen.

The following prayer (Amidah) to "as in ancient years," is to be said standing.

O Lord, open you my lips, and my mouth shall declare your praise.

Blessed are you, O Lord our God and God of our fathers, God of Abraham, God of Isaac, and God of Jacob, the great, mighty and revered God, the most high God, who bestows loving-kindnesses, and possesses all things; who remembers the pious deeds of the patriarchs, and in love will bring a redeemer to their children's children for your name's sake.

During the Ten Days of Penitence say—

Remember us unto life, O King, who delights in life, and inscribe us in the book of life, for your own sake, O living God.

O King, Helper, Savior and Shield. Blessed are you, O Lord, the Shield of Abraham.

You, O Lord, are mighty forever, you quicken the dead, you are mighty to save.

From the Eighth Day of Solemn Assembly until the First Day of Passover say—

You cause the wind to blow and the rain to fall.

You sustain the living with loving-kindness, quickens the dead with great mercy, supports the falling, heals the sick, loose the bound, and keeps your faith to them that sleep in the dust. Who is like unto you, Lord of mighty acts, and who resembles you, O King, who kills and quickens, and causes salvation to spring forth?

During the Ten Days of Penitence say—

Who is like unto you, Father of mercy, who in mercy remembers your creatures unto life?

Yea, faithful are you to quicken the dead. Blessed are you, O Lord, who quickens the dead.

You are holy, and your name is holy, and holy beings praise you daily. (Selah.) Blessed are you, O Lord, the holy God.

During the Ten Days of Penitence conclude the blessing thus—
the holy King.

You favor man with knowledge, and teach mortals understanding.

At the conclusion of Sabbath or of a Festival say—

You have favored us with knowledge of your Torah, and has taught us to perform the statutes of your will. You have made a distinction, O Lord our God, between holy and profane, between light and darkness, between Israel and other nations, between the seventh day and the six working days. O our Father, our King, grant that the days which are approaching us may begin for us in peace, and that we may be withheld from all sin and cleansed from all iniquity, and cleave to the fear of you

O favor us with knowledge, understanding and discernment from you. Blessed are you. O Lord, gracious Giver of knowledge.

Cause us to return, O our Father, unto your Torah; draw us near, O our King, unto your service, and bring us back in perfect repentance unto your presence. Blessed are you, O Lord, who delights in repentance.

Forgive us, O our Father, for we have sinned; pardon us, O our King, for we have transgressed; for you dost pardon and forgive. Blessed are you, O Lord, who are gracious, and do abundantly forgive.

Look upon our affliction and plead our cause, and redeem us speedily for your name's sake; for you are a mighty Redeemer. Blessed are you, O Lord, the Redeemer of Israel.

Heal us, O Lord, and we shall be healed; save us and we shall be saved; for you are our praise. Vouchsafe a perfect healing to all our wounds; for you, almighty King, are a faithful and merciful Physician. Blessed are you, O Lord, who heals the sick of your people Israel.

Bless this year unto us, O Lord our God, together with every kind of the produce thereof, for our welfare; give a blessing

During the Winter Season substitute for the last sentence—
Give dew and rain for a blessing upon the face of the earth.

upon the face of the earth. O satisfy us with your goodness, and bless our year like other good years. Blessed are you, O Lord, who blesses the years.

Sound the great horn for our freedom; lift up the ensign to gather our exiles, and gather us from the four corners of the earth. Blessed are you, O Lord, who gathers the banished ones of your people Israel.

Restore our judges as at the first, and our counsellors as at the beginning; remove from us grief and suffering; reign you over us, O Lord, you alone, in loving-kindness and tender mercy, and justify us in judgment. Blessed are you O Lord, the King who loves righteousness and judgment.

During the Ten Days of Penitence conclude the blessing thus—
the King of Judgment.

And for slanderers let there be no hope, and let all wickedness perish as in a moment; let all your enemies be speedily cut off, and the dominion of arrogance do you uproot and crush, cast down and humble speedily in our days. Blessed are you, O Lord, who breaks the enemies and humbles the arrogant.

Towards the righteous and the pious, towards the elders of your people the house of Israel, towards the remnant of their scribes, towards the proselytes of righteousness, and towards us also may your tender mercies be stirred, O Lord our God; grant a good reward unto all who faithfully trust in your name; set our portion with them forever, so that we may not be put to shame; for we have trusted in you. Blessed are you, O Lord, the stay and trust of the righteous.

And to Jerusalem, your city, return in mercy, and dwell therein as you have spoken; rebuild it soon in our days as an everlasting building, and speedily set up therein the throne of David. Blessed are you, O Lord, who rebuilds Jerusalem.

Speedily cause the offspring of David, your servant, to flourish, and let his horn be exalted by your salvation, because we wait for your salvation all the day. Blessed are you, O Lord, who causes the horn of salvation to flourish.

Hear our voice, O Lord our God; spare us and have mercy upon us, and accept our prayer in mercy and favor; for you are a God who hearkens unto prayers and supplications: from your presence, O our King, turn us not empty away; for you hearken in mercy to the prayer of your people Israel. Blessed are you, O Lord, who hearkens unto prayer.

Accept, O Lord our God, your people Israel and their prayer; restore the service to the oracle of your house; receive in love and favor both the fire-offerings of Israel and their prayer; and may the service of your people Israel be ever acceptable unto you.

On New Moon and the Intermediate Days of Passover and Sukkot the following is added—

Our God and God of our fathers! May our remembrance rise, come and be accepted before you, with the remembrance of our fathers, of Messiah the son of David your servant, of Jerusalem your holy city, and of all your people the house of Israel, bringing deliverance and well-being, grace, loving-kindness and mercy, life and peace on this day of

On New Moon say—
the New Moon.
On Passover—

the Feast of Unleavened Bread.
On Sukkot—
The Feast of Sukkot.

Remember us, O Lord our God, thereon for our wellbeing; be mindful of us for blessing, and save us unto life: by your promise of salvation and mercy, spare us and be gracious unto us; have mercy upon us and save us; for our eyes are bent upon you, because you are a gracious and merciful God and King.

And let our eyes behold your return in mercy to Zion. Blessed are you, O Lord, who restores your divine presence unto Zion.

We give thanks unto you, for you are the Lord our God and the God of our fathers forever and ever; you are the Rock of our lives, the Shield of our salvation through every generation. We will give thanks unto you and declare your praise for our lives which are committed unto your hand, and for our souls which are in your charge, and for your miracles, which are daily with us, and for your wonders and your benefits, which are wrought at all times, evening, morn and noon. O you who are all-good, whose mercies fail not; you, merciful Being, whose loving-kindnesses never cease, we have ever hoped in you.

On Chanukah and Purim say—
We thank you, etc.

For all these things your name, O our King, shall be continually blessed and exalted forever and ever.

During the Ten Days of Penitence say—

O inscribe all the children of your covenant for a happy life.

And everything that lives shall give thanks unto you forever, and shall praise your name in truth, O God, our salvation and our help. Blessed are you, O Lord, whose name is All-good, and unto whom it is becoming to give thanks.

Grant abundant peace unto Israel your people forever; for you are the sovereign Lord of all peace; and may it be good in your sight to bless your people Israel at all times and in every hour with your peace

During the Ten Days of Penitence say—

In the book of life, blessing, peace and good sustenance may we be remembered and inscribed before you, we and all your people the house of Israel, for a happy life and for peace. Blessed are you, O Lord, who makes peace.

Blessed are you, O Lord, who blesses your people Israel with peace.

O my God! guard my tongue from evil and my lips from speaking guile; and to such as curse me let my soul be dumb, yea, let my soul be unto all as the dust. Open my heart to your Torah, and let my soul pursue your commandments. If any design evil against me, speedily make their counsel of none effect, and frustrate their designs. Do it for the sake of your name, do it for the sake of your right hand, do it for the sake of your holiness, do it for the sake of your Torah. In order that your beloved ones may be delivered, O save with your right hand, and answer me. Let the words of my mouth and the meditation of my heart be acceptable before you, O Lord, my Rock and my Redeemer. He who makes peace in his high places, may he make peace for us and for all Israel, and say ye, Amen.

May it be your will, O Lord our God and God of our fathers, that the temple be speedily rebuilt in our days, and grant our portion in your Torah. And there we will serve you with awe, as in the days of old, and as in ancient years. Then shall the offering of Judah and Jerusalem be pleasant unto the Lord, as in the days of old, and as in ancient years.

Reader.—Magnified and sanctified be his great name in the world which he has created according to his will. May he establish his kingdom during your life and during your days, and during the life of all the house of Israel, even speedily and at a near time, and say ye, Amen.

Cong. and Reader.—Let his great name be blessed forever and to all eternity.

Reader.—Blessed, praised and glorified, exalted, extolled and honored, magnified and lauded be the name of the Holy One, blessed be he; though he be high above all the blessings and hymns, praises and consolations, which are uttered in the world; and say ye. Amen.

Cong.—Accept our prayer in mercy and in favor.

Reader.—May the prayers and supplications of all Israel be accepted by their Father who is in heaven; and say ye, Amen.

Reader.—May there be abundant peace from heaven, and life for us and for all Israel; and say ye, Amen.

Cong.—My help is from the Lord, who made heaven and earth.

Reader.—He who makes peace in his high places, may he make peace for us and for all Israel; and say ye, Amen.

It is our duty to praise the Lord of all things, to ascribe greatness to him who formed the world in the beginning, since he has not made us like the nations of other lands, and has not placed us like other families of the earth, since he has not assigned unto us a portion as unto them, nor a lot as unto all their multitude. For we bend the knee and offer worship and thanks before the supreme King of kings, the Holy One, blessed be he, who stretched forth the heavens and laid the foundations of the earth, the seat of whose glory is in the heavens above, and the abode of whose might is in the loftiest heights. He is our God; there is none else: in truth he is our King; there is none besides him; as it is written in his Torah, And you shall know this day, and lay it to your heart, that the Lord he is God in heaven above and upon the earth beneath: there is none else.

We therefore hope in you, O Lord our God, that we may speedily behold the glory of your might, when you will remove the abominations from the earth and the idols will be utterly cut off, when the world will be perfected under the kingdom of the Almighty and all the children of flesh will call upon your name, then you will turn unto yourself all the wicked of le earth. Let all the inhabitants of the world perceive and know that unto you every knee must bow, every tongue must swear. Before you, O Lord our God, let them bow and fall; and unto your glorious name let them give honor; let them all accept the yoke of your kingdom, and do you reign over them speedily, and forever and ever. For the kingdom is yours, and to all eternity you will reign in glory; as it is written in your Torah, The Lord shall reign forever and ever. And it is said, And the Lord shall be king over all the earth: in that day shall the Lord be One, and his name One.

The following Kaddish is said by a Mourner.

Mourner.—Magnified and sanctified be his great name in the world which he has created according to his will. May he establish his kingdom during your life and during your days, and during the life of all the house of Israel, even speedily and at a near time, and say ye, Amen.

Cong. and Mourner.—Let his great name be blessed forever and to all eternity.

Mourner.—Blessed, praised and glorified, exalted, extolled and honored, magnified and lauded be the name of the Holy One, blessed be he;, though he be high above all the blessings and hymns, praises and consolations, which are uttered in the world; and say ye, Amen.

Cong.—Let the name of the Lord be blessed from this time forth and forevermore.

Mourner.—May there be abundant peace from heaven, and life for us and for all Israel; and say ye, Amen.

Cong.—My help is from the Lord, who made heaven and earth.

Mourner.—He who makes peace in his high places, may he make peace for us and for all Israel; and say ye, Amen.

INAUGURATION OF THE SABBATH.

On kindling the Sabbath lights say—

Blessed are you, O Lord our God, King of the universe, who has sanctified us by your commandments, and commanded us to kindle the Sabbath light.

Psalm xcv.

O come, let us exult before the Lord: let us shout for joy to the rock of our salvation. Let us come before his presence with thanksgiving: let us shout for joy unto him with psalms. For the Lord is a great God, and a great king above all gods. In his hand are the deep places of the earth; the heights of the mountains are his also. The sea is his, and he made it; and his hands formed the dry land. O come, let us worship and bow down; let us kneel before the Lord our maker. For he is our God, and we are the people of his pasture, and the sheep of his hand. To-day, oh that you would hearken to his voice! Harden not your hearts as at Meribah, as in the day of Massah in the wilderness: when your fathers tempted me, and proved me, although they had seen my work. Forty years long was I wearied with that generation, and said, It is a people that do err in their heart, and they have not known my ways. Wherefore I swore in my wrath, that they should not enter into my rest.

Psalm xcvi.

O sing unto the Lord a new song: sing unto the Lord, all the earth. Sing unto the Lord, bless his name: proclaim his salvation from day to day. Recount his glory among the nations, his wondrous works among all the peoples. For great is the Lord, and exceedingly to be praised: he is to be revered above all gods. For all the gods of the peoples are things of naught: but the Lord made the heavens. Splendor and majesty are before him: strength and beauty are in his sanctuary. Give unto the Lord, you families of the peoples, give unto the Lord glory and strength. Give unto the Lord the glory due unto his name: take an offering, and come into his courts. O worship the Lord in the beauty of holiness; tremble before him, all the earth. Say among the nations, the Lord reigns: the world also is set firm that it cannot be moved: he shall judge the peoples with equity. Let the heavens rejoice, and let the earth be glad; let the sea roar, and the fullness thereof; let the plain triumph and all that is therein; yea, let all the trees of the forest exult before the Lord, for he comes; for he comes to judge the earth: he will judge the world with righteousness, and the peoples in his faithfulness.

Psalm xcvii.

The Lord reigns; let the earth be glad; let the many coast-lands rejoice. Clouds and darkness are round about him: righteousness and justice are the foundation of his throne. A fire goes before him, and burns up his adversaries round about. His lightnings illumine the world: the earth sees and trembles. The mountains melt like wax before the Lord, before the Lord of the whole earth. The heavens declare his righteousness, and all the peoples behold his glory. Ashamed are all they that serve graven images, that make their boast of things of naught: worship him, all you gods. Zion hears and rejoices, and the daughters of Judah are glad because of your judgments, O Lord. For you, Lord, are most high above all the earth: you are exalted far above all gods. O you that love the Lord, hate evil: he preserves the souls of his loving ones; he delivers them out of the hand of the wicked. Light is sown for the righteous, and joy for the upright in heart. Rejoice in the Lord, you righteous; and give thanks to his holy name.

Psalm xcviii.

A Psalm. O sing unto the Lord a new song; for he has done marvelous things: his right hand, and his holy arm, has wrought salvation for him. The Lord has made known his salvation: his righteousness has he revealed in the sight of the nations. He has remembered his loving-kindness and his faithfulness toward the house of Israel: all the ends of the earth have seen the salvation of our God. Shout for joy unto the Lord, all the earth; break forth into exultation, and sing praises. Sing praises unto the Lord with the lyre; with the lyre and the sound of song. With trumpets and the sound of the horn shout for joy before the king the Lord. Let the sea roar, and the fullness thereof, the world, and they that dwell therein. Let the streams clap their hands, let the mountains exult together before the Lord, for he comes to judge the earth: he will judge the world with righteousness, and the peoples with equity.

Psalm xcix.

The Lord reigns; let the peoples tremble: he sits above the cherubim; let the earth be moved. The Lord is great in Zion; and he is high above all the peoples. Let them give thanks to your great and dreaded name; holy is he. And the strength of a king that loves justice you did establish in equity; you have wrought justice and righteousness in Jacob. Exalt you the Lord our God, and worship at his footstool: holy is he. Moses and Aaron among his priests, and Samuel among them that call upon his name, called upon the Lord, and he answered them. He spoke to them in the pillar of cloud: they kept his testimonies, and the statute that he gave them. You did answer them, O Lord our God: a forgiving God you wast unto them, though you took vengeance on their misdeeds. Exalt you the Lord our God, and worship at his holy mount; for the Lord our God is holy.

Psalm xxix.

A Psalm of David. Give unto the Lord, O you children of the mighty, give unto the Lord glory and strength. Give unto the Lord the glory due unto his name; worship the Lord in the beauty of holiness. The voice of the Lord is upon the waters: the God of glory thunders, even the Lord upon the great waters. The voice of the Lord is powerful; the voice of the Lord is full of majesty. The voice of the Lord breaks the cedars; yea, the Lord breaks in pieces the cedars of Lebanon. He makes them also to skip like a calf; Lebanon and Sirion like a young wild-ox. The voice of the Lord cleaves flames of fire; the voice of the Lord makes the wilderness to tremble; the Lord makes tremble the wilderness of Kadesh. The voice of the Lord makes the hinds to travail, and strips the forests bare: and in his temple everything says, Glory. The Lord sat as king at the flood; yea, the Lord sits as king forever. The Lord will give strength unto his people; the Lord will bless his people with peace.

 Come, my friend, to meet the bride; let us welcome the presence of the Sabbath.

"Observe" and "Remember the Sabbath day," the only God caused us to hear in a single utterance: the Lord is One, and his name is One to his renown and his glory and his praise. Come, my friend, to meet the bride; let us welcome the presence of the Sabbath.

Come, let us go to meet the Sabbath, for it is a well-spring of blessing; from the beginning, from of old it was ordained,—last in production, first in thought. Come, my friend, to meet the bride; let us welcome the presence of the Sabbath.

O sanctuary of our King, O regal city, arise, go forth from your overthrow; long enough have you dwelt in the valley of weeping; verily He will have compassion upon you. Come, my friend, to meet the bride; let us welcome the presence of the Sabbath.

Shake yourself from the dust, arise, put on the garments of your glory, O my people! Through the son of Jesse, of Bethlehem, draw You nigh unto my soul, redeem it. Come, my friend, to meet the bride; let us welcome the presence of the Sabbath.

Arouse yourself, arouse yourself, for your light is come: arise, shine; awake, awake; give forth a song; the glory of the Lord is revealed upon you. Come, my friend, to meet the bride; let us welcome the presence of the Sabbath.

Be not ashamed, neither be confounded. Why are you cast down, and why are you disquieted? The poor of my people trust in you, and the city shall be built on her own mound. Come, my friend, to meet the bride; let us welcome the presence of the Sabbath.

And they that spoil you shall be a spoil, and all that would swallow you shall be far away: your God shall rejoice over you, as a bridegroom rejoices over his bride. Come, etc. You shall spread abroad on the right hand and on the left, and you shall reverence the Lord. Through the offspring of Perez we also shall rejoice and be glad. Come, my friend, to meet the bride; let us welcome the presence of the Sabbath.

Come in peace, you crown of your husband, with rejoicing and with cheerfulness, in the midst of the faithful of the chosen people: come, O bride; come, O bride.

Come, my friend, to meet the bride; let us welcome the presence of the Sabbath.

Psalm xcii.

A Psalm, a Song for the Sabbath Day. It is a good thing to give thanks unto the Lord, and to sing praises unto your name, O Most High: to declare your loving-kindness in the morning, and your faithfulness every night, with an instrument of ten strings and with a harp, with thoughtful music upon the lyre. For you, O Lord, have made me rejoice through your work: I will exult in the works of your hands. How great are your works, O Lord: your thoughts are very deep. A brutish man knows it not, neither does a fool understand this: when the wicked sprang up as the grass, and all the workers of iniquity flourished, it was that they might be destroyed forever. But you, O Lord, are on high forevermore. For, lo, your enemies, O Lord, for, lo, your enemies shall perish; all the workers of iniquity shall be scattered. But my horn have you exalted, like that of the wild-ox: I am anointed with fresh oil. My eye also has seen my desire on my enemies; my ears have heard my desire of them that rose up against me, doers of evil. The righteous shall spring up like a palm-tree; he shall grow tall like a cedar in Lebanon. Planted in the house of the Lord, they shall blossom in the courts of our God. They shall still shoot forth in old age; they shall be full of sap and green: to declare that the Lord is upright; he is my rock, and there is no unrighteousness in him.

Psalm xciii.

The Lord reigns; he has robed him in majesty; the Lord has robed him, yea, he has girded himself with strength: the world also is set firm, that it cannot be moved. Your throne is set firm from of old: you are from everlasting. The streams have lifted up, O Lord, the streams have lifted up their voice; the streams lift up their roaring. Than the voices of many waters, mighty waters, breakers of the sea, more mighty is the Lord on high. Your testimonies are very faithful: holiness becomes your house, O Lord, forevermore.

The following Kaddish is said by a Mourner.

Mourner.—Magnified and sanctified be his great name in the world which he has created according to his will. May he establish his kingdom during your life and during your days, and during the life of all the house of Israel, even speedily and at a near time, and say ye, Amen.

Cong. and Mourner.—Let his great name be blessed forever and to all eternity.

Mourner.—Blessed, praised and glorified, exacted extolled and honored, magnified and lauded be the name of the Holy One, blessed be he; though he be high above all the blessings and hymns, praises and consolations, which are uttered in the world; and say ye, Amen.

Cong.—Let the name of the Lord be blessed from this time forth and forevermore.

Mourner.—May there be abundant peace from heaven, and life for us and for all Israel; and say ye, Amen.

Cong.—My help is from the Lord, who made heaven and earth.

Mourner.—He who makes peace in his high places, may he make peace for us and for all Israel; and say ye, Amen.

When a Festival or one of the Intermediate Days of a Festival falls on Sabbath, the Inauguration Service commences with "A Psalm, a Song, etc."

EVENING SERVICE FOR SABBATHS AND FESTIVALS

Reader.—Bless you the Lord who is to be blessed.

Congregation in an undertone:

Blessed, praised, glorified, exalted and extolled be the name of the supreme King of kings, the Holy One, blessed be he, who is the first and the last, and beside him there is no God. Extol you him that rides upon the heavens by his name Yah, and rejoice before him. His name is exalted above all blessing and praise. Blessed be His name, whose glorious kingdom is forever and ever. Let the name of the Lord be blessed from this time forth and forevermore.

Cong. and Reader.—Blessed is the Lord who is to be blessed forever and ever.

Blessed are you, O Lord our God, King of the universe, who at your word brings on the evening twilight, with wisdom opens the gates of the heavens, and with understanding changes times and varies the seasons, and arranges the stars in their watches in the sky, according to your will. You creates day and night; you rolls away the light from before the darkness, and the darkness from before the light; you makes the day to pass and the night to approach, and divides the day from the night, the Lord of hosts is your name; a God living and enduring continually, may you reign over us forever and ever. Blessed are you, O Lord, who brings on the evening twilight.

With everlasting love you have loved the house of Israel, your people; a Torah and commandments, statutes and judgments have you taught us. Therefore. O Lord our God, when we lie down and when we rise up we will meditate on your statutes: yea, we will rejoice in the words of your Torah and in your commandments forever; for they are our life and the length of our days and we will meditate on them day and night. And may you never take away your love from us. Blessed are you, O Lord, who loves your people Israel.

When Prayers are not said with the Congregation, add—

God, faithful King!

Deut. vi. 4-9.

Hear, O Israel, the Lord our God, the Lord is One.

Blessed be His name, whose glorious kingdom is forever and ever.

And you shall love the Lord your God with all your heart, and with all your soul, and with all your might. And these words, which I command you this day, shall be upon your heart: and you shall teach them diligently unto your children, and shall talk of them when you sit in your house, and when you walk by the way, and when you lie down, and when you rise up. And you shall bind them for a sign upon your hand, and they shall be for frontlets between your eyes. And you shall write them upon the door posts of your house, and upon your gates.

Deut. xi. 13-21.

And it shall come to pass, if you shall hearken diligently unto my commandments which I command you this day, to love the Lord your God, and to serve him with all your heart and with all your soul, that I will give the rain of your land in its season, the former rain and the latter rain, that you may gather in your corn, and your wine, and your oil. And I will give grass in your field for your cattle, and you shall eat and be satisfied. Take heed to yourselves, lest your heart be deceived, and you turn aside, and serve other gods, and worship them; and the anger of the Lord be kindled against you, and he shut up the heaven, that there be no rain, and that the land yield not her fruit; and you perish quickly from off the good land which the Lord gives you. Therefore shall you lay up these my words in your heart and in your soul: and you shall bind them for a sign upon your hand, and they shall be for frontlets between your eyes. And you shall teach them your children, talking of them when you sit in your house, and when you walk by the way, and when you lie down, and when you rise up. And you shall write them upon the door posts of your house, and upon your gates: that your days may be multiplied, and the days of your children, upon the land which the Lord swore to your fathers to give them, as the days of the heavens above the earth.

Numbers xv. 37-41.

And the Lord spoke to Moses, saying, Speak unto the children of Israel, and bid them that they make them a fringe upon the corners of their garments throughout their generations, and that they put upon the fringe of each corner a cord of blue: and it shall be unto you for a fringe, that you may look upon it, and remember all the commandments of the Lord, and do them; and that you go not about after your own heart and your own eyes, after which you use to go astray: that you may remember and do all my commandments, and be holy unto your God. I am the Lord your God, who brought you out of the Land of Egypt, to be your God; I am the Lord your God.

True and trustworthy is all this, and it is established with us that he is the Lord our God, and there is none beside him, and that we, Israel, are his people. It is he who redeemed us from the hand of kings, even our King, who delivered us from the grasp of all the terrible ones; the God, who on our behalf dealt out punishment to our adversaries, and requited all the enemies of our soul; who does great things past finding out, yea, and wonders without number; who holds our soul in life, and has not suffered our feet to be moved; who made us tread upon the high places of our enemies, and exalted our horn over all them that hated us; who wrought for us miracles and vengeance upon Pharaoh, signs and wonders in the land of the children of Ham; who in his wrath smote all the first-born of Egypt, and brought forth his people Israel from among them to everlasting freedom; who made his children pass between the divisions of the Red Sea, but sank their pursuers and their enemies in the depths. Then his children beheld his might; they praised and gave thanks unto his name, and willingly accepted his sovereignty. Moses and the children of Israel sang a song unto you with great joy, saying, all of them,

Who is like unto you, O Lord, among the mighty ones? Who is like unto you, glorious in holiness, revered in praises, doing wonders?

Your children beheld your sovereign power, as you did cleave the sea before Moses: they exclaimed, This is my God! and said,

The Lord shall reign forever and ever.

And it is said, For the Lord has delivered Jacob, and redeemed him from the hand of him that was stronger than he. Blessed are you, O Lord, who has redeemed Israel.

Cause us, O Lord our God, to lie down in peace, and raise us up, O our King, unto life. Spread over us the tabernacle of your peace; direct us right through your own good counsel; save us for your name's sake; be you a shield about us; remove from is every enemy, pestilence, sword, famine and sorrow; remove also the adversary from before us and from behind us. O shelter us beneath the shadow of your wings; for you, O God, are our Guardian and our Deliverer; yea, you, O God, are a gracious and merciful King; and guard our going out and our coming in unto life and unto peace from this time forth and forevermore; yea, spread over us the tabernacle of your peace. Blessed are you, O Lord, who spreads the tabernacle of peace over us and over all your people Israel, and over Jerusalem.

On Sabbaths—

Exodus xxxi. 16, 17.

And the children of Israel shall keep the Sabbath, to observe the Sabbath throughout their generations, for an everlasting covenant. It is a sign between me and the children of Israel forever, that in six days the Lord made the heavens and the earth, and on the seventh day he rested, and ceased from his work.

On Passover, Pentecost and Sukkot, say—

And Moses declared the set feasts of the Lord unto the children of Israel.

On New Year—

Blow the horn on the new moon, at the beginning of the month, for our day of festival: for it is a statute for Israel, a decree of the God of Jacob.

On the Day of Atonement—

For on this day shall atonement be made for you to cleanse you; from all your sins shall you be clean before the Lord.

Reader.—Magnified and sanctified be his great -name in the world which he has created according to his will. May he establish his kingdom during your life and during your days, and during the life of all the house of Israel, even speedily and at a near time, and say ye, Amen.

Cong. and Reader.—Let his great name be blessed. forever and to all eternity.

Reader.—Blessed, praised and glorified, exalted, extolled and honored, magnified and lauded be the name of the Holy One, blessed be he; though he be high above all the blessings and hymns, praises and consolations, which are uttered in the world; and say ye,. Amen.

On Festivals say the appropriate Amidot.

O Lord, open you my lips, and my mouth shall declare your praise.

Blessed are you, O Lord our God and God of our fathers, God of Abraham, God of Isaac, and God of Jacob, the great, mighty and revered God, the most high God, who bestows loving-kindnesses, and possesses all things; who remembers the pious deeds of the patriarchs, and in love will bring a redeemer to their children's children for your name's sake.

On the Sabbath of Penitence say—

Remember us unto life, O King, who delights in. life, and inscribe us in the book of life, for your own sake, O living God.

O King, Helper, Savior and Shield. Blessed are you, O Lord, the Shield of Abraham.

You, O Lord, are mighty forever, you quicken the dead, you are mighty to save.

From the Sabbath after the Eighth Day of Solemn Assembly until the First Day of Passover say—

You cause the wind to blow and the rain to fall.

You sustain the living with loving-kindness, quicken the dead with great mercy, supports the falling, heals the sick, loose the bound, and keeps your faith to them that sleep in the dust. Who is like unto you, Lord of mighty acts, and who resembles you, O King, who kills and quickens, and causes salvation to spring forth?

On the Sabbath of Penitence say—

Who is like unto you, Father of mercy, who in mercy remembers your creatures unto life?

Yea, faithful are you to quicken the dead. Blessed are you, O Lord, who quickens the dead.

You are holy, and your name is holy, and holy beings praise you daily. (Selah.) Blessed are you, O Lord, the holy God.

On the Sabbath of Penitence conclude the blessing thus—
the holy King.

You did hallow the seventh day unto your name, as the end of the creation of heaven and earth; you did bless it above all days, and did hallow it above all seasons; and thus it is written in your Torah:

And the heaven and the earth were finished and all their host. And on the seventh day God had finished his work which he had made; and he rested on the seventh day from all his work which he had made. And God blessed the seventh day, and he hallowed it because he rested thereon from all his work which God had created and made.

Our God and God of our fathers, accept our rest; sanctify us by your commandments, and grant our portion in your Torah; satisfy us with your goodness, and gladden us with your salvation; purify our hearts to serve you in truth; and in your love and favor, O Lord our God, let us inherit your holy Sabbath; and may Israel, who hallow your name, rest thereon. Blessed are you, O Lord, who hallows the Sabbath.

Accept, O Lord our God, your people Israel and their prayer; restore the service to the oracle of your house; receive in love and favor both the fire-offerings of Israel and their prayer; and may the service of your people Israel be ever acceptable unto you.

On New Moon and the Intermediate Days of Passover and Sukkot the following is added—

Our God and God of our fathers! May our remembrance rise, come and be accepted before you, with the remembrance of our fathers, of Messiah the son of David your servant, of Jerusalem your holy city, and of all your people the house of Israel, bringing deliverance and well-being, grace, loving-kindness and mercy, life and peace on this day of

On the New Moon—
the New Moon.
On Passover—
the Feast of Unleavened Bread.
On Sukkot—
the Feast of Sukkot.

Remember us, O Lord our God, thereon for our well-being; be mindful of us for blessing, and save us unto life: by your promise of salvation and mercy, spare us and be gracious unto us; have mercy upon us and save us; for our eyes are bent upon you, because you are a gracious and merciful God and King.

And let our eyes behold your return in mercy to Zion. Blessed are you, O Lord, who restores your divine presence unto Zion.

We give thanks unto you, for you are the Lord our God and the God of our fathers forever and ever; you are the Rock of our lives, the Shield of our salvation through every generation. We will give thanks unto you and declare your praise for our lives which are committed unto your hand, and for our souls which are in your charge, and for your miracles, which are daily with us, and for your wonders and your benefits which are wrought at all times, evening, morn and noon. O you who are all-good, whose mercies fail not; you, merciful Being, whose loving-kindnesses never cease, we have ever hoped in you

On Chanukah say—
We thank you, etc.

For all these things your name, O our King, shall be continually blessed and exalted forever and ever

On the Sabbath of Penitence say—

O inscribe all the children of your covenant for a happy life.

And everything that lives shall give thanks unto you forever, and shall praise your name in truth, O God, our salvation and our help. Blessed are you, O Lord, whose name is All-good, and unto whom it is becoming to give thanks.

Grant abundant peace unto Israel your people forever; for you are the sovereign Lord of all peace; and may it be good in your sight to bless your people Israel at all times and at every hour with your peace.

On the Sabbath of Penitence say—

In the book of life, blessing, peace and good sustenance may we be remembered and inscribed before you, we and all the people of the rouse of Israel, for a happy life and for peace. Blessed are you, O Lord; who makes peace.

Blessed are you, O Lord, who blesses your people Israel with peace.

O my God! guard my tongue from evil and my lips from speaking guile; and to such as curse me let my soul be dumb, yea, let my soul be unto all as the dust. Open my heart to your Torah, and let my soul pursue your commandments. If any design evil against me, speedily make their counsel of none effect, and frustrate their designs. Do it for the sake of your name, do it for the sake of your right hand, do it for the sake of your holiness, do it for the sake of your Torah. In order that your beloved ones may be delivered, O save with your right hand, and answer me. Let the words of my mouth and the meditation of my heart be acceptable before you, O Lord, my Rock and my Redeemer. He who makes peace in his high places, may he make peace for us and for all Israel, and say ye, Amen.

May it be your will, O Lord our God and God of our fathers, that the temple be speedily rebuilt in our days, and grant our portion in your Torah. And there we will serve you with awe, as in the days of old, and as in ancient years. Then shall the offering of Judah and Jerusalem be pleasant unto the Lord, as in the days of old, and as in ancient years.

The Reader and Congregation repeat from "And the heaven" to "and made."

And the heaven and the earth were finished and all their host. And on the seventh day God had finished his work which he had made; and he rested on the seventh day from all his work which he had made. And God blessed the seventh day, and he hallowed it, because he rested thereon from all his work which God had created and made.

The following to "the Sabbath," is omitted when Prayers are not said with the Congregation—

Reader.—Blessed are you, O Lord our God and God of our fathers, God of Abraham, God of Isaac and God of Jacob, the great, mighty and revered God, the most high God, Possessor of heaven and earth.

Reader and Cong.—He with his word was a shield to our forefathers, and by his bidding will quicken the dead; the holy God (on the Sabbath of Penitence say, "holy King"), like unto whom there is none; who gives rest to his people on his holy Sabbath day, because he took pleasure in them to grant them rest. Him we will serve with fear and awe, and daily and constantly we will give thanks unto his name in the fitting forms of Blessings. He is the God to who, thanksgivings are due, the Lord of peace, who hallows the Sabbath and blesses the seventh day, and in holiness gives rest unto a people sated with delights, in remembrance of the creation.

Reader.—Our God and God of our fathers, accept our rest; sanctify us by your commandments, and grant our portion in your Torah; satisfy us with your goodness, gladden us with your salvation; purify our hearts to serve you in truth; and in your love and favor, O Lord our God, let us inherit your holy Sabbath; and may Israel, who hallow your name, rest thereon. Blessed are you, O Lord, who hallows the Sabbath.

Reader.—Magnified and sanctified be his great name in the world which he has created according to his will. May he establish his kingdom during your life and during your days, and during the life of all the house of Israel, even speedily and at a near time, and say ye, Amen.

Cong. and Reader.—Let his great name be blessed forever and to all eternity.

Reader.—Blessed, praised and glorified, exalted, extolled and honored, magnified and lauded be the name of the Holy One, blessed be he; though he be high above all the blessings and hymns, praises and consolations, which are uttered in the world; and say ye, Amen.

Cong.—Accept our prayer in mercy and in favor.

Reader.—May the prayers and supplications of all Israel be accepted by their Father who is in heaven; and say ye, Amen.

Cong.—Let the name of the Lord be blessed from this time forth and forevermore.

Reader.—May there be abundant peace from heaven, and life for us and for all Israel; and say ye, Amen.

Cong.—My help is from the Lord, who made heaven and earth.

Reader.—He who makes peace in his high places, may he make peace for us and for all Israel; and say ye, Amen.

The following is not said on Festivals, on the Intermediate Sabbath of a Festival, or on the evening after a Festival—

Mishnah, Treatise Sabbath, ch. ii.

1. With what materials may the Sabbath lamp be lighted, and with what may it not be lighted? It may not be lighted with cedar-bast, nor with uncombed flax, nor with floss-silk, nor with willow-fiber, nor with nettle fiber, nor with waterweeds (all these forming imperfect wicks). It may also not be lighted with pitch, nor with liquid wax, nor with oil made from the seeds of the cotton plant, nor with oil which, having been set apart as a heave-offering and having become defiled, is condemned to be destroyed by burning, nor with the fat from the tails of sheep, nor with tallow. Nahum the Mede, says one may use tallow when it has been boiled, but the other sages say, that whether so prepared or not, it may not be used.

2. On a festival one may not use such consecrated oil as has been condemned, after defilement, to be burnt. R. Ishmael says, one may not, from respect to the Sabbath, use tar. The sages permit the use of all kinds of oil; the oil of sesamum, of nuts, of radish seeds, of fish, of colocynth seeds, as well as tar and naphtha. R. Tarphon says, one may use no other than olive oil for lighting the Sabbath lamp.

3. No part of a tree may be used as a wick for lighting, with the exception of flax (spoken of in Joshua ii. 6 as "the flax of a tree"); nor is any part of a tree, if used in the construction of a tent, capable of acquiring pollution according to the law concerning the pollution of tents, except flax. If a slip of cloth has been folded but not singed, R. Eliezer says it may become unclean, and may not be used as a wick for lighting; R. Akiba says it remains clean, and may be used.

4. One may not perforate an egg-shell, fill it with oil, and place it above the opening of the lamp, so that drops of oil may fall therein; he may not even employ an earthenware vessel in this manner; but R. Yehudah permits it. If, however, the potter had originally joined the two parts, then it is allowed, because it is actually only one vessel. A person may not fill a bowl with oil, place it by the side of the lamp, and put the end of the wick into it, so that it may draw the oil to the flame; but R. Yehudah permits it.

5. He who extinguishes the light, because he is in fear of heathens, or robbers, or of en evil spirit, or to enable a sick person to sleep, is absolved; if his object is to save the lamp, the oil, or the wick, he is guilty of a breach of the Sabbath law. R. Jose absolves from such guilt in every case except in that of the one whose object is to save the wick, because by thus extinguishing it, he converts it into a coal.

6. For three transgressions women die in childbirth: because they have been negligent in regard to their periods of separation, in respect to the consecration of the first cake of the dough, and in the lighting of the Sabbath lamp.

7. Three things a man must say to his household on Sabbath eve towards dusk: Have you separated the tithe? Have you made the Erub? Kindle the Sabbath lamp. If it be doubtful whether it is dark, that which is certainly untithed must not then be tithed, vessels must not be immersed to purify them from their defilement, nor must the Sabbath lamps be lighted; but that which is doubtfully untithed may be tithed, the Erub may be made, and hot victuals may be covered to retain their heat.

Talmud Babli. End of Treatise Berakhot.

R. Eleazar said in the name of R. Hanina, The disciples of the sages increase peace throughout the world, as it is said, And all your children shall be taught of the Lord; and great shall be the peace of your children. (Read not here banayich, by children, but bonayich, your builders.)—Great peace have they who love your Torah; and there is no stumbling for them. Peace be within your rampart, prosperity within your palaces. For my brethren and companions' sakes I would fain speak peace concerning you. For the sake of the house of the Lord our God I would seek your good. The Lord will give strength unto his people; the Lord will bless his people with peace.

Kiddush is said by the Reader.

It is our duty to praise the Lord of all things, to ascribe greatness to him who formed the world in the beginning, since he has not made us like the nations of other lands, and has not placed us like other families of the earth, since he has not assigned unto us a portion as unto them, nor a lot as unto all their multitude. For we bend the knee and offer worship and thanks before the supreme King of kings, the Holy One, blessed be he, who stretched forth the heavens and laid the foundations of the earth, the seat of whose glory is in the heavens above, and the abode of whose might is in the loftiest heights. He is our God; there is none else; in truth he is our King; there is none besides him; as it is written in his Torah, And you shall know this day, and lay it to your heart, that the Lord he is God in heaven above and upon the earth beneath: there is none else.

We therefore hope in you, O Lord our God, that we may speedily behold the glory of your might, when you will remove the abominations from the earth, and the idols will be utterly cut off, when the world will be perfected under the kingdom of the Almighty, and all the children of flesh will call upon your name, when you will turn unto yourself all the wicked of the earth. Let all the inhabitants of the world perceive and know that unto you every knee must bow, every tongue must swear. Before you, O Lord our God, let them bow and fall; and unto your glorious name let them give honor; let them all accept the yoke of your kingdom, and do you reign over them speedily, and forever and ever. For the kingdom is yours, and to all eternity you will reign in glory; as it is written in your Torah, The Lord shall reign forever and ever. And it is said, And the Lord shall be king over all the earth: in that lay shall the Lord be One, and his name One.

The following Kaddish is said by a Mourner.

Mourner.—Magnified and sanctified be his great name in the world which he has created according to his will. May he establish his kingdom during your life and during your days, and during the life of all the house of Israel, even speedily and at a near time, and say ye, Amen.

Cong. and Mourner.—Let his great name be blessed forever and to all eternity.

Mourner.—Blessed, praised and glorified, exalted, extolled and honored, magnified and lauded be the name of the Holy One, blessed be he; though he be high above all the blessings and hymns, praises and consolations, which are uttered in the world; and say ye, Amen.

Cong.—Let the name of the Lord be blessed from this time forth and forevermore.

Mourner.—May there be abundant peace from heaven, and life for us and for all Israel; and say ye, Amen.

Cong.—My help is from the Lord, who made heaven and earth.

Mourner.—He who makes peace in his high places, may he make peace for us and for all Israel; and say ye, Amen.

1. Magnified and praised be the living God: he is, and there is no limit in time unto his being.
2. He is One, and there is no unity like unto his unity; inconceivable is he, and unending is his unity.
3. He has neither bodily form nor substance: we can compare naught unto him in his holiness.
4. He was before anything that has been created—even the first: but his existence had no beginning.
5. Behold he is the Lord of the universe: to every creature he teaches his greatness and his sovereignty.
6. The rich gift of his prophecy he gave to the men of his choice, in whom he gloried.
7. There has never yet arisen in Israel a prophet like unto Moses, one who has beheld his similitude.
8. The Torah of truth God gave unto his people by the hand of his prophet, who was faithful in his house.
9. God will not alter nor change his Torah to ever, lasting for any other.
10. He watches and knows our secret thoughts: he beholds the end of a thing before it exists.
11. He bestows loving-kindness upon a man according to his work; he gives to the wicked evil according to his wickedness.
12. He will send our anointed at the end of days, to redeem them that wait for the end—his salvation.
13. In the abundance of his loving-kindness God will quicken the dead. Blessed forevermore be his glorious name.

On the Eve of Sabbaths and of Holydays it is customary for Parents, either at the conclusion of the Service in Synagogue, or upon reaching their Home, to pronounce the following Benediction upon their Children—

To Sons say—

God make you as Ephraim and Manasseh.

To Daughters say—

God make you as Sarah, Rebekah, Rachel and Leah.

To Sons and Daughters—

The Lord bless you, and keep you: the Lord make his face to shine upon you, and be gracious unto you: the Lord turn his face unto you, and give you peace.

The following is said in the Home by the Master of the House—

Proverbs xxxi. 10-31.

A woman of worth who can find? For her price is far above rubies. The heart of her husband trusts in her; and he shall have no lack of gain. She does him good and not evil all the days of her life. She seeks wool and flax, and works willingly with her hands. She is like the merchant-ships; she brings her food from afar. She rises also while it is yet night, and sets forth provision for her household, and their portion for her maidens. She considers a field, and buys it: with the fruit of her hands she plants a vineyard. She girds her loins with strength, and makes strong her arms. She perceives that her earnings are good: her lamp goes not out by night. She puts her hands to the distaff, and her hands hold the spindle. She stretches out her hand to the poor; yea, she puts forth her hands to the needy. She is not afraid of the snow for her household; for all her household are clothed with scarlet. She makes for herself coverings of tapestry; her clothing is fine linen and purple. Her husband is known in the gates, when he sits among the elders of the land. She makes linen garments and sells them; and delivers girdles unto the merchant. Strength and majesty are her clothing; and she laughs at the time to come. She opens her mouth with wisdom; and the Torah of loving-kindness is on her tongue. She looks well to the ways of her household, and eats not the bread of idleness. Her children rise up and call her happy; her husband also, and he praises her, saying, Many daughters have done worthily, but you excel them all. Favor is false, and beauty is vain; but a woman that fears the Lord, she shall be praised. Give her of the fruit of her hands; and let her works praise her in the gates.

KIDDUSH FOR SABBATH EVENING

The following is said in the Home by the Master of the House, previous to partaking of the Sabbath Meal—

And it was evening and it was morning—the sixth day.

And the heaven and the earth were finished and all their host. And on the seventh day God had finished his work which he had made; and he rested on the seventh day from all his work which he had made. And God blessed the seventh day, and he hallowed it, because he rested thereon from all his work which God had created and made.

Blessed are you, O Lord our God, King of the universe, who creates the fruit of the vine.

Blessed are you, O Lord our God, King of the universe, who has sanctified us by your commandments and has taken pleasure in us, and in love and favor has given us your holy Sabbath as an inheritance, a memorial of the creation—that day being also the first of the holy convocations, in remembrance of the departure from Egypt. For you have chosen us and sanctified us above all nations, and in love and favor has given us your holy Sabbath as an inheritance. Blessed are you, O Lord, who hallows the Sabbath.

Blessed are you, O Lord our God, King of the universe, who brings forth bread from the earth.

MORNING SERVICE FOR SABBATHS AND FESTIVALS.
Recite to "the Lord is One." Then continue as follows—

The breath of every living being shall bless your name, O Lord our God, and the spirit of all flesh shall continually glorify and exalt your memorial, O our King; from everlasting to everlasting you are God; and beside you we have no King who redeems and saves, sets free and delivers, who supports and has mercy in all times of trouble and distress; yea, we have no King but you.

He is God of the first and of the last, the God of all creatures, the Lord of all generations, who is extolled with many praises, and guides his world with loving-kindness and his creatures with tender mercies. The Lord slumbers not, nor sleeps; he arouses the sleepers and awakens the slumberers; he makes the dumb to speak, looses the bound, supports the falling, and raises up the bowed.

To you alone we give thanks. Though our mouths were full of song as the sea, and our tongues of exultation as the multitude of its waves, and our lips of praise as the wide-extended firmament; though our eyes shone with light like the sun and the moon, and our hands were spread forth like the eagles of heaven, and our feet were swift as hinds, we should still be unable to thank you and to bless your name, O Lord our God and God of our fathers, for one thousandth or one ten thousandth part of the bounties which you have bestowed upon our fathers and upon us. You did redeem us from Egypt, O Lord our God, and did release us from the house of bondage; during famine you did feed us, and did sustain us in plenty; from the sword you did rescue us, from pestilence you did save us, and from sore and lasting diseases you did deliver us. Hitherto your tender mercies have helped us, and your loving-kindnesses have not left us: forsake us not, O Lord our God, forever. Therefore the limbs which you have spread forth upon us, and the spirit and breath which you have breathed into our nostrils, and the tongue which you have set in our mouths, lo, they shall thank, bless, praise, glorify, extol, reverence, hallow and assign kingship to your name, O Our King. For every mouth shall give thanks unto you, and every tongue shall swear unto you; every knee shall bow to you, and whatsoever is lofty shall prostrate itself before you; all hearts shall fear you, and all the inward parts and reins shall sing unto your name, according to the word that is written, All my bones shall say, Lord, who is like unto you? You deliver the poor from him that is stronger than he, the poor and the needy from him that robs him. Who is like unto you, who is equal to you, who can be compared unto you, O God, great, mighty, and awful, most high God, Possessor of heaven and earth? We will praise, laud and glorify you, and we will bless your holy name, as it is said, (A Psalm of David,) Bless the Lord, O my soul; and all that is within me, bless his holy name. You are God in your power and might, great in your glorious name, mighty forever and awful by your awful acts, the King who sits upon a high and lofty throne.

He who inhabits eternity, exalted and holy is his name; and it is written, Exult in the Lord, O you righteous; praise is seemly for the upright.

By the mouth of the upright you shall be praised, by the words of the righteous you shall be blessed, by the tongue of the loving ones you shall be extolled, and in the midst of the holy you shall be hallowed.

In the assemblies also of the tens of thousands of your people, the house of Israel, your name, O our King, shall be glorified with joyous dies in every generation; for such is the duty of all creatures in your presence, O Lord our God and God of our fathers, to thank, praise, laud, glorify, extol, honor, bless, exalt and adore you, even beyond all the words of song and praise of David the son of Jesse, your servant and anointed.

Praised be your name forever, O our King, the great and holy God and King, in heaven and on earth; for unto you, O Lord our God and God of our fathers, song and praise are becoming, hymn and psalm, strength and dominion, victory, greatness and might, renown and glory, holiness and sovereignty, blessings and thanksgivings from henceforth even forever. Blessed are you, O Lord, God and King, great in praises, God of thanksgivings, Lord of wonders, who makes choice of song and psalm, O King and God, the life of all worlds.

Reader.—Magnified and sanctified be his great name in the world which he has created according to his will. May he establish his kingdom during your life and during your days, and during the life of all the house of Israel, even speedily and at a near time, and say ye, Amen.

Cong. and Reader.—Let his great name be blessed forever and to all eternity.

Reader.—Blessed, praised and glorified, exalted, extolled and honored, magnified and lauded be the name of the Holy One, blessed be he; though he be high above all the blessings and hymns, praises and consolations, which are uttered in the world; and say ye. Amen.

Reader.—Bless you the Lord who is to be blessed.

Cong. and Reader.—Blessed is the Lord who is to be blessed forever and ever.

Blessed are you, O Lord our God, King of the universe, who forms light and creates darkness, who makes peace and creates all things.

Congregation in an undertone.

Blessed, praised, glorified, exalted and extolled be the name of the supreme King of kings, the Holy One, blessed be he, who is the first and the last, and beside him there is no God. Extol him that rides upon the heavens by his name Yah, and rejoice before him. His name is exalted above all blessing and praise. Blessed be His name, whose glorious kingdom is forever and ever. Let the name of the Lord be blessed from this time forth and forevermore.

On Festivals falling, on week-days say, "Who in mercy."

All shall thank you, and all shall praise you, and all shall say, There is none holy like the Lord. All shall extol you forever, you Creator of all things, O God who opens every day the doors of the gates of the East, and cleaves the windows of the firmament, bringing forth the sun from his place, and the moon from her dwelling, giving light to the whole world and to its inhabitants whom you creates by your attribute of mercy. In mercy you give light to the earth and to there that dwell thereon, and in your goodness renews the creation every day continually; O King, who alone was exalted from aforetime, praised, glorified and extolled from days of old. O everlasting God, in your abundant mercies, have mercy upon us, Lord of our strength, Rock of our stronghold, Shield of our salvation, you Stronghold of ours! There is none to be compared unto you, neither is there any beside you; there is none but you: who is like unto you? There is none to be compared unto you, O Lord our God, in this world, neither is there any beside you, O our King, for the life of the world to come; there is none but you, O our Redeemer, for the days of the Messiah; neither is there any like unto you. O our Savior, for the resurrection of the dead.

God, the Lord over all works, blessed is he, and ever to be blessed by the mouth of everything that has breath. His greatness and goodness fill the universe; knowledge and understanding surround him: he is exalted above the holy Chayoth and is adorned in glory above the celestial chariot, purity and rectitude are before his throne, loving-kindness and tender mercy before his glory. The luminaries are good which our God has created: he formed them with knowledge, understanding and discernment; he gave them might and power to rule in the midst of the world. They are full of luster, and they radiate brightness: beautiful is their luster throughout all the world. They rejoice in their going forth, and are glad in their returning; they perform with awe the will of their Master. Glory and honor they render unto his name, exultation and rejoicing at the remembrance of his sovereignty. He called unto the sun, and it shone forth in light: he looked, and ordained the figure of the moon. All the hosts on high render praise unto him, the Seraphim, the Ophanim and the holy Chayoth ascribing glory and greatness

To the God who rested from all his works, and on the seventh day exalted himself and sat upon the throne of his glory; who robed himself in glory on the day of rest, and called the Sabbath day a delight. This is the praise of the Sabbath day, that God rested thereon from all his work, when the Sabbath day itself offered praise and said, "A Psalm, a song of the Sabbath day, It is good to give thanks into the Lord." Therefore let all his creatures glorify and bless God; let them render praise, honor and greatness to the God and King who is Creator of all things, and who, in his holiness, gives an inheritance of rest to his people Israel on the holy Sabbath day. Your name, O Lord our God, shall be hallowed, and your remembrance, O our King, shall be glorified in heaven above and on earth beneath. Be you blessed, O our Savior, for the excellence of your handiwork, and for the bright luminaries which you have made: they shall glorify you forever.

Be you blessed, O our Rock, our King and Redeemer, Creator of holy beings, praised be your name forever, O our King; Creator of ministering spirits, all of whom stand in the heights of the universe, and proclaim with awe in unison aloud the words of the living God and everlasting King. All of them are beloved, pure and mighty, and all of them in dread and awe do the will of their Master: and all of them open their mouths in holiness and purity, with song and psalm, while they bless and praise, glorify and reverence, sanctify and ascribe sovereignty to—

The name of the Divine King, the great, mighty and dreaded One, holy is he; and they all take upon themselves the yoke of the kingdom of heaven one from the other, and give sanction to one another to hallow their Creator: in tranquil joy of spirit, with pure speech and holy melody they all respond in unison, and exclaim with awe:

Holy, holy, holy is the Lord of hosts: the whole earth is full of his glory.

And the Ophanim and the holy Chayoth with a noise of great rushing, upraising themselves towards the Seraphim, thus over against them offer praise and say:

Blessed be the glory of the Lord from his place.

To the blessed God they offer pleasant melodies; to the King, the living and ever-enduring God, they utter hymns and make their praises heard; for he alone performs mighty deeds, and makes new things; he is the Lord of battles; he sows righteousness, causes salvation to spring forth, creates remedies, and is revered in praises. He is the Lord of wonders, who in his goodness renews the creation every day continually; as it is said, (O give thanks) to him that makes great lights, for his loving-kindness endures forever. O cause a new light to shine upon Zion, and may we all be worthy soon to enjoy its brightness. Blessed are you, O Lord, Creator of the luminaries.

With abounding love have you loved us, O Lord our God, with great and exceeding pity have you pitied us. O our Father, our King, for our fathers' sake, who trusted in you, and whom you did teach the statutes of life, be also gracious unto us and teach us. O our Father, merciful Father, ever-compassionate, have mercy upon us: O put it into our hearts to understand and to discern, to mark, learn and teach, to heed, to do and to fulfil in love all the words of instruction in your Torah. Enlighten our eyes in your Torah, and let our hearts cleave to your commandments, and unite our hearts to love and fear your name, so that we be never put to shame. Because we have trusted in your holy, great and revered name, we shall rejoice and be glad in your salvation. O bring us in peace from the four corners of the earth, and make us go upright to our land; for you are a God who works salvation. You have chosen us from all peoples and tongues, and has brought us near unto your great name forever in faithfulness, that we might in love give thanks unto you and proclaim your unity. Blessed are you, O Lord, who has chosen your people Israel in love.

When Prayers are not said with the Congregation, add—

God, faithful King!

Deut. vi. 4-9.

Hear, O Israel: the Lord our God, the Lord is One.

Blessed be His name, whose glorious kingdom is forever and ever.

And you shall love the Lord your God with all your heart, and with all your soul, and with all your might. And these words, which I command you this day, shall be upon your heart: and you shall teach them diligently unto your children, and shall talk of them when you sit in your house, and when you walk by the way, and when you lie down, and when you rise up. And you shall bind them for a sign -upon your hand, and they shall be for frontlets between your eyes. And you shall write them upon the door posts of your house, and upon your gates.

Deut. xi. 13-21.

And it shall come to pass, if you shall hearken diligently unto my commandments which I command you this day, to love the Lord your God and to serve him with all your heart and with all your soul, that I will give the rain of your land in its season, the former rain and the latter rain, that you may gather in your corn, and your wine, and your oil. And I will give grass in your field for your cattle, and you shall eat and be satisfied. Take heed to yourselves, lest your heart be deceived and you turn aside, and serve other gods, and worship them; and the anger of the Lord be kindled against you, and he shut up the heaven, that there be no rain, and the land yield not her fruit; and you perish quickly from off the good land which the Lord gives you. Therefore shall you lay up these my words in your heart and in your soul; and you shall bind them for a sign upon your hand, and they shall be for frontlets between your eyes. And you shall teach them your children, talking of them when you sit in your house, and when you walk by the way, and when you lie down, and when you rise up. And you shall write them upon the door posts of your house, and upon your gates: that your days may be multiplied, and the days of your children, upon the land which the Lord swore to your fathers to give them, as the days of the heavens above the earth.

Numbers xv. 37-41.

And the Lord spoke to Moses, saying, Speak unto the children of Israel,. and bid them that they make them a fringe upon the corners of their garments throughout their generations, and that they put upon the fringe of each corner a cord of blue: and it shall be unto you for a fringe, that you may look upon it, and remember all the commandments of the Lord, and do them; and that you go not about after your own heart and your own eyes, after which you use to go astray: that you may remember and do all my commandments, and be holy unto your God. I am the Lord your God, who brought you out of the land of Egypt, to be your God: I am the Lord your God.

True and firm, established and enduring, right and faithful, beloved and precious, desirable and pleasant, revered and mighty, well-ordered and acceptable, good and beautiful is this your word unto us forever and ever. It is true, the God of the universe is our King, the Rock of Jacob, the Shield of our salvation: throughout all generations he endures and his name endures; his throne is established, and his kingdom and his faithfulness endure forever. His words also live and endure; they are faithful and desirable forever and to all eternity, as for our fathers so also for us, our children, our generations, and for all the generations of the seed of Israel his servants.

For the first and for the last ages your word is good and endures forever and ever; it is true and trust, worthy, a statute which shall not pass away. True it is that you are indeed the Lord our God and the God of our fathers, our King, our fathers' King, our Redeemer, the Redeemer of our fathers, our Maker, the Rock of our salvation; our Deliverer and Rescuer from everlasting, such is your name; there is no God beside you.

You have been the help of our fathers from of old, a Shield and Savior to their children after them in every generation: in the heights of the universe is your habitation, and your judgments and your righteousness reach to the furthest ends of the earth. Happy is the man who hearkens unto your commandments, and lays up your Torah and your word in his heart. True it is that you are indeed the Lord of your people, and a mighty King to plead their cause. True it is that you are indeed the first and you are the last beside you we have no King, Redeemer and Savior. From Egypt you did redeem us, O Lord our God, and from the house of bondmen you did deliver us; all their first-born you did slay, but your first-born you did redeem; you did divide the Red Sea, and drown the proud; but you made the beloved to pass through, while the waters covered their adversaries, not one of whom was left. Wherefore the beloved praised and extolled God, and offered hymns, songs, praises, blessings and thanksgivings to the King and God, who lives and endures; who is high and exalted, great and revered; who brings low the haughty, and raises up the lowly, leads forth the prisoners, delivers the meek, helps the poor, and answers his people when they cry unto him; even praises to the Most High God, blessed is he, and ever to be blessed. Moses and the children of Israel sang a song unto you with great joy, saying. all of them,

Who is like unto you, O Lord, among the mighty ones? Who is like unto you, glorious in holiness, revered in praises, doing marvels?

With a new song the redeemed people offered praise unto your name at the sea shore; they all gave thanks in unison, and proclaimed your sovereignty, and said,

The Lord shall reign forever and ever.

O Rock of Israel, arise to the help of Israel, and deliver, according to your promise, Judah and Israel. Our Redeemer, the Lord of hosts is his name, the Holy One of Israel. Blessed are you, O Lord, who has redeemed Israel.

The following prayer (Amidah) to "as in ancient years," is to be said standing.

O Lord, open you my lips, and my mouth shall declare your praise.

Blessed are you, O Lord our God and God of our fathers, God of Abraham, God of Isaac, and God of Jacob, the great, mighty and revered God, the most high God, who bestows loving-kindnesses, and possesses all things; who remembers the pious deeds of the patriarchs, and in love will bring a redeemer to their children's children for your name's sake.

On the Sabbath of Penitence say—

Remember us unto life, O King, who delights in life, and inscribe us in the book of life, for your own sake, O living God.

O King, Helper, Savior and Shield. Blessed are you, O Lord, the Shield of Abraham.

You, O Lord, are mighty forever, you quicken the dead, you are mighty to save.

From the Sabbath after the Eighth Day of Solemn Assembly until the First Day of Passover, say—

You cause the wind to blow and the rain to fall.

You sustain the living with loving-kindness, quicken the dead with great mercy, support the falling, heal the sick, loose the bound, and keep your faith to them that sleep in the dust. Who is like unto you, Lord of mighty acts, and who resembles you, O King, who kills and quickens, and causes salvation to spring forth?

On the Sabbath of Penitence say—

Who is like unto you, Father of mercy, who in mercy remembers your creatures unto life?

Yea, faithful are you to quicken the dead. Blessed are you, O Lord, who quickens the dead.

You are holy, and your name is holy, and holy beings praise you daily. (Selah.) Blessed are you, O Lord, the holy God.

On the Sabbath of Penitence conclude the Blessing thus—
the Holy King.

When the Reader repeats the Amidah, the following is said, to "holy God."

Reader.—We will sanctify your name in the world even as they sanctify it in the highest heavens, as it is written by the hand of your prophet: And they called one unto the other and said,

Cong.—Holy, holy, holy is the Lord of hosts: the whole earth is full of his glory.

Reader.—Then with a noise of great rushing, mighty and strong, they make their voices heard, and, upraising themselves toward the Seraphim, they exclaim over against them, Blessed—

Cong.—Blessed be the glory of the Lord from his place.

Reader.—From your place shine forth, O our King, and reign over us, for we wait for you. When will you reign in Zion? Speedily, even in our days, do you dwell there, and forever. May you be magnified and sanctified in the midst of Jerusalem your city throughout all generations and to all eternity. O let our eyes behold your kingdom, according to the word that was spoken in the songs of your might by David, your righteous anointed:

Cong.—The Lord shall reign forever, your God, O Zion, unto all generations. Praise you the Lord.

Reader.—Unto all generations we will declare your greatness, and to all eternity we will proclaim your holiness, and your praise, O our God, shall not depart from our mouth forever, for you are a great and holy God and King. Blessed are you, O Lord, the holy God.

On the Sabbath of Penitence conclude the blessing thus—
the holy King.

Moses rejoiced in the gift of his portion, for you did call him a faithful servant: a diadem of glory did you place upon his head, when he stood before you upon Mount Sinai; and in his hand he brought down the two tables of stone, upon which the observance of the Sabbath was prescribed, and. thus it is written in your Torah:

Exodus xxxi. 16, 17.

And the children of Israel shall keep the Sabbath, to observe the Sabbath throughout their generations, for an everlasting covenant. It is a sign between me and the children of Israel forever, that in six days the Lord made the heavens and the earth, and on the seventh day he rested, and ceased from his work.

And you did not give it, O Lord our God, unto the nations of other lands, nor did you, O our King, make it the heritage of worshipers of idols, nor do the uncircumcised dwell in its rest; but unto your people Israel you did give it in love, unto the seed of Jacob whom you did choose. The people that hallow the seventh day, even all of them shall be satiated and delighted with your goodness, seeing that you did find pleasure in the seventh day, and did hallow it; you did call it the desirable of days, in remembrance of the creation.

Our God and God of our fathers, accept our rest; sanctify us by your commandments, and grant our portion in your Torah; satisfy us with your goodness, and gladden us with your salvation; purify our hearts to serve you in truth; and in your love and favor, O Lord our God, let us inherit your holy Sabbath; and may Israel, who hallow your name, rest thereon. Blessed are you, O Lord, who hallows the Sabbath,

Accept, O Lord our God, your people Israel and their prayer; restore the service to the oracle of your house; receive in love and favor both the fire-offerings of Israel and their prayer; and may the service of your people Israel be ever acceptable unto you.

On New Moon and the Intermediate Days of Passover and Sukkot say—

Our God and God of our fathers! May our rise, come and be accepted before you, with the remembrance of our fathers, of Messiah the son of David your servant, of Jerusalem your holy city, and of all your people the house of Israel, bringing deliverance and well-being, grace, loving-kindness and mercy, life and peace on this day of

On the New Moon—
the New Moon.
On Passover—
the Feast of Unleavened Bread.
On Sukkot—
the Feast of Sukkot.

Remember us, O Lord our God, thereon for our wellbeing; he mindful of us for blessing and save us unto life: by your promise of salvation and mercy, spare us and be gracious unto us; have mercy upon us and save Is; for our eyes are bent upon you, because you are a gracious and merciful God and King.

And let our eyes behold your return in mercy to Zion. Blessed are you, O Lord, who restores your divine presence unto Zion.

We give thanks unto you, for you are the Lord our God and the God of our fathers forever and ever; you are the Rock of our lives, the Shield of our salvation through every generation. We will give thanks unto you and declare your praise for our lives which are committed into your hand, and for our souls which are in your charge, and for your miracles, which are daily with us, and for your wonders and your benefits, which are wrought at all times, evening, morn and noon. O you who are all-good, whose mercies fail not; you, merciful Being, whose loving-kindnesses never cease, we have ever hoped in you.\

Congregation in an undertone—

We give thanks unto you, for you are the Lord our God and the God of our fathers, the God of all flesh, our Creator and the Creator of all things in the beginning. Blessings and thanksgivings be to your great and holy name, because you have kept us in life and has preserved us; so may you continue to keep us in life and to preserve us. O gather our exiles to your holy courts to observe your statutes, to do your will, and to serve you with a perfect heart; seeing that we give thanks unto you. Blessed be the God to whom thanksgivings are due.

(On Chanukah say "We thank you also.")
For all these things your name, O our King shall be continually blessed and exalted forever and ever.
On the Sabbath of Penitence say—
O inscribe all the children of your covenant for a happy life.

And everything that lives shall give thanks unto you forever, and shall praise your name in truth, O God, our salvation and our help. Blessed are you, O Lord, whose name is All-good, and unto whom it is becoming to give thanks.

At the repetition of the Amidah by the Reader the following is introduced—

Our God and God of our fathers, bless us with the three-fold blessing of your Torah written by the hand of Moses your servant, which was spoken by Aaron and his sons, the priests, your holy people, as it is said, The Lord bless you, and keep you: the Lord make his face to shine upon you, and be gracious unto you: the Lord turn his face unto you, and give you peace.

Grant peace, welfare, blessing, grace, loving-kindness and mercy unto us and unto all Israel, your people. Bless us, O our Father, even all of us together, with the light of your countenance; for by the light of your countenance you have given us, O Lord our God, the Torah of life, loving-kindness and righteousness, blessing, mercy, life and peace; and may it be good in your sight to bless your people Israel at all times and in every hour with your peace.

On the Sabbath of Penitence say—

In the book of life, blessing, peace and good sustenance may we be remembered and inscribed before you, we and all your people the house of Israel, for a happy life and for peace. Blessed are you, O Lord, who makes peace.

Blessed are you, O Lord, who blesses your people Israel with peace.

O my God! guard my tongue from evil and my lips from speaking guile; and to such as curse me let my soul be dumb, yea, let my soul be unto all as the dust. Open my heart to your Torah, and let my soul pursue your commandments. If any design evil against me, speedily make their counsel of none effect, and frustrate their designs. Do it for the sake of your name, do it for the sake of your right hand, do it for the sake of your holiness, do it for the sake of your Torah. In order that your beloved ones may be delivered, O save with your right hand, and answer me. Let the words of my mouth and the meditation of my heart be acceptable before you, O Lord, my Rock and my Redeemer. He who makes peace in his high places, may he make peace for us and for all Israel, and say ye, Amen.

May it be your will, O Lord our God and God of our fathers, that the temple be speedily rebuilt in our days, and grant our portion in your Torah. And there we will serve you with awe, as in the days of old, and as in ancient years. Then shall the offering of Judah and Jerusalem be pleasant unto the Lord, as in the days of old, and as in ancient years.

On New Moon, Festivals, and the Intermediate Days of Festivals and on Chanukah, Hallel is said after the Amidah.

Reader.—Magnified and sanctified be his great name in the world which he has created according to his will. May he establish his kingdom during your life and during your days, and during the life of all the house of Israel, even speedily and at a near time, and say ye, Amen.

Cong. and Reader.—Let his great name be blessed forever and to all eternity.

Reader.—Blessed, praised and glorified, exalted, extolled and honored, magnified and lauded be the name of the Holy One, blessed be he; though he be high above all the blessings and hymns, praises and consolations, which are uttered in the world; and say ye, Amen.

Cong.—Accept our prayer in mercy and in favor.

Reader.—May the prayers and supplications of all Israel be accepted by their Father who is in heaven; and say ye, Amen.

Cong.—Let the name of the Lord be blessed from this time forth and forevermore.

Reader.—May there be abundant peace from heaven and life for us and for all Israel; and say ye, Amen.

Cong.—My help is from the Lord, who made heaven and earth.

Reader.—He who makes peace in his high places, may he make peace for us and for all Israel; and say ye, Amen.

On Festivals falling on Week-days.

Who in mercy gives light to the earth and to them that dwell thereon, and in your goodness renews the creation every day continually. How manifold are your works, O Lord! In wisdom have you made them all: the earth is full of your possessions. O King, who alone was exalted from aforetime, praised, glorified and extolled from days of old; O everlasting God, in your abundant mercies, have mercy upon us, Lord of our strength Rock of our stronghold, Shield of our salvation, you Stronghold of ours! The blessed God, great in knowledge, prepared and formed the rays of the sun: it was a boon he produced as a glory to his name: he set the luminaries round about his strength. The chiefs of his hosts are holy beings that exalt the Almighty, and continually declare the glory of God and his holiness. Be you blessed, O Lord our God, for the excellence of your handiwork, and for the bright luminaries which you have made: they shall glorify you forever.

Continue "Be you blessed," see above.

ORDER OF READING THE TORAH ON SABBATHS AND FESTIVALS

There is none like unto you among the gods, O Lord; and there are no works like unto yours. Your kingdom is an everlasting kingdom, and your dominion endures throughout all generations. The Lord reigns; the Lord has reigned; the Lord shall reign forever and ever. The Lord will give strength unto his people; the Lord will bless his people with peace.

Father of mercies, do good in your favor unto Zion; build you the walls of Jerusalem. For in you alone do we trust, O King, high and exalted God, Lord of worlds.

The Ark is opened.

Reader and Cong.—And it came to pass, when the ark set forward, that Moses said, Rise up, O Lord, and your enemies shall be scattered, and they that hate you shall flee before you. For out of Zion shall go forth the Torah, and the word of the Lord from Jerusalem.

The Reader takes the Scroll of the Torah and says—

Blessed be he who in his holiness gave the Torah to his people Israel.

In some Congregations the following is said—

Zohar, Parshas Vayakhel.

Blessed be the name of the Sovereign of the universe. Blessed be your crown and your abiding-place. Let your favor rest with your people Israel forever: show them the redemption of your right hand in your holy temple. Vouchsafe unto us the benign gift of your light, and in mercy accept our supplications. May it be your will to prolong our life in well-being. Let me also be numbered among the righteous, so that you may be merciful unto me, and have me in your keeping, with all that belong to me and to your people Israel. You are he that feeds and sustains all; you are he that rules over all; you are he that rules over kings, for dominion is yours. I am the servant of the Holy One, blessed be he, before whom and before whose glorious Torah I prostrate myself at all times: not in man do I put my trust, nor upon any angel do I rely, but upon the God of heaven, who is the God of truth, and whose Torah is truth, and whose prophets are prophets of truth, and who abounds in deeds of goodness and truth. In him I put my trust, and unto his holy and glorious name I utter praises. May it be your will to open my heart unto your Torah, and to fulfil the wishes of my heart and of the hearts of all your people Israel for good, for life, and for peace.

On Festivals the following is said—

The Lord, the Lord is a merciful and gracious God, slow to anger and abounding in loving-kindness and truth; keeping loving-kindness for thousands, forgiving iniquity and transgression and sin. (*To be said three times.*)

Lord of the universe, fulfil the wishes of my heart for good; grant my desire, give me my request, even unto me, your servant, — the son of — (thy maid servant — the daughter of —), and make me worthy (together with my wife,) (my husband,) (my children,) to do your will with a perfect heart; and deliver me from the evil inclination. O grant our portion in your Torah; make us worthy to have your divine presence abiding with us; vouchsafe unto us the spirit of wisdom and understanding, the spirit of counsel and might, the spirit of knowledge and fear of the Lord. So also may it be your will, O Lord our God and God of our fathers, that I may be fitted to do such deeds as are good in your sight, and to walk in the way of the upright before you. Sanctify us by your commandments that we may merit the long and blessed life of the world to come: guard us from evil deeds, and also from evil hours that visit and afflict this world. As for him who trusts in the Lord, let loving-kindness surround him Amen.

Let the words of my mouth and the meditation of my heart be acceptable before you, O Lord, my Rock and my Redeemer.

And as for me, may my prayer unto you, O Lord, be in an acceptable time: O God, in the abundance of your loving-kindness, answer me in the truth of your salvation.

(This verse is said three times.)

The Reader takes the Scroll of the Torah, and the following is said—

Reader and Cong.—Hear, O Israel: the Lord our God, the Lord is One.

Reader and Cong.—One is our God; great is our Lord; holy is his name.

Reader.—Magnify the Lord with me, and let us exalt his name together.

Reader and Cong.—Yours, O Lord, is the greatness, and the power, and the glory, and the victory, and the majesty: for all that is in the heaven and in the earth is yours; yours, O Lord, is the kingdom, and the supremacy as head over all. Exalt you the Lord our God, and worship at his footstool: holy is he. Exalt you the Lord our God, and worship at his holy mount; for the Lord our God is holy.

Magnified and hallowed, praised and glorified, exalted and extolled above all be the name of the Supreme King of Kings, the Holy One, blessed be he, in the worlds which he has created,—this world and the world to come,—in accordance with his desire, and with the desire of them that fear him, and of all the house of Israel: the Rock everlasting, the Lord of all creatures, the God of all souls, who dwells in the wide-extended heights, who inhabits the heaven of heavens of old; whose holiness is above the Chayoth and above the throne of glory. Now, therefore, your name, O Lord our God, shall be hallowed amongst us in the sight of all living. Let us sing a new song be, fore him, as it is written, Sing unto God, sing praises unto his name, extol you him that rides upon the heavens by his name Yah, and exult before him. And may we see him, eye to eye, when he returns to his habitation, as it is written, For they shall see eye to eye, when the Lord returns unto Zion. And it is said, And the glory of the Lord shall be revealed, and all flesh shall see it together; for the mouth of the Lord has spoken it.

May the Father of mercy have mercy upon a people that have been borne by him. May he remember the covenant with the patriarchs, deliver our souls from evil hours, check the evil inclination in them that have been carried by him, grant us of his grace an everlasting deliverance, and in the attribute of his goodness fulfil our desires by salvation and mercy.

The Scroll of the Torah is placed upon the desk, and the Reader says the following—

And may he help, shield and save all who trust in him, and let us say, Amen. Ascribe all of you greatness unto our God, and render honor to the Torah.

Here the Reader names the Person who is called to the Reading of the Torah.

Blessed be he, who in his holiness gave the Torah unto his people Israel. The Torah of the Lord is perfect, restoring the soul: the testimony of the Lord is faithful, making wise the simple. The precepts of the Lord are right, rejoicing the heart: the commandment of the Lord is pure, enlightening the eyes. The Lord will give strength unto his people, the Lord will bless his people with peace. As for God his way is perfect: the word of the Lord is tried: he is a shield unto all them that trust in him.

Cong. and Reader.—And you that cleave unto the Lord your God are alive every one of you this day.

Those who are called to the Reading of the Torah say the following Blessing—

Bless you the Lord who is to be blessed.

Cong.—Blessed be the Lord, who is to be blessed forever and ever.

The Response of the Congregation is repeated, and the Blessing continued—

Blessed are you, O Lord our God, King of the universe, who has chosen us from all peoples, and has given us your Torah. Blessed are you, O Lord, who gives the Torah.

After the reading of a Section of the Torah, the following Blessing is said—

Blessed are you, O Lord our God, King of the universe, who east given us the Torah of truth, and has planted everlasting life in our midst. Blessed are you, O Lord, who gives the Torah.

Persons who have been in peril of their lives, during journeys by sea or land, in captivity or sickness, upon their deliverance or recovery say the following, after the conclusion of the last Blessing—

"Blessed are you, O Lord our God, King of the universe, who vouchsafes benefits unto the undeserving, who has also vouchsafed all good unto me.

The Congregation responds—

He who has vouchsafed all good unto you, may he vouchsafe all good unto you forever.

The following is said by the Father of a Bar-Mitzvah, when the latter has concluded the Blessing after having been called to the Reading of the Torah.

Blessed be he who has freed me from the responsibility for this child.

After the Reading of the Torah, the Scroll is held up, and the Congregation says the following—

And this is the Torah which Moses set before the children of Israel, according to the commandment of the Lord by the hand of Moses. It is a tree of life to them that grasp it, and of them that uphold it every one is rendered happy. Its ways are ways of pleasantness, and all its paths are peace. Length of days is in its right hand; in its left hand are riches and honor. It pleased the Lord, for his righteousness' sake, to magnify the Torah and to make it honorable.

Before the Lesson from the Prophets the following is said—

Blessed are you, O Lord our God, King of the universe, who has chosen good prophets, and has found pleasure in their words which were spoken in truth. Blessed are you, O Lord, who has chosen the Torah, and Moses your servant, and Israel your people, and prophets of truth and righteousness.

After the Lesson from the Prophets the following is said—

Blessed are you, O Lord our God, King of the universe, Rock of all worlds, righteous through all generations, O faithful God, who says and does, who speaks and fulfills, all whose words are truth and righteousness. Faithful are you, O Lord our God, and faithful are your words, and not one of your words shall return void, for you are a faithful and merciful God and King. Blessed are you, O Lord, God, who are faithful in all your words.

Have mercy upon Zion, for it is the home of our life, and save her that is grieved in spirit speedily, even iii our days. Blessed are you, O Lord, who makes Zion joyful through her children.

Gladden us, O Lord our God, with Elijah the prophet, your servant, and with the kingdom of the house of David, your anointed. Soon may he come and rejoice our hearts. Suffer not a stranger to sit upon his throne, nor let others any longer inherit his glory; for by your holy name you did swear unto him, that his right should not be quenched forever. Blessed are you, O Lord, the Shield of David.

On Sabbaths, including the Intermediate Sabbath of Passover, say—

For the Torah, for the divine service, for the prophets, and for this Sabbath day, which you, O Lord our God, has given us for holiness and for rest, for honor and for glory.

For all these we thank and bless you, O Lord our God, blessed be your name by the mouth of every living being continually and forever. Blessed are you, O Lord, who sanctifies the Sabbath.

On the Three Festivals, as also on the Intermediate Sabbath of Sukkot, say—
For the Torah, for the divine service, for the prophets;
On the Sabbath—
for this Sabbath day,
On Passover—
and for this day of the Feast of Unleavened Bread.
On Pentecost—
and for this day of the Feast of Weeks.
On Sukkot—
and for this day of the Feast of Sukkot.

On the Eighth Day of Solemn Assembly: and for this Eighth-day feast of Solemn Assembly, which you, O Lord our God, has given us (on Sabbath add, for holiness and for rest,) for joy and gladness, for honor and glory,—f or all these we thank and bless you, O Lord our God, blessed be your name by the mouth of every living being continually and forever. Blessed are you, O Lord, who sanctifies (on Sabbath add, the Sabbath) Israel and the Festivals.

On the New Year say—

For the Torah, for the divine service, for the prophets (on Sabbath add, and for this Sabbath Day), and for this Day of Memorial, which you, O Lord our God, has given us (on Sabbath add, for holiness and for rest) for honor and glory—for all these we thank and bless you, O Lord our God, blessed be your name by the mouth of every living being continually and forever your word is true and endures forever. Blessed are you, O Lord, King over the whole earth, who sanctifies (on Sabbath add, the Sabbath) Israel and the Day of Memorial.

On the Day of Atonement say—

For the Torah, for the divine service, for the prophets (on Sabbath add, for this Sabbath day), and for this Day of Atonement, which you, O Lord our God, has given us (on Sabbath add, for holiness and for rest) for forgiveness, pardon and atonement, for honor and for glory—for all these we thank and bless you, O Lord our God, blessed be your name by the mouth of every living being continually and forever: your word is true and endures forever. Blessed are you, O Lord, you King, who pardons and forgives our iniquities and the iniquities of your people, the house of Israel, and makes our trespasses to pass away year by year; King over the whole earth, who sanctifies (on Sabbath add, the Sabbath) Israel and the Day of Atonement

The following three paragraphs are not said on Festivals occurring on Weekdays.

May salvation from heaven, with grace, loving-kindness, mercy, long life, ample sustenance, heavenly aid, health of body, a higher enlightenment, and a living and abiding offspring, that will not break with, for neglect any of the words of the Torah, be vouchsafed unto the teachers and rabbis of the holy community, who are in the land of Israel, and in the land of Babylon, and in all the lands of our dispersion; unto the heads of the academies, the chiefs of the captivity, the heads of the colleges, and the judges in the gates; unto all their disciples, unto all the disciples of their disciples, and unto all who occupy themselves with the study of the Torah. May the King of the universe bless them, prolong their lives, increase their days, and add to their years, and may they be saved and delivered from every trouble and mishap. May the Lord of heaven be their help at all times and seasons; and let us say, Amen.

The following two paragraphs are only said when Service is held with a Congregation.

May salvation from heaven, with grace, loving-kindness, mercy, long life, ample sustenance, heavenly aid, health of body, a higher enlightenment, and a living and abiding offspring, that will not break with nor neglect any of the words of the Torah, be vouchsafed unto all this holy congregation, great and small, children and women. May the King of the universe bless you, prolong your lives, increase your days and add to your years, and may you be saved and delivered from every trouble and mishap. May the Lord of heaven be your help at all times and seasons; and let us say, Amen.

May he who blessed our fathers, Abraham, Isaac and Jacob, bless all this holy congregation, together with all other holy congregations: them, their wives, their sons and daughters, and all that belong to them; those also who unite to form Synagogues for prayer, and those who enter therein to pray; those who give the lamps for lighting, and wine for Kiddush and Havdalah, bread to the wayfarers, and charity to the poor, and all such as occupy themselves in faithfulness with the wants of the congregation. May the Holy One, blessed be he, give them their recompense; may he remove from them all sickness, heal all their body, forgive all their iniquity, and send blessing and prosperity upon all the work of their hands, as well as upon all Israel, their brethren; and let us say, Amen.

The Reader takes the Scroll of the Torah, and says the following prayers.

Prayer for the State of Israel—

Our Father in Heaven, Rock and Redeemer of Israel, bless the State of Israel, the first manifestation of the approach of our redemption. Shield it with Your lovingkindness, envelop it in Your peace, and bestow Your light and truth upon its leaders, ministers, and advisors, and grace them with Your good counsel. Strengthen the hands of those who defend our holy land, grant them deliverance, and adorn them in a mantle of victory. Ordain peace in the land and grant its inhabitants eternal happiness.

Lead them, swiftly and upright, to Your city Zion and to Jerusalem, the abode of Your Name, as is written in the Torah of Your servant Moses: "Even if your outcasts are at the ends of the world, from there the Lord your God will gather you, from there He will fetch you. And the Lord your God will bring you to the land that your fathers possessed, and you shall possess it; and He will make you more prosperous and more numerous than your fathers." Draw our hearts together to revere and venerate Your name and to observe all the precepts of Your Torah, and send us quickly the Messiah son of David, agent of Your vindication, to redeem those who await Your deliverance.

Manifest yourself in the splendor of Your boldness before the eyes of all inhabitants of Your world, and may everyone endowed with a soul affirm that the Lord, God of Israel, is king and his dominion is absolute. Amen forevermore.

Prayer for the Government—

He who gives salvation unto kings and dominion unto princes, whose kingdom is an everlasting kingdom, who delivered his servant David from the hurtful sword, who makes a way in the sea and a path in the mighty waters.—may he bless, guard, protect, and help, exalt, magnify, and highly aggrandize THE CONSTITUTED OFFICERS OF THIS GOVERNMENT.

May the Supreme King of Kings in his mercy preserve them in life and deliver them from all trouble and hurt. May the Supreme King of Kings in his mercy exalt them and raise them on high, and grant them a long and prosperous rule. May the Supreme King of Kings in his mercy inspire them and all their counsellors and officers with benevolence toward us, and all Israel our brethren. In their days and in ours may Judah be saved and Israel dwell securely; and may the redeemer come unto Zion. O that this may be his will, and let us say, Amen.

On the Sabbath preceding New Moon the following is said—

May it be your will, O Lord our God and God of our fathers, to renew unto us this coming month for good and for Blessing.

O grant us long life, a life of peace, of good, of blessing, of sustenance, of bodily vigor, a life marked by the fear of Heaven and the dread of sin, a life free from shame and reproach, a life of prosperity and honor, a life in which the love of the Torah and the fear of Heaven shall cleave to us, a life in which the desires of our heart shall be fulfilled for good. Amen. (Selah.)

Reader.—He who wrought miracles for our fathers, and redeemed them from slavery unto freedom, may he speedily redeem us, and gather our exiles from the four corners of the earth, even all Israel united in fellowship; and let us say, Amen.

The New Moon of (naming the month) will be on (naming the day or days). May it come to us and to all Israel for good.

Cong. and Reader.—May the Holy One, blessed be he, renew it unto us and unto all his people, the house of Israel, for life and peace, for gladness and joy, for salvation and consolation; and let us say, Amen.

In many Congregations the following is said only on the Sabbaths preceding Yom Kippur and the Fast of the Ninth of Ab—

May the Father of mercies, who dwells on high in his mighty compassion, remember those loving, upright and blameless ones, the holy congregations, who laid down their lives for the sanctification of the divine name, who were lovely and pleasant in their lives, and in their death were not divided; swifter than eagles, stronger than lions to do the will of their Master and the desire of their Rock. May our God remember them for good with the other righteous of the world, and avenge the blood of his servants which has been shed; as it is written in the Torah of Moses, the man of God, Rejoice, O you nations, with his people, for he will avenge the blood of his servants, and will render vengeance to his adversaries, and will make atonement for his land and for his people. And by the hands of your servants, the prophets, it is written saying, I will cleanse their blood that I have not yet cleansed: for the Lord dwells in Zion. And in the Holy Writings it is said, Wherefore should the nations say, Where is their God? Let there be made known among the nations in our sight the revenging of the blood of your servants which has been shed. And it is said, For he that makes inquisition for blood remembers them; he forgets not the cry of the humble. And it is further said, He judges among the nations; the land is full of corpses: he smites the head over a wide land. He drinks of the brook in the way: therefore shall he lift up the head.

Happy are they that dwell in your house: they will be ever praising you. (Selah.)
Happy is the people that is in such a case: happy is the people, whose God is the Lord.
Psalm cxlv. A Psalm of Praise: of David.
I will extol you, my God, O King; and I will bless your name forever and ever.
Every day will I bless you; and I will praise your name forever and ever.
Great is the Lord, and exceedingly to be praised; and his greatness is unsearchable.
One generation shall laud your works to another, and shall declare your mighty acts.
On the majestic glory of your grandeur, and on your marvelous deeds, will I meditate.
And men shall speak of the might of your awful acts; and I will recount your greatness.
They shall pour forth the fame of your great goodness, and shall exult in your righteousness.
The Lord is gracious and merciful; slow to anger and of great loving-kindness.
The Lord is good to all; and his tender mercies are over all his works.
All your works shall give thanks unto you, O Lord; and your loving ones shall bless you.
They shall speak of the glory of your kingdom, and talk of your power.
To make known to the sons of men his mighty acts, and the majestic glory of his kingdom.
Your kingdom is an everlasting kingdom, and your dominion endures throughout all generations.
The Lord upholds all that fall, and raises up all those that are bowed down.
The eyes of all wait upon you; and you give them their food in due season.
You open your hand and satisfy every living thing with favor.
The Lord is righteous in all his ways, and loving in all his works.
The Lord is nigh unto all them that call upon hire to all that call upon him in truth.
He will fulfil the desire of them that fear him; he also will hear their cry, and will save them.
The Lord guards all them that love him; but all the wicked will he destroy.
My mouth shall speak of the praise of the Lord; and let all flesh bless his holy name forever and ever.
But we will bless the Lord from this time forth and forevermore. Praise you the Lord.

On returning the Scroll of the Torah to the Ark the Reader says—

Let them praise the name of the Lord; for his name alone is exalted:

Congregation.—His grandeur is above the earth and heaven: and he has lifted up a horn for his people, to the praise of all his loving ones, even of the children of Israel, the people near unto him. Praise you the Lord.

On Sabbaths and on Festivals occurring on Sabbaths say—

Psalm xxix.

A Psalm of David. Give unto the Lord, O you children of the mighty, give unto the Lord glory and strength. Give unto the Lord the glory due unto his name; worship the Lord in the beauty of holiness. The voice of the Lord is upon the waters: the God of glory thunders, even the Lord upon the great waters the voice of the Lord is powerful; the voice of the Lord is full of majesty. The voice of the Lord breaks the cedars; yea, the Lord breaks in pieces the cedars of Lebanon. He makes them also to skip like a calf; Lebanon and Sirion like a young wild-ox. The voice of the Lord cleaves flames of fire; the voice of the Lord makes the wilderness to tremble; the Lord makes tremble the wilderness of Kadesh. The voice of the Lord makes the hinds to travail, and strips the forests bare: and in his temple everything says, Glory. The Lord sat as king at the flood; yea, the Lord sits as king forever. The Lord will give strength unto his people; the Lord will bless his people with peace.

On Festivals occurring on Week-days say—

Psalm xxiv.

A Psalm of David. The earth is the Lord's, and the fullness thereof; the world, and they that dwell therein. For it is he that has founded it upon the seas, and established it upon the floods. Who may ascend the mountain of the Lord? And who may stand in his holy place? He that has clean hands and a pure heart; who has not set his desire upon vanity, and has not sworn deceitfully. He shall receive a blessing from the Lord, and righteousness from the God of his salvation. This is the generation of them that seek after him that seek your face (O God of) Jacob! (Selah.) Lift up your heads, O you gates; and be you lifted up, you everlasting doors, that the King of glory may come in. Who, then, is the King of glory? The Lord strong and mighty, the Lord mighty in battle. Lift up your heads, O you gates; yea, lift them up, you everlasting doors that the King of glory may come in. Who, then, is the King of glory? The Lord of hosts, he is the King of glory. (Selah.)

While the Scroll of the Torah is being placed in the Ark, the following to "as of old" is said—

And when it rested, he said, Return, O Lord, unto the ten thousands of the thousands of Israel. Arise, O Lord, unto your resting place; you, and the ark of your strength. Let your priests be clothed with righteousness; and let your loving ones shout for joy. For the sake of David your servant, turn not away the face of your anointed. For I give you good doctrine; forsake you not my Torah. It is a tree of life to them that grasp it, and of them that uphold it every one is rendered happy. Its ways are ways of pleasantness, and all its paths are peace. Turn you us unto you, O Lord, and we shall return: renew our days as of old.

Reader.—Magnified and sanctified be his great name in the world which he has created according to his will. May he establish his kingdom during your life and during your days, and during the life of all the house of Israel, even speedily and at a near time, and say ye, Amen.

Cong. and Reader.—Let his great name be blessed forever and to all eternity.

Reader.—Blessed, praised and glorified, exalted, extolled and honored, magnified and lauded be the name of the Holy One, blessed be he; though he be high above all the blessings and hymns, praises and consolations, which are uttered in the world; and say ye, Amen.

ADDITIONAL SERVICE FOR SABBATHS.

For the Additional Service on the Intermediate Sabbath of a Festival see Service for the Festivals.

The following prayer (Amidah) to "as in ancient years," is said standing.

O Lord, open you my lips, and my mouth shall declare your praise.

Blessed are you, O Lord our God and God of our fathers, God of Abraham, God of Isaac and God of Jacob, the great, mighty and revered God, the most high God, who bestows loving-kindnesses, and possesses all things; who remembers the pious deeds of the patriarchs, and in love will bring a redeemer to their children's children for your name's sake.

On the Sabbath of Penitence say—

Remember us unto life, O King, who delights in life, and inscribe us in the book of life, for your own sake, O living God.

O King, Helper, Savior and Shield. Blessed are you, O Lord, the Shield of Abraham.

You, O Lord, are mighty forever, you quicken the dead, you are mighty to save.

From the Sabbath after the Eighth Day of Solemn Assembly until the First day of Passover say—

You cause the wind to blow and the rain to fall.

You sustain the living with loving-kindness, quicken the dead with great mercy, support the falling, heal the sick, loose the bound, and keep your faith to them that sleep in the dust Who is like unto you, Lord of mighty acts, and who resembles you, O King, who kills and quickens, and causes salvation to spring forth?

On the Sabbath of Penitence say—

Who is like unto you, Father of mercy, who in mercy remembers your creatures unto life?

Yea, faithful are you to quicken the dead. Blessed are you, O Lord, who quickens the dead.

You are holy, and your name is holy, and holy beings praise you daily. (Selah.) Blessed are you, O Lord, the holy God.

On the Sabbath of Penitence, conclude the blessing thus—
the holy King.

Cong.—Holy, holy, holy is the Lord of hosts: the whole earth is full of his glory.

Reader.—His glory fills the universe: his ministering angels ask one another, Where is the place of his glory? Those over against them say, Blessed—

Cong.—Blessed be the glory of the Lord from his place.

Reader.—From his place may he turn in mercy and be gracious unto a people who, evening and morning, twice every day, proclaim with constancy the unity of his name, saying in love, Hear—

Cong.—Hear, O Israel: the Lord our God, the Lord is One.

Reader.—One is our God; he is our Father; he is our King; he is our Savior; and he of his mercy will let us hear a second time, in the presence of all living (his promise), "To be to you for a God."

Cong.—"I am the Lord your God."

Reader.—And in your Holy Words it is written, saying,

Cong.—The Lord shall reign forever, your God, O Zion, unto all generations. Praise you the Lord.

Reader.—Unto all generations we will declare your greatness, and to all eternity we will proclaim your holiness, and your praise, O our God, shall not depart from our mouth forever, for you are a great and holy God and King. Blessed are you, O Lord, the holy God.

On the Sabbath of Penitence, conclude the last blessing thus—
the holy King.

 You did institute the Sabbath, and did accept its offerings; you did command its special obligations with the order of its drink offerings. They that find delight in it shall inherit glory forever lasting; they that taste it are worthy of life; while such as love its teachings have chosen true greatness. Already from Sinai they were commanded concerning it; and you have also commanded us, O Lord our God, to bring thereon the additional offering of the Sabbath as is meet. May it be your will, O Lord our God and God of our fathers, to lead us up in joy unto our land, and to plant us within our borders, where we will prepare unto you the offerings that are obligatory for us, the continual offerings according to their order, and the additional offerings according to their enactment; and the additional offering of this Sabbath day we will prepare and offer up unto you in love, according to the precept of your will, as you have prescribed for us in your Torah through the hand of Moses your servant, by the mouth of your glory, as it is said:

And on the Sabbath day two he-lambs of the first year, without blemish, and two tenth parts of an ephah of fine flour for a meal offering, mingled with oil, and the drink offering thereof: this is the burnt offering of every Sabbath, beside the continual burnt offering and the drink offering thereof.

They that keep the Sabbath and call it a delight shall rejoice in your kingdom; the people that hallow the seventh day, even all of them shall be satiated and delighted with your goodness, seeing that you did find pleasure in the seventh day and did hallow it; you did call it the desirable of days, in remembrance of the creation.

Our God and God of our fathers, accept our rest; sanctify us by your commandments, and grant our portion in your Torah; satisfy us with your goodness, and gladden us with your salvation; purify our hearts to serve you in truth; and in your love and favor, O Lord our God, let us inherit your holy Sabbath; and may Israel, who hallow your name, rest thereon. Blessed are you, O Lord, who hallows the Sabbath.

Accept, O Lord our God, your people Israel and their prayer; restore the service to the oracle of your house; receive in love and favor both the fire-offerings of Israel and their prayer; and may the service of your people Israel be ever acceptable unto you.

And let our eyes behold your return in mercy to Zion. Blessed are you, O Lord, who restores your divine presence unto Zion.

We give thanks unto you, for you are the Lord our God and the God of our fathers forever and ever; you are the Rock of our lives, the Shield of our salvation through every generation. We will give thanks unto you and declare your praise for our lives which are committed unto your hand, and for our souls which are in your charge, and for your miracles, which are daily with us, and for your wonders and your benefits, which are wrought at all times, evening, morn and noon. O you who are all-good, whose mercies fail not; you, merciful Being, whose loving-kindnesses never cease, we have ever hoped in you.

Congregation in an undertone:

We give thanks unto you, for you are the Lord our God and the God of our fathers, the God of all flesh, our Creator and the Creator of all things in the beginning. Blessings and thanksgivings be to your great and holy name, because you have kept us in life and has preserved us: so may you continue to keep us in life and to preserve us. O gather our exiles to your holy courts to observe your statutes, to do your will, and to serve you with a perfect heart; seeing that we give thanks unto you. Blessed be the God to whom thanksgivings are due.

On Chanukah say, "We thank you also," etc.

For all these things your name, O our King, shall be continually blessed and exalted forever and ever.

On the Sabbath of Penitence say—

O inscribe all the children of your covenant for a happy life.

And everything that lives shall give thanks unto you forever, and shall praise your name in truth, O God, our salvation and our help. Blessed are you, O Lord, whose name is All-good, and unto whom it is becoming to give thanks.

At the repetition of the Amidah by the Reader, the following is introduced—

Our God and God of our fathers, bless us with the three-fold blessing of your Torah written by the hand of Moses your servant, which was spoken by Aaron and his sons, the priests, your holy people, as it is said, The Lord bless you, and keep you: the Lord make his face to shine upon you, and be gracious unto you: the Lord turn his face unto you, and give you peace.

Grant peace, welfare, blessing, grace, loving-kindness and mercy unto us and unto all Israel, your people. Bless us, O our Father, even all of us together, with the light of your countenance; for by the light of your countenance you have given us, O Lord our God, the Torah of life, loving-kindness and righteousness, blessing, mercy, life and peace; and may it be good in your sight to bless your people Israel at all tinges and in every hour with your peace.

On the Sabbath of Penitence say—

In the book of life, blessing, peace and good may we be remembered and inscribed before you, us and all your people the house of Israel, for a happy life and for peace. Blessed are you, O Lord, who makes peace.

Blessed are you, O Lord, who blesses your people Israel with peace.

O my God! guard my tongue from evil and my lips from speaking guile; and to such as curse me let my soul be dumb, yea, let my soul be unto all as the dust. Open my heart to your Torah, and let my soul pursue your commandments. If any design evil against me, speedily make their counsel of none effect, and frustrate their designs. Do it for the sake of your name, do it for the sake of your right hand, do it for the sake of your holiness, do it for the sake of your Torah. In order that your beloved ones may be delivered, O save with your right hand, and answer me. Let the words of my mouth and the meditation of my heart be acceptable before you, O Lord, my Rock and my Redeemer. He who makes peace in his high places, may he make peace for us and for all Israel, and say ye, Amen.

May it be your will, O Lord our God and God of our fathers, that the temple be speedily rebuilt in our days, and grant our portion in your Torah. And there we will serve you with awe, as in the days of old, and as in ancient years. Then shall the offering of Judah and Jerusalem be pleasant unto the Lord, as in the days of old, and as in ancient years.

Reader.—Magnified and sanctified be his great name in the world which he has created according to his will. May he establish his kingdom during your life and during your days, and during the life of all the house of Israel, even speedily and at a near time, and say ye, Amen.

Cong. and Reader.—Let his great name be blessed forever and to all eternity.

Reader.—Blessed, praised and glorified, exalted, extolled and honored, magnified and lauded be the name of the Holy One, blessed be he; though he be high above all the blessings, praises and consolations, which are uttered in the world; and say ye, Amen.

Cong.—Accept our prayer in mercy and in favor.

Reader.—May the prayers and supplications of all Israel be accepted by their Father who is in heaven; and say ye, Amen.

Cong.—Let the name of the Lord be blessed from this time forth and forevermore.

Reader.—May there be abundant peace from heaven, and life for us and for all Israel; and say ye, Amen.

Cong.—My help is from the Lord who made heaven and earth.

Reader.—He who makes peace in his high places, may be make peace for us and for all Israel; and say ye, Amen.

There is none like our God: none like our Lord.

There is none like our King: none like our Savior.

Who is like our God: who is like our Lord? Who is like our King: who is like our Savior?

We will give thanks unto our God: we will give thanks unto our Lord.

We will give thanks unto our King: we will give thanks unto our Savior?

Blessed be our God: blessed be our Lord. Blessed be our King: blessed be our Savior. You are our God: you are our Lord. You are our King: you are our Savior. You are he unto whom our fathers burnt incense of spices.

Talmud Babli: Treatise Kerithot 6a.

The compound forming the incense consisted of balm, onycha, galbanum and frankincense, in quantities weighing seventy manehs each; of myrrh, cassia, spikenard and saffron, each sixteen manehs by weight; of costus twelve, of aromatic bark three, and of cinnamon nine manehs; of lye obtained from a species of leek, nine kabs; of Cyprus wine three seahs and three kabs: though, if Cyprus wine was not procurable, old white wine might be used; of salt of Sodom the fourth part of a kab, and of the herb Maaleh Ashan a minute quantity. R. Nathan says, a minute quantity was also required of the odoriferous herb Cippath, that grew on the banks of the Jordan; if, however, one added honey to the mixture, he rendered the incense unfit for sacred use, while he who, in preparing it, omitted one of its necessary ingredients, was liable to the penalty of death. Rabban Simeon, son of Gamaliel, says, the balm is a resin that exudes from the wood of the balsam tree. The lye obtained from a species of leek was rubbed over the onycha to improve it, while the Cyprus wine was used to steep it in, so that its odor might be more pungent.

Mishnah: End of Treatise Tamid.

These were the Psalms which the Levites used to recite in the Temple—

On the first day of the week they used to recite (Psalm xxiv.), The earth is the Lord's and the fullness thereof; the world and they that dwell therein.

On the second day (Psalm xlviii.), Great is the Lord and exceedingly to be praised, in the city of our God, in his holy mountain.

On the third day (Psalm lxxxii.), God stands in the congregation of the mighty; he judges among the judges.

On the fourth day (Psalm xciv.), God of vengeance, Lord, God of vengeance, shine forth.

On the fifth day (Psalm lxxxi.), Exult aloud unto God our strength; shout for joy unto the God of Jacob.

On the sixth day (Psalm xciii.), The Lord reigns; he has robed him in majesty; the Lord has robed him, yea, he has girded himself with strength: the world also is set firm, that it cannot be moved.

On the Sabbath (Psalm xcii.), A psalm, a song for the Sabbath Day. It is the psalm and song also for the hereafter, for the day which will be wholly a Sabbath, and will bring rest in life everlasting.

Talmud Babli. End of Treatise Berakhot.

R. Eleazer said in the name of R. Hanina, The disciples of the sages increase peace throughout the world, as it is said, And all your children shall be taught of the Lord; and great shall be the peace of your children. Read not here *banayich*, your children (or disciples), but *bonayich*, your builders.—Great peace have they who love your Torah; and there is no stumbling for them. Peace be within your rampart, prosperity within your palaces. For my brethren and companions' sake, I would fain speak peace concerning you. For the sake of the house of the Lord our God I would seek your good. The Lord will give strength unto his people; the Lord will bless his people with peace.

It is our duty to praise the Lord of all things, to ascribe greatness to him who formed the world in the beginning, since he has not made us like the nations of other lands, and has not placed us like other families of the earth, since he has not assigned unto us a portion as unto them, nor a lot as unto all their multitude. For we bend the knee and offer worship and thanks before the supreme King of kings, the Holy One, blessed be he, who stretched forth the heavens and laid the foundations of the earth, the seat of whose glory is in the heavens above, and the abode of whose might is in the loftiest heights. He is our God; there is none else: in truth he is our King; there is none besides him; as it is written in his Torah, And you shall know this day, and lay it to your heart, that the Lord he is God in heaven above and upon the earth beneath: there is none else.

We therefore hope in you, O Lord our God, that we may speedily behold the glory of your might, when you will remove the abominations from the earth, and the idols will be utterly cut off, when the world will be perfected under the kingdom of the Almighty, and all the children of flesh will call upon your name, when you will turn unto yourself all the wicked of the earth. Let all the inhabitants of the world perceive and know that unto you every knee must bow, every tongue must swear. Before you, O Lord our God, let them bow and fall; and unto your glorious name let them give honor; let them all accept the yoke of your kingdom, and do you reign over them speedily, and forever and ever. For the kingdom is yours, and to all eternity you will reign in glom; as it is written in your Torah, The Lord shall reign forever and ever. And it is said, And the Lord shall be King over all the earth: in that day shall the Lord be One, and his name One.

The following Kaddish is said by a Mourner.

And now, I pray you, let the power of the Lord be great, according as you have spoken. Remember, O Lord, your tender mercies and your loving-kindnesses; for they have been ever of old.

Mourner.—Magnified and sanctified be his great name in the world which he has created according to his will. May he establish his kingdom during your life and during your days, and during the life of all the house of Israel, even speedily and at a near time, and say ye, Amen.

Cong. and Mourner.—Let his great name be blessed forever and to all eternity.

Mourner.—Blessed, praised and glorified, exalted, extolled and honored, magnified and lauded be the name of the Holy One, blessed be he; though he be high above all the blessings and hymns, praises and consolations, which are uttered in the world; and say ye, Amen.

Cong.—Let the name of the Lord be blessed from this time forth and forevermore.

Mourner.—May there be abundant peace from heaven and life for us and for all Israel; and say ye, Amen.

Cong.—My help is from the Lord, who made heaven and earth.

Mourner.—He who makes peace in his high place, may he make peace for us and for all Israel; and say ye, Amen.

He is Lord of the universe, who reigned before any creature yet was formed:

At the time when all things were made by his desire, then was his name proclaimed King.

And after all things shall have had an end, he alone, the dreaded one, shall reign;

Who was, who is, and who will be in glory. And he is One, and there is no second to compare to him, to consort with him:

Without beginning, without end; to him belong strength and dominion.

And he is my God—my Redeemer lives—and a rock in my travail in time of distress;

And he is my banner and my refuge, the portion of my cup on the day when I call.

Into his hand I commend my spirit, when I sleep and when I wake;

And with my spirit, my body also: the Lord is with me, and I will not fear.

UNITY HYMN FOR THE SABBATH DAY

In some Congregations the following is said before "Blessed be he who spoke."

Of old you did rest on the seventh day; you did therefore bless the Sabbath.

For every work of yours praise is prepared for you; your loving ones bless you at all times.

Blessed be the Lord, the Maker of them all, the living God and everlasting King.

For from of old there has rested upon your servants the abundance of your mercies and your loving kindnesses.

But in Egypt you did begin to make known that you are exalted far.

Above all gods, when you did execute great judgment: upon the Egyptians and upon their gods.

When you did cleave the Red Sea, your people saw your great hand, and they feared.

You did guide your people, so that you might make unto yourself a name of glory to manifest your greatness.

You spoke also with them from the heavens, when the clouds dropped water.

You knew their wanderings in the wilderness, in a land of drought, where none passed through.

You gave to your people the corn of heaven, flesh abundant as the dust, and water from the rock.

You did drive out many nations, and they took possession of their land and of the labor of the peoples;

That they might observe your statutes and laws, the words of the Lord, which are pure words.

And they delighted themselves with fat pastures, and with rivers of oil from the flinty rock.

When they rested, they built your holy city, and adorned the house of your sanctuary.

Then you said, Here will I dwell for length of days: I will surely bless her provision.

There they shall sacrifice sacrifices of righteousness; your priests also shall be clothed with righteousness.

The house of Levi also shall chant pleasant songs; they shall shout for joy and sing unto you.

The house of Israel and they that fear the Lord shall give glory and thanks unto your name, O Lord.

You have dealt out exceeding kindness to the earliest ages; deal thus kindly also with the latest.

O Lord, rejoice over us, even as you did rejoice over our fathers,

To multiply us and deal kindly with us; and we will forever give thanks unto you for your goodness.

O Lord, rebuild your city speedily, for it is called by your name.

And make the horn of David to flourish therein, and dwell in the midst thereof forever, O Lord.

There we will offer sacrifices of righteousness, and there may our offering be pleasant as in former days.

Bless your people with the light of your countenance; for they desire to do your will.

And in your good will fulfil our desire; look, we beseech you, we are your people, all of us.

You have chosen us to be unto you a treasured people: let your blessing be upon your people forever.

And we will continually declare your praise, and praise your glorious name.

Of your blessing let your people be blessed, for every one whom you blesses is blessed.

As for me, while I have my being, I will praise my Creator, and I will bless him all the days of my appointed time.

Let the name of the Lord be blessed forever, from everlasting even to everlasting.

As it is written: Blessed be the Lord, the God of Israel, from everlasting even to everlasting. And all the people said, Amen, and praised the Lord. Daniel answered and said, Blessed be the name of God forever and ever: for wisdom and might are his. And it is said: Then the Levites, Jeshua, Kadmiel, Bani, Hashabneiah, Sherebiah, Hodiah, Shebaniah, and Pethahiah said, Stand up and bless the Lord your God from everlasting to everlasting: and let them bless your glorious name, that is exalted above all blessing and praise. And it is said: Blessed be the Lord, the God of Israel, from everlasting even to everlasting: and let all the people say, Amen: praise you the Lord. And it is said, And David blessed the Lord in the presence of all the congregation: and David said, blessed are you, O Lord, the God of Israel our father, from everlasting to everlasting.

You did form your world from of old; you had finished your work on the seventh day; you have loved us and taken pleasure in us, has exalted us above all tongues, has sanctified us by your commandments, has brought us near, O our King unto your service, and called us by your great and holy name. You, O Lord our God, also gave us in love Sabbaths for rest and New Moons for atonement. But because we sinned against you, both we and our fathers, our city has been laid waste, our sanctuary is desolate, our splendor has gone into exile, and the glory has been removed from the house of our life, so that we are not able to perform our obligations in your chosen house, in that great and holy house which was called by your name, because of the hand that has been stretched out against your sanctuary. May it be your will, O Lord our God and God of our fathers, to lead us up in joy unto our land, and to plant us within our borders, where we will prepare unto you the offerings that are obligatory for us, the continual offerings according to their order, and the additional offerings according to their enactment; and the additional offerings of this Sabbath day and of this New Moon we will prepare and offer up unto you in love, according to the precept of your will, as you have prescribed for us in your Torah through the hand of Moses your servant, by the mouth of your glory, as it is said: And on the Sabbath day two he-lambs of the first year without blemish, and two tenth parts of an ephah of fine flour for a meal offering, mingled with oil, and the drink offering thereof: this is the burnt offering of every Sabbath, beside the continual burnt offering and the drink offering thereof.

And in the beginnings of your months you shall offer a burnt offering unto the Lord; two young bullocks and one ram, seven he-lambs of the first year without blemish. And their meal offering and their drink offerings as has been ordained, three tenth parts of an ephah for each bullock, and two tenth parts for the ram, and one tenth part for each lamb, with wine according to the drink offering thereof, and a he-goat with which to make atonement, and the two continual offerings according to their enactment.

They that keep the Sabbath and call it a delight shall rejoice in your kingdom; the people that hallow the seventh day, even all of them shall be satiated and delighted with your goodness, seeing that you did find pleasure in the seventh day, and did hallow it; thon did call it the desirable of days, in remembrance of the creation.

Our God and God of our fathers, accept our rest, and on this Sabbath day renew this New Moon unto us for good and for blessing, for joy and for gladness, for salvation and comfort, for sustenance and maintenance, for life and peace, for pardon of sin and forgiveness of iniquity (during Leap Year— and for atonement of transgression); for you have chosen your people Israel from among all nations, and have made your holy Sabbath known unto them, and has appointed unto them statutes for the beginnings of the months. Blessed are you, O Lord, who sanctifies the Sabbath, Israel and the beginnings of the months.

HYMN OF GLORY.

The Ark is opened and the following Hymn is chanted in alternate verses by the Reader and Congregation.

I will chant sweet hymns and compose songs; for my soul pants after you.

My soul has longed to be beneath the shadow of your hand, to know all your secret mysteries.

Even while I speak of your glory, my heart yearns for your love.

Therefore will I speak glorious things of you, and will honor your name with songs of love.

I will declare your glory, though I have not seen you; under images will I describe you, though I have not known you.

By the hand of your prophets, in the mystic utterance of your servants, you have imaged forth the grandeur and the glory of your majesty.

Your greatness and your might they described in accordance with the power made manifest in your acts.

In images they told of you, but not according to your essence; they but likened you in accordance with your works.

They figured you in a multitude of visions; behold you are One under all images.

They saw in you both age and youth, the hair of your head now grey as in old age, now black as in youth.

Age in the Day of Judgment, and youth in the day of battle; as a man of war he strives with his hands:

He has bound a helmet of victory upon his head; his right hand, and his holy arm, has wrought victory for him:

With dew of light his head is filled, and his locks with drops of the night.

He shall be glorified by me for he delights in me; yea, he shall be to me a crown of beauty.

His head is like fine, pure gold; upon his forehead is impressed the glory of his holy name.

For grace and glory, beauty and splendor his people has encircled him with a crown.

The plaited hair of his head seemed as in the days of youth, his black locks were flowing in curls.

The abode of righteousness—his glorious beauty—may he prefer it above his chief joy.

May his treasured people be a crown in his hand, a royal diadem of glorious beauty.

They were borne by him, he carried them; with a crown he adorned them; for that they were precious in his sight he honored them.

His glory rests upon me, and mine upon him; and he is nigh unto me, when I cry unto him.

He is bright and ruddy in red apparel, when he comes front treading the winepress in Edom.

The symbol of his all-embracing providence he showed to the meek Moses, when the similitude of the Lord was before his eyes.

Taking pleasure in his people, he will glorify the meek; that, dwelling amid praises, he may be glorified by them.

The sum of your word is truth; O you, who has called every generation from the beginning, seek the people that seeks you.

Accept, I beseech you, the multitude of my songs, and let my joyous cry come near unto you.

Let my praise be a crown unto your head, and my prayer be set forth before you as incense.

Let the song of the poor be precious in your sight as the song that was sung at your offerings.

May my blessing rise to the bountiful God, who creates and produces, who is just and mighty.

And when I bless you, incline your head unto me, and take what I offer as though it were the choicest spices.

May my meditation be pleasant unto you, for my soul pants after you.

Psalm xcii.

A Psalm, a Song for the Sabbath Day. It is a good thing to give thanks unto the Lord, and to sing praises unto your name, O Most High: to declare your loving-kindness in the morning, and your faithfulness every night, with an instrument of ten strings and with a harp, with thoughtful music upon the lyre. For you, O Lord, have made me rejoice through your work: I will exult in the works of your hands. How great are your works, O Lord: the thoughts are very deep. A brutish man knows it not, neither does a fool understand this: when the wicked sprang up as the grass, and all the workers of iniquity flourished, it was that they might be destroyed forever. But you, O Lord, are on high forevermore. For, lo, your enemies, O Lord, for, lo, your enemies shall perish; all the workers of iniquity shall be scattered. But my horn have you exalted, like that of the wild-ox: I am anointed with fresh oil. My eye also has seen my desire on my enemies; my ears have heard my desire of them that rose up against me, doers of evil. The righteous shall spring up like a palm-tree; he shall grow tall like a cedar in Lebanon. Planted in the house of the Lord, they shall blossom in the courts of our God. They shall still shoot forth in old age; they shall be full of sap and green: to declare that the Lord is upright; he is my rock, and there is no unrighteousness in him.

The Mourner's Kaddish.

KIDDUSH FOR SABBATH MORNING.
Exodus xxxi. 16, 17.

And the children of Israel shall keep the Sabbath, to observe the Sabbath throughout their generations, for an everlasting covenant. It is a sign between me and the children of Israel forever, that in six days the Lord made the heavens and the earth, and on the seventh day he rested, and ceased from his work.

Exod. xx. 8-11.

Remember the Sabbath day to keep it holy. Six days shall you labor, and do all your work: but the seventh day is a Sabbath unto the Lord your God: in it you shall not do any work, you, nor your son, nor your daughter, your man-servant, nor your maidservant, nor your cattle, nor your stranger that is within your gates: for in six days the Lord made heaven and earth, the sea and all that is therein, and rested on the seventh day; wherefore the Lord blessed the Sabbath day and hallowed it.

Blessed are you, O Lord our God, King of the universe, who creates the fruit of the vine.

Blessed are you, O Lord our God, King of the universe, who brings forth bread from the earth.

AFTERNOON SERVICE FOR SABBATHS.

Happy are they that dwell in your house: they will be ever praising you. (Selah.)

Happy is the people that is in such a case: happy the people, whose God is the Lord.

Psalm cxlv. A Psalm of Praise: of David.

I will extol you, my God, O King; and I will bless your name forever and ever.

Every day will I bless you; and I will praise your name forever and ever.

Great is the Lord, and exceedingly to be praised: and his greatness is unsearchable.

One generation shall laud your works to another, and shall declare your mighty acts.

On the majestic glory of your grandeur, and on your marvelous deeds, will I meditate.

And men shall speak of the might of your awful acts; and I will recount your greatness.

They shall pour forth the fame of your great goodness, and shall exult in your righteousness.

The Lord is gracious and merciful; slow to anger and of great loving-kindness.

The Lord is good to all; and his tender mercies are over all his works.

All your works shall give thanks unto you, O Lord; and your loving ones shall bless you.

They shall speak of the glory of your kingdom, and talk of your power.

To make known to the sons of men his mighty acts, and the majestic glory of his kingdom.

Your kingdom is an everlasting kingdom, and your dominion endures throughout all generations.

The Lord upholds all that fall, and raises up all those that are bowed down.

The eyes of all wait upon you; and you gives them their food in due season.

You open your hand, and satisfies every living thing with favor.

The Lord is righteous in all his ways, and loving in all his works.

The Lord is nigh unto all them that call upon him, to all that call upon him in truth.

He will fulfil the desire of them that fear him; he also will hear their cry, and will save them.

The Lord guards all them that love him; but all the wicked will he destroy.

My mouth shall speak of the praise of the Lord: and let all flesh bless his holy name forever and ever.

But we will bless the Lord from this time forth and forevermore. Praise you the Lord.

And a redeemer shall come to Zion and to them that turn from transgression in Jacob, says the Lord. And as for me, this is my covenant with them, says the Lord: my spirit that is upon you, and my words which I have put in your mouth, shall not depart out of your mouth, nor out of the mouth of your seed, nor out of the mouth of your seed's seed, says the Lord, from henceforth and forever.

But you are holy, O you that dwell amid the praises of Israel. And one cried unto another, and said, Holy, holy, holy is the Lord of hosts: the whole earth is full of his glory. And they receive sanction the one from the other, and say, Holy in the highest heavens, the place of his divine abode; holy upon earth, the work of his might; holy forever and to all eternity is the Lord of hosts; the whole earth is full of the radiance of his glory. Then a wind lifted me up, and I heard behind me the voice of a great rushing (saying), Blessed be the glory of the Lord from his place. Then a wind lifted me up, and I heard behind me the voice of a great rushing, of those who uttered praises, and said, Blessed be the glory of the Lord from the region of his divine abode. The Lord shall reign forever and ever. The kingdom of the Lord endures forever and to all eternity. O Lord, the God of Abraham, of Isaac and of Israel, our fathers, keep this forever in the imagination of the thoughts of the heart of your people, and direct their heart unto you. Arid he, being merciful, forgives iniquity and destroys not: yea, many a time he turns his anger away, and does not stir up all his wrath. For you, O Lord, are good and forgiving, and abounding in loving-kindness to all them that call upon you. Your righteousness is an everlasting righteousness, and your Torah is truth. You will show truth to Jacob and loving kindness to Abraham, according as you have sworn unto our fathers from the days of old. Blessed be the Lord day by day; if one burdens us. God is our salvation. (Selah.) The Lord of hosts is with us; the God of Jacob is our stronghold. (Selah.) O Lord of hosts, happy is the man who trusts in you. Save, Lord: may the King answer us on the day when we call. Blessed is our God, who has created us for his glory, and has separated us from them that go astray, and has given us the Torah of truth and planted everlasting life in our midst. May he open our heart unto his Torah, and place his love and fear within our hearts, that we may do his will and serve him with a perfect heart, that we may not labor in vain, nor bring forth for confusion. May it be your will, O Lord our God and God of our fathers that we may keep your statutes in this world, and be worthy to live to witness and inherit happiness and blessing in the days of the Messiah and in the life of the world to come. To the end that my glory may sing praise unto you, and not be silent: O Lord my God, I will give thanks unto you forever. Blessed is the man that trusts in the Lord, and whose trust the Lord is. Trust you in the Lord forever; for in Yah the Lord is an everlasting rock. And they that know your name will put their trust in you; for you have not forsaken them that seek you, Lord. It pleased the Lord, for his righteousness' sake, to magnify the Torah and to make it honorable.

Reader.—Magnified and sanctified be his great name in the world which he has created according to his will. May he establish his kingdom during your life and during your days, and during the life of all the house of Israel, even speedily and at a near time, and say ye, Amen.

Cong. and Reader.—Let his great name be blessed forever and to all eternity.

Reader.—Blessed, praised and glorified, exalted, extolled and honored, magnified and lauded be the name of the Holy One, blessed be he; though he be high above all the blessings and hymns, praises and consolations, which are uttered in the world; and say ye, Amen.

And as for me, may my prayer unto you, O Lord, be in an acceptable time: O God, in the abundance of your loving-kindness, answer me in the truth of your salvation.

The first section of the Lesson from the Pentateuch of the following Sabbath is read.

For Order of Reading the Torah see above.

While the vestments are being replaced upon the Scroll, Psalm, xcii, is said.

The following prayer (Amidah) to "as in ancient years," is to be said standing.

O Lord, open you my lips, and my mouth shall declare your praise.

Blessed are you, O Lord our God and God of our fathers, God of Abraham, God of Isaac, and God of Jacob, the great, mighty and revered God, the most high God, who bestows loving-kindnesses, and possesses all things; who remembers the pious deeds of the patriarchs, and in love will bring a redeemer to their children's children for your name's sake.

During the Ten Days of Penitence say—

Remember us unto life, O King, who delights in life, and inscribe us in the book of life, for your own sake, O living God.

O King, Helper, Savior and Shield. Blessed are you, O Lord, the Shield of Abraham.

You, O Lord, are mighty forever, you quicken the dead, you are mighty to save.

From the Sabbath after the Eighth Day of Solemn Assembly until the First Day of Passover say—

You cause the wind to blow and the rain to fall,

You sustain the living with loving-kindness, quicken the dead with great mercy, support the falling, heal the sick, loose the bound, and keep your faith to them that sleep in the dust. Who is like unto you, Lord of mighty acts, and who resembles you, O King, who kills and quickens and causes salvation to spring forth?

On the Sabbath of Penitence say—

Who is like unto you, Father of mercy, who in mercy remembers your creatures unto life?

Yea, faithful are you to quicken the dead. Blessed are you, O Lord, who quickens the dead.

You are holy, and your name is holy, and holy beings praise you daily. (Selah.) Blessed are you, O Lord, the holy God.

On the Sabbath of Penitence conclude the Blessing thus:
the holy King.

When the Reader repeats the Amidah, the following is said, to "holy God."

Reader.—We will sanctify your name in the world even as they sanctify it in the highest heavens, as it is written by the hand of your prophet: And they called one unto the other and said,

Cong.—Holy, holy, holy is the Lord of hosts: the whole earth is full of his glory.

Reader.—Those over against them say, Blessed—

Cong.—Blessed be the glory of the Lord from his place.

Reader.—And in your Holy Words it is written, saying,

Cong.—The Lord shall reign forever, your God, Zion, unto all generations. Praise you the Lord.

Reader.—Unto all generations we will declare your greatness, and to all eternity we will proclaim your holiness, and your praise, O our God, shall not depart from our mouth forever, for you are a great and holy God and King. Blessed are you, O Lord, the holy God.

During the Ten Days of Penitence conclude the blessing thus—
the holy King.

You are One and your name is One, and who, is like your people Israel, an unique nation on the earth? Glorious greatness and a crown of salvation, even the day of rest and holiness, you have given unto your people—Abraham was glad, Isaac rejoiced, Jacob and his sons rested thereon—a rest vouchsafed in generous love, a true and faithful rest, a rest in peace and tranquility, in quietude and safety, a perfect rest wherein you delight. Let your children perceive and know that their rest is from you, and by their rest may they hallow your name.

Our God and God of our fathers, accept our rest; sanctify us by your commandments, and grant our portion in your Torah; satisfy us with your goodness, and gladden us with your salvation; purify our hearts to serve you in truth; and in your love and favor, O Lord our God, let us inherit your holy Sabbath; and may Israel, who hallow your name, rest thereon. Blessed are you, O Lord, who hallows the Sabbath.

Accept, O Lord our God, your people Israel and their prayer; restore the service to the oracle of your house; receive in love and favor both the fire-offerings of Israel and their prayer; and may the service of your people Israel be ever acceptable unto you.

On New Moon and the Intermediate Days of Passover and Sukkot the following is added—

Our God and God of our fathers! May our remembrance rise, come and be accepted before you, with the remembrance of our fathers, of Messiah the son of David your servant, of Jerusalem your holy city, and of all your people the house of Israel, bringing deliverance and well-being, grace, loving-kindness and mercy, life and peace on this day of

On the New Moon—
the Feast of the New Moon.
On Passover—
the Feast of Unleavened Bread.
On Sukkot—
Sukkot.

Remember us, O Lord our God, thereon for our wellbeing; be mindful of us for blessing, and save us unto life: by your promise of salvation and mercy, spare us and be gracious unto us; have mercy upon us and save us; for our eyes are bent upon you, because you are a gracious and merciful God and King.

And let our eyes behold your return in mercy to Zion. Blessed are you, O Lord, who restores your divine presence unto Zion.

We give thanks unto you, for you are the Lord our God and the God of our fathers forever and ever; you are the Rock of our lives, the Shield of our salvation through every generation. We will give thanks unto you and declare your praise for our lives which are committed unto your hand, and for our souls which are in your charge, and for your miracles, which are daily with us, and for your wonders and your benefits, which are wrought at all times, evening, morn and noon. O you who are all-good, whose mercies fail not; you, merciful Being, whose loving-kindnesses never cease, we have ever hoped in you.

Congregation in an undertone.

We give thanks unto you, for you are the Lord our God and the God of our fathers, the God of all flesh, our Creator and the Creator of all things in the beginning. Blessings and thanksgivings be to your great and holy name because you have kept us in life and has preserved us: so may you continue to keep us in life and to preserve us. O gather our exiles to your holy courts to observe your statutes, to do your will, and to serve you with a perfect heart; seeing that we give thanks unto you. Blessed be the God to whom thanksgivings are due.

On Sabbath of Chanukah say: We thank you, etc.
For all these things your name, O our King, shall be continually blessed and exalted forever and ever.
On the Sabbath of Penitence say—
O inscribe all the children of your covenant for a happy life.

And everything that lives shall give thanks unto you forever, and shall praise your name in truth, O God, our salvation and our help. Blessed are you, O Lord, whose name is All-good, and unto whom it is becoming to give thanks.

Grant abundant peace unto Israel your people forever; for you are the sovereign Lord of all peace; and may it be good in your sight to bless your people Israel at all times and in every hour with your peace.

On the Sabbath of Penitence say—
In the book of life, blessing, peace and good sustenance may we be remembered and inscribed before you, us and all your people the house of Israel, for a happy life and for peace. Blessed are you, O Lord, who makes peace.

Blessed are you, O Lord, who blesses your people Israel with peace.

O my God! guard my tongue from evil and my lips from speaking guile; and to such as curse me let my soul be dumb, yea, let my soul be unto all as the dust. Open my heart to your Torah, and let my soul pursue your commandments. If any design evil against me, speedily make their counsel of none effect, and frustrate their designs. Do it for the sake of your name, do it for the sake of your right hand, do it for the sake of your holiness, do it for the sake of your Torah. In order that your beloved ones may be delivered, O save with your right hand, and answer me. Let the words of my mouth and the meditation of my heart be acceptable before you, O Lord, my Rock and my Redeemer. He who makes peace in his high places, may he make peace for us and for all Israel, and say ye, Amen.

May it be your will, O Lord our God and God of our fathers, that the temple be speedily rebuilt in our days, and grant our portion in your Torah. And there we will serve you with awe, as in the days of old, and as in ancient years. Then shall the offering of Judah and Jerusalem be pleasant unto the Lord, as in the days of old, and as in ancient years.

The following is omitted on such occasions as those on which Tachanun is omitted on Week-days—

Your righteousness is an everlasting righteousness, and your Torah is truth. Your righteousness also, O God, is very high; you who has done great things, O God, who is like unto you? your righteousness is like the mountains of God; your judgments are a great deep; man and beast you save, O Lord.

Reader.—Magnified and sanctified be his great name in the world which he has created according to his will. May he establish his kingdom during your life and during your days, and during the life of all the house of Israel, even speedily and at a near time, and say ye, Amen.

Cong. and Reader.—Let his great name be blessed forever and to all eternity.

Reader.—Blessed, praised and glorified, exalted, extolled and honored, magnified and lauded be the name of the Holy One, blessed be he; though he be high above all the blessings and hymns, praises and consolations, which are uttered in the world; and say ye, Amen.

Cong.—Accept our prayer in mercy and in favor.

Reader.—May the prayers and supplications of all Israel be accepted by their Father who is in heaven; and say ye, Amen.

Cong.—Let the name of the Lord be blessed from this time forth and forevermore.

Reader.—May there be abundant peace from heaven, and life for us and for all Israel; and say ye, Amen.

Cong.—My help is from Lord who made heaven and earth.

Reader.—He who makes peace in his high places may he make peace for us and for all Israel; and say ye, Amen.

It is our duty to praise the Lord of all things, to ascribe greatness to him who formed the world in the beginning, since he has not made us like the nations of other lands, and has not placed us like other families of the earth, since he has not assigned unto us a portion as unto them, nor a lot as unto all their multitude. For we bend the knee and offer worship and thanks before the supreme King of kings, the Holy One, blessed be he, who stretched forth the heavens and laid the foundations of the earth, the seat of whose glory is in the heavens above, and the abode of whose might is in the loftiest heights. He is our God; there is none else: in truth he is our King; there is none besides him; as it is written in his Torah, And you shall know this day, and lay it to your heart, that the Lord he is God in heaven above and upon the earth beneath: there is none else.

We therefore hope in you, O Lord our God, that we may speedily behold the glory of your might, when you will remove the abominations from the earth, and the idols will be utterly cut off, when the world will be perfected under the kingdom of the Almighty, and all the children of flesh will call upon your name, when you will turn unto yourself all the wicked of the earth. Let all the inhabitants of the world perceive and know that unto you every knee must bow, every tongue must swear. Before you, O Lord our God, let them bow and fall; and unto your glorious name let them give honor; let them all accept the yoke of your kingdom, and do you reign over them speedily, and forever and ever. For the kingdom is yours, and to all eternity you will reign in glory; as it is written in your Torah, The Lord shall reign forever and ever. And it is said, And the Lord shall be king over all the earth: in that day shall the Lord be One, and his name One.

The following Kaddish is said by a Mourner

Mourner.—Magnified and sanctified be his great name in the world which he has created according to his will. May he establish his kingdom during your life and during your days, and during the life of all the house of Israel, even speedily and at a near time, and say ye, Amen.

Cong. and Mourner.—Let his great name be blessed forever and to all eternity.

Mourner.—Blessed, praised and glorified, exalted, extolled and honored, magnified and lauded be the name of the Holy One, blessed be he; though he be high above all the blessings and hymns, praises and consolations, which are uttered in the world; and say ye, Amen.

Cong.—Let the name of the Lord be blessed from this time forth and forevermore.

Mourner.—May there be abundant peace from heaven, and life for us and for all Israel; and say ye, Amen.

Cong.—My help is from the Lord, who made heaven and earth.

Mourner.—He who makes peace in his high places, may he make peace for us and for all Israel; and say ye, Amen.

From the Sabbath after "the Rejoicing of the Torah" until the Sabbath before Passover, the following Psalms are read—

Psalm civ.

Bless the Lord, O my soul: O Lord my God, you are very great; you have robed you in splendor and majesty. He covers himself with light as with a garment; he stretches out the heavens like a curtain: he lays the beams of his upper chambers in the waters; he makes the clouds his chariot; he walks upon the wings of the wind. He makes winds his messengers; his ministers flaming fire: he founded the earth upon its bases, that it might not be moved forever. You did cover it with the deep as with a vesture; the waters stood above the mountains. At your rebuke they fled; at the voice of your thunder they hasted away. The mountains rose, the valleys sank unto the place which you had founded for them. You have set a bound that they may not pass over; that they turn not again to cover the earth. He sends forth springs into the valleys; they run among the mountains. They give drink to every beast of the plain; the wild asses quench their thirst. By them the birds of the heaven have their dwelling; they utter their voice from among the branches. He gives drink to the mountains from his upper chambers: the earth is satisfied with the fruit of your works. He causes grass to grow for the cattle, and herbs for the service of man; that he may bring forth bread from the earth; and wine that makes glad the heart of man, and oil to make his face to shine, and bread that strengthens man's heart. The trees of the Lord are satisfied; the cedars of Lebanon which he has planted; where the birds make their nests: as for the stork, the fir trees are her house. The high mountains are for the wild goats; the rocks are a refuge for the conies. He made the moon for seasons: the sun knows its going down. You make darkness, and it is night; wherein all the beasts of the forest do move. The young lions roar after their prey, and seek their food from God. The sun arises, they get them away, and lay them down in their dens. Man goes forth unto his work and to his labor until the evening. How manifold are your works, O Lord! In wisdom have you made them all: the earth is full of your possessions. Yonder is the sea, great and of wide extern therein are moving things innumerable, living creatures both small and great. There the ships make their course; there is leviathan whom you have formed to sport therein. These all wait upon you, that you may give them their food in due season. You give unto them, they gather; you open your hand, they are satisfied with good. You hide your face, they are confounded; you gather in their breath, they die, and return to their dust. You send forth your spirit, they are created; and you renew the face of the ground. Let the glory of the Lord endure forever; let the Lord rejoice in his works. He looks on the earth, and it trembles; he touches the mountains, and they smoke. I will sing unto the Lord as long as I live; I will sing praise to my God while I have my being. May my meditation be sweet unto him: as for me, I will rejoice in the Lord. Sinners shall be consumed out of the earth, and the wicked shall be no more. Bless the Lord, O my soul: praise you the Lord.

Psalm cxx.

A Song of Degrees. In my distress I cried unto the Lord, and he answered me. Deliver my soul, O Lord, from a lying lip, and from a deceitful tongue. What shall he give unto you, and what shall he add unto you, you deceitful tongue? Sharpened arrows of a mighty man with coals of juniper. Woe is me, that I sojourn in Mesech, that I dwell among the tents of Kedar. My soul has full long had her dwelling with him that hates peace. I am all peace; but when I speak, they are for war.

Psalm cxxi.

A Song of Degrees. I lift up my eyes unto the hills: From where will my help come? My help is from the Lord, the maker of heaven and earth. He will not suffer your foot to slip: he that guards you will not slumber. Behold, he that guards Israel will neither slumber nor sleep. The Lord is your guardian: the Lord is your shade upon your right hand. The sun shall not smite you by day, nor the moon by night. The Lord shall guard you from all evil; he shall guard your soul. The Lord shall guard your going out and your coming in, from this time forth and forevermore.

Psalm cxxii.

A Song of Degrees; of David. I was glad when they said unto me, Let us go unto the house of the Lord. Our feet stood within your gates, O Jerusalem; Jerusalem that are built up as a city that is compact together: whither the tribes go up, even the tribes of the Lord, for a testimony unto Israel, to give thanks unto the name of the Lord. For there are set thrones for judgment, the thrones of the house of David. Pray for the peace of Jerusalem; may they prosper that love you. Peace be within your rampart, prosperity within your palaces. For my brethren and companions' sakes I would fain speak peace concerning you. For the sake of the house of the Lord our God I would seek your good.

Psalm cxxiii.

A Song of Degrees. Unto you do I lift up my eyes, O you that dwell in the heavens. Behold, as the eyes of servants look unto the hand of their master, as the eyes of a maiden unto the hand of her mistress, so our eyes look unto the Lord our God, until he have pity upon us. Have pity upon us, O Lord, have pity upon us: for we are full sated with contempt. Our soul is full sated with the mocking of those that are at ease, with the contempt of the proud.

Psalm cxxiv.

A Song of Degrees; of David. If it had not been the Lord who was on our side, let Israel now say: if it had not been the Lord who was on our side, when men rose up against us, then they had swallowed us up alive, when their wrath was kindled against us; then the waters had overwhelmed us, the stream had gone over our soul; then the proud waters had gone over our soul. Blessed be the Lord, who has not given us a prey to their teeth. Our soul escaped as a bird out of the snare of the fowlers: the snare was broken, and we escaped. Our help is in the name of the Lord, who made heaven and earth.

Psalm cxxv.

A Song of Degrees. They that trust in the Lord are as Mount Zion, which cannot be moved, but abides forever. The mountains are round about Jerusalem, and the Lord is round about his people, from this time forth and forevermore. For the scepter of wickedness shall not rest upon the lot of the righteous, that the righteous put not forth their hands unto iniquity. Do good, O Lord, unto those that are good, and to them that are upright in their hearts. But as for such as turn aside unto their crooked ways, the Lord will destroy them with the workers of iniquity. Peace be upon Israel.

Psalm cxxvi.

A Song of Degrees. When the Lord turned again the captivity of Zion, we were like unto them that dream. Then was our mouth filled with laughter, and our tongue with exultation: then said they among the nations, The Lord has done great things for them. The Lord has done great things for us; whereat we rejoiced. Bring back our captivity, O Lord, as the streams in the south. They that sow, in tears shall reap in joy. Though he goes on his way weeping, hearing the store of seed, he shall come back with joy, bearing his sheaves.

Psalm cxxvii.

A Song of Degrees; of Solomon. Except the Lord build the house, they labor in vain that build it: except the Lord watch over the city, the watchman wakes but in vain. It is vain for you to rise up early, and so late take rest, and eat the bread of toil: such things he gives unto his beloved in sleep. Lo, children are a heritage of the Lord: the fruit of the womb is his reward. As arrows in the hand of a mighty man, so are the children of youth. Happy is the man that has filled his quiver with them: they shall not be ashamed, when they speak with enemies in the gate.

Psalm cxxviii.

A Song of Degrees. Happy is every one that fears the Lord, that walks in his ways. When you shall eat the labor of your hands, happy shall you be, and it shall be well with you. Your wife shall be as a fruitful vine, in the recesses of your house: your children like olive plants, round about your table. Behold thus shall the man be blessed that fears the Lord. May the Lord bless you out of Zion: may you see the good of Jerusalem all the days of your life. Yea, may you see your children's children. Peace be upon Israel.

Psalm cxxix.

A Song of Degrees. To the full have they afflicted me from my youth up, let Israel now say; to the full have they afflicted me from my youth up: yet have they not prevailed against me. The plower; plowed upon my back, they made long their furrows. The Lord is righteous: he has cut asunder the cords of the wicked. Let them be ashamed and turned backward, all they that hate Zion. Let them be as the grass upon the housetops, which withers before it shoots forth: with which the mower fills not his hand, nor he that binds sheaves his bosom: neither do they which go by say, The blessing of the Lord be upon you; we bless you in the name of the Lord.

Psalm cxxx.

A Song of Degrees. Out of the depths have I cried unto you, O Lord. Lord, hear my voice: let your ears be attentive to the voice of my supplications. If you, Lord, should mark iniquities, O Lord, who could stand? But there is forgiveness with you, that you may be feared. I wait for the Lord, my soul does wait, and in his word do I hope. My soul waits for the Lord, more than watchmen wait for the morning; yea, more than watchmen for the morning. O let Israel hope in the Lord; for with the Lord there is loving-kindness, and with him is plenteous deliverance. And he shall deliver Israel from all his iniquities.

Psalm cxxxi.

A Song of Degrees; of David. Lord, my heart is not haughty, nor my eyes lofty, neither do I exercise myself in great matters, or in things too marvelous for me. Surely I have stilled and quieted my soul, like a weaned child with his mother; my soul is with me like a weaned child. O Israel, hope in the Lord from this time forth and forevermore.

Psalm cxxxii.

A Song of Degrees. Lord, remember for David all his affliction; how he swore to the Lord, and vowed unto the Mighty One of Jacob: Surely I will not come into the tent of my house, nor go up unto the couch of my rest; I will not give sleep to my eyes, or slumber to my eyelids; until I find out a place for the Lord, a habitation for the Mighty One of Jacob. Lo, we heard of it in Ephrathah: we found it in the fields of Yaar. Let us go into his habitation; let us worship at his footstool. Arise, O Lord, unto your resting place; you, and the ark of your strength. Let your priests be clothed with righteousness; and let your loving ones exult. For the sake of David your servant turn not away the face of your anointed. The Lord has sworn unto David in truth—he will not turn from it—: of the fruit of your body will I set upon your throne. If your children will keep my covenant, and my testimonies that I shall teach them, their children also shall sit upon your throne forevermore. For the Lord has chosen Zion; he has desired it for his habitation. This is my resting-place forever: here will I dwell; for I have desired it. I will abundantly bless her provision: I will satisfy her needy with bread. Her priests also will I clothe with salvation; and her loving ones shall exult aloud. There will I make a horn to spring forth unto David: I have prepared a lamp for my anointed. His enemies will I clothe with shame; but upon him his crown shall shine.

Psalm cxxxiii.

A Song of Degrees; of David. Behold, how good and pleasant it is for brethren to dwell together in unity! It is like the goodly oil upon the head, that runs down upon the beard, even Aaron's beard; that runs down upon the skirt of his garments; like the dew of Hermon, that runs down upon the mountains of Zion: for there the Lord commandment the blessing, even life forevermore.

Psalm cxxxiv.

A Song of Degrees. Behold, bless you the Lord, all you servants of the Lord, who stand in the house of the Lord in the night seasons. Lift up your hands towards the sanctuary, and bless you the Lord. The Lord bless you out of Zion; even he that made heaven and earth.

"It is our duty."

Mourner's Kaddish

ETHICS OF THE FATHERS
One of the following chapters is read on each Sabbath from the Sabbath after Passover until the Sabbath before New Year.

All Israel have a portion in the world to come, as it is said (Isaiah lx, 21), And your people shall be all righteous; they shall inherit the land forever, the branch of my planting, the work of my hands, that I may be glorified.

CHAPTER I

(1.) Moses received the Torah on Sinai, and handed it down to Joshua; Joshua to the elders; the elders to the prophets; and the prophets handed it down to the men of the Great Synagogue. They said three things: Be deliberate in judgment; raise up many disciples, and make a fence round the Torah. (2.) Simon the Just was one of the last survivors of the Great Synagogue. He used to say, Upon three things the world is based: upon the Torah, upon the Temple service, and upon the practice of charity. (3.) Antigonos of Socho received the tradition from Simon the Just. He used to say, Be not like servants who minister to their master upon the condition of receiving a reward; but be like servants who minister to their master without the condition of receiving a reward; and let the fear of Heaven be upon you. (4.) Yose, the son of Yoezer, of Zeredah, and Yose, the son of Yochanan, of Jerusalem, received the tradition from the preceding. Yose, the son of Yoezer, of Zeredah, said, Let your house be a meeting house for the wise; sit amid the dust of their feet, and drink their words with thirst. (5.) Yose, the son of Yochanan, of Jerusalem, said, Let your house be open wide; let the poor be the members of your household, and engage not in much gossip with women. This applies even to one's own wife; how much more then to the wife of one's neighbor. Hence the sages say, Who engages in much gossip with women brings evil upon himself, neglects the study of the Torah, and will in the end inherit Gehinnom. (6.) Joshua, the son of Perachyah, and Nittai, the Arbelite, received the tradition from the preceding. Joshua, the son of Perachyah, said, Provide yourself a teacher, and get you a companion, and judge all men in the scale of merit. (7.) Nittai, the Arbelite, said, Keep you far from a bad neighbor, associate not with the wicked, and abandon not the belief in retribution. (8.) Judah, the son of Tabbai, and Simeon, the son of Shatach, received the tradition from the preceding. Judah, the son of Tabbai, said, (In the judge's office) act not the counsel's part; when the parties to a suit are standing before you, let them both be regarded by you as guilty, but when they are departed from your presence, regard them both as innocent, the verdict having been acquiesced in by them. (9.) Simeon, the son of Shatach, said, Be very searching in the examination, of witnesses, and be heedful of your words, lest through them they learn to falsify. (10.) Shemayah and Abtalyon received the tradition from the preceding. Shemayah said, Love work, hate lordship, and seek no intimacy with the ruling power (11.) Abtalyon said, you sages, be heedful of your words, lest you incur the penalty of exile and be exiled to a place of evil waters, and the disciples who come after you drink thereof and die, and the Heavenly Name be profaned. (12.) Hillel and Shammai received the tradition from the preceding. Hillel said, Be of the disciples of Aaron, loving peace and pursuing peace, loving your fellow-creatures, and drawing them near to the Torah. (13.) He used to say, A name made great is a name destroyed; he who does not increase his knowledge decreases it; and he who does not study deserves to die; and he who makes a worldly use of the crown of the Torah shall waste away. (14.) He used to say, If I am not for myself, who will be for me? And being for my own self, what am I? And if not now, when? (15). Shammai said, Fix a period for your study of the Torah; say little and do much; and receive all men with a cheerful countenance. (16.) Rabban Gamaliel said, Provide yourself a teacher, and be quit of doubt, and accustom not yourself to give tithes by a conjectural estimate. (17.) Simeon, his son, said, All my days I have grown up amongst the wise, and I have found naught of better service than silence; not learning but doing is the chief thing; and who is profuse of words causes sin. (18.) Rabban Simeon, the son of Gamaliel, said, By three things is the world preserved: by truth, by judgment, and by peace, as it is said, Judge you the truth and the judgment of peace in your gates (Zech. viii. 16).

Rabbi Hananya, the son of Akashya, said, The Holy One, blessed be he, was pleased to make Israel worthy; wherefore he gave them a copious Torah and many commandments, as it is said, It pleased the Lord, for his righteousness' sake, to magnify the Torah and make it honorable (Isaiah xlii, 21).

CHAPTER II

All Israel have a portion in the world to come, as it is said (Isaiah lx. 21), And your people shall be all righteous; they shall inherit the land forever, the branch of my planting, the work of my hands, that I may be glorified.

(1.) Rabbi said, What is the right course that a man should choose for himself? That which he feels to be honorable to himself, and which also brings him honor from mankind. Be heedful of a light precept as of a grave one, for you know not the grant of reward for each precept. Reckon the loss incurred by the fulfilment of a precept against the reward secured by its observance, and the gain gotten by a transgression against the loss it involves. Reflect upon three things, and you will not come within the power of sin; Know what is above you—a seeing eye, and a hearing ear, and all your deeds written in a book. (2.) Rabban Gamaliel, the son of Rabbi Judah the Prince, said, An excellent thing is the study of the Torah combined with some worldly occupation, for the labor demanded by them both makes sin to be forgotten. All study of the Torah without work must in the end be futile and become the cause of sin. Let all who are employed with the congregation act with them for Heaven's sake, for then the merit of their fathers sustains them, and their righteousness endures forever. And as for you, (God will then say,) I account you worthy of great reward, as if you had wrought it all yourselves. (3.) Be on your guard against the ruling power; for they who exercise it draw no man near to them except for their own interests; appearing as friends when it is to their own advantage, they stand not by a man in the hour of his need. (4.) He used to say, Do His will as if it were your will, that He may do your will as if it were His will. Nullify your will before His will, that He may nullify the will of others before your will. (5) Hillel said, Separate not yourself from the congregation; trust not in yourself until the day of your death; judge not your neighbor until you are come into his place; and say not anything which cannot be understood at once, in the hope that it will be understood in the end; neither say, When I have leisure I will study; perchance you will have no leisure. (6.) He used to say, An empty-headed man cannot be a sin fearing man, nor can an ignorant person be pious, nor can a shamefaced man learn, nor a passionate man teach, nor can one who is engaged overmuch in business grow wise. In a place where there are no men, strive to be a man. (7.) Moreover, he saw a skull floating on the surface of the water: he said to it, Because you drowned others, they have drowned you, and at the last they that drowned you shall themselves be drowned. (8.) He used to say, The more flesh, the more worms; the more property, the more anxiety; the more women, the more witchcraft; the more maid-servants, the more lewdness; the more men-servants, the more robbery;—the more Torah, the more life; the more schooling, the more wisdom; the more counsel, the more understanding; the more charity, the more peace. He who has acquired a good name, has acquired it for himself; he who has acquired for himself words of Torah, has acquired for himself life in the world to come. (9.) Rabban Yochanan, the son of Zacchai received the tradition from Hillel and Shammai. He used to say, if you have learnt much Torah, ascribe not any merit to yourself, for thereunto were you created. (10.) Rabban Yochanan, the son of Zacchai, had five disciples, and these are they, Rabbi Eliezer, the son of Hyrcanus, Rabbi Joshua, the son of Chananya, Rabbi Jose, the Priest, Rabbi Simeon, the son of Nathaniel, and Rabbi Eleazar, the son of Arach. (11.) He used thus to recount their praise: Eliezer, the son of Hyrcanus, is a cemented cistern, which loses not a drop; Joshua, the son of Chananya—happy is she that bore him; Jose, the Priest, is a pious man; Simeon, the son of Nathaniel, is a fearer of sin; Eleazar, the son of Arach, is like a spring flowing ever-sustaining vigor. (12.) He used to say, If all the sages of Israel were in one scale of the balance, and Eliezer, the son of Hyrcanus, in the other, he would outweigh them all. Abba Saul said in his name, If all the sages of Israel were in one scale of the balance, and Eliezer, the son of Hyrcanus, also with them, and Eleazar, the son of Arach, in the other scale, he would outweigh them all. (13.) He said to them, Go forth and see which is the good way to which a man should cleave. R. Eliezer said, A good eye; R. Joshua said, A good friend; R. Jose said, A good neighbor; R. Simeon said, One who foresees the fruit of an action; R. Eleazar said, A good heart. Thereupon he said to them, I approve the words of Eleazar, the son of Arach, rather than your words, for in his words yours are included. (14.) He said to them, Go forth and see which is the evil way that a man should shun. R. Eliezer said, An evil eye; R. Joshua said, A bad friend; R. Jose said, A bad neighbor; R. Simeon said, One who borrows and does not repay,—it is the same whether one borrows from man or from the all-present God; as it is said, The wicked borrows, and pays not again, but the righteous deals graciously and gives (Psalm xxxvii. 21); R. Eleazar said, A bad heart. Thereupon he said to them, I approve the words of Eleazar, the son of Arach, rather than your words, for in his words yours are included. (15.) They each said three things. R. Eliezer said, Let your friend's honor be as dear to you as your own; and be not easily moved to anger; and repent one day before your death. And (he further said), Warm yourself by the fire of the wise; but beware of their glowing coals, lest you be burnt, for their bite is the bite of the fox, and their sting is the scorpion's sting, and their hiss is the serpent's hiss, and all their words are like coals of fire. (16.) R. Joshua said, The evil eye, the evil inclination, and hatred of his fellow-creatures put a man out of the world. (17.) R. Jose said, Let the property of your friend be as dear to you as your own; qualify yourself for the study of the Torah, since the knowledge of it is not an inheritance of yours, and let all your deeds be done for the sake of Heaven. (18.) R. Simeon said, Be careful to read the Shema' and to say the Amidah; and when you pray, regard not your prayer as a fixed mechanical task, but as an appeal for mercy and grace before the All-present, as it is said, For he is gracious and full of mercy, slow to anger and abounding in loving-kindness, and repents him of the evil (Joel ii. 13); and be not wicked in your own esteem. (19.) R. Eleazar said, Be watchful in the study of the Torah, and know what answer to give to the unbeliever; know also before whom you toil, and who your Employer is, who will pay you the reward of your labor. (20.) Rabbi Tarfon said. The day is short, and the work is great, and the laborers are sluggish, and the reward is much, and the Master of the house is urgent. (21.) He used also to say, It is not your duty to complete the work, but neither are you free to desist from it; if you have studied much Torah, much reward will be given you; and faithful is your Employer to pay you the reward of your labor; and know that the grant of reward unto the righteous will be in the time to come.

Rabbi Chananya, the son of Akashya, said, The Holy One, blessed be he, was pleased to make Israel worthy; wherefore he gave them a copious Torah and many commandments, as it is said, It pleased the Lord, for his righteousness' sake, to magnify the Torah and make it honorable (Isaiah xlii. 21).

CHAPTER III

All Israel have a portion in the world to come, as it is said (Isaiah lx. 21), And your people shall be all righteous; they shall inherit the land forever, the branch of my planting, the work of my hands, that I may be glorified.

(1.) Akabya, the son of Mahalalel, said, Reflect upon three things, and you will not come within the power of sin: know from where you came, and whither you are going, and before whom you will in future have to give account and reckoning. From where you came—from a putrefying drop; whither you are going—to a place of dust, worms and maggots; and before whom you will in future have to give account and reckoning—before the Supreme King of kings, the Holy One, blessed be he. (2.) R. Chanina, the Vice-High-Priest, said, Pray for the welfare of the government, since but for the year thereof men would swallow each other alive. (3.) R. Chananya, the son of Teradyon, said, If two sit together and interchange no words of Torah, they are a meeting of scorners, concerning whom it is said, The godly man sits not in the seat of the scorners (Ps. i. 1); but if two sit together and interchange words of Torah, the Divine Presence abides between them; as it is said, Then they that feared the Lord snake one with the other: and the Lord hearkened and heard, and a book of remembrance was written before him, for them that feared the Lord, and that thought upon his name (Mal. iii. 16). Now, the Scripture enables me to draw this inference in respect to two persons; whence can it be deduced that if even one person sedulously occupies himself with the Torah, the Holy One, blessed be he, appoints unto him a reward? Because it is said, Though he sit alone, and meditate in stillness, yet he takes it (the reward) upon him (Lam. iii. 27). (4.) R. Simeon said, If three have eaten at a table and have spoken there no words of Torah, it is as if they had eaten of sacrifices to dead idols, of whom it is said, For all their tables are full of vomit and filthiness; the All-present is not (in their thoughts) (Isa. xxviii. 8). But if three have eaten at a table and have spoken there words of Torah, it is as if they had eaten at the table of the All-present, to which the Scripture may be applied, And he said unto me, This is the table that is before the Lord (Ezek. xli. 22). (5.) R. Chanina, the son of Chachinai, said, He who keeps awake at night, and goes on his way alone, while turning his heart to vanity, such a one forfeits his own life. (6.) R. Nechunya, son of Hakkanah, said, Who receives upon himself the yoke of the Torah, from him the yoke of the kingdom and the yoke of worldly care will be removed; but who breaks off from him the yoke of the Torah, upon him will be laid the yoke of the kingdom and the yoke of worldly care. (7.) R. Chalafta, the son of Dosa, of the village of Chananya, said, When ten people sit together and occupy themselves with the Torah, the Shechinah abides among them, as it is said, God stands in the congregation of the godly (Psalm lxxxii. 1). And whence can it be shown that the same applies to five? Because it is said, He has founded his band upon the earth (Amos ix. 6). And whence can it be shown that the same applies to three? Because it is said, He judges among the judges (Psa. lxxxii. 1). And whence can it be shown that the same applies to two? Because it is said, Then they that feared the Lord spoke one with the other; and the Lord hearkened, and heard (Mal. iii. 16). And whence can it be shown that the same applies even to one? Because it is said, In every place where I cause my name to be remembered I will come unto you and I will bless you (Exod. xx. 24). (8.) R. Eleazar, of Bertotha, said, Give unto Him of what is His, seeing that you and what you have are His: this is also found expressed by David, who said, For all things come of you, and of Your own we have given You (1 Chron. xxix. 14). (9.) R. Jacob said, He who is walking by the way and studying, and breaks off his study and says, How fine is that tree, how fine is that fallow, him the Scripture regards as if he had forfeited his life. (10.) R. Dostai, the son of Yannai, said in the name of R. Meir, Who forgets one word of his study, him the Scripture regards as if he had forfeited his life, for it is said, Only take heed to yourself, and keep your soul diligently, lest you forget the things which your eyes have seen (Deut. iv. 9). Now, one might suppose that the same result follows even if a man's study has been too hard for him. To guard against such an inference, it is said (ibid.), And lest they depart from your mouth all the days of your life. Thus, a person's guilt is not established until he deliberately and of set purpose removes those lessons from his heart. (11.) R. Chanina, the son of Dosa, said, He in whom the fear of sin comes before wisdom, his wisdom shall endure; but he in whom wisdom comes before the fear of sin, his wisdom will not endure. (12.) He used to say, He whose works exceed his wisdom, his wisdom shall endure; but he whose wisdom exceeds his works, his wisdom will not endure. (13.) He used to say, He in whom the spirit of his fellow-creatures takes delight, in him the Spirit of the All-present takes delight; and he in whom the spirit of his fellow-creatures takes not delight, in him the Spirit of the All-present takes not delight. (14.) R. Dosa, the son of Horkinas, said Morning sleep, and midday wine, and children's talk, and attending the houses of assembly of the ignorant put a man out of the world. (15.) R. Eleazar Hammudai said, He who profanes things sacred, and despises the festivals, and puts his fellow-man to shame in public, and makes void the covenant of Abraham our father, and makes the Torah bear a meaning other than the right, such a one, even though knowledge of the Torah and good deeds be his, has no share in the world to come. (16.) R. Ishmael said, Be submissive to a superior, affable to a suppliant, and receive all men with cheerfulness. (17.) R. Akiba said, Jesting and levity lead a man on to lewdness. The Massorah is a fence to the Torah. Tithes are a fence to riches; vows are a fence to abstinence; a fence to wisdom is silence. (18.) He used to say, Beloved is man, for he was created in the image of God; but it was by a special love that it was made known to him that he was created in the image of God, as it is said, For in the image of God made he man (Gen. ix. 6). Beloved are Israel, for they were called children of the All-present; but it was by a special love that it was made known to them that they were called children of the All-present, as it is said, you are children unto the Lord your God (Deut. xiv. 1). Beloved are Israel, for unto them was given the desirable instrument; but it was by a special love that it was made known to them that that desirable instrument was theirs, through which the world was created, as it is said, For I give you good doctrine: forsake you not my Law (Prov. iv. 2). (19.) Everything is foreseen, yet freedom of choice is given; and the world is judged by grace, yet all is according to the amount of the work. (20.) He used to say, Everything is given on pledge, and a net is spread for all the living: the shop is open; and the dealer gives credit; and the ledger lies open; and the hand writes; and whoever wishes to borrow may come and borrow; but the collectors regularly make their daily round, and exact payment from man whether he be content or not, and they have that whereon they can rely in their demand, and the judgment is a judgment of truth; and everything is prepared for the feast. (21.) R. Eleazar, the son of Azariah, said, Where there is no Torah, there are no manners; where there are no manners, there is no Torah: where there is no wisdom, there is no fear of God; where there is no fear of God, there is no wisdom; where there is no knowledge, there is no understanding; where there is no understanding, there is no knowledge: where there is no meal, there is no Torah; where there is no Torah, there is no meal. (22.) He used to say, He whose wisdom exceeds his works, to what is he like? To a tree whose branches are many, but whose roots are few; and the wind comes and plucks it up and overturns it upon its face, as it is said, And he shall be like a lonely juniper tree in the desert, and shall not see when good comes but shall inhabit the parched places in the wilderness, a salt land and not inhabited (Jeremiah xvii. 6). But he whose works exceed his wisdom, to what is he like? To a tree whose branches are few, but whose roots are many, so that even if all the winds in the world come and blow upon it, it cannot be stirred from its place, as it is said, And he shall be as a tree planted by the waters; and that spreads out its roots by the river, and shall not perceive when heat comes, but his leaf shall be green; and shall not be troubled in the year of drought, neither shall cease from yielding fruit (Jeremiah xvii. 8). (23.) R. Eleazar Chisma said, The laws concerning the sacrifices of birds and the purification of women are ordinances of moment; astronomy and geometry are the after-courses of wisdom.

Rabbi Chananya, the son of Akashya, said, The Holy One, blessed be he, was pleased to make Israel worthy; wherefore he gave them a copious Torah and many commandments, as it is said, It pleased the Lord, for his righteousness' sake, to magnify the Torah and make it honorable (Isaiah xlii. 21).

CHAPTER IV

All Israel have a portion in the world to come, as it is said (Isaiah lx. 21), And your people shall be all righteous; they shall inherit the land forever, the branch of my planting, the work of my hands, that I may be glorified.

(1.) Ben Zoma said, Who is wise? He who learns from all men, as it is said, From all my teachers I have gotten understanding (Psalm cxix. 99). Who is mighty? He who subdues his passions, as it is said, He that is slow to anger is better than the mighty, and he that rules over his spirit than he that takes a city (Prov. xvi. 32). Who is rich? He who rejoices in his portion, as it is said, When you eat the labor of your hands, happy are you, and it shall be well with you (Psalm cxxviii. 2); happy are you in this world, and it shall be well with you in the world to come. Who is honored? He who honors others, as it is said, For them that honor me I will honor, and they that despise me shall be held in contempt (1 Sam. ii. 30). (2.) Ben Azzai said, Run to do even a slight precept, and flee from transgression; for precept draws precept in its train, and transgression, transgression; for the recompense of a precept is a precept, and the recompense of a transgression, a transgression. (3.) He used to say, Despise not any man, and carp not at anything; for there is not a man that has not his hour, and there is not a thing that has not its place. (4.) R. Levitas, of Yavneh, said, Be exceedingly lowly of spirit, since the hope of man is but the worm. (5.) R. Yochanan, the son of Berokah, said, Whoever profanes the Name of Heaven in secret will suffer the penalty for it in public; and this, whether the Heavenly Name be profaned in ignorance or in willfulness. (6.) R. Ishmael, his son, said, He who learns in order to teach, to him the means will be vouchsafed both to learn and to teach; but he who learns in order to practice, to him the means will be vouchsafed to learn and to teach, to observe and to practice. (7.) R. Zadok said, Separate not yourself from the congregation; (in the judge's office) act not the counsel's part; make not of the Torah a crown with which to aggrandize yourself, nor a spade with which to dig. So also used Hillel to say, He who makes a worldly use of the crown of the Torah shall waste away. Hence you may infer, that whoever derives a profit for himself from the words of the Torah is helping on his own destruction. (8.) R. Jose said, Who honors the Torah will himself be honored by mankind, but who dishonors the Torah will himself be dishonored by mankind. (9.) R. Ishmael, his son, said, He who shuns the judicial office rids himself of hatred, robbery and vain swearing; but he who presumptuously lays down is foolish, wicked and of an arrogant spirit. (10.) He used to say, Judge not alone, for none may judge alone save One; neither say (to your judicial colleagues), Accept my view, for the choice is theirs (to concur); and it is not for you (to compel concurrence). (11.) R. Jonathan said, Who fulfils the Torah in the midst of poverty shall in the end fulfil it in the midst of wealth; and who neglects the Torah in the midst of wealth shall in the end neglect it in the midst of poverty. (12.) R. Meir said, Lessen your toil for worldly goods, and be busy in the Torah; be humble of spirit before all men; if you neglect the Torah, many causes for neglecting it will present themselves to you, but if you labor in the Torah, He has abundant recompense to give you. (13.) R. Eliezer, the son of Jacob, said, He who does one precept has gotten himself one advocate; and he who commits one transgression has gotten himself one accuser. Repentance and good deeds are as a shield against punishment. (14.) R. Yochanan, the sandal maker, said, Every assembly which is in the Name of Heaven will in the end be established, but that which is not in the Name of Heaven will not in the end be established. (15.) R. Eleazar, the son of Shammua, said, Let the honor of your disciple be as dear to you as your own, and the honor of your associate be like the fear of your master, and the fear of your master like the fear of Heaven. (16.) Judah said, Be cautious in study, for an error in study may amount to presumptuous sin. (17.) R. Simeon said, There are three crowns: the crown of Torah, the crown of priesthood, and the crown of kingdom; but the crown of a good name excels them all. (18.) R. Nehorai said, Wander forth to a home of the Torah, and say not that the Torah will come after you; for there your associates will establish you in the possession of it; and lean not upon your own understanding. (19.) R. Yannai said, It is not in our power to explain either the prosperity of the wicked or the afflictions of the righteous. (20.) R. Mattithyah, the son of Cheresh, said, Be beforehand in the salutation of peace to all men; and be rather a tail to lions than a head to foxes. (21.) R. Jacob said, This world is like a vestibule before the world to come; prepare yourself in the vestibule, that you may enter into the hall. (22.) He used to say, Better is one hour of repentance and good deeds in this world than the whole life of the world to come; and better is one hour of blissfulness of spirit in the world to come than the whole life of this world (23.) R. Simeon, the son of Eleazar, said, Do not appease your fellow in the hour of his anger, and comfort him not in the hour when his dead lies before him, and question him not in the hour of his vow, and strive not to see him in the hour of his disgrace. (24.) Samuel the younger used to quote, Rejoice not when your enemy falls, and let not your heart be glad when he stumbles: lest the Lord see it and it displease him, and he turn away his wrath from him (Prov. xxiv. 17, 18). (25.) Elisha, the son of Abuyah, said, If one learns as a child, what is it like? Like ink written on clean paper. If one learns as an old man, what is it like? Like ink written on blotted paper. (26.) R. Jose, the son of Judah, of Chephar Babli, said, He who learns from the young, to what is he like? To one who eats unripe grapes, and drinks wine from his vat. And he who learns from the old, to what is he like? To one who eats ripe grapes, and drinks old wine. (27.) R. Meir said, Look not at the flask, but at what it contains: there may be a new flask full of old wine, and an old flask that has not even new wine in it. (28.) R. Eleazar Hakkappar said, Envy, cupidity and ambition take a man from the world. (29.)He used to say, They that are born are destined to die; and the dead to be brought to life again; and the living to be judged, to know, to make known, and to be made conscious that he is God, he the Maker, he the Creator, he the Discerner, he the Judge, he the Witness, he the Complainant; he it is that will in future judge, blessed be he, with whom there is no unrighteousness, nor forgetfulness, nor respect of persons, nor taking of bribes: know also that everything is according to the reckoning: and let not your imagination give you hope that the grave will be a place of refuge for you; for perforce you were formed, and perforce you were born, and you live perforce, and perforce you will die, and perforce you will in the future have to give account and reckoning before the Supreme King of kings, the Holy One, blessed be he.

Rabbi Chananya, the son of Akashya, said, The Holy One blessed be he, was pleased to make Israel worthy; wherefore he gave them a copious Torah and many commandments, as it is said, It pleased the Lord, for his righteousness' sake, to magnify the Torah and make it honorable (Isaiah xlii. 21).

CHAPTER V

All Israel have a portion in the world to come, as it is said (Isaiah lx. 21), And your people shall be all righteous; they shall inherit the land forever, the branch of my planting, the work of my hands, that I may be glorified.

(1) With ten Sayings the world was created. What does this teach us? Could it not have been created with one Saying? It is to make known the punishment that will befall the wicked who destroy the world that was created with ten Sayings, as well as the goodly reward that will be bestowed upon the just who preserve the world that was created with ten sayings. (2.) There were ten generations from Adam to Noah, to make known how longsuffering God is, seeing that all those generations continued provoking him, until he brought upon them the waters of the flood. (3.) There were ten generations from Noah to Abraham, to make known how longsuffering God is, seeing that all those generations continued provoking him, until Abraham our father came, and received the reward they should all have earned. (4.) With ten trials our father Abraham was tried, and he stood firm in them all, to make known how great was the love of our father Abraham. (5.) Ten miracles were wrought for our fathers in Egypt, and ten at the Sea. (6.) Ten plagues did the Holy One, blessed be he, bring upon the Egyptians in Egypt, and ten at the Sea. (7.) With ten temptations did our fathers tempt the Holy One, blessed be he, in the wilderness, as it is said, And they have tempted me these ten times, and have not hearkened to my voice (Numb. xiv. 22). (8.) Ten miracles were wrought for our fathers in the Temple: no woman miscarried from the scent of the holy flesh; the holy flesh never became putrid; no fly was seen in the slaughter house: no unclean accident ever befell the high priest on the Day of Atonement; the rain never quenched the fire of the wood-pile on the altar; neither did the wind overcome the column of smoke that arose therefrom; nor was there ever found any disqualifying defect in the omer (of new barley, offered on the second day of Passover), or in the two loaves (the first fruits of the wheat-harvest, offered on Pentecost), or in the showbread; though the people stood closely pressed together, they found ample space to prostrate themselves; never did serpent or scorpion injure any one in Jerusalem; nor did any man ever say to his fellow, The place is too strait for me to lodge overnight in Jerusalem. (9.) Ten things were created on the eve of Sabbath in the twilight: the mouth of the earth (Numb. xvi. 32); the mouth of the well (Ibid. xxi. 16); the mouth of the ass (Ibid. xxii. 28); the rainbow; the manna; the rod (Exod. iv. 17); the Shamir; the shape of the written characters; the writing, and the tables of stone: some say the destroying spirits also, and the sepulcher of Moses, and the ram of Abraham our father; and others say, tongs also made with tongs. (10.) There are seven marks of an uncultured, and seven of a wise man. The wise man does not speak before him who is greater than he in wisdom; and does not break in upon the speech of his fellow; he is not hasty to answer; he questions according to the subject matter, and answers to the point; he speaks upon the first thing first, and upon the last last; regarding that which he has not understood he says, I do not understand it, and he acknowledges the truth. The reverse of all this is to be found in an uncultured man. (11.) Seven kinds of punishment come into the world for seven important transgressions. If some give their tithes and others do not, a dearth ensues

from drought, and some suffer hunger while others are full. If they all determine to give no tithes, a dearth ensues from tumult and drought. If they further resolve not to give the dough-cake (Numb. xv. 20), an exterminating dearth ensues. Pestilence comes into the world to fulfil those death penalties threatened in the Torah, the execution of which, however, is not within the function of a human tribunal, and for the violation of the law regarding the fruits of the seventh year (Levit. xxv. 1-7). The sword comes into the world for the delay of justice, and for the perversion of justice, and on account of the offence of those who interpret the Torah not according to its true sense. Noxious beasts come into the world for vain swearing, and for the profanation of the Divine Name. Captivity comes into the world on account of idolatry, immorality, bloodshed, and the neglect of the year of rest for the soil. (12.) At four periods pestilence grows apace: in the fourth year, in the seventh, at the conclusion of the seventh year, and at the conclusion of the Feast of Sukkot in each year: in the fourth year, for default of giving the tithe to the poor in the third year (Deut. xiv. 28, 29); in the seventh year, for default of giving the tithe to the poor in the sixth year; at the conclusion of the seventh year, for the violation of the law regarding the fruits of the seventh year, and at the conclusion of the Feast of Sukkot in each year, for robbing the poor of the grants legally assigned to them. (13.) There are four characters among men: he who says, What is my is my and what is yours is yours, his is a neutral character—some say, this is a character like that of Sodom; he who says, What is my is yours and what is yours is mine, is a boor; he who says, What is my is yours and what is yours is yours, is a saint; he who says, What is yours is my and what is my is mine, is a wicked man. (14.) There are four kinds of tempers: he whom it is easy to provoke and easy to pacify, his loss disappears in his gain; he whom it is hard to provoke and hard to pacify, his gain disappears in his loss; he whom it is hard to provoke and easy to pacify is a saint; he whom it is easy to provoke and hard to pacify is a wicked man. (15.) There are four qualities in disciples: he who quickly understands and quickly forgets, his gain disappears in his loss; he who understands with difficulty and forgets with difficulty, his loss disappears in his gain; he who understands quickly and forgets with difficulty, his is a good portion; he who understands with difficulty and forgets quickly, his is an evil portion. (16.) As to almsgiving there are four dispositions: he who desires to give, but that others should not give, his eye is evil towards what appertains to others (since almsgiving brings blessing to the giver); he who desires that others should give, but will not give himself, his eye is evil against what is his own; he who gives and wishes others to give is a saint; he who will not give and does not wish others to give is a wicked man. (17.) There are four characters suggested by those who attend the house of study: he who goes and does not practice secures the reward for going; he who practices but does not go secures the reward for practicing; he who goes and practices is a saint; he who neither goes nor practices is a wicked man. (18.) There are four qualities among those that sit before the wise: they are like a sponge, a funnel, a strainer, or a sieve: a sponge, which sucks up everything; a funnel, which lets in at one end and out at the other; a strainer, which lets the wine pass out and retains the lees; a sieve, which lets out the bran and retains the fine flour. (19.) Whenever love depends upon some material cause, with the passing away of that cause, the love too passes away; but if it be not dependent upon such a cause, it will not pass away forever. Which love was that which depended upon a material cause? Such was the love of Amnon and Tamar. And that which depended upon no such cause? Such was the love of David and Jonathan. (20.) Every controversy that is in the Name of Heaven shall in the end lead to a permanent result, but every controversy that is not in the Name of Heaven shall not lead to a permanent result. Which controversy was that which was in the Name of Heaven? Such was the controversy of Hillel and Shammai. And that which was not in the Name of Heaven? Such was the controversy of Korah and all his company. (21.) Whoever causes the multitude to be righteous, through him no sin shall be brought about: but he who causes the multitude to sin shall not have the means to repent (the sins of others being beyond the remedial action of his repentance). Moses was righteous and made the multitude righteous; the righteousness of the multitude was laid upon him, as it is said, He executed the justice of the Lord and his judgments with Israel (Deut. xxxiii. 21). Jeroboam, the son of Nebat, sinned and caused the multitude to sin: the sin of the multitude was laid upon him, as it is said, For the sins of Jeroboam which he sinned and which he made Israel to sin (1 Kings xv. 30). (22.) Whoever has these three attributes is of the disciples of Abraham our father, but whoever has three other attributes is of the disciples of Balaam the wicked. A good eye, a humble mind and a lowly spirit (are the tokens) of the disciples of Abraham our father; an evil eye, a haughty mind and a proud spirit (are the signs) of the disciples of Balaam the wicked. What is the difference between the disciples of Abraham our father and those of Balaam the wicked? The disciples of Abraham our father enjoy this world and inherit the world to come, as it is said, That I may cause those that love me to inherit substance, and may fill all their treasuries (Prov. viii. 21); the disciples of Balaam the wicked inherit Gehinnom and descend into the pit of destruction, as it is said, But you, O God, will bring them down into the pit of destruction: bloodthirsty and deceitful men shall not live out half their days; but I will trust in you (Psalm lv. 24). (23.) Judah, the son of Tema, said, Be strong as a leopard, light as an eagle, fleet as a hart, and strong as a lion, to do the will of your Father who is in heaven. He used to say, The bold-faced are for Gehinnom, the shame-faced for the Garden of Eden. (He said further) May it be your will, O Lord our God and God of our fathers, that the Temple be speedily rebuilt in our days, and grant our portion in your Torah. (24.) He used to say, At five years the age is reached for the study of the Scripture, at ten for the study of the Mishnah, at thirteen for the fulfilment of the commandments, at fifteen for the study of the Talmud, at eighteen for marriage, at twenty for seeking a livelihood, at thirty for entering into one's full strength, at forty for understanding, at fifty for counsel, at sixty a man attains old age, at seventy the hoary head, at eighty the gift of special strength (Psalm xc. 10), at ninety he bends beneath the weight of years, at a hundred he is as if he were already dead and had passed away from the world. (25.) Ben Bag Bag said, Turn it (the Torah) and turn it over again, for everything is in it, and contemplate it, and wax gray and old over it, and stir not from it, for you canst have no better rule than this. (26.) Ben He He said, According to the labor is the reward.

Rabbi Hananya, the son of Akashya, said, The Holy One, blessed be he, was pleased to make Israel worthy; wherefore he gave them a copious Torah and many commandments, as it is said, It pleased the Lord, for his righteousness' sake, to magnify the Torah and make it honorable (Isaiah xlii. 21).

CHAPTER VI

All Israel have a portion in the world to come, as it is said (Isaiah lx. 21), And your people shall be all righteous; they shall inherit the land forever, the branch of my planting, the work of my hands, that I may be glorified.

The sages taught the following in the style of the Mishnah,—Blessed be he that made choice of them and their Mishnah. (1.) R. Meir said. Whoever labors in the Torah for its own sake merits many things;

and not only so, but the whole world is indebted to him: he is called friend, beloved, a lover of the All-present, a lover of mankind: it clothes him in meekness and reverence; it fits him to become just, pious, upright and faithful; it keeps him far from sin, and brings him near to virtue: through him the world enjoys counsel and sound knowledge, understanding and strength, as it is said, Counsel is mine, and sound knowledge; I am understanding; I have strength (Prov. viii. 14): and it gives him sovereignty and dominion and discerning judgment; to him the secrets of the Torah are revealed; he is made like a never-failing fountain, and like a river that flows on with ever-sustained vigor he becomes modest, longsuffering, and forgiving of insults; and it magnifies and exalts him above all things. (2.) R. Joshua, the son of Levi, said, Every day a Bath-kol (a heavenly voice) goes forth from Mount Sinai, proclaiming these words, Woe to mankind for contempt of the Torah, for whoever does not labor in the Torah is said to be under the divine censure, as it is said, As a ring of gold in a swine's snout, so is a fair woman who turns aside from discretion (Prov. xi. 22); and it says, And the tables were the work of God, and the writing was the writing of God, graven upon the tables. Read not charuth (graven), but cheruth (freedom), for no man is free but he who labors in the Torah. But whoever labors in the Torah, behold he shall be exalted, as it is said, And from Mattanah to Nachaliel, and from Nachaliel to Bamoth (Numb. xxi. 19). (3.) He who learns from his fellow a single chapter, a single rule, a single verse, a single expression, or even a single letter, ought to pay him honor, for so we find with David, King of Israel, who learnt only two things from Ahitophel, and yet regarded him as his master, His guide and his familiar friend, as it is said, But it was you, a man, my equal, my guide, and my familiar friend (Psalm lv. 14). Now, is it not an argument from minor to major? Ii David, the King of Israel, who learned only two things from Ahitophel, regarded him as his master, guide and familiar friend, how much more ought one who learns from his fellow a chapter, rule, verse, expression, or even a single letter, to pay him honor? And honor is nothing but Torah, as it is said, The wise shall inherit honor (Prov. iii. 35); and the perfect shall inherit good (Ibid. xxviii. 10). And good is nothing but Torah, as it is said, For I give you good doctrine, forsake you not my Torah (Ibid. iv. 2). (4.) This is the way that is becoming for the study of the Torah: a morsel of bread with salt you must eat, and water by measure you must drink, you must sleep upon the ground, and live a life of trouble the while you toil in the Torah. If you do this, Happy shall you be and it shall be well with you (Psalm cxxviii. 2); happy shall you be in this world, and it shall be well with you in the world to come. (5.) Seek not greatness for yourself, and court not honor; let your works exceed your learning; and crave not after the table of kings; for your table is greater than theirs, and your crown is greater than theirs, and your Employer is faithful to pay you the reward of your work. (6.) The Torah is greater than the priesthood and than royalty, seeing that royalty demands thirty qualifications, the priesthood twenty-four, while the Torah is acquired by forty-eight. And these are they: By audible study; by distinct pronunciation; by understanding and discernment of the heart; by awe, reverence, meekness, cheerfulness; by ministering to the sages, by attaching oneself to colleagues, by discussion with disciples; by sedateness; by knowledge of the Scripture and of the Mishnah; by moderation in business, in intercourse with the world, in pleasure, in sleep, in conversation, in laughter; by longsuffering; by a good heart; by faith in the wise; by resignation under chastisement; by recognizing one's place, rejoicing in one's portion, putting a fence to one's words, claiming no merit for oneself; by being beloved, loving the All-present, loving mankind, loving just courses, rectitude and reproof; by keeping oneself far from honor, not boasting of one's learning, nor delighting in giving decisions; by bearing the yoke with one's fellow, judging him favorably, and leading him to truth and peace; by being composed in one's study; by asking and answering, hearing and adding thereto (by one's own reflection); by learning with the object of teaching, and by learning with the object of practicing; by making one's master wiser, fixing attention upon his discourse, and reporting a thing in the name of him who said it. So you have learnt, Whoever reports a thing in the name of him who said it brings deliverance into the world, as it is said, And Esther told the king in the name of Mordecai (Esther ii. 22). (7.) Great is the Torah which gives life to those that practice it in this world and in the world to come, as it is said, For they are life unto those that find them, and health to all their flesh (Prov. iv. 22); and it says, It shall be health to your navel, and marrow to your bones (Ibid. iii. 8); and it says, It is a tree of life to them that grasp it, and of them that uphold it every one is rendered happy (Ibid. iii. 18); and it says, For they shall be a chaplet of grace unto your head, and chains about your neck (Ibid. i. 9); and it says, It shall give to your head a chaplet of grace: a crown of glory it shall deliver to you (Ibid. iv. 9); and it says, For by me your days shall be multiplied, and the years of your life shall be increased (Ibid. ix. 11); and it says, Length of days is in its right hand; in its left hand are riches and honor (Ibid. iii. 16); and it says, For length of days, and years of life, and peace shall they add to you (Ibid. iii. 2). (8.) R. Simeon, the son of Judah, in the name of R. Simeon, the son of Yochai, said, Beauty, strength, riches, honor, wisdom, old age and a hoary head and children are comely to the righteous and comely to the world, as it is said, The hoary head is a crown of glory, if it be found in the way of righteousness (Ibid. xvi. 31); and it says, The glory of young men is their strength, and the adornment of old men is the hoary head (Ibid. xx. 29); and it says, A crown unto the wise is their riches (Ibid. xiv. 24); and it says, Children's children are the crown of old men, and the adornment of children are their fathers (Ibid. xvii. 6); and it is said, Then the moon shall be confounded and the sun ashamed; for the Lord of hosts shall reign in Mount Zion and in Jerusalem, and before his elders shall be glory (Isaiah xxiv. 23). R. Simeon, the son of Menasya, said, These seven qualifications which the sages enumerated as becoming to the righteous were all realized in Rabbi Judah the Prince, and in his sons. (9.) R. Jose, the son of Kisma, said, I was once walking by the way, when a man met me and saluted me, and I returned the salutation. He said to me, Rabbi, from what place are you? I said to him, I come from a great city of sages and scribes. He said to me, If you are willing to dwell with us in our place, I will give you a thousand thousand golden dinars and precious stones and pearls. I said to him, Were you to give me all the silver and gold and precious stones and pearls in the world, I would not dwell anywhere but in a home of the Torah; and thus it is written in the book of Psalms by the hands of David, King of Israel, The law of your mouth is better unto me than thousands of gold and silver (Psalm cxix. 72); and not only so, but in the hour of man's departure neither silver nor gold nor precious stones nor pearls accompany him, but only Torah and good works, as it is said, When you walk it shall lead you; when you lie down it shall watch over you; and when you awake it shall talk with you (Prov. vi. 22)—when you walk it shall lead you—in this world; when you lie down it shall watch over you—in the grave; and when you awake it shall talk with you—in the world to come. And it says, The silver is mine, and the gold is mine, says the Lord of hosts (Haggai ii. 8). (10.) Five pos. sessions the Holy One, blessed be he, made especially his own in his world, and these are they, The Torah, heaven and earth, Abraham, Israel, and the house of the sanctuary. Whence know we this of the Torah? Because it is written, The Lord possessed me as the beginning of his way, before his works, from of old (Prov. viii. 22). Whence of heaven and earth? Because it is written, Thus says the Lord, The heaven is my throne, and the earth is my footstool: what manner of house will you build unto me? and what manner of place for my rest? (Isaiah lxvi. 1); and it says, How manifold are your works, O Lord! In wisdom have you made them all: the earth is full of your possessions (Psalm civ. 24). Whence of Abraham? Because it is written, And he blessed him, and said, Blessed be Abram of the Most High God, possessor of heaven and earth (Genesis xiv. 19). Whence of Israel? Because it is written, Till your people pass over, O Lord, till the people pass over which you have acquired (Exod. xv. 16); and it says, As for the saints that are in the earth, they are noble ones in whom is all my delight (Psalm xvi. 3). Whence of the house of the sanctuary? Because it is written, The place, O Lord, which you have made for you to dwell in, the sanctuary, O Lord, which your hands have prepared (Exod. xv. 17); and it says, And he brought them to the border of his sanctuary, to this mountain which his right hand had acquired (Psalm lxxviii. 54). (11). Whatsoever the Holy One, blessed be he, created, in his world he created but for his glory, as it is said, Everything that is called by my name, it is for my glory I have created it, I have formed it, yea, I have made it (Isaiah xliii. 7); and it says, The Lord shall reign forever and ever (Exod. xv. 18).

Rabbi Hananya, the son of Akashya, said, The Holy One, blessed be he, was pleased to make Israel worthy; wherefore he gave them a copious Torah and many commandments, as it is said, It pleased the Lord, for his righteousness' sake, to magnify the Torah and make it honorable (Isaiah xlii. 21).

"It is our duty," etc. *Mourner's Kaddish.*

SERVICE FOR THE CONCLUSION OF THE SABBATH
Psalm cxliv.

A Psalm of David. Blessed be the Lord my rock, who teaches my hands to war, and my fingers to fight: my loving-kindness, and my fortress, my stronghold, and my deliverer; my shield, and he in whom I take refuge: who subdues my people under me. Lord, what is man, that you regard him? or the son of man, that you take account of him? Man is like to vanity: his days are as a shadow that passes away. Bow your heavens, O Lord, and come down: touch the mountains, and they shall smoke. Flash forth lightning, and scatter them: send out your arrows, and discomfit them. Stretch forth your hands from above; rescue me, and deliver me out of great waters, out of the hand of strangers; whose mouth speaks vanity, and their right hand is a right hand of falsehood. I will sing a new song unto you, O God: upon a harp of ten strings will I sing praises unto you. It is he that gives salvation unto kings: who rescues David his servant from the hurtful sword. Rescue me, and deliver me out of the hand of strangers, whose mouth speaks vanity, and their right hand is a right hand of falsehood.—When our sons shall be as plants grown tall in their youth, and our daughters as corner-stones hewn after the fashion of a palace; when our garners are full, affording all manner of store, and our sheep bring forth by thousands; yea, are multiplied by tens of thousands in our fields; when our oxen are well laden; when there is no breach and no surrender; and no lamentation in our streets; happy is the people, that is in such a case: yea, happy is the people, whose God is the Lord.

Psalm lxvii.

For the Chief Musician; on Neginoth. A Psalm, A Song. May God be gracious unto us, and bless us; may he cause his face to shine upon us. (Selah.) That your way may be known upon the earth, your salvation among all nations. Let the peoples give thanks unto you, O God; let all the peoples give thanks unto you.

O let the nations rejoice and exult: for you will judge the peoples with equity, and lead the nations upon the earth. (Selah.) Let the peoples give thanks unto you, O God; let all the peoples give thanks unto you. The earth has yielded her increase: God, even our God, shall bless us. God shall bless us; and all the ends of the earth shall fear him.

For Evening Service, Amidah and Kaddish to "And say you Amen." Then say the following:

And let the pleasantness of the Lord our God be upon us: and establish you the work of our hands upon us; yea, the work of our hands establish you it.

Psalm xci.

He that dwells in the shelter of the Most High abides under the shadow of the Almighty. I say of the Lord, He is my refuge and my fortress; my God in whom I trust.—For he shall deliver you from the snare of the fowler, and from the noisome pestilence. He shall cover you with his pinions, and under his wings shall you take refuge: his truth shall be a shield and a buckler. You shall not be afraid of the terror by night, nor of the arrow that flies by day; of the pestilence that walks in darkness, nor of the plague that ravages at noon day. A thousand may fall at your side, and ten thousand at your right hand; it shall not come nigh unto you. Only with your eyes shall you look on, and see the retribution of the wicked. For you, O Lord, are my refuge.—You have made the Most High your dwelling place; there shall no evil befall you, neither shall any scourge come nigh your tent. For he shall give his angels charge over you, to keep you in all your ways. They shall bear you upon their hands, lest you strike your foot against a stone. You shall tread upon the lion and the adder: upon the young lion and the serpent shall you trample.— Because he has set his love upon me, therefore will I deliver him: I will set him on high, because he knows my name. When he calls upon me, I will answer him; I will be with him in trouble: I will deliver him and honor him. With length of days will I satisfy him, and will let him see my salvation. Repeat the last verse.

But you are holy, O you that dwell amid the praises of Israel And one cried unto another, and said, Holy, holy, holy is the Lord of hosts: the whole earth is full of his glory. And they receive sanction the one from the other, and say, Holy in the highest heavens, the place of his divine abode; holy upon earth, the work of his might; holy forever and to all eternity is the Lord of hosts; the whole earth is full of the radiance of his glory. Then a wind lifted me up, and I heard behind me the voice of a great rushing (saying), Blessed be the glory of the Lord from his place. Then a wind lifted me up, and I heard behind me the voice of a great rushing, of those who uttered praises, and said, Blessed be the glory of the Lord from the region of his divine abode. The Lord shall reign forever and ever. The kingdom of the Lord endures forever and to all eternity. O Lord, the God of Abraham, of Isaac and of Israel, our fathers, keep this forever in the imagination of the thoughts of the heart of your people, and direct their heart unto you. And he, being merciful, forgives iniquity and destroys not: yea, many a time he turns his anger away, and does not stir up all his wrath. For you, O Lord, are good and forgiving, and abounding in loving-kindness to all them that call upon you. Your righteousness is an everlasting righteousness, and your Torah is truth. You will show truth to Jacob and loving-kindness to Abraham, according as you have sworn unto our fathers from the days of old. Blessed be the Lord day by day; if one burdens us, God is our salvation. (Selah). The Lord of hosts is with us; the God of Jacob is our stronghold. (Selah.) O Lord of hosts, happy is the man who trusts in you. Save, Lord: may the King answer us on the day when we call. Blessed is our God, who has created us for his glory, and has separated us from them that go astray, and has given us the Torah of truth and planted everlasting life in our midst. May he open our heart unto his Torah, and place his love and fear within our hearts, that we may do his will and serve him with a perfect heart, that we may not labor in vain, nor bring forth for confusion. May it be your will, O Lord our God and God of our fathers, that we may keep your statutes in this world, and be worthy to live to witness and inherit happiness and blessing in the days of the Messiah and in the life of the world to come. To the end that my glory may sing praise unto you, and not be silent: O Lord my God, I will give thanks unto you forever. Blessed is the man that trusts in the Lord, and whose trust the Lord is. Trust you in the Lord forever; for in Yah the Lord is an everlasting rock. And they that know your name will put their trust in you; for you have not forsaken them that seek you, Lord. It pleased the Lord, for his righteousness' sake, to magnify the Torah and to make it honorable.

Should a Festival occur on any day of the following week, "And let the pleasantness," etc., and "But you are holy," are not said. If the Fast of the Ninth of Ab commences at the termination of the Sabbath, "And let the pleasantness," etc., is omitted.

Reader.—Magnified and sanctified be his great name in the world which he has created according to his will. May he establish his kingdom during your life and during your days; and during the life of all the house of Israel, even speedily and at a near time, and say ye, Amen.

Cong. and Reader.—Let his great name be blessed forever and to all eternity.

Reader.—Blessed, praised and glorified, exalted. extolled and honored, magnified and lauded be the name of the Holy One, blessed be he.; though he be high above all the blessings and hymns, praises and consolations, which are uttered in the world; and say you Amen.

Cong.—Accept our prayer in mercy and in favor.

Reader.—May the prayers and supplications of all Israel be accepted by their Father who is in heaven; and say ye, Amen.

Cong.—Let the name of the Lord be blessed from this time forth and forevermore.

Reader.—May there be abundant peace from heaven, and life for us and for all Israel; and say ye, Amen.

Cong.—My help is from the Lord, who made heaven and earth.

Reader.—He who makes peace in his high places, may he make peace for us and for all Israel; and say ye, Amen.

On Chanukah the lights are here kindled by the Reader.

And God give you of the dew of heaven, and of the fatness of the earth, and plenty of corn and wine: let peoples serve you, and nations bow down to you: be lord over your brethren, and let your mother's sons bow down to you: cursed be every one that curses you, and blessed be every one that blesses you. And God Almighty bless you, and make you fruitful, and multiply you, that you may be a company of peoples; and give you the blessing of Abraham, to you and to your seed with you; that you may inherit the land of your sojourning, which God gave unto Abraham. From the God of your father— may he help you,—and the Almighty—may he bless you with blessings of the heavens above, blessings of the deep that couches beneath, blessings of the breasts and the womb. The blessings of your father have prevailed above the blessings of my progenitors unto the utmost bound of the everlasting hills: may they be on the head of Joseph, and on the crown of the head of him that is prince among his brethren. And he will love you, and bless you, and multiply you: he will also bless the fruit of your body and the fruit of your ground, your corn and your wine and your oil, the offspring of your kine and the young of your flock, in the land which he swore to your fathers to give you. You shall be blessed above all peoples: there shall not be male or female barren among you, or among your cattle. And the Lord will take away from you all sickness; and he will put none of the evil diseases of Egypt, which you know, upon you, but will lay them upon all them that hate you.

The angel who has redeemed me from all evil bless the lads; and let my name be named on them, and the name of my fathers Abraham and Isaac; and let them grow into a multitude in the midst of the earth. The Lord your God has multiplied you, and behold you are this day as the stars of heaven for multitude. The Lord, the God of your fathers, make you a thousand times so many more as you are, and bless you, as he has promised you.

Blessed shall you be in the city, and blessed shall you be in the field. Blessed shall you be when you come in, and blessed shall you be when you go out. Blessed shall be your basket and your kneading-trough. Blessed shall be the fruit of your body, and the fruit of your ground, and the fruit of your cattle, the offspring of your kine, and the young of your flock. The Lord shall command the blessing upon you in your barns, and in all that you put your hand unto; and he shall bless you in the land which the Lord your God gives you. The Lord shall open unto you his good treasury, the heavens, to give the rain of your land in its season, and to bless all the work of your hand: and you shall lend unto many nations, but you shall not borrow. For the Lord your God will bless you, as he promised you: and you shall lend unto many nations, but you shall not borrow; and you shall rule over many nations, but they shall not rule over you. Happy are you, O Israel: who is like unto you, a people saved by the Lora, the shield of your help, and that is the sword of your majesty! And your enemies shall submit themselves unto you; and you shall tread upon their high places.

I have blotted out, as a cloud, your transgressions, and, as a mist, your sins; return unto me, for I have redeemed you. Sing, O you heavens, for the Lord has done it; shout, you nethermost parts of the earth; break forth into singing, you mountains, and forest, and every tree therein; for the Lord has redeemed Jacob, and will glorify himself in Israel. Our Redeemer, the Lord of hosts is his name, the Holy One of Israel.

Israel is saved by the Lord with an everlasting salvation: you shall not be ashamed nor confounded forever and ever. And you shall eat in plenty and be satisfied, and shall praise the name of the Lord your God, that has dealt wondrously with you: and my people shall never be ashamed. And you shall know that I am in the midst of Israel, and that I am the Lord your God, and there is none else: and my people shall never be ashamed. For you shall go out with joy, and be led forth with peace: the mountains and the hills shall break forth before you into singing, and all the trees of the field shall clap their hands. Behold, God is my salvation; I will trust, and will not be afraid: for Yah the Lord is my strength and song; and he is become my salvation. Therefore with joy shall you draw water out of the wells of salvation. And in that day shall you say, Give thanks unto the Lord, call upon his name, declare his doings among the peoples, make mention that his name is exalted. Sing unto the Lord; for he has done excellent things: this is made known in all the earth. Cry aloud and shout, you inhabitant of Zion: for great is the Holy One of Israel in the midst of you. And one shall say in that day, Lo, this is our God; we have waited for him that he should save us: this is the Lord; we have waited for him, let us be glad and rejoice in his salvation.

O house of Jacob, come ye, and let us walk in the light of the Lord. And abundance of salvation, wisdom and knowledge shall be the steadfastness of your times: the fear of the Lord is his treasure. And David prospered in all his ways; and the Lord was with him. He has rescued my soul in peace so that none might come nigh me, for they were many that were striving with me. And the people said unto Saul, Shall Jonathan die who has wrought this great salvation in Israel? Far be it; as the Lord lives, there shall not one hair of his head fall to the ground; for he has wrought with God this day. So the people rescued Jonathan that he died not. And the rescued of the Lord shall return, and come with singing unto Zion; and everlasting joy shall be upon their heads: they shall obtain gladness and joy, and sorrow and sighing shall flee away. You have turned for me my mourning into dancing; you have loosed my sackcloth and girded me with gladness And the Lord your God would not hearken unto Balaam; but the Lord your God turned the curse into a blessing unto you, because the Lord your God loved you. Then shall the virgin rejoice in the dance, and the young men and the old together; for I will turn their mourning into joy, and will comfort them, and make them rejoice from their sorrow.

He creates the fruit of the lips: Peace, peace to him that is far off and to him that is near, says the Lord, and I will heal him. Then the spirit came upon Amasai, who was chief of the captains (and he said), Yours are we, David, and on your side, O son of Jesse; peace, peace be unto you, and peace be to him that helps you; for your God helps you. Then David received them, and made them chiefs of the band. And thus you shall say, All hail, and peace be unto you, and peace be to your house, and peace be unto all that you have. The Lord will give strength unto his people; the Lord will bless his people with peace.

Rabbi Yochanan said, In every passage where you find the greatness of God mentioned, there you find also his humility. This is written in the Torah, repeated in the Prophets, and a third time stated in the Writings. It is written in the Torah, for the Lord your God, he is God of gods, and Lord of lords, the great, mighty and revered God, who regards not persons, nor takes a bribe. And it is written afterwards, He does execute the judgment of the fatherless and widow, and loves the stranger, in giving him food and raiment. It is repeated in the Prophets, as it is written, For thus says the high and lofty One that inhabits eternity, and whose name is holy, I dwell in the high and holy place, with him also that is of a contrite and humble spirit, to revive the spirit of the humble, and to revive the heart of the contrite ones. It is a third time stated in the Writings, Sing unto God, sing praises to his name: extol you him that rides upon the heavens by his name Yah, and I rejoice before him. And it is written afterwards, A father of the fatherless, and a judge of the widows, is God in his holy habitation. The Lord our God be with us, as he was with our fathers: let him not leave us, nor forsake us. And you that cleave unto the Lord your God are alive every one of you this day. For the Lord has comforted Zion: he has comforted all her waste places, and has made her wilderness like Eden, and her desert like the garden of the Lord; joy and gladness shall be found therein, thanksgiving and the voice of melody. It pleased the Lord for his righteousness' sake, to magnify the Torah and to make it honorable.

Psalm cxxviii.

A Song of Degrees. Happy is every one that fears the Lord, that walks in his ways. When you shall eat the labor of your hands, happy shall you be, and it shall be well with you. Your wife shall be as a fruitful vine, in the recesses of your house: your children like olive plants, round about your table. Behold thus shall the man be blessed that fears the Lord. May the Lord bless you out of Zion: may you see the good of Jerusalem all the days of your life. Yea, may you see your children's children. Peace be upon Israel.

The Reader says Havdalah (below), omitting the Introductory Verses.

It is our duty to praise the Lord of all things, to ascribe greatness to him who formed the world in the beginning, since he has not made us like the nations of other lands, and has not placed us like other families of the earth, since he has not assigned unto us a portion as unto them, nor a lot as unto all their multitude. For we bend the knee and offer worship and thanks before the supreme King of kings, the Holy One, blessed be he, who stretched forth the heavens and laid the foundations of the earth, the seat of whose glory is in the heavens above, and the abode of whose might is in the loftiest heights. He is our God; there is none else: in truth he is our King; there is none besides him; as it is written in his Torah, And you shall know this day, and lay it to your heart, that the Lord he is God in heaven above and upon the earth beneath: there is none else.

We therefore hope in you, O Lord our God, that we may speedily behold the glory of your might, when you will remove the abominations from the earth, and the idols will be utterly cut off, when the world will be perfected under the kingdom of the Almighty, and all the children of flesh will call upon your name, when you will turn unto yourself all the wicked of the earth. Let all the inhabitants of the world perceive and know that unto you every knee must bow, every tongue must swear. Before you, O Lord our God, let them bow and fall; and unto your glorious name let them give honor; let them all accept the yoke of your kingdom, and do you reign over them speedily, and forever and ever. For the kingdom is yours, and to all eternity you will reign in glory; as it is written in your Torah, The Lord shall reign forever and ever. And it is said, And the Lord shall be king over all the earth: in that day shall the Lord be One, and his name One.

The following Kaddish is said by a Mourner.

Mourner.—Magnified and sanctified be his great name in the world which he has created according to his will. May he establish his kingdom during your life and during your days, and during the life of all the house of Israel, even speedily and at a near time, and say ye, Amen.

Cong. and Mourner.—Let his great name be blessed forever and to all eternity.

Mourner.—Blessed, praised and glorified, exalted, extolled and honored, magnified and lauded be the name of the Holy One, blessed be he; though he be high above all the blessings and hymns, praises and consolations, which are uttered in the world; and say ye, Amen.

Cong.—Let the name of the Lord be blessed from this time forth and forevermore.

Mourner.—May there be abundant peace from heaven, and life for us and for all Israel; and say ye, Amen.

Cong.—My help is from the Lord, who made heaven and earth.

Mourner.—He who makes peace in his high places, may he make peace for us and for all Israel; and say ye, Amen.

THE HAVDALAH SERVICE

A cup of wine is taken in the right hand, and the following is said—

Behold, God is my salvation; I will trust, and will not be afraid: for Yah the Lord is my strength and song, and he is become my salvation. Therefore with joy shall you draw water out of the wells of salvation. Salvation belongs unto the Lord: your blessing be upon your people. (Selah.) The Lord of hosts is with us; the God of Jacob is our refuge. (Selah.) The Jews had light and joy and gladness and honor. So be it with us. I will lift the cup of salvation, and call upon the name of the Lord.

Blessed are you, O Lord our God, King of the universe who creates the fruit of the vine.

The spice-box is taken, and the following is said—

Blessed are you, O Lord our God, King of the universe who creates divers kinds of spices.

The hands are spread towards the light, and the following is said—

Blessed are you, O Lord our God, King of the universe, who creates the light of the fire.

The cup is again taken in the right hand, and the following is said—

Blessed are you, O Lord our God, King of the universe, who makes a distinction between holy and profane, between light and darkness, between Israel and other nations, between the seventh day and the six working days. Blessed are you, O Lord, who makes a distinction between holy and profane.

May he who makes a distinction between holy and profane pardon our sins; our offspring and our possessions may he multiply as the sand, and as the stars in the night.

The day has declined like the palm tree's shade; I call upon God who performs all things for me; the watchman says, the morning comes, though it now be night.

Your righteousness is like Mount Tabor: O pass you wholly over my sins; let them be as yesterday which is past, and as a watch in the night.

The season of my offerings is over: would that rest again were mine! I am weary with my groaning; in my tears I melt away every night.

Hear my voice, lee it not be cast away; open to me the lofty gate, for my head is filled with dew, my locks with the drops of the night.

Be entreated, O dreaded and awful God; while I cry, grant me your redemption, in the twilight, in the evening of the day, yea, in the blackness of the night.

I call upon you, Lord, save you me; make me to know the path of life; from pining sickness snatch you me, from day to night.

Cleanse the impurity of my deeds, lest my foes should say, Where is the God that made me, who gives songs in the night?

We are like clay in your hand; forgive, we beseech you, our sins both light and grave, and day shall pour forth the word unto day, and night unto night.

May he who makes a distinction between holy and profane pardon our sins; our offspring and our possessions may he multiply as the sand, and as the stars in the night.

MEDITATION AND BLESSINGS ON TAKING THE LULAB
On Sukkot, previous to Hallel, being said, the Lulab is taken, and the following Meditation and Blessings are read—

Lo, I am prepared and ready to fulfil the command of my Creator, who has commanded us in his Torah, And you shall take you on the first day the fruit of the tree Hadar, branches of palm trees, a bough of the tree Aboth, and willows of the brook. While I wave them, may the stream of blessings flow in upon me, together with holy thoughts which tell that he is the God of gods and Lord of lords, governing below and above, whose kingdom rules over all. May this my observance of the precept of the Four Species be accounted as though I had fulfilled it in all its details and particulars. And let the pleasantness of the Lord our God be upon us, and establish you the work of our hands upon us; yea, the work of our hands establish you it. Blessed be the Lord forever, Amen, and Amen.

Blessed are you, O Lord our God, King of the universe, who has sanctified us by your commandments, and has given us command concerning the taking of the Lulab.

Blessed are you, O Lord our God, King of the universe, who has kept us in life, and has preserved us, and enabled us to reach this season.

The latter Blessing is said on the First Day of the Festival only. Should the First Day, however, fall on Sabbath, it is said on the Second Day.

HALLEL

The following Prayer (Hallel) is said on New Moon, on Passover, Pentecost and Sukkot, and on Chanukah.

On the Intermediate Days of Festivals the Tefillin are removed before Hallel; on New Moon, before the Additional Service.

Blessed are you, O Lord our God, King of the universe, who has sanctified us by your commandments, and has commanded us to read the Hallel.

Psalm cxiii.

Praise you the Lord. Praise, O you servants of the Lord, praise the name of the Lord. Let the name of the Lord be blessed from this time forth and forevermore. From the rising of the sun unto the going down thereof the Lord's name is to be praised. The Lord is high above all nations, and his glory above the heavens. Who is like unto the Lord our God, that dwells so high; that looks down so low upon the heavens and the earth? He raises up the lowly out of the dust, and lifts up the needy from the dunghill; that he may set him with princes, even with the princes of his people. He makes the barren woman dwell in her house as a joyful mother of children. Praise you the Lord.

Psalm cxiv.

When Israel went forth out of Egypt, the house of Jacob from a people of strange language; Judah became his sanctuary, Israel his dominion. The sea saw it, and fled; Jordan turned back. The mountains skipped like rams, the hills like lambs. What ails you, O you sea, that you flee? You Jordan, that you turns back? you mountains, that you skip like rams? you hills, like lambs? At the presence of the Lord tremble, O earth, at the presence of the God of Jacob; who turned the rock into a pool of water, the flint into a fountain of waters.

On New Moon and the last Six Days of Passover omit the following paragraph—

Psalm cxv.

Not unto us, O Lord, not unto us, but unto your name give glory, for your loving-kindness and for the truth's sake. Wherefore should the nations say, Where, then, is their God? But our God is in the heavens, he does whatsoever he pleases. Their idols are silver and gold, the work of men's hands. They have mouths, but they speak not; eyes have they, but they see not. They have ears, but they hear not; noses have they, but they smell not. As for their hands, they touch not; as for their feet, they walk not; they give no sound through their throat. They that make them shall be like unto them; yea, every one that trusts in them. O Israel, trust you in the Lord: he is their help and their shield. O house of Aaron, trust in the Lord: he is their help and their shield. You that fear the Lord, trust in the Lord: he is their help and their shield.

The Lord has been mindful of us; he will bless, he will bless the house of Israel; he will bless the house of Aaron. He will bless them that fear the Lord both small and great. May the Lord increase you, you and your children. Blessed are you of the Lord, why, made heaven and earth. The heavens are the heavens of the Lord; but the earth has he given to the children of men. The dead praise not the Lord, neither any that go down into silence; but we will bless the Lord from this time forth and forevermore. Praise you the Lord.

On New Moon and the last Sir Days of Passover omit the following paragraph—

Psalm cxvi.

I love the Lord, because he hears my voice and my supplications. Because he has inclined his ear unto me, therefore will I call upon him as long as I live. The cords of death had encompassed me, and the straits of the grave had come upon me: I found trouble and sorrow. Then I called upon the name of the Lord: O Lord, I beseech you, deliver my soul. Gracious is the Lord and righteous: yea, our God is merciful. The Lord guards the simple: I was brought low, and he saved me. Return unto your rest, O my soul; for the Lord has dealt bountifully with you. For you have delivered my soul from death, my eyes from tears, my feet from falling. I shall walk before the Lord in the land of the living. I kept my faith in God ever when I spoke, I am greatly afflicted; even when I said in my haste, All men are liars.

What can I render unto the Lord for all his benefits towards me? I will lift the cup of salvation, and call upon the name of the Lord. I will pay my vows unto the Lord, yea, in the presence of all his people. Precious in the sight of the Lord is the death of his loving ones. Ah, Lord, truly I am your servant: I am your servant, the son of your handmaid; you have loosed my bonds. I will offer to you the sacrifice of thanksgiving, and will call upon the name of the Lord. I will pay my vows unto the Lord, yea, in the presence of all his people; in the courts of the Lord's house, in the midst of you, O Jerusalem. Praise you the Lord.

Psalm cxvii.

O praise the Lord, all you nations; laud him, all you peoples. For his loving-kindness is mighty over us; and the truth of the Lord endures forever. Praise you the Lord.

The following verses are chanted by the Reader, the Congregation at the end of each verse repeating, "O give thanks," etc., to "ever."

Psalm cxviii.

O give thanks unto the Lord; for he is good: for his loving-kindness endures forever.

O let Israel say, that his loving-kindness endures forever.

O let the house of Aaron say that his loving-kindness endures forever.

O let them that fear the Lord say that his loving-kindness endures forever.

Out of my straits I called upon the Lord: the Lord answered me with enlargement. The Lord is for me, I will not fear: what can man do unto me? The Lord is for me among them that help me; therefore shall I see my desire on them that hate me. It is better to trust in the Lord than to confide in man. It is better to trust in the Lord than to confide in princes. All nations compassed me about: in the name of the Lord I surely cut them down. They compassed me about; yea, they compassed me about: in the name of the Lord I surely cut them down. They compassed me about like bees;—they were extinguished as a fire of thorns—in the name of the Lord I surely cut them down. You did thrust sore at me that I might fall: but the Lord helped me. The Lord is my strength and song; and he is become my salvation. The voice of exulting and salvation is in the tents of the righteous: the right hand of the Lord does valiantly. The right hand of the Lord is exalted: the right hand of the Lord does valiantly. I shall not die, but live, and recount the works of the Lord. The Lord has chastened me sore: but he has not given me over unto death. Open to me the gates of righteousness: I will enter into them, I will give thanks unto the Lord. This is the gate of the Lord; the righteous may enter into it.

I will give thanks unto you, for you have answered me, and are become my salvation.

Repeat this and the next three verses.

The stone which the builders rejected is become the head-stone of the corner.

This was the Lord's doing; it is marvelous in our eyes.

This is the day which the Lord has made; we will be glad and rejoice thereon.

Reader and Congregation—

Save, we beseech you, O Lord.

Save, we beseech you, O Lord.

We beseech you, O Lord, send prosperity.

We beseech you, O Lord, send prosperity.

Blessed be he that comes in the name of the Lord: we bless you out of the house of the Lord.

Repeat this and the next three verses.

The Lord is God, he has given us light: bind the festal offering with cords, even unto the horns of the altar.

You are my God, and I will give thanks unto you: you are my God, I will exalt you.

O give thanks unto the Lord; for he is good: for his loving-kindness endures forever.

All your works shall praise you, O Lord our God, and your pious ones, the just who do your will, together with all your people, the house of Israel, shall with exultation thank, bless, praise, glorify, exalt, reverence, sanctify and ascribe sovereignty unto your name, O our King; for it is good to give thanks unto you, and becoming to sing praises unto your name, because from everlasting to everlasting you are God. Blessed are you, O Lord, a King extolled with praises.

Kaddish.

Order of Service at the Reading of the Torah on New Moons and the Intermediate Days of Festivals; on Festivals and on New Moons falling on Sabbaths.

On New Moons and the Intermediate Days of Festivals—

   "Happy are they."

   "And a redeemer," to "honorable."

Say Kaddish to "in the world, and say ye, Amen."

On New Moons continue with the following Amidah.

On Festivals, and on the Intermediate Days of Festivals, say the appropriate Amidot of the Additional Service.

ADDITIONAL SERVICE FOR THE NEW MOON
The following prayer (Amidah) to "as in ancient years," is to be said standing.

O Lord, open you my lips, and my mouth shall declare your praise.

Blessed are you, O Lord our God and God of our fathers, God of Abraham, God of Isaac, and God of Jacob, the great, mighty and revered God, the most high God, who bestows loving-kindnesses, and possesses all things; who remembers the pious deeds of the patriarchs, and in love will bring a redeemer to their children's children for your name's sake.

O king, Helper, Savior and shield. Blessed are you, O Lord, the Shield of Abraham.

You, O Lord, are mighty forever, you quicken the dead, you are mighty to save.

From the Eighth Day of Solemn Assembly until the First Day, of Passover say—

You cause the wind to blow and the rain to fall.

You sustain the living with loving-kindness, quicken the dead with great mercy, support the falling, heals the sick, loose the bound, and keep your faith to them that sleep in the dust. Who is like unto you, Lord of mighty acts, and who resembles you, O King, who kills and quickens, and causes salvation to spring forth?

Yea, faithful are you to quicken the dead. Blessed are you, O Lord, who quickens the dead.

You are holy, and your name is holy, and holy beings praise you daily. (Selah.) Blessed are you, O Lord the holy God.

When the Reader repeats the Amidah, the following is said, to "holy God."

Reader.—We will sanctify your name in the world even as they sanctify it in the highest heavens, as it is written by the hand of your prophet:

And they called one unto the other and said,

Cong.—Holy, holy, holy is the Lord of hosts: the whole earth is full of his glory.

Reader.—Those over against them say, Blessed—

Cong.—Blessed be the glory of the Lord from his place.

Reader.—And in your Holy Words it is written, saying,

Cong.—The Lord shall reign forever, your God, O Zion, unto all generations. Praise you the Lord.

Reader.—Unto all generations we will declare your greatness, and to all eternity we will proclaim your holiness, and your praise, O our God, shall not depart from our mouth forever, for you are a great and holy God and King. Blessed are you, O Lord, the holy God.

The beginnings of the months you did assign unto your people for a season of atonement throughout their generations. While they offered unto you acceptable sacrifices, and goats for a sin offering to atone for them, these were to be a memorial for them all, and the salvation of their soul from the hand of the enemy. O do you establish a new altar on Zion, and we will offer upon it the burnt offering of the New Moon, and prepare he-goats for your acceptance; while we all of us rejoice in the service of the sanctuary, and in the songs of David your servant, Which shall then be heard in your city and chanted before your altar. O vouchsafe unto them everlasting love, and the covenant of the fathers remember unto the children. Bring us with exultation to Zion your city, and to Jerusalem your sanctuary with everlasting joy, and there will we prepare unto you the offerings that are obligatory for us, the continual offerings according to their order, and the additional offerings according to their enactment; and the additional offering of this New Moon we will prepare and offer unto you in love according to the precept of your will, as you have prescribed for us in your Torah through the hand of Moses your servant, by the mouth of your glory, as it is said:

And in the beginnings of your months you shall offer a burnt offering unto the Lord; two young bullocks and one ram, seven he-lambs of the first year without blemish. And their meal offering and their drink offerings as has been ordained, three tenth parts of an ephah of fine flour for each bullock, two tenth parts for the ram, one tenth for each lamb, and wine according to the drink offering of each, a goat for atonement, and two daily offerings according to their institution.

Our God and God of our fathers, renew this month unto us for good and for blessing, for joy and gladness, for salvation and consolation, for support and sustenance, for life and peace, for pardon of sin and forgiveness of iniquity, (in Leap Year add, and for atonement of transgression); for you have chosen your people Israel from all nations, and has appointed unto them statutes for the beginnings of the months. Blessed are you, O Lord, who sanctifies Israel and the beginnings of the months.

Accept, O Lord our God, your people Israel and their prayer; restore the service to the oracle of your house; receive in love and favor both the fire offerings of Israel and their prayer; and may the service of your people Israel be ever acceptable unto you.

And let our eyes behold your return in mercy to Zion. Blessed are you, O Lord, who restores your divine presence unto Zion.

We give thanks unto you, for you are the Lord our God and the God of our fathers forever and ever; you are the Rock of our lives, the Shield of our salvation through every generation. We will give thanks unto you and declare your praise for our lives which are committed unto your hand, and for our souls which are in your charge, and for your miracles, which are daily with us, and for your wonders and your benefits, which are wrought at all times, evening, morn, and noon. O you who are all-good, whose mercies fail not; you, merciful Being, whose loving-kindnesses never cease, we have ever hoped in you.

Congregation in an undertone

We give thanks unto you, for you are the Lord our God and the God of our fathers, the God of all flesh, our Creator and the Creator of all things in the beginning. Blessings and thanksgivings be to your great and holy name, because you have kept us in life and has preserved us: so may you continue to keep us in life and to preserve us. O gather our exiles to your holy courts to observe your statutes, to do your will, and to serve you with a perfect heart; seeing that we give thanks unto you. Blessed be the God to whom thanksgivings are due.

On Chanukah say, "We thank you also," etc.

For all these things your name, O our King, shall be continually blessed and exalted forever and ever.

And everything that lives shall give thanks unto you forever, and shall praise your name in truth, O God, our salvation and our help. Blessed are you, O Lord, whose name is All-good, and unto whom it is becoming to give thanks.

At the repetition of the Amidah by the Reader, the following is introduced—

Our God and God of our fathers, bless us with the three-fold blessing of your Torah written by the hand of Moses your servant, which was spoken by Aaron and his sons, the priests, your holy people, as it is said, The Lord bless you, and keep you: the Lord make his face to shine upon you, and be gracious unto you: the Lord turn his face unto you, and give you peace.

Grant peace, welfare, blessing, grace, loving-kindness and mercy unto us and unto all Israel, your people. Bless us, O our Father, even all of us together, with the light of your countenance; for by the light of your countenance you have given us, O Lord our God, the Torah of life, loving-kindness and righteousness, blessing mercy, life and peace; and may it be good in your sight to bless your people Israel at all times and in every hour with your peace.

Blessed are you, O Lord, who blesses your people Israel with peace.

O my God! guard my tongue from evil and my lips from speaking guile; and to such as curse me let my soul be dumb, yea, let my soul be unto all as the dust. Open my heart to your Torah, and let my soul pursue your commandments. If any design evil against me, speedily make their counsel of none effect, and frustrate their designs. Do it for the sake of your name, do it for the sake of your right hand, do it for the sake of your holiness, do it for the sake of your Torah. In order that your beloved ones may be delivered, O save with your right hand, and answer me. Let the words of my mouth and the meditation of my heart be acceptable before you. O Lord, my Rock and my Redeemer. He who makes peace in his high places, may he make peace for us all and for all Israel, and say ye, Amen.

May it be your will, O Lord our God and God of our fathers, that the temple be speedily rebuilt in our days, and grant our portion in your Torah. And there we will serve you with awe, as in the days of old, and as in ancient years. Then shall the offering of Judah and Jerusalem be pleasant unto the Lord, as in the days of old, and as in ancient years.

Kaddish.
"It is our duty."
Mourner's Kaddish.
Psalm civ.

SERVICE FOR FESTIVALS

On lighting the Festival Lamp in the Home, the following is said—

Blessed are you, O Lord our God, King of the universe, who has sanctified us by your commandments, and has commanded us to kindle [on Friday add: the Sabbath and] the Festival light.

On the Eve of Festivals, Afternoon Service is said as on Weekdays, but omitting "And David said," "O Guardian of Israel," "It is our duty" and "Kaddish."

Evening Service. Should the evening of the Festival fall on Friday, the Evening Service commences with "A Psalm, a Song for the Sabbath Day."

The following Amidah is said at the Evening, Morning and Afternoon Services of Passover, Pentecost, Sukkot, and the Eighth Day of Solemn Assembly and the Rejoicing of the Torah.

O Lord, open you my lips, and my mouth shall declare your praise.

Blessed are you, O Lord our God and God of our fathers, God of Abraham, God of Isaac, and God of Jacob, the great, mighty and revered God, the most high God, who bestows loving-kindnesses, and possesses all things; who remembers the pious deeds of the patriarchs, and in love will bring a redeemer to their children's children for your name's sake.

O king, Helper, Savior and shield. Blessed are you, O Lord, the Shield of Abraham.

You, O Lord, are mighty forever, you quicken the dead, you are mighty to save.

From the Sabbath after the Eighth Day of Solemn Assembly until the First Day of Passover say—

You cause the wind to blow and the rain to fall.

You sustain the living with loving-kindness, quicken the dead with great mercy, support the falling, heals the sick, loose the bound, and keep your faith to them that sleep in the dust. Who is like unto you, Lord of mighty acts, and who resembles you, O King, who kills and quickens, and causes salvation to spring forth?

Yea, faithful are you to quicken the dead. Blessed are you, O Lord, who quickens the dead.

You are holy, and your name is holy, and holy beings praise you daily. (Selah.) Blessed are you, O Lord, the holy God.

When the Reader repeats the Amidah, the following is said, to "holy God."

Reader.—We will sanctify your name in the world even as they sanctify, it in the highest heavens, as it is written by the hand of your prophet:

And they called one unto the other and said,

Cong.—Holy, holy, holy is the Lord of hosts: the whole earth is full of his glory.

Reader.—Then with a noise of great rushing, mighty and strong, they make their voices heard, and, upraising themselves towards the Seraphim, they exclaim over against them, Blessed—

Cong.—Blessed be the glory of the Lord from his place.

Reader.—From your place shine forth, O our King, and reign over us, for we wait for you. When will you reign in Zion? Speedily, even in our days, do you dwell there, and forever. May you be magnified and sanctified in the midst of Jerusalem your city throughout all generations and to all eternity. O let our eyes behold your kingdom, according to the word that was spoken in the songs of your might by David, your righteous anointed:

Cong.—The Lord shall reign forever, your God, O Zion, unto all generations. Praise you the Lord.

Reader.—Unto all generations we will declare your greatness, and to all eternity we will proclaim your holiness, and your praise, O our God, shall not depart from our mouth forever, for you are a great and holy God and King. Blessed are you, O Lord, the holy God.

You have chosen us from all peoples; you have loved us and taken pleasure in us, and has exalted us above all tongues; you have sanctified us by your commandments, and brought us near unto your service, O our King, and has called us by your great and holy name.

On Saturday Night add the following—

You, O Lord our God, have made known unto us the judgments of your righteousness; you have taught us to perform the statutes of your will; you have given us, O Lord our God, righteous judgments, true laws, good statutes and commandments. You have also caused us to inherit seasons of joy, appointed times of holiness, and feasts of free will gifts, and has given us as a heritage the holiness of the Sabbath, the glory of the appointed time, and the celebration of the festival. You have made a distinction, O Lord our God, between holy and profane, between light and darkness, between Israel and other nations, between the seventh day and the six working days; you have made a distinction between the holiness of the Sabbath and that of the festival, and has hallowed the seventh day above the six working days: you have distinguished and sanctified your people Israel by your holiness.

On Sabbath add the words in brackets.

And you have given us in love, O Lord our God, [Sabbaths for rest,] appointed times for gladness, festivals and seasons for joy; [this Sabbath Day, and] this day of—

On Passover—
The Feast of Unleavened Bread, the season of our Freedom;
On Pentecost—
The Feast of Weeks, the season of the Giving of our Torah;
On Sukkot—
The Feast of Sukkot, the season of our Gladness;
On the Eighth Day of Solemn Assembly and on the Rejoicing of the Torah—
The Eighth-day Feast of Solemn Assembly, the season of our Gladness.

[in love]; a holy convocation, as a memorial of the departure from Egypt.

Our God and God of our fathers! May our remembrance rise and come and be accepted before you, with the remembrance of our fathers, of Messiah the son of David your servant, of Jerusalem your holy city, and of all your people the house of Israel, bringing deliverance and well-being, grace, loving-kindness and mercy, life and peace on this day of

On Passover—
The Feast of Unleavened Bread;
On Pentecost—
The Feast of Weeks;
On Sukkot—
The Feast of Sukkot;
On the Eighth Day of Solemn Assembly, and on the Rejoicing of the Torah—
The Eighth-day Feast of Solemn Assembly.

Remember us, O Lord our God, thereon for our wellbeing; be mindful of us for blessing, and save us unto life: by your promise of salvation and mercy, spare us and be gracious unto us; have mercy upon us and save us; for our eyes are bent upon you, because you are a gracious and merciful God and King.

O Lord our God, bestow upon us the blessing of your appointed times for life and peace, for joy and gladness, even as you have been pleased to promise that you would bless us. [Our God and God of our fathers, accept our rest.] Sanctify us by your command with your goodness, and gladden us with your salvation, and grant our portion in your Torah; satisfy us purify our hearts to serve you in truth; and let us inherit, O Lord our God, [in love and favor,] with joy and gladness your holy [Sabbath and] appointed times; and may Israel, who hallow your name, rejoice in you. Blessed are you, O Lord, who hallows [the Sabbath and] Israel and the seasons.

Accept, O Lord our God, your people Israel and their prayer; restore the service to the oracle of your house; receive in love and favor both the fire offerings of Israel and their prayer; and may the service of your people Israel be ever acceptable unto you.

And let our eyes behold your return in mercy to Zion. Blessed are you, O Lord, who restores your divine presence unto Zion.

We give thanks unto you, for you are the Lord our God and the God of our fathers forever and ever; you are the Rock of our lives, the Shield of our salvation through every generation. We will give thanks unto you and declare your praise for our lives which are committed unto your hand, and for our souls which are in your charge, and for your miracles, which are daily with us, and for your wonders and your benefits, which are wrought at all times, evening, morn and noon. O you who are all-good, whose mercies fail not; you, merciful Being, whose loving-kindnesses never cease, we have ever hoped in you.

Congregation in an undertone

We give thanks unto you, for you are the Lord our God and the God of our fathers, the God of all flesh, our Creator and the Creator of all things in the beginning. Blessings and thanksgivings be to your great and holy name, because you have kept us in life and has preserved us: so may you continue to keep us in life and to preserve us. O gather our exiles to your holy courts to observe your statutes, to do your will, and to serve you with a perfect heart; seeing that we give thanks unto you. Blessed he the God to whom thanksgivings are due.

For all these things your name, O our King, shall be continually blessed and exalted forever and ever.

And everything that lives shall give thanks unto you forever, and shall praise your name in truth, O God, our salvation and our help. Blessed are you, O Lord, whose name is All-good, and unto whom it is becoming to give thanks.

At the repetition of the Amidah by the Reader the following is introduced—

Our God and God of our fathers, bless us with the three-fold blessing of your Torah written by the hand of Moses your servant, which was spoken by Aaron and his sons, the priests, your holy people, as it is said, The Lord bless you, and keep you: the Lord make his face to shine upon you, and be gracious unto you: the Lord turn his face unto you, and give you peace.

At the Morning Service say—

Grant peace, welfare, blessing, grace, loving-kindness and mercy unto us and unto all Israel, your people. Bless us, O our Father, even all of us together, with the light of your countenance; for by the light of your countenance you have given us. O Lord our God, the Torah of Life, loving-kindness and righteousness, blessing, mercy, life and peace; and may it be good in your sight to bless your people Israel at all times and in every hour with your peace.

At the Afternoon and Evening Services say—

Grant abundant peace unto Israel your people forever; for you are the sovereign Lord of all peace; and may it be good in your sight to bless your people Israel at all times and in every hour with your peace.

Blessed are you, O Lord, who blesses your people Israel with peace.

O my God! guard my tongue from evil and my lips from speaking guile; and to such as curse me let my soul be dumb, yea, let my soul be unto all as the dust. Open my heart to your Torah, and let my soul pursue your commandments. If any design evil against me, speedily make their counsel of none effect, and frustrate their designs. Do it for the sake of your name, do it for the sake of your right hand, do it for the sake of your holiness, do it for the sake of your Torah. In order that your beloved ones may be delivered, O save with your right hand and answer me. Let the words of my mouth and the meditation of my heart be acceptable before you, O Lord, my Rock and my Redeemer. He who makes peace in his high places, may he make peace for us and for all Israel, and say ye, Amen.

May it be your will, O Lord our God and God of our fathers, that the temple be speedily rebuilt in our days, and grant our portion in your Torah. And there we will serve you with awe, as in the days of old, and as in ancient years. Then shall the offering of Judah and Jerusalem be pleasant unto the Lord, as in the days of old, and as in ancient years.

KIDDUSH FOR FESTIVALS
To be said on Passover, Pentecost and Sukkot.

When the Festival occurs on Sabbath begin here—

And it was evening and it was morning,—the sixth day.

And the heaven and the earth were finished and all their host. And on the seventh day God had finished his work which he had made: and he rested on the seventh day from all his work which he had made. And God blessed the seventh day, and he hallowed it, because he rested thereon from all his work which God had created and made.

Blessed are you, O Lord our God, King of the universe, who creates the fruit of the vine.

On Sabbath add the words in brackets.

Blessed are you, O Lord our God, King of the universe, who has chosen us from all peoples, and exalted us above all tongues, and sanctified us by your commandments. And you have given us in love, O Lord our God, [Sabbaths for rest,] appointed times for gladness, festivals and seasons for joy; [this Sabbath day and] this day of—

On Passover—
The Feast of Unleavened Bread, the season of our Freedom;
On Pentecost—
The Feast of Weeks, the season of the Giving of our Torah;
On Sukkot—
The Feast of Sukkot, the season of our Gladness;
On the Eighth Day of Solemn Assembly and on the Rejoicing of the Torah—
The Eighth-day Feast of Solemn Assembly, the season of our Gladness.
[in love]; a holy convocation, as a memorial of the departure from Egypt; for you have chosen us, and sanctified us above all peoples, and your holy [Sabbath and] appointed times you have caused us to inherit [in love and favor] in joy and gladness. Blessed are you, O Lord, who sanctifies [the Sabbath,] Israel and the festive seasons.

On Saturday night the following is added—

Blessed are you, O Lord our God, King of the universe, who creates the light of the fire.

Blessed are you, O Lord our God, King of the universe, who makes a distinction between holy and profane, between light and darkness, between Israel and other nations, between the seventh day and the six working days. You have made a distinction between the holiness of the Sabbath and that of the festival, and has hallowed the seventh day above the six working days; you have distinguished and sanctified your people Israel by your holiness. Blessed are you, O Lord, who makes a distinction between holy and holy.

Blessed are you, O Lord our God, King of the universe, who has kept us in life, and has preserved us, and enabled us to reach this season.

The last Blessing is said on the following occasions—The first two nights of Passover; the two nights of Pentecost; the first two nights of Sukkot; on the night of the Eighth Day of Solemn Assembly, and on that of the Rejoicing of the Torah.

MEDITATION AND BLESSINGS IN THE SUKKAH
To be said in the sukkah on the first night of the festival.

May it be your will, O Lord my God and God of my fathers, to let your divine presence abide among us. Spread over us the tabernacle of your peace in recognition of the precept of the sukkah which we are now fulfilling, and whereby we establish in fear and love the unity of your holy and blessed name. O surround us with the pure and holy radiance of your glory that is spread over our heads as the eagle over the nest he stirs up: and thence bid the stream of life flow in upon your servant (thy handmaid). And seeing that I have gone forth from my house abroad, and am speeding the way of your commandments, may it be accounted unto me as though I had wandered far in your cause. O wash me thoroughly from my iniquity, and cleanse me from my sin. Keep me in life, O Lord; vouchsafe unto me the abundance of your blessings; and to such as are hungry and thirsty give bread and water unfailingly. Make me worthy to dwell trustingly in the covert of your shadowing wings at the time when I part from the world. O deal graciously with us in the decree to which you set your seal, and make us worthy to dwell many days upon the land, the holy land, ever serving and fearing you. Blessed be the Lord forever. Amen and Amen.

Blessed are you, O Lord our God, King of the universe, who has sanctified us by your commandments, and has commanded us to dwell in the sukkah.

Blessed are you, O Lord our God, King of the universe, who has kept us in life, and has preserved us, and enabled us to reach this season.

ADDITIONAL SERVICE FOR THE FESTIVALS
To be said on Passover, Pentecost and Sukkot, and on the intermediate days of Festivals.

The following prayer (Amidah) to "as in ancient years," is said standing.

O Lord, open you my lips, and my mouth shall declare your praise.

Blessed are you, O Lord our God and God of our fathers, God of Abraham, God of Isaac, and God of Jacob, the great, mighty and revered God, the most high God, who bestows loving-kindnesses, and possesses all things; who remembers the pious deeds of the patriarchs, and in love will bring a redeemer to their children's children for your name's sake.

O king, Helper, Savior and shield. Blessed are you, O Lord, the Shield of Abraham.

You, O Lord, are mighty forever, you quicken the dead, you are mighty to save.

From the Sabbath after the Eighth Day of Solemn Assembly until the First Day of Passover say—

You cause the wind to blow and the rain to fall.

You sustain the living with loving-kindness, quicken the dead with great mercy, support the falling, heals the sick, loose the bound, and keep your faith to them that sleep in the dust. Who is like unto you, Lord of mighty acts, and who resembles you, O King, who kills and quickens, and causes salvation to spring forth?

Yea, faithful are you to quicken the dead. Blessed are you, O Lord, who quickens the dead.

You are holy, and your name is holy, and holy beings praise you daily. (Selah.) Blessed are you, O Lord, the holy God.

When the Reader repeats the Amidah, the following is added to "holy God."

Reader.—We will reverence and sanctify you according to the mystic utterance of the Holy Seraphim, who hallow your name in the sanctuary, as it is written by the hand of your prophet, And they called one unto the other and said,

Cong.—Holy, holy, holy is the Lord of hosts: the whole earth is full of his glory.

Reader.—His glory fills the universe: his ministering angels ask one another, Where is the place of his glory? Those over against them say, Blessed—

Cong.—Blessed be the glory of the Lord from his place.

Reader.—From his place may he turn in mercy and be gracious unto a people who, evening and morning, twice every day, proclaim with constancy the unity of his name, saying in love, Hear—

Cong.—Hear, O Israel: the Lord our God, the Lord is One.

Reader.—One is Our God; he is our Father; he is our King, he is our Savior; and he of his mercy will let us hear a second time, in the presence of all living (his promise), "To be to you for a God."

Cong.—"I am the Lord your God

Reader.—And in your Holy Words it is written, saying,

Cong.—The Lord shall reign forever, your God, O Zion, unto all generations. Praise you the Lord.

Reader.—Unto all generations we will declare your greatness, and to all eternity we will proclaim your holiness, and your praise, O our God, shall not depart front our mouth forever, for you are a great and holy God and King. Blessed are you, O Lord, the holy God.

You have chosen us from all peoples; you have, loved us and taken pleasure in us, and has exalted us above all tongues; you have sanctified us by your commandments, and brought us near unto your service, O our King, and has called us by your great and holy name.

On Sabbath add the words in brackets.

And you have given us in love, O Lord our God, [Sabbaths for rest,] appointed times for gladness, festivals and seasons for joy; [this Sabbath day and] this day of

On Passover—
The Feast of Unleavened Bread, the season of our Freedom;
On Pentecost—
The Feast of Weeks, the season of the Giving of our Torah;
On Sukkot—
The Feast of Sukkot, the season of our Gladness:
On the Eighth Day of Solemn Assembly and on the Rejoicing of the Torah.
The Eighth-day Feast of Solemn Assembly, the season of our Gladness.

[in love]; a holy convocation, as a memorial of the departure from Egypt.

But on account of our sins we were exiled from our land, and removed far from our country, and we are unable to go up in order to appear and prostrate ourselves before you, and to fulfil our obligations in your chosen house, that great and holy temple which was called by your name, because of the hand that has been stretched out against your sanctuary. May it be your will, O Lord our God and God of our fathers, merciful King, that you may again in your abundant compassion have mercy upon us and upon your sanctuary, and may speedily rebuild it and magnify its glory. Our Father, our King, do you speedily make the glory of your kingdom manifest upon us; shine forth and exalt yourself upon us in the sight of all living; bring our scattered ones among the nations near unto you, and gather our dispersed from the ends of the earth. Lead us with exultation unto Zion your city, and unto Jerusalem the place of your sanctuary with everlasting joy; and there we will prepare before you the offerings that are obligatory for us, the continual offerings according to their order, and the additional offerings according to their enactment; and the additional offering of [this Sabbath day with the additional offering of] this

On Passover—
Feast of Unleavened Bread—
On Pentecost—
Feast of Weeks—
On Sukkot—
Feast of Sukkot—
On the Eighth Day of Solemn Assembly and on the Rejoicing of the Torah.
Eighth-day Feast of Solemn Assembly we will prepare and offer unto you in love according to the precept of your will, as you have prescribed for us in your Torah through the hand of Moses your servant, by the mouth of your glory, as it is said:

[And on the Sabbath day two he-lambs of the first year without blemish, and two-tenth parts of an ephah of fine flour for a meal offering, mingled with oil, and the drink offering thereof; this is the burnt offering of every Sabbath, beside the continual burnt offering and the drink offering thereof.]

On the first two days of Passover say—

And in the first month, on the fourteenth day of the month, is the Passover unto the Lord. And on the fifteenth day of this month shall be a feast: seven days shall unleavened bread be eaten. On the first day shall be a holy convocation; you shall do no servile work.

And you shall offer an offering made by fire, a burnt offering unto the Lord; two young bullocks and one ram, and seven he-lambs of the first year; they shall be unto you without blemish.

On Passover, after the first two days, say the last paragraph only.

On Pentecost say—

And on the day of the first fruits, when you offer a new meal offering unto the Lord in your Feast of Weeks, you shall have a holy convocation; you shall do no servile work; you shall offer a burnt offering for a sweet savor unto the Lord; two young bullocks, one ram, seven he-lambs of the first year.

On the first two days of Sukkot say—

And on the fifteenth day of the seventh month you shall have a holy convocation; you shall do no servile work, and you shall keep a feast unto the Lord seven days. And you shall offer a burnt offering, an offering made by fire, of a sweet savor unto the Lord; thirteen young bullocks, two rams, fourteen he-lambs of the first year; they shall be without blemish.

On all Festivals say—

And their meal offering and their drink offerings as has been ordained; three-tenth parts of an ephah for each bullock, and two-tenth parts for the ram, and one-tenth part for each lamb, with wine according to the drink offering thereof, and a he-goat with which to make atonement, and the two continual offerings according to their enactment.

On the first of the Intermediate Days of Sukkot say—

And on the second day you shall offer twelve young bullocks, two rams, fourteen he-lambs of the first year without blemish. And their meal offering, etc.

And on the third day you shall offer eleven bullocks, two rams, fourteen he-lambs of the first year without blemish. And their meal offering, etc.

On the second of the Intermediate Days of Sukkot, say—

And on the third day you shall offer eleven bullocks two rams, fourteen he-lambs of the first year without blemish. And their meal offering, etc.

And on the fourth day you shall offer ten bullocks, two rams, fourteen he-lambs of the first year without blemish. And their meal offering, etc.

On the third of the Intermediate Days of Sukkot, say—

And on the fourth day you shall offer ten bullocks, two rams, fourteen he-lambs of the first year without blemish. And their meal offering, etc.

And on the fifth day you shall offer nine bullocks, two rams, fourteen he-lambs of the first year without blemish. And their meal offering, etc.

On the fourth of the Intermediate Days of Sukkot, say—

And on the fifth day you shall offer nine bullocks, two rams, fourteen he-lambs of the first year without blemish. And their meal offering, etc.

And on the sixth day you shall offer eight bullocks, two rams, fourteen he-lambs of the first year without blemish. And their meal offering, etc.

On the fifth of the Intermediate Days of Sukkot (Hoshana Rabba), say—

And on the sixth day you shall offer eight bullocks, two rams, fourteen he-lambs of the first year without blemish. And their meal offering, etc.

And on the seventh day you shall offer seven bullocks, two rams, fourteen lie-lambs of the first year without blemish. And their meal offering, etc.

On the Eighth Day of Solemn Assembly, and on the Rejoicing of the Torah, say—

On the eighth day you shall have a solemn assembly; you shall do no servile work. And you shall offer a burnt offering, an offering made by fire, of a sweet savor unto the Lord: one bullock, one ram, seven he-lambs of the first year without blemish. And their meal offering, etc.

[They that keep the Sabbath and call it a delight shall rejoice in your kingdom; the people that hallow the seventh day, even all of them shall be satiated and delighted with your goodness, seeing that you did find pleasure in the seventh day, and did hallow it; you did call it the desirable of days, in remembrance of the creation.]

Our God and God of our fathers, merciful King, have mercy upon us, O you good and beneficent Being, suffer yourself to be sought of us; return unto us in your yearning compassion for the fathers' sake who did your will; rebuild your house as at the beginning, and establish your sanctuary upon its site; grant that we may see it in its rebuilding, and make us rejoice in its re-establishment; restore the priests to their service, the Levites to their song and psalmody, and Israel to their habitations: and there we will go up to appear and prostrate ourselves before you at the three periods of our festivals, according as it is written in your Torah, Three times in the year shall all your males appear before the Lord your God in the place which he shall choose, on the feast of unleavened bread; and on the feast of weeks, and on the feast of Sukkot: and they shall not appear before the Lord empty. Every man shall bring according as he is able, according to the blessing of the Lord your God which he has given you.

O Lord our God, bestow upon us the blessing of your appointed times for life and peace, for joy and gladness, even as you have been pleased to promise that you would bless us. [Our God and God of our fathers, accept our rest.] Sanctify us by your commandments, and grant our portion in your Torah; satisfy us with your goodness, and gladden us with your salvation; purify our hearts to serve you in truth; and let us inherit, O Lord our God [in love and favor,] with joy and gladness your holy [Sabbath and] appointed times; and may Israel who hallow your name rejoice in you. Blessed are you, O Lord, who hallows [the Sabbath and] Israel and the seasons.

Accept, O Lord our God, your people Israel and their prayer; restore the service to the oracle of your house; receive in love and favor both the fire offerings of Israel and their prayer; and may the service of your people Israel be ever acceptable unto you.

And let our eyes behold your return in mercy to Zion. Blessed are you, O Lord, who restores your divine presence unto Zion.

Congregation in an undertone:

We give thanks unto you, for you are the Lord our God and the God of our fathers, the God of all flesh, our Creator and the Creator of all things in the beginning. Blessings and thanksgivings be to your great and holy name, because you have kept us in life and has preserved us; so may you continue to keep us in life and to preserve us. O gather our exiles to your holy courts to observe your statutes, to do your will, and to serve you with a perfect heart; seeing that we give thanks unto you. Blessed be the God to whom thanksgivings are due.

We give thanks unto you, for you are the Lord our God and the God of our fathers forever and ever; you are the Rock of our lives, the shield of our salvation through every generation. We will give thanks unto you and declare your praise for our lives which are committed unto your hand, and for our souls which are in your charge, and for your miracles, which are daily with us, and for your wonders and your benefits, which are wrought at all times, evening, morn and noon. O you who are all-good, whose mercies fail not; you, merciful Being, whose loving-kindnesses never cease, we have ever hoped in you.

For all these things your name, O our King, shall be continually blessed and exalted forever and ever.

And everything that lives shall give thanks unto you forever, and shall praise your name in truth, O God, our salvation and our help. Blessed are you, O Lord, whose name is All-good, and unto whom it is becoming to give thanks.

At the repetition of the Amidah by the Reader, the following is introduced—

Our God and God of our fathers, bless us with the three-fold blessing of your Torah written by the hand of Moses your servant, which was spoken by Aaron and his sons, the priests, your holy people, as it is said, The Lord bless you, and keep you: the Lord make his face to shine upon you, and be gracious unto you: the Lord turn his face unto you, and give you peace.

Grant peace, welfare, blessing, grace, loving-kindness and mercy unto us and unto all Israel, your people. Bless us, O our Father, even all of us together, with the light of your countenance; for by the light of your countenance you have given us, O Lord our God, the Torah of life, loving-kindness and righteousness, blessing, mercy, life and peace; and may it be good in your sight to bless your people Israel at all times and in every hour with your peace.

Blessed are you, O Lord, who blesses your people Israel with peace.

O my God! guard my tongue from evil and my lips from speaking guile; and to such as curse me let my soul be dumb, yea, let my soul be unto all as the dust. Open my heart to your Torah, and let my soul pursue your commandments. If any design evil against me, speedily make their counsel of none effect, and frustrate their designs. Do it for the sake of your name, do it for the sake of your right hand, do it for the sake of your holiness, do it for the sake of your Torah. In order that your beloved ones may be delivered, O save with your right hand, and answer me. Let the words of my mouth and the meditation of my heart be acceptable before you, O Lord, my Rock and my Redeemer. He who makes peace in his high places, may he make peace for us and for all Israel, and say ye, Amen.

May it be your will, O Lord our God and God of our fathers, that the temple be speedily rebuilt in our days, and grant our portion in your Torah. And there we will serve you with awe, as in the days of old, and as in ancient years. Then shall the offering of Judah and Jerusalem be pleasant unto the Lord, as in the days of old, and as in ancient years.

THE ORDER OF THE BLESSING OF THE PRIESTS

On Festivals, except on Sabbath, the following Order of the Blessing of the Priests is added in the Additional Amidah after "acceptable unto you."

The Priests ascend the steps of the Ark.

Cong. and Reader.—And may our prayer be acceptable unto you as burnt offering and as sacrifice. O you who are merciful, we beseech you, in your abundant mercy to restore your divine presence unto Zion, and the ordained service to Jerusalem. And let our eyes behold your return in mercy to Zion, and there will we worship you in awe, as in the days of old and as in ancient years.

Reader.—Blessed are you, O Lord, whom alone we serve in awe.

Continue "We give thanks unto you," to "it is becoming to give thanks."

The Reader says to "and his sons," in an undertone.

Our God and God of our fathers, bless us with the three-fold blessing of your Torah written by the hand of Moses your servant, which was spoken by Aaron and his sons,

Reader.—The priests,

Cong.—Your holy people, as it is said:

The Priests pronounce the following blessing:

Blessed are you, O Lord our God, King of the universe, who has sanctified us with the sanctity of Aaron and has commanded us to bless your people Israel in love.

Reader followed by the Priests, word for word.

The Lord bless you and keep you: Amen.

The Lord make his face to shine upon you and be gracious unto you: Amen,

The Lord turn his face unto you and give you peace. Amen. Selah.

Continue "Grant peace," etc., to the end of the Amidah.

SERVICE FOR NEW YEAR

The lighting of the Festival Lamp.

Afternoon Service as on Fridays. Evening Service. Should the first evening of the New Year fall on Friday, the Evening Service commences with "A Psalm, a Song for the Sabbath Day."

The following Amidah is said at the Evening, Morning and Afternoon Services.

O Lord, open you my lips, and my mouth shall declare your praise.

Blessed are you, O Lord our God and God of our fathers, God of Abraham, God of Isaac, and God of Jacob, the great, mighty and revered God, the most high God, who bestows loving-kindnesses, and possesses all things; who remembers the pious deeds of the patriarchs, and in love will bring a redeemer to their children's children for your name's sake.

Remember us unto life, O King, who delights in life, and inscribe us in the book of life, for your own sake, O living God.

O King, Helper, Savior and Shield. Blessed are you, O Lord, the Shield of Abraham.

You, O Lord, are mighty forever, you quicken the dead, you are mighty to save.

You sustain the living with loving-kindness, quicken the dead with great mercy, support the falling, heals the sick, loose the bound, and keep your faith to them that sleep in the dust. Who is like unto you, Lord of mighty acts, and who resembles you, O King, who kills and quickens, and causes salvation to spring forth?

Who is like unto you, Father of mercy, who in mercy remembers your creatures unto life?

Yea, faithful are you to quicken the dead. Blessed are you, O Lord, who quickens the dead.

You are holy, and your name is holy, and holy beings praise you daily. (Selah.)

Now, therefore, O Lord our God, impose your awe upon all your works, and your dread upon all that you have created, that all works may fear you and all creatures prostrate themselves before you, that they may all form a single band to do your will with a perfect heart, even as we know, O Lord our God, that dominion is yours, strength is in your hand, and might in your right hand, and that your name is to be feared above all that you have created.

Give then glory, O Lord, unto your people, praise to them that fear you, hope to them that seek you, and free speech to them that wait for you, joy to your land, gladness to your city, a flourishing horn unto David your servant, and a clear shining light unto the son of Jesse, your anointed, speedily in our days.

Then shall the just also see and be glad, and the upright shall exult, and the pious triumphantly rejoice, while iniquity shall close her mouth, and all wickedness shall be wholly consumed like smoke, when you make the dominion of arrogance to pass away from the earth.

And you, O Lord, shall reign, you alone over all your works on Mount Zion, the dwelling place of your glory, and in Jerusalem, your holy city, as it is written in your Holy Words, The Lord shall reign forever, your God, O Zion; unto all generations. Praise you the Lord.

Holy are you, and dreaded is your name, and there is no God beside you, as it is written, And the Lord of hosts is exalted in judgment, and the holy God is sanctified in righteousness. Blessed are you, O Lord, the holy King.

You have chosen us from all peoples, you have loved us and taken pleasure in us, and has exalted us above all tongues; you have sanctified us by your commandments and brought us near unto your service, O our King, and called us by your great and holy name.

On Saturday Night add the following—

You, O Lord our God, have made known unto us the judgments of your righteousness; you have taught us to perform the statutes of your will; you have given us, O Lord our God, righteous judgments, true laws, good statutes and commandments. You have also caused us to inherit seasons of joy, appointed times of holiness, and feasts of free will gifts, and has given us as a heritage the holiness of the Sabbath, the glory of the appointed time, and the celebration of the festival. You have made a distinction, O Lord our God, between holy and profane, between light and darkness, between Israel and other nations, between the seventh day and the six working days; you have made a distinction between the holiness of the Sabbath and that of the festival, and has hallowed the seventh day above the six working days; you have distinguished and sanctified your people Israel by your holiness.

On Sabbath add the words in brackets.

And you have given us in love, O Lord our God [this Sabbath Day and] this Day of Memorial, a day of blowing the Shofar, [on Sabbath substitute for the last phrase—a day of remembrance of blowing the Shofar, in love]; a holy convocation as a memorial of the departure from Egypt.

Our God and God of our fathers! May our remembrance rise and come and be accepted before you, with the remembrance of our fathers, of Messiah the son of David your servant, of Jerusalem your holy city, and of all your people the house of Israel, bringing deliverance and well-being, grace, loving-kindness and mercy, life and peace on this Day of Memorial. Remember us, O Lord our God, thereon for our wellbeing; be mindful of us for blessing, and save us unto life: by your promise of salvation and mercy, spare us and be gracious unto us; have mercy upon us and save us; for our eyes are bent upon you, because you are a gracious and merciful God and King.

Our God and God of our fathers, reign you in your glory over the whole universe, and be exalted above all the earth in your honor, and shine forth in the splendor and excellence of your might upon all the inhabitants of your world, that whatsoever has been made may know that you have made it, and whatsoever has been created may understand that you have created it, and whatsoever has breath in its nostrils may say, The Lord God of Israel is King, and his dominion rules over all. [Our God and God of our fathers, accept our rest.] Sanctify us by your commandments, and grant our portion in your Torah; satisfy us with your goodness, and gladden us with your salvation [and in your love and favor, O Lord our God, let us inherit your holy Sabbath; and may Israel, who hallow your name, rest thereon.] O purify our hearts to serve you in truth, for you are God in truth and your word is truth, and endures forever. Blessed are you, O Lord, King over all the earth, who sanctifies [the Sabbath and] Israel and the Day of Memorial.

Accept, O Lord our God, your people Israel and their prayer; restore the service to the oracle of your house; receive in love and favor both the fire offerings of Israel and their prayer; and may the service of your people Israel be ever acceptable unto you.

And let our eyes behold your return in mercy to Zion. Blessed are you, O Lord, who restores your divine presence unto Zion.

We give thanks unto you, for you are the Lord our God and the God of our fathers forever and ever; you are the Rock of our lives, the Shield of our salvation through every generation. We will give thanks unto you and declare your praise for our lives which are committed unto your hand, and for our souls which are in your charge, and for your miracles, which are daily with us, and for your wonders and your benefits, which are wrought at all times, evening, morn and noon. O you who are all-good, whose mercies fail not; you, merciful Being, whose loving-kindnesses never cease, the have ever hoped in you.

Congregation in an undertone

We give thanks unto you, for you are the Lord our God and the God of our fathers, the God of all flesh, our Creator and the Creator of all things in the beginning. Blessings and thanksgivings be to your great and holy name, because you have kept us in life and has preserved us; so may you continue to keep us in life and to preserve us. O gather our exiles to your holy courts to observe your statutes, to do your will, and to serve you with a perfect heart; seeing that we give thanks unto you. Blessed be the God to whom thanksgivings are due.

For all these things your name, O our King, shall be continually blessed and exalted forever and ever.

O inscribe all the children of your covenant for a happy life.

And everything that lives shall give thanks unto you forever, and shall praise your name in truth, O God, our salvation and our help. Blessed are you; O Lord, whose name is All-good, and unto whom it is becoming to give thanks.

At the repetition of the Amidah by the Reader the following is introduced—

Our God and God of our fathers, bless us with the three-fold blessing of your Torah written by the hand of Moses your servant, which was spoken by Aaron and his sons, the priests, your holy people, as it is said, The Lord bless you and keep you: the Lord make his face to shine upon you, and be gracious unto you: the Lord turn his face unto you, and give you peace.

At the Morning Service say—

Grant peace, welfare, blessing, grace, loving-kindness and mercy unto us and unto all Israel, your people. Bless us, O our Father, even all of us together, with the light of your countenance; for by the light of your countenance you have given us, O Lord our God, the Torah of life, loving-kindness and righteousness, blessing, mercy, life and peace; and may it be good in your sight to bless your people Israel at all times and in every hour with your peace.

At the Afternoon and Evening Service Say—

Grant abundant peace unto Israel your people forever; for you are the sovereign Lord of all peace; and may it be good in your sight to bless your people Israel at all times and at every hour with your peace.

In the book of life, blessing, peace and good sustenance may we be remembered and inscribed before you, we and all your people the house of Israel, for a happy life and for peace. Blessed are you, O Lord, who makes peace.

O my God! guard my tongue from evil and my lips from speaking guile; and to such as curse me let my soul be dumb, yea, let my soul be unto all as the dust. Open my heart to your Torah, and let my soul pursue your commandments. If any design evil against me, speedily make their counsel of none effect, and frustrate their designs. Do it for the sake of your name, do it for the sake of your right hand, do it for the sake of your holiness, do it for the sake of your Torah. In order that your beloved ones may be delivered, O save with your right hand, and answer me. Let the words of my mouth and the meditation of my heart be acceptable before you, O Lord, my Rock and my Redeemer. He who makes peace in his high places, may he make peace for us and for all Israel, and say ye, Amen.

May it be your will, O Lord our God and God of our fathers, that the temple be speedily rebuilt in our days, and grant our portion in your Torah. And there we will serve you with awe, as in the days of old, and Is in ancient years. Then shall the offering of Judah and Jerusalem be pleasant unto the Lord, as in the lays of old, and as in ancient years.

The following form of greeting is used on New Year:

May you be inscribed for a happy year.

KIDDUSH FOR NEW YEAR
When New Year occurs on Sabbath begin here—

And it was evening and it was morning, the sixth day.

And the heaven and the earth were finished and all their host. And on the seventh day God had finished his work which he had made; and he rested on the seventh day from all his work which he had made.

And God blessed the seventh day, and he hallowed it, because he rested thereon from all his work which God had created and made.

Blessed are you, O Lord our God, King of the universe, who creates the fruit of the vine.

On Sabbath add the words in brackets.

Blessed are you, O Lord our God, King of the universe, who has chosen us from all peoples and exalted us above all tongues, and sanctified us by your commandments. And you have given us in love, O Lord our God, [this Sabbath day and] this Day of Memorial, a day of blowing the Shofar [on Sabbath substitute for the last phrase—a day of remembrance of blowing the Shofar, in love]; a holy convocation, as a memorial of the departure from Egypt. For you have chosen us and has sanctified us above all nations; and your word is truth and endures forever. Blessed are you, O Lord, King over all the earth, who sanctifies [the Sabbath and] Israel and the Day of Memorial.

On Saturday night the following is added:

Blessed are you, O Lord our God, King of the universe, who creates the light of the fire.

Blessed are you, O Lord our God, King of the universe, who makes a distinction between holy and profane, between light and darkness, between Israel and other nations, between the seventh day and the six working days. You have made a distinction between the holiness of the Sabbath and that of the festival, and has hallowed the seventh day above the six working days; you have distinguished and sanctified your people Israel by your holiness. Blessed are you, O Lord, who makes a distinction between holy and holy.

Blessed are you, O Lord our God, King of the universe, who has kept us in life, and has preserved us, and enabled us to reach this season.

Kiddush and the Blessing over the Bread having been said, an apple, dipped in honey, is taken, before partaking of which the following is said—

Blessed are you, O Lord our God, King of the universe, who creates the fruit of the tree.

After having partaken of the apple and honey, say—

May it be your will, O Lord our God, and God of our fathers, to renew unto us a happy and pleasant year.

ADDITIONAL SERVICE FOR NEW YEAR

O Lord, open you my lips, and my mouth shall declare your praise.

Blessed are you, O Lord our God and God of our fathers, God of Abraham, God of Isaac, and God of Jacob, the great, mighty and revered God, the most high God, who bestows loving-kindnesses, and possesses all things; who remembers the pious deeds of the patriarchs, and in love will bring a redeemer to their children's children for your name's sake.

Remember us unto life, O King, who delights in life, and inscribe us in the book of life, for your own sake, O living God.

O King, Helper, Savior and Shield. Blessed are you, O Lord, the Shield of Abraham.

You, O Lord, are mighty forever, you quicken the dead, you are mighty to save.

You sustain the living with loving-kindness, quicken the dead with great mercy, support the falling, heals the sick, loose the bound, and keep your faith to them that sleep in the dust. Who is like unto you, Lord of mighty acts, and who resembles you, O King, who kills and quickens, and causes salvation to spring forth?

Who is like unto you, Father of mercy, who in mercy remembers your creatures unto life?

Yea, faithful are you to quicken the dead. Blessed are you, O Lord, who quickens the dead.

You are holy, and your name is holy, and holy beings praise you daily. (Selah.)

Now, therefore, O Lord our God, impose your awe upon all your works, and your dread upon all that you have created, that all works may fear you and all creatures prostrate themselves before you, that they may all form a single band to do your will with a perfect heart, even as we know, O Lord our God, that dominion is yours, strength is in your hand, and might in your right hand, and that your name is to be feared above all that you have created.

Give then glory, O Lord, unto your people, praise to them that fear you, hope to them that seek you, and free speech to them that wait for you, joy to your land, gladness to your city, a flourishing horn unto David your servant, and a clear shining light unto the son of Jesse, your anointed, speedily in our days.

Then shall the just also see and be glad, and the upright shall exult, and the pious triumphantly rejoice, while iniquity shall close her mouth, and all wickedness shall be wholly consumed like smoke, when you make the dominion of arrogance to pass away from the earth.

And you, O Lord, shall reign, you alone over all your works on Mount Zion, the dwelling place of your glory, and in Jerusalem, your holy city, as it is written in your Holy Words, The Lord shall reign forever, your God, O Zion, unto all generations. Praise you the Lord.

Holy are you, and dreaded is your name, and there is no God beside you, as it is written, And the Lord of hosts is exalted in judgment, and the holy God is sanctified in righteousness. Blessed are you, O Lord, the holy King.

You have chosen us from all peoples; you have loved us and taken pleasure in us, and has exalted us above all tongues; you have sanctified us by your commandments, and brought us near unto your service, O our King, and called us by your great and holy name.

On Sabbath add the words in brackets.

And you have given us in love, O Lord our God, [this Sabbath day and] this Day of Memorial, a day of blowing the Shofar [on Sabbaths substitute for the last phrase—a day of remembrance of blowing the Shofar, in love]; a holy convocation, as a memorial of the departure from Egypt.

But on account of our sins we were exiled from our land, and removed far from our country, and we are unable to fulfil our obligations in your chosen house, that great and holy temple which was called by your name, because of the hand that has been stretched out against your sanctuary. May it be your will, O Lord our God and God of our fathers, merciful King, that you may again in your abundant compassion have mercy upon us and upon your sanctuary, and may speedily rebuild it and magnify its glory. Our Father, our King, do you speedily make the glory of your kingdom manifest upon us; shine forth and exalt yourself upon us in the sight of all living; bring our scattered ones among the nations near unto you, and gather our dispersed from the ends of the earth. Lead us with exultation unto Zion your city, and unto Jerusalem the place of your sanctuary with everlasting joy; and there we will prepare before you the offerings that are obligatory for us, the continual offerings according to their order, and the additional offerings according to their enactment; and the additional offerings of [this Sabbath day and] this Day of Memorial, we will prepare and offer unto you in love according to the precept of your will, as you have prescribed for us in your Torah through the hand of Moses your servant, by the mouth of your glory, as it is said:

[And on the Sabbath day two he-lambs of the first year without blemish, and two-tenth parts of an ephah of fine flour for a meal offering, mingled with oil, and the drink offering thereof; this is the burnt offering of every Sabbath, beside the continual burnt offering and the drink offering thereof.]

And in the seventh month, on the first day of the month, you shall have a holy convocation; you shall do no servile work: it shall be a day of blowing the Shofar unto you. And you shall offer a burnt offering for a sweet savor unto the Lord; one young bullock, one ram, seven he-lambs of the first year without blemish. And their meal offering and their drink offerings as has been ordained; three-tenth parts of an ephah for each bullock, and two-tenth parts for the ram, and one-tenth part for each lamb, with wine according to the drink offering thereof, and two he-goats with which to make atonement, and the two continual offerings according to their enactment; beside the burnt offering of the New Moon and the meal offering thereof, and the continual burnt offering and the meal offering thereof, and their drink offerings, according to their ordinance, for a sweet savor, an offering made by fire unto the Lord.

[They that keep the Sabbath and call it a delight shall rejoice in your kingdom; the people that hallow the seventh day, even all of them, shall be satiated and delighted with your goodness, seeing that you did find pleasure in the seventh day, and did hallow it; you did call it the desirable of days, in remembrance of the creation.]

It is our duty to praise the Lord of all things, to ascribe greatness to him who formed the world in the beginning, since he has not made us like the nations of other lands, and has not placed us like other families of the earth, since he has not assigned unto us a portion as unto them, nor a lot as unto all their multitude. For we bend the knee and offer worship and thanks before the supreme King of kings, the Holy One, blessed be he, who stretched forth the heavens and laid the foundations of the earth, the seat of whose glory is in the heavens above, and the abode of whose might is in the loftiest heights. He is our God; there is none else: in truth he is our King; there is none besides him; as it is written in his Torah, And you shall know this day, and lay it to your heart, that the Lord he is God in heaven above and upon the earth beneath: there is none else.

We therefore hope in you, O Lord our God, that we may speedily behold the glory of your might, when you will remove the abominations from the earth, and the idols will be utterly cut off, when the world will be perfected under the kingdom of the Almighty, and all the children of flesh will call upon your name, when you will turn unto yourself all the wicked of the earth. Let all the inhabitants of the world perceive and know that unto you every knee must bow, every tongue must swear. Before you, O Lord our God, let them bow and fall; and unto your glorious name let them give honor; let them all accept the yoke of your kingdom, and do you reign over them speedily, and forever and ever. For the kingdom is yours, and to all eternity you will reign in glory; as it is written in your Torah, The Lord shall reign forever and ever.

And it is said, He has not beheld iniquity in Jacob, neither has he seen perverseness in Israel: the Lord his God is with him, and the trumpet shout of a King is among them. And it is said, And he became King in Yeshurun, when the heads of the people were gathered, the tribes of Israel together. And in your Holy Words it is written, saying, For the kingdom is the Lord's, and he is ruler over the nations. And it is said, The Lord reigns; he has robed him in majesty; the Lord has robed him, yea, he has girded himself with strength: the world also is set firm, that it cannot be moved. And it is said, Lift up your heads, O you gates, and be you lifted up, you everlasting doors, that the King of glory may come in. Who, then, is the King of glory? The Lord, strong and mighty, the Lord mighty in battle. Lift up your heads, O you gates; yea, lift them up, you everlasting doors, that the King of glory may come in. Who, then, is the King of glory? The Lord of hosts, he is the King of glory. (Selah.) And by the hands of your servants, the prophets, it is written, saying, Thus says the Lord, the King of Israel and his Redeemer, the Lord of hosts: I am the first, and I am the last; and beside me there is no God. And it is said, And saviors shall come up on Mount Zion to judge the Mount of Esau, and the kingdom shall be the Lord's. And it is said, And the Lord shall be King over all the earth: in that day shall the Lord be One and his name One. And in your Torah it is written saying, Hear, O Israel: the Lord our God, the Lord is One.

Our God and God of our fathers, reign you in your glory over the whole universe, and be exalted above all the earth in your honor, and shine forth in the splendor and excellence of your might upon all the inhabitants of your world, that whatsoever has been made may know that you have made it, and whatsoever has been created may understand that you have created it, and whatsoever has breath in its nostrils may say, the Lord God of Israel is King and his dominion rules over all. [Our God and God of our fathers, accept our rest.] Sanctify us by your commandments, and grant our portion in your Torah; satisfy us with your goodness, and gladden us with your salvation: [and in your love and favor, O Lord our God, let us inherit your holy Sabbath; and may Israel, who hallow your name, rest thereon]. O purify our hearts to serve you in truth, for you are God in truth, and your word is truth, and endures forever. Blessed are you, O Lord,) King over all the earth, who sanctifies [the Sabbath and] Israel and the Day of Memorial.

You remember what was wrought from eternity and are mindful of all that has been formed from of old: before you all secrets are revealed and the multitude of hidden things from the beginning; for there is no forgetfulness before the throne of your glory; nor is there naught hidden from your eyes. You remember every deed that has been done: not a creature is concealed from you: all things are manifest and known unto you, O Lord our God, who looks and sees to the end of all generations. For you will bring on the appointed time of memorial when every spirit and soul shall be visited, and the multitudinous works be remembered with the innumerable throng of your creatures. From the beginning you did make this your purpose known, and from aforetime you did disclose it. This day, on which was the beginning of your work, is a memorial of the first day, for it is a statute for Israel, a decree of the God of Jacob. Thereon also sentence is pronounced upon countries,—which of them is destined to the sword and which to peace, which to famine and which to plenty; and each separate creature is visited thereon, and recorded for life or for death. Who is not visited on this day? For the remembrance of every creature comes before you, each man's deeds and destiny, his works and ways, his thoughts and schemes, his imaginings and achievements. Happy is the man who forgets you not, and the son of man who strengthens himself in you; for they that seek you shall never stumble, neither shall any be put to shame who trust in you. Yea, the remembrance of all works comes before you, and you enquire into the doings of them all. Of Noah also you were mindful in your love, and did visit him with a promise of salvation and mercy, when you brought the waters of the flood to destroy all flesh on account of their evil deeds. So his remembrance came before you, O Lord our God, to increase his seed like the dust of the earth, and his offspring like the sand of the sea: as it is written in your Torah, And God remembered Noah, and every living thing, and all the cattle that were with him in the ark: and God made a wind to pass over the earth, and the waters subsided. And it is said, And God heard their groaning, and God remembered his covenant with Abraham, with Isaac and with Jacob. And it is said, Then will I remember my covenant with Jacob; and also my covenant with Isaac, and also my covenant with Abraham will I remember; and I will remember the land. And in your Holy Words it is written saying, He has made a memorial for his wondrous works: the Lord is gracious and full of compassion. And it is said, He has given food unto them that fear him: he will ever be mindful of his covenant. And it is said, And he remembered for them his covenant, and repented according to the multitude of his loving-kindnesses. And by the hands of your servants, the prophets, it is written saying, Go and cry in the ears of Jerusalem, saying, Thus says the Lord, I remember for you the kindness of your youth, the love of your bridal state; how you went after me in the wilderness, in a land that was not sown. And it is said, Nevertheless, I will remember my covenant with you in the days of your youth, and I will establish unto you an everlasting covenant. And it is said, Is Ephraim a precious son unto me? Is he a caressed child? As often as I spoke against him, I earnestly remembered him. Therefore my heart yearns for him: I will surely have mercy upon him, says the Lord.

Our God and God of our fathers, let us be remembered by you for good: grant us a visitation of salvation and mercy from your heavens, the heavens of old; and remember unto us, O Lord our God, the covenant and the loving-kindness and the oath which you swore unto Abraham our father on Mount Moriah: and may the binding with which Abraham our father bound his son Isaac on the altar appear before you. How he overbore his compassion in order to perform your will with a perfect heart. So may your compassion overbear your anger against us; in your great goodness may the fierceness of your wrath turn aside from your people, your city and your inheritance. Fulfil unto us, O Lord our God, the word in which you have bidden us trust in your Torah through the hand of Moses your servant, from the mouth of your glory, as it is said, But I will remember unto them the covenant of their ancestors, whom I brought forth out of the land of Egypt in the sight of the nations, that I might be their God: I am the Lord. For you are he who remembers from eternity all forgotten things, and before the throne of whose glory there is no forgetfulness. O remember the binding of Isaac this day in mercy unto his seed. Blessed are you, O Lord, who remembers the covenant.

You did reveal yourself in a cloud of glory unto your holy people in order to speak with them. Out of heaven you did make them hear your voice and was revealed unto them in clouds of purity. The whole world trembled at your presence, and the works of creation were in awe of you, when you did thus reveal yourself, O our King, upon Mount Sinai to teach your people the Torah and commandments, and did make them hear your majestic voice and your holy utterances out of flames of fire. Amid thunders and lightning you did manifest yourself to them, and while the Shofar sounded you did shine forth upon them; as it is written in your Torah, And it came to pass on the third day, when it was morning, that there were thunders and lightning, and a thick cloud upon the mount, and the sound of the Shofar exceeding loud; and all the people that were in the camp trembled. And it is said, And the sound of the Shofar waxed louder and louder; Moses spoke, and God answered him by a voice. And it is said, And all the people perceived the thundering and the lightning, and the sound of the Shofar, and the mountain smoking: and when the people saw it, they were moved and stood afar off. And in your Holy Words it is written, saying, God is gone up with a shout, the Lord with the sound of a Shofar. And it is said, With trumpets and sound of Shofar shout joyously before the King, the Lord. And it is said, Blow the Shofar on the new moon, at the beginning of the month, for our day of festival; for it is a statute for Israel, a decree of the God of Jacob. And it is said, Praise you the Lord. Praise God in his sanctuary: praise him in the firmament of his power. Praise him for his mighty acts: praise him according to his abundant greatness. Praise him with the blast of the Shofar: praise him with the harp and the lyre. Praise him with the timbrel and dance: praise him with stringed instruments and the pipe, Praise him with the clear-toned cymbals: praise him with the loud-sounding cymbals. Let everything that has breath praise the Lord. Praise you the Lord. And by the hands of your servants, the prophets, it is written saying, All you inhabitants of the world, and you dwellers on the earth, when an ensign is lifted up on the mountains, see ye, and when the Shofar is blown, hear ye. And it is said, And it shall come to pass on that day, that a great Shofar shall be blown; and they shall come who were lost in the land of Assyria, and they that were outcasts in the land of Egypt; and they shall worship the Lord in the holy mountain at Jerusalem. And it is said, And the Lord shall be seen over them, and his arrow shall go forth as the lightning: and the Lord God shall blow the Shofar, and shall go with the whirlwinds of the south. The Lord of hosts shall be a shield unto them. So be a shield unto your people Israel with your peace.

Our God and God of our fathers, sound the great Shofar for our freedom, lift up the ensign to gather our exiles; bring our scattered ones among the nations near unto you, and gather our dispersed from the ends of the earth. Lead us with exultation unto Zion, your city, and unto Jerusalem the place of your sanctuary with everlasting joy; and there we will prepare before you the offerings that are obligatory for us, as is commanded us in your Torah through the hand of Moses your servant, from the mouth of your glory, as it is said, And in the day of your gladness, and in your set feasts, and in the beginnings of your months, you shall blow with the trumpets over your burnt offerings, and over the sacrifices of your peace offerings; and they shall be to you for a memorial before your God: I am the Lord your God. For you hear the sound of the Shofar and give heed to the trumpet-blast, and there is none like unto you. Blessed are you, O Lord, who in mercy hears the sound of the trumpet-blast of your people Israel.

Accept, O Lord our God, your people Israel and their prayer; restore the service to the oracle of your house; receive in love and favor both the fire offerings of Israel and their prayer; and may the service of your people Israel be ever acceptable unto you.

And let our eyes behold your return in mercy to Zion. Blessed are you, O Lord, who restores your divine presence unto Zion.

We give thanks unto you, for you are the Lord our God and the God of our fathers forever and ever; you are the Rock of our lives, the Shield of our salvation through every generation. We will give thanks unto you and declare your praise for our lives which are committed unto your hand, and for our souls which are in your charge, and for your miracles, which are daily with us, and for your Wonders and your benefits, which are wrought at all times, evening, morn and noon. O you who are all-good, whose mercies fail not; you, merciful Being, whose loving-kindnesses never cease, we have ever hoped in you.

Congregation in an undertone

We give thanks unto you, for you are the Lord our God and the God of our fathers, the God of all flesh, our Creator and the Creator of all things in the beginning. Blessings and thanksgivings be to your great and holy name, because you have kept us in life and has preserved us so may you continue to keep us in life and to preserve us. O gather our exiles to your holy courts to observe your statutes, to do your will, and to serve you with a perfect heart; seeing that we give thanks unto you. Blessed be the God to whom thanksgivings are due.

For all these things your name, O our King, shall be continually blessed and exalted forever and ever.

O inscribe all the children of your covenant for a happy life.

And everything that lives shall give thanks unto you forever, and shall praise your name in truth, O God, our salvation and our help. Blessed are you, O Lord, whose name is All-good, and unto whom it is becoming to give thanks.

At the repetition of the Amidah by the Reader, the following is introduced—

Our God and God of our fathers, bless us with the three-fold blessing of your Torah written by the hand of Moses your servant, which was spoken by Aaron and his sons, the priests, your holy people, as it is said, The Lord bless you, and keep you: the Lord make his face to shine upon you, and be gracious unto you: the Lord turn his face unto you, and give you peace.

Grant peace, welfare, blessing, grace, loving-kindness and mercy unto us and unto all Israel, your people. Bless us, O our Father, even all of us together, with the light of your countenance; for by the light of your countenance you have given us, O Lord our God, the Torah of life, loving-kindness and righteousness, blessing, mercy, life and peace; and may it be good it your sight to bless your people Israel at all times and in every hour with your peace.

In the book of life, blessing, peace and good sustenance may we be remembered and inscribed before you, we and all your people the house of Israel, for a happy life and for peace. Blessed are you, O Lord who makes peace.

O my God! guard my tongue from evil and my lips from speaking guile; and to such as curse me let my soul be dumb, yea, let my soul be unto all as the dust. Open my heart to your Torah, and let my soul pursue your commandments. If any design evil against me, speedily make their counsel of none effect, and frustrate their designs. Do it for the sake of your name, do it for the sake of your right hand, do it for the sake of your holiness, do it for the sake of your Torah. In order that your beloved ones may be delivered, O save with your right hand, and answer me. Let the words of my mouth and the meditation of my heart be acceptable before you, O Lord, my Rock and my Redeemer. He who makes peace in his high places, may he make peace for us and for all Israel, and say ye, Amen.

May it be your will, O Lord our God and God of our fathers, that the temple be speedily rebuilt in our days, and grant our portion in your Torah. And there we will serve you with awe, as in the days of old, and as in ancient years. Then shall the offering of Judah and Jerusalem be pleasant unto the Lord, as in the days of old, and as in ancient years.

The Blessing of the Priests when the New Year falls on a week-day.

On the Day of New Year, or, when New Year falls on Sabbath, on the Second Day, after the Afternoon Service, it is customary to go to the banks of a river, or of any other piece of water, and to say the following—

Who is a God like unto you that pardons iniquity and passes by the transgression of the remnant of his heritage? He retains not his anger forever, because he delights in loving-kindness. He will turn again and have mercy upon us; he will subdue our iniquities. And you will cast all their sins into the depths of the sea. O may you cast all the sins of your people, the house of Israel, into a place where they shall be no more remembered or visited, or ever again come to mind. You will show faithfulness to Jacob, and loving-kindness to Abraham as you have sworn unto our fathers from the days of old.

SERVICE FOR THE EVE OF THE DAY OF ATONEMENT

On the day previous to the Fast of Atonement, Afternoon Service is said as on Fridays, but earlier than usual, After "who makes peace," say "Our God . . . let our prayer come," to the end of the Amidah for the Day of Atonement.

"It is our duty."

Before going to Synagogue the lamp is lighted, and the following Blessing is said—

Blessed are you, O Lord our God, King of the universe, who has sanctified us by your commandments, and commanded us to kindle the light of the [Sabbath and the] Day of Atonement.

SERVICE FOR THE DAY OF ATONEMENT

O Lord, open you my lips, and my mouth shall declare your praise.

Blessed are you, O Lord our God and God of our fathers, God of Abraham, God of Isaac, and God of Jacob, the great, mighty and revered God, the most high God, who bestows loving-kindnesses, and possesses all things; who remembers the pious deeds of the patriarchs, and in love will bring a redeemer to their children's children for your name's sake.

Remember us unto life, O King, who delights in life, and inscribe us in the book of life, for your own sake, O living God.

O King, Helper, Savior and Shield. Blessed are you, O Lord, the Shield of Abraham.

You, O Lord, are mighty forever, you quicken the dead, you are mighty to save.

You sustain the living with loving-kindness, quicken the dead with great mercy, support the falling, heals the sick, loose the bound, and keep your faith to them that sleep in the dust. Who is like unto you, Lord of mighty acts, and who resembles you, O King, who kills and quickens, and causes salvation to spring forth?

Who is like unto you, Father of mercy, who in mercy remembers your creatures unto life?

Yea, faithful are you to quicken the dead. Blessed are you, O Lord, who quickens the dead.

You are holy, and your name is holy, and holy beings praise you daily. (Selah.)

Now, therefore, O Lord our God, impose your awe upon all your works, and your dread upon all that you have created, that all works may fear you and all creatures prostrate themselves before you, that they may all form a single band to do your will with a perfect heart, even as we know, O Lord our God, that dominion is yours, strength is in your hand, and might in your right hand, and that your name is to be feared above all that you have created.

Give then glory, O Lord, unto your people, praise to them that fear you, hope to them that seek you, and free speech to them that wait for you, joy to your land, gladness to your city, a flourishing horn unto David your servant, and a clear shining light unto the son of Jesse, your anointed, speedily in our days.

Then shall the just also see and be glad, and the upright shall exult, and the pious triumphantly rejoice, while iniquity shall close her mouth, and all wickedness shall be wholly consumed like smoke, when you make the dominion of arrogance to pass away from the earth.

And you, O Lord, shall reign, you alone over all your works on Mount Zion, the dwelling place of your glory, and in Jerusalem, your holy city, as it is written in your Holy Words, The Lord shall reign forever, your God, O Zion, unto all generations. Praise you the Lord.

Holy are you, and dreaded is your name, and there is no God beside you, as it is written, And the Lord of hosts is exalted in judgment, and the holy God is sanctified in righteousness. Blessed are you, O Lord, the holy King.

You have chosen us from all peoples, you have loved us and taken pleasure in us, and has exalted us above all tongues; you have sanctified us by your commandments, and brought us near unto your service, O our King, and has called us by your great and holy name.

On Sabbath add the words in brackets.

And you have given us in love, O Lord our God, [this Sabbath day for holiness and rest, and] this Day of Atonement for pardon, forgiveness, and atonement, that we may [in love] obtain pardon thereon for all our iniquities; a holy convocation, as a memorial of the departure from Egypt.

Our God and God of our fathers! May our remembrance rise and come and be accepted before you, with the remembrance of our fathers, of Messiah, the son of David your servant, of Jerusalem your holy city, and of all your people the house of Israel, bringing deliverance and well-being, grace, loving-kindness and mercy, life and peace on this Day of Atonement. Remember us, O Lord our God, thereon for our wellbeing; be mindful of us for blessing, and save us unto life; by your promise of salvation and mercy, spare us and be gracious unto us; have mercy upon us and save us; for our eyes are bent upon you, because you are a gracious and merciful God and King.

Our God and God of our fathers, pardon our iniquities [on this Sabbath day, and] on this Day of Atonement; blot out our transgressions and our sins, and make them pass away from before your eyes; as it is said, I even I, am he that blots out your transgressions for my own sake; and I will not remember your sins. And it is said, I have blotted out, as a cloud, your transgressions, and, as a mist, your sins: return unto me, for I have redeemed you. And it is said, For on this day shall atonement be made for you, to cleanse you; from all your sins shall you be clean before the Lord. [Our God and God of our fathers, accept our rest.] Sanctify us by your commandments, and grant our portion in your Torah; satisfy us with your goodness, and gladden us with your salvation; [and let us inherit, O Lord our God, in love and favor, your holy Sabbath; and may Israel, who hallow your name, rejoice thereon]; and purify our hearts to serve you in truth; for you are the forgiver of Israel and the pardoner of the tribes of Yeshurun in every generation, and beside you we have no king who pardons and forgives. Blessed are you, O Lord, you King, who pardons and forgives our iniquities and the iniquities of your people, the house of Israel, who makes our trespasses to pass away year by year, King over all the earth, who sanctifies [the Sabbath and] Israel and the day of Atonement.

Accept, O Lord our God, your people Israel and their prayer; restore the service to the oracle of your house; receive in love and favor both the fire offerings of Israel and their prayer; and may the service of your people Israel be ever acceptable unto you.

And let our eyes behold your return in mercy to Zion. Blessed are you, O Lord, who restores your divine presence unto Zion.

We give thanks unto you, for you are the Lord our God and the God of our fathers forever and ever; you are the Rock of our lives, the Shield of our salvation through every generation. We will give thanks unto you and declare your praise for our lives which are committed unto your hand, and for our souls which are in your charge, and for your miracles, which are daily with us, and for your wonders and your benefits, which are wrought at all times, evening, morn and noon. O you who are all-good, whose mercies fail not; you, merciful Being whose loving-kindnesses never cease, we have ever hoped in you.

Congregation in an undertone

We give thanks unto you, for you are the Lord our God and the God of our fathers, the God of all flesh, our Creator and the Creator of all things in the beginning. Blessings and thanksgivings be to your great and holy name because you have kept us in life and has preserved us so may you continue to keep us in life and to preserve us. O gather our exiles to your holy courts to observe your statutes, to do your will, and to serve you with a perfect heart; seeing that we give thanks unto you. Blessed be the God to whom thanksgivings are due.

For all these things your name, O our King, shall be continually blessed and exalted forever and ever.

O inscribe all the children of your covenant for a happy life.

And everything that lives shall give thanks unto you forever, and shall praise your name in truth, O God, our salvation and our help. Blessed are you, O Lord, whose name is All-good, and unto whom it is becoming to give thanks.

At the repetition of the Amidah by the Reader the following is introduced—

Our God and God of our fathers, bless us with the three-fold blessing of your Torah written by the hand of Moses your servant, which was spoken by Aaron and his sons, the priests, your holy people, as it is said, The Lord bless you, and keep you: the Lord make his face to shine upon you, and be gracious unto you: the Lord turn his face unto you, and give you peace.

At the Morning Service say—

Grant peace, welfare, blessing, grace, loving-kindness and mercy unto us and unto all Israel, your people. Bless us, O our Father, even all of us together, with the light of your countenance; for by the light of your countenance you have given us, O Lord our God, the Torah of life, loving-kindness and righteousness, blessing, mercy, life and peace; and may it be good in your sight to bless your people Israel at all times and in every hour with your peace.

At the Afternoon and Evening Service say—

Grant abundant peace unto Israel your people forever; for you are the sovereign Lord of all peace; and may it be good in your sight to bless your people Israel at all times and at every hour with your peace.

In the book of life, blessing, peace and good sustenance may we be remembered and inscribed before you, we and all your people the house of Israel, for a happy life and for peace. Blessed are you, O Lord, who makes peace.

Our God and God of our fathers,

let our prayer come before you; hide not yourself from our supplication, for we are not arrogant and stiff-necked, that we should say before you, O Lord our God and God of our fathers, we are righteous and have not sinned; but verily, we have sinned.

We have trespassed, we have been faithless, we have robbed, we have spoken basely, we have committed iniquity, we have wrought unrighteousness, we have been presumptuous, we have done violence, we have forged lies, we have counselled evil, we have spoken falsely, we have scoffed, we have revolted, we have blasphemed, we have been rebellious, we have acted perversely, we have transgressed, we have persecuted, we have been stiff-necked, we have done wickedly, we have corrupted ourselves, we have committed abomination, we have gone astray, and we have led astray.

We have turned aside from your commandments and good judgments, and it has profited us naught. But you are righteous in all that is come upon us; for you have acted truthfully, but we have wrought unrighteousness.

What shall we say before you, O you who dwells on high, and what shall we recount unto you, you who abides in the heavens? Do you not know all things, both the hidden and the revealed?

You know the secrets of eternity and the most hidden mysteries of all living. You search the innermost recesses, and try the reins and the heart. Naught is concealed from you, or hidden from your eyes.

May it then be your will, O Lord our God and God of our fathers, to forgive us for all our sins, to pardon us for all our iniquities, and to grant us remission for all our transgressions.

For the sin which we have committed before you tinder compulsion, or of our own will;
And for the sin which we have committed before you in hardening of the heart:
For the sin which we have committed before you unknowingly;
And for the sin which we have committed before you with utterance of the lips:
For the sin which we have committed before you by unchastity;
And for the sin which we have committed before you openly and secretly:
For the sin which we have committed before you knowingly and deceitfully:
And for the sin which we have committed before you in speech:
For the sin which we have committed before you by wronging our neighbor;
And for the sin which we have committed before you by the sinful meditating of the heart:
For the sin which we have committed before you by association with impurity;
And for the sin which have committed before you by confession with the mouth alone:
For the sin which we have committed before you by despising parents and teachers;
And for the sin which we have committed before you in presumption or in error:

For the sin which we have committed before you by violence;

And for the sin which we have committed before you by the profanation of the divine Name:

For the sin which we have committed before you by unclean lips;

And for the sin which we have committed before you by folly of the mouth:

For the sin which we have committed before you by the evil inclination;

And for the sin which we have committed before you wittingly or unwittingly:

For all these, O God of forgiveness, forgive us, pardon us, grant us remission.

For the sin which we have committed before you by denying and lying;

And for the sin which we have committed before you by taking of bribes:

For the sin which we have committed before you by scoffing;

And for the sin which we have committed before you by slander:

For the sin which we have committed before you in business;

And for the sin which we have committed before you in eating and drinking:

For the sin which we have committed before you by usury and interest;

And for the sin which we have committed before you by the stretched forth neck of pride:

For the sin which we have committed before you by the conversation of our lips;

And for the sin which we have committed before you with wanton looks:

For the sin which we have committed before you with haughty eyes;

And for the sin which we have committed before you by effrontery:

For all these, O God of forgiveness, forgive us, pardon us, grant us remission.

For the sin which we have committed before you by breaking off the yoke of your commandments;

And for the sin which we have committed before them by contentiousness:

For the sin which we have committed before you by ensnaring our neighbor;

And for the sin which we have committed before you by envy:

For the sin which we have committed before you by levity;

And for the sin which we have committed before you by being stiff-necked:

For the sin which we have committed before you by running to do evil;

And for the sin which we have committed before you by tale-bearing:

For the sin which we have committed before you by vain oaths;

And for the sin which we have committed before you by causeless hatred:

For the sin which we have committed before you by breach of trust;

And for the sin which we have committed before you with confusion of mind:

For all these, O God of forgiveness, forgive us, pardon us, grant us remission.

And also for the sins for which we owe a burnt offering:

And for the sins for which we owe a sin offering:

And for the sins for which we owe an offering, varying according to our means:

And for the sins for which we owe an offering, whether for certain or for doubtful trespass.

And for the sins for which we are liable to the penalty of chastisement:

And for the sins for which we are liable to the penalty of forty stripes:

And for the sins for which we are liable to the penalty of death by the hand of heaven:

And for the sins for which we are liable to the penalty of excision and childlessness:

For all these, O God of forgiveness, forgive us, pardon us, grant us remission.

And also for the sins for which we are liable to any of the four death penalties inflicted by the court, stoning, burning, beheading, and strangling; for the violation of positive, or for the violation of negative precepts, whether these latter do or do not admit of a remedy by the subsequent fulfilment of a positive command; for all our sins, whether they be or be not manifest to us. Such sins as are manifest to us, we have already declared and confessed unto you, while such as are not manifest unto us, are manifest and known unto you, according to the word that has been spoken, The secret things belong unto the Lord our God; but the things that are revealed belong unto us and to our children forever, that we may do all the words of this Torah. For you are the forgiver of Israel and the pardoner of the tribes of Yeshurun in every generation, and beside you we have no king, who pardons and forgives.

O my God, before I was formed I was nothing worth, and now that I have been formed I am but as though I had not been formed. Dust am I in my life: how much more so in my death. Behold I am before you like a vessel filled with shame and contusion, O may it be your will, O Lord my God and God of my fathers, that I may sin no more, and as to the sins I have committed, purge them away in your abounding compassion though not by means of affliction and sore diseases.

O my God! guard my tongue from evil and my lips from speaking guile; and to such as curse me let my soul be dumb, yea, let my soul be unto all as the dust. Open my heart to your Torah, and let my soul pursue your commandments. If any design evil against me, speedily make their counsel of none effect, and frustrate their designs. Do it for the sake of your name, do it for the sake of your right hand, do it for the sake of your holiness, do it for the sake of your Torah, In order that your beloved ones may be delivered, O save with your right hand, and answer me. Let the words of my mouth and the meditation of my heart be acceptable before you, O Lord, my Rock and my Redeemer. He who makes peace in his high places, may he make peace for us and for all Israel, and say ye, Amen.

May it be your will, O Lord our God and God of our fathers, that the temple be speedily rebuilt in our days, and grant our portion in your Torah. And there we will serve you with awe, as in the days of old, and as in ancient years. Then shall the offering of Judah and Jerusalem be pleasant unto the Lord, as in the days of old, and as in ancient years.

ADDITIONAL SERVICE FOR THE DAY OF ATONEMENT

O Lord, open you my lips, and my mouth shall declare your praise.

Blessed are you, O Lord our God and God of our fathers, God of Abraham, God of Isaac, and God of Jacob, the great, mighty and revered God, the most high God, who bestows loving-kindnesses, and possesses all things; who remembers the pious deeds of the patriarchs, and in love will bring a redeemer to their children's children for your name's sake.

Remember us unto life, O King, who delights in life, and inscribe us in the book of life, for your own sake, O living God.

O King, Helper, Savior and Shield. Blessed are you, O Lord, the Shield of Abraham.

You, O Lord, are mighty forever, you quicken the dead, you are mighty to save.

You sustain the living with loving-kindness, quicken the dead with great mercy, support the falling, heals the sick, loose the bound, and keep your faith to them that sleep in the dust. Who is like unto you, Lord of mighty acts, and who resembles you, O King, who kills and quickens, and causes salvation to spring forth?

Who is like unto you, Father of mercy, who in mercy remembers your creatures unto life?

Yea, faithful are you to quicken the dead. Blessed are you, O Lord, who quickens the dead.

You are holy, and your name is holy, and holy beings praise you daily. (Selah.)

Now, therefore, O Lord our God, impose your awe upon all your works, and your dread upon all that you have created, that all works may fear you and all creatures prostrate themselves before you, that they may all form a single band to do your will with a perfect heart, even as we know, O Lord our God, that dominion is yours, strength is in your hand, and might in your right hand, and that your name is to be feared above all that you have created.

Give then glory, O Lord, unto your people, praise to them that fear you, hope to them that seek you, and free speech to them that wait for you, joy to your land, gladness to your city, a flourishing horn unto David your servant, and a clear shining light unto the son of Jesse, your anointed, speedily in our days.

Then shall the just also see and be glad, and the upright shall exult, and the pious triumphantly rejoice, while iniquity shall close her mouth, and all wickedness shall be wholly consumed like smoke, when you make the dominion of arrogance to pass away from the earth.

And you, O Lord, shall reign, you alone over all your works on Mount Zion, the dwelling place of your glory, and in Jerusalem, your holy city, as it is written in your Holy Words, The Lord shall reign forever, your God, O Zion, unto all generations. Praise you the Lord.

Holy are you, and dreaded is your name, and there is no God beside you, as it is written, And the Lord of hosts is exalted in judgment, and the holy God is sanctified in righteousness. Blessed are you, O Lord, the holy King.

You have chosen us from all peoples, you have loved us and taken pleasure in us, and has exalted us above all tongues; you have sanctified us by your commandments, and has brought us near unto your service, O our King, and has called us by your great and holy name.

On Sabbath add the words in brackets.

And you, has given us in love, O Lord our God, [this Sabbath day for holiness and rest, and] this Day of Atonement for pardon, forgiveness and atonement, that we may [in love] obtain pardon thereon for all our iniquities; a holy convocation, as a memorial of the departure from Egypt.

But on account of our sins we were exiled from our land, and removed far from our country, and we are unable to fulfil our obligations in your chosen house, that great and holy temple which was called by your name because of the hand that has been stretched out against your sanctuary. May it be your will, O Lord our God and God of our fathers, merciful King, that you may again in your abundant compassion have mercy upon us and upon your sanctuary, and may speedily rebuild it and magnify its glory. Our Father, our King, do you speedily make the glory of your kingdom manifest upon us; shine forth and exalt yourself upon us in the sight of all living; bring our scattered ones among the nations near unto you, and gather our dispersed from the ends of the earth. Lead us with exultation unto Zion your city, and unto Jerusalem the place of your sanctuary, with everlasting joy; and there we will prepare before you the offerings that are obligatory for us, the continual offerings according to their order, and the additional offerings according to their enactment: and the additional offerings of [this Sabbath day and] this day of Atonement we will prepare and offer unto you in love according to the precept of your will, as you have prescribed for us in your Torah through the hand of Moses your servant, by the mouth of your glory, as it is said—

[And on the Sabbath day two he-lambs of the first year without blemish, and two-tenth parts of an ephah of fine flour for a meal offering, mingled with oil, and the drink offering thereof; this is the burnt offering of every Sabbath, beside the continual burnt offering and the drink offering thereof.]

And on the tenth day of this seventh month there shall be a holy convocation unto you; and you shall afflict your souls, you shall do no manner of work. And you shall offer a burnt offering unto the Lord for a sweet savor; one young bullock, one ram, seven he-lambs of the first year; they shall be unto you without blemish. And their meal offering and their drink offerings as has been ordained; three-tenth parts of an ephah for each bullock, and two-tenth parts for the ram, and one-tenth part for each lamb, with wine according to the drink offering thereof, and two he-goats with which to make atonement, and the two continual offerings according to their enactment.

[They that keep the Sabbath and call it a delight shall rejoice in your kingdom; the people that hallow the seventh day, even all of them shall be satiated and delighted with your goodness, seeing that you did find pleasure in the seventh day and did hallow it; you did call it the desirable of days, in remembrance of the creation.]

Our God and God of our fathers, pardon our iniquities [on this Sabbath day, and] on this Day of Atonement; blot out our transgressions and our sins, and make them pass away from before your eyes; as it is said, I, even I, am he that blots out your transgressions for my own sake; and I will not remember your sins. And it is said, I have blotted out, as a cloud, your transgressions, and, as a mist, your sins: return unto me, for I have redeemed you. And it is said, For on this day shall atonement be made for you, to cleanse you; from all your sins shall you be clean before the Lord. [Our God and God of our fathers, accept our rest.] Sanctify us by your commandments, and grant our portion in your Torah; satisfy us with your goodness and gladden us with your salvation; [and let us inherit, O Lord our God, in love and favor, your holy Sabbath and may Israel, who hallow your name, rejoice thereon] and purify our hearts to serve you in truth; for you are the forgiver of Israel and the pardoner of the tribes of Yeshurun in every generation, and beside you We have no king who pardons and forgives. Blessed are you, O Lord, you King who pardons and forgives our iniquities and the iniquities of your people, the house of Israel, who makes our trespasses to pass away year by year, King over all the earth, who sanctifies [the Sabbath and] Israel and the day of Atonement.

Accept, O Lord our God, your people Israel and their prayer; restore the service to the oracle of your house; receive in love and favor both the fire offerings of Israel and their prayer; and may the service of your people Israel be ever acceptable unto you.

And let our eyes behold your return in mercy to Zion. Blessed are you, O Lord, who restores your divine presence unto Zion.

We give thanks unto you, for you are the Lord our God and the God of our fathers forever and ever; you are the Rock of our lives, the Shield of our salvation through every generation. We will give thanks unto you and declare your praise for our lives which are committed unto your hand, and for our souls which are in your charge, and for your miracles, which are daily with us, and for your wonders and your benefits, which are wrought at all times, evening, morn and noon. O you who are all-good, whose mercies fail not; you, merciful Being, whose loving-kindnesses never cease, we have ever hoped in you.

Congregation in an undertone

We give thanks unto you, for you are the Lord our God and the God of our fathers, the God of all flesh, our Creator and the Creator of all things in the beginning. Blessings and thanksgivings be to your great and holy name, because you have kept us in life and has preserved us: so may you continue to keep us in life and to preserve us. O gather our exiles to your holy courts to observe your statutes, to do your will, and to serve you with a perfect heart; seeing that we give thanks unto you. Blessed be the God to whom thanksgivings are due.

For all these things your name, O our King, shall be continually blessed and exalted forever and ever.

O inscribe all the children of your covenant for a happy life.

And everything that lives shall give thanks unto you forever, and shall praise your name in truth, O God, our salvation and our help. Blessed are you, O Lord, whose name is All-good, and unto whom it is becoming to give thanks.

At the repetition of the Amidah by the Reader, the following is introduced—

Our God and God of our fathers, bless us with the three-fold blessing of your Torah written by the hand of Moses your servant, which was spoken by Aaron and his sons, the priests, your holy people, as it is said, The Lord bless you, and keep you: the Lord make his face to shine upon you, and be gracious unto you: the Lord turn his face unto you, and give you peace.

Grant peace, welfare, blessing, grace, loving-kindness and mercy unto us and unto all Israel, your people. Bless us, O our Father, even all of us together, with the light of your countenance; for by the light of your countenance you have given us, O Lord our God, the Torah of life, loving-kindness and righteousness, blessing, mercy, life and peace; and may it be good in your sight to bless your people Israel at all times and in every hour with your peace.

In the book of life, blessing, peace and good sustenance may we be remembered and inscribed before you, we and all your people the house of Israel, for a happy life and for peace. Blessed are you, O Lord, who makes peace.

Our God and God of our fathers,

Let our prayer come before you; hide not yourself from our supplication, for we are not arrogant and stiff-necked, that we should say before you, O Lord our God and God of our fathers, we are righteous and have not sinned; but verily, we have sinned We have trespassed, we have been faithless, we have robbed, we have spoken basely, we have committed iniquity, we have wrought unrighteousness, we have been presumptuous, we have done violence, we have forged lies, we have counselled evil, we have spoken falsely, we have scoffed, we have revolted, we have blasphemed, we have been rebellious, we have acted perversely, we have transgressed, we have persecuted we have been stiff-necked, we have done wickedly, we have corrupted ourselves, we have committed abomination, we have gone astray, and we have led astray.

We have turned aside from your commandments and good judgments, and it has profited us naught. But you are righteous in all that is come upon us; for you have acted truthfully, but we have wrought unrighteousness.

What shall we say before you, O you who dwells on high, and what shall we recount unto you, you who abides in the heavens? Do you not know all things, both the hidden and the revealed?

You know the secrets of eternity and the most hidden mysteries of all living. You search the innermost recesses, and try the reins and the heart. Naught is concealed from you, or hidden from your eyes.

May it then be your will, O Lord our God and God of our fathers, to forgive us for all our sins, to pardon us for all our iniquities, and to grant us remission for all our transgressions.

For the sin which we have committed before you under compulsion, or of our own will;
And for the sin which we have committed before you in hardening of the heart:
For the sin which we have committed before you unknowingly;
And for the sin which we have committed before you with utterance of the lips:
For the sin which we have committed before you by unchastity;
And for the sin which we have committed before you openly and secretly:
For the sin which we have committed before you knowingly and deceitfully:
And for the sin which we have committed before you in speech:
For the sin which we have committed before you by wronging our neighbor;
And for the sin which we have committed before you by the sinful meditating of the heart:
For the sin which we have committed before you by association with impurity;
And for the sin which we have committed before you by confession with the mouth alone:

For the sin which we have committed before you by despising parents and teachers;

And for the sin which we have committed before you in presumption or in error:

For the sin which we have committed before you by violence;

And for the sin which we have committed before you by the profanation of the divine Name:

For the sin which we have committed before you by unclean lips;

And for the sin which we have committed before you by folly of the mouth:

For the sin which we have committed before you by the evil inclination;

And for the sin which we have committed before you wittingly or unwittingly:

For all these, O God of forgiveness, forgive us, pardon us, grant us remission.

For the sin which we have committed before you by denying and lying;

And for the sin which we have committed before you by the taking of bribes:

For the sin which we have committed before you by scoffing;

And for the sin which we have committed before you by slander:

For the sin which we have committed before you in business;

And for the sin which we have committed before you in eating and drinking:

For the sin which we have committed before you by usury and interest;

And for the sin which we have committed before you by the stretched forth neck of pride:

For the sin which we have committed before you by the conversation of our lips;

And for the sin which we have committed before you with wanton looks

For the sin which we have committed before you with haughty eyes;

And for the sin which we have committed before you by effrontery:

For all these, O God of forgiveness, forgive us, pardon us, grant us remission.

For the sin which we have committed before you by breaking off the yoke of your commandments;

And for the sin which we have committed before you by contentiousness:

For the sin which we have committed before you by ensnaring our neighbor;

And for the sin which we have committed before you by envy:

For the sin which we have committed before you by levity;

And for the sin which we have committed before you by being stiff-necked:

For the sin which we have committed before you by running to do evil;

And for the sin which we have committed before you by tale-bearing:

For the sin which we have committed before you by vain oaths;

And for the sin which we have committed before you by causeless hatred:

For the sin which we have committed before you by breach of trust;

And for the sin which we have committed before you with confusion of mind:

For all these, O God of forgiveness, forgive us pardon us, grant us remission.

And also for the sins for which we owe a burnt offering:

And for the sins for which we owe a sin offering:

And for the sins for which we owe an offering, varying according to our means:

And for the sins for which we owe an offering, whether for certain or for doubtful trespass.

And for the sins for which we are liable to the penalty of chastisement:

And for the sins for which we are liable to the penalty of forty stripes:

And for the sins for which we are liable to the penalty of death by the hand of heaven:

And for the sins for which we are liable to the penalty of excision and childlessness:
For all these, O God of forgiveness, forgive us, pardon us, grant us remission;

And also for the sins for which we are liable to any of the four death penalties inflicted by the court,—stoning, burning, beheading, and strangling; for the violation of positive, or for the violation of negative precepts, whether these latter do or do not admit of a remedy by the subsequent fulfilment of a positive command; for all our sins, whether they be or be not manifest to us. Such sins as are manifest to us, we have already declared and confessed unto you, while such as are not manifest unto us, are manifest and known unto you, according to the word that has been spoken, The secret things belong unto the Lord our God; but the things that are revealed belong unto us and to our children forever, that we may do all the words of this Torah. For you are the forgiver of Israel and the pardoner of the tribes of Yeshurun in every generation, and beside you we have no king, who pardons and forgives.

O my God, before I was formed I was nothing worth, and now that I have been formed I am but as though I had not been formed. Dust am I in my life: how much more so in my death. Behold I am before you like a vessel filled with shame and confusion. O may it be your will, O Lord my God and God of my fathers, that I may sin no more, and as to the sins I have committed, purge them away in your abounding compassion though not by means of affliction and sore diseases.

O my God! guard my tongue from evil and my lips from speaking guile; and to such as curse me let my soul be dumb, yea, let my soul be unto all as the dust. Open my heart to your Torah, and let my soul pursue your commandments. If any design evil against me, speedily make their counsel of none effect, and frustrate their designs. Do it for the sake of your name, do it for the sake of your right hand, do it for the sake of your holiness, do it for the sake of your Torah. In order that your beloved ones may be delivered, O save with your right hand, and answer me. Let the words of my mouth and the meditation of my heart be acceptable before you, O Lord, my Rock and my Redeemer. He who makes peace in his high places, may he make peace for us and for all Israel, and say ye, Amen.

May it be your will, O Lord our God and God of our fathers, that the temple be speedily rebuilt in our days, and grant our portion in your Torah. And there we will serve you with awe, as in the days of old, and as in ancient years. Then shall the offering of Judah and Jerusalem be pleasant unto the Lord, as in the days of old, and as in ancient years.

Recite the Blessing of the Priests when the Day of Atonement falls on a week-day.

AFTERNOON SERVICE FOR THE DAY OF ATONEMENT
Amidah.

CONCLUSION SERVICE FOR THE DAY OF ATONEMENT
"Happy are they," etc., "And a redeemer," etc., and "Kaddish."

O Lord, open you my lips, and my mouth shall declare your praise.

Blessed are you, O Lord our God and God of our fathers, God of Abraham, God of Isaac, and God of Jacob, the great, mighty and revered God, the most high God, who bestows loving-kindnesses, and possesses all things; who remembers the pious deeds of the patriarchs, and in love will bring a redeemer to their children's children for your name's sake.

Remember us unto life, O King, who delights in life, and seal us in the book of life, for your own sake, O living God.

O King, Helper, Savior and Shield. Blessed are you, O Lord, the Shield of Abraham.

You, O Lord, are mighty forever, you quicken the dead, you are mighty to save.

You sustain the living with loving-kindness, quicken the dead with great mercy, support the falling, heals the sick, loose the bound, and keep your faith to them that sleep in the dust. Who is like unto you, Lord of mighty acts, and who resembles you, O King, who kills and quickens, and causes salvation to spring forth?

Who is like unto you, Father of mercy, who in mercy remembers your creatures unto life?

Yea, faithful are you to quicken the dead. Blessed are you, O Lord, who quickens the dead.

You are holy, and your name is holy, and holy beings praise you daily. (Selah.)

Now, therefore, O Lord our God, impose your awe upon all your works, and your dread upon all that you have created, that all works may fear you and all creatures prostrate themselves before you, that they may all form a single band to do your will with a perfect heart, even as we know, O Lord our God, that dominion is yours, strength is in your hand, and might in your right hand, and that your name is to be feared above all that you have created.

Give then glory, O Lord, unto your people, praise to them that fear you, hope to them that seek you, and free speech to them that wait for you, joy to your land, gladness to your city, a flourishing horn unto David your servant, and a clear shining light unto the son of Jesse your anointed, speedily in our days.

Then shall the just also see and be glad, and the upright shall exult, and the pious triumphantly rejoice, while iniquity shall close her mouth, and all wickedness shall be wholly consumed like smoke, when you makes the dominion of arrogance to pass away from the earth.

And you, O Lord, shall reign, you alone over all your works on Mount Zion, the dwelling place of your glory, and in Jerusalem, your holy city, as it is written in your Holy Words, The Lord shall reign forever, your God, O Zion, unto all generations. Praise you the Lord.

Holy are you, and dreaded is your name, and there is no God beside you, as it is written, And the Lord of hosts is exalted in judgment, and the holy God is sanctified in righteousness. Blessed are you, O Lord the holy King.

You have chosen us from all peoples, you have loved us and taken pleasure in us, and has exalted us above all tongues; you have sanctified us by your commandments, and brought us near unto your service, O our King, and has called us by your great and holy name.

On Sabbath add the words in brackets.

And you have given us in love, O Lord our God [this Sabbath day for holiness and rest, and] this Day of Atonement for pardon, forgiveness, and atonement, that we may [in love] obtain pardon thereon for all our iniquities; a holy convocation. as a memorial of the departure from Egypt.

Our God and God of our fathers! May our remembrance rise and come and be accepted before you, with the remembrance of our fathers, of Messiah the son of David your servant, of Jerusalem your holy city, and of all your people the house of Israel, bringing deliverance and well-being, grace, loving-kindness and mercy, life and peace on this Day of Atonement. Remember us, O Lord our God, thereon for our wellbeing; be mindful of us for blessing, and save us unto life: by your promise of salvation and mercy, spare us and be gracious unto us; have mercy upon us and save us; for our eyes are bent upon you, because you are a gracious and merciful God and King.

Our God and God of our fathers, pardon our iniquities [on this Sabbath day, and] on this Day of Atonement; blot out our transgressions and our sins, and make them pass away from before your eyes; as it is said, I, even I, am he that blots out your transgressions for my own sake; and I will not remember your sins. And it is said, I have blotted out, as a cloud, your transgressions, and, as a mist, your sins: return unto me, for I have redeemed you. And it is said, For on this day shall atonement be made for you, to cleanse you; from all your sins shall you be clean before the Lord. [Our God and God of our fathers, accept our rest.] Sanctify us by your commandments, and grant our portion in your Torah; satisfy us with your goodness, and gladden us with your salvation; [and let us inherit, O Lord our God, in love and favor, your holy Sabbath; and may Israel, who hallow your name, rejoice thereon]; and purify our hearts to serve you in truth; for you are the forgiver of Israel and the pardoner of the tribes of Yeshurun in every generation, and beside you we have no king who pardons and forgives. Blessed are you, O Lord, you King who pardons and forgives our iniquities and the iniquities of your people, the house of Israel, who makes our trespasses to pass away year by year, King over all the earth, who sanctifies [the Sabbath and] Israel and the day of Atonement.

Accept, O Lord our God, your people Israel and their prayer; restore the service to the oracle of your house; receive in love and favor both the fire offerings of Israel and their prayer; and may the service of your people Israel be ever acceptable unto you.

And let our eyes behold your return in mercy to Zion. Blessed are you, O Lord, who restores your divine presence unto Zion.

We give thanks unto you, for you are the Lord our God and the God of our fathers forever and ever; you are the Rock of our lives, the Shield of our salvation through every generation. We will give thanks unto you and declare your praise for our lives which are committed unto your hand, and for our souls which are in your charge, and for your miracles, which are daily with us, and for your wonders and your benefits, which are wrought at all times, evening, morn and noon. O you who are all-good, whose mercies fail not; you, merciful Being, whose loving-kindnesses never cease, we have ever hoped in you.

Congregation in an undertone

We give thanks unto you, for you are the Lord our God and the God of our fathers, the God of all flesh, our Creator and the Creator of all things in the beginning. Blessings and thanksgivings be to your great and holy name, because you have kept us in life and has preserved us: so may you continue to keep us in life and to preserve us. O gather our exiles to your holy courts to observe your statutes, to do your will, and to serve you with a perfect heart; seeing that we give thanks unto you. Blessed be the God to whom thanksgivings are due.

For all these things your name, O our King, shall be continually blessed and exalted forever and ever.

O seal all the children of your covenant for a happy life.

And everything that lives shall give thanks unto you forever, and shall praise your name in truth, O God, our salvation and our help. Blessed are you, O Lord, whose name is All-good, and unto whom it is becoming to give thanks.

At the repetition of the Amidah by the Reader the following is introduced—

Our God and God of our fathers, bless us with the three-fold blessing of your Torah written by the hand of Moses your servant, which was spoken by Aaron and his sons, the priests, your holy people, as it is said, The Lord bless you, and keep you: the Lord make his face to shine upon you, and be gracious unto you: the Lord turn his face unto you, and give you peace.

Grant peace, welfare, blessing, grace, loving-kindness and mercy unto us and unto all Israel, your people. Bless us, O our Father, even all of us together, with the light of your countenance; for by the light of your countenance you have given us, O Lord our God, the Torah of life, loving-kindness and righteousness, blessing, mercy, life and peace; and may it be good in your sight to bless your people Israel at all times and in every hour with your peace.

In the book of life, blessing, peace and good sustenance may we be remembered and sealed before you, we and all your people the house of Israel, for a happy life and for peace. Blessed are you, O Lord, who makes peace.

Our God and God of our fathers

Let our prayer come before you; hide not yourself from our supplication, for we are not arrogant and stiff-necked, that we should say before you, O Lord our God and God of our fathers, we are righteous and have not sinned; but verily, we have sinned.

We have trespassed, we have been faithless, we have robbed, we have spoken basely, we have committed iniquity, we have wrought unrighteousness, we have been presumptuous, we have done violence, we have forged lies, we have counselled evil, we have spoken falsely, we have scoffed, we have revolted, we have blasphemed, we have been rebellious, we have acted perversely, we have transgressed, we have persecuted, we have been stiff-necked, we have done wickedly, we have corrupted ourselves, we have committed abomination, we have gone astray, and we have led astray.

We have turned aside from your commandments and good judgments, and it has profited us naught. But you are righteous in all that is come upon us; for you have acted truthfully, but we have wrought unrighteousness.

What shall we say before you, O you who dwells on high, and what shall we recount unto you, you who abide in the heavens? Do you not know all things, both the hidden and the revealed?

You give a hand to transgressors, and your right hand is stretched out to receive the penitent; you have taught us, O Lord our God, to make confession unto you of all our sins, in order that we may cease from the violence of our hands, that you may receive us into your presence in perfect repentance, even as fire offerings and sweet savors, for your words' sake which you have spoken. Endless would be the fire offerings required for our guilt, and numberless the sweet savors for our trespasses; but you know that our latter end is the worm, and has therefore multiplied the means of our forgiveness. What are we? What is our life? What is our piety? What our righteousness; What our helpfulness? What our strength? What our might? What shall we say before you, O Lord our God and God of our fathers? Are not all the mighty men as naught before you, the men of renown as though they had not been, the wise as if without knowledge, and the men of understanding as if without discernment? For most of their works are void, and the days of their lives are vanity before you, and the pre-eminence of man over the beast is naught, for all is vanity.

You have distinguished man from the beginning, and have recognized his privilege that he might stand before you; far who shall say unto you, What do you? And if he be righteous what can he give you? But you of your love has given us, O Lord our God [this Sabbath day and] this Day of Atonement to be the end of, as well as the season of pardon and forgiveness for, all our iniquities, that we may cease from the violence of our hands, and may return unto you to do the statutes of your will with a perfect heart. O do you, in your abounding compassion, have mercy upon us, for you delight not in the destruction of the world, as it is said, Seek you the Lord, while he may be found, call you upon him while he is near. And it is said, Let the wicked forsake his way, and the man of iniquity his thoughts; and let him return unto the Lord, and he will have mercy upon him; and to our God for he will abundantly pardon. But you are a God ready to forgive, gracious and merciful, slow to anger, plenteous in loving-kindness, and abounding in goodness; you delight in the repentance of the wicked, and have no pleasure in their death; as it is said, Say unto them, As I live, says the Lord God, I have no pleasure in the death of the wicked; but that the wicked turn from his way and live: turn ye, turn you from your evil ways; for why will you die, O house of Israel? And it is said, Have I at all any pleasure in the death of the wicked, says the Lord God, and not rather that he should return from his way, and live? And it is said, For I have no pleasure in the death of him that dies, says the Lord God; wherefore turn yourselves and live. For you are the pardoner of Israel and the forgiver of the tribes of Yeshurun in every generation, and beside you we have no King who pardons and forgives.

O my God, before I was formed I was nothing worth, and now that I have been formed I am but as though I had not been formed. Dust am I in my life: how much more so in my death. Behold I am before you like a vessel filled with shame and confusion. O may it be your will, O Lord my God and God of my fathers, that I may sin no more, and as to the sins I have committed, purge them away in your abounding compassion though not by means of affliction and sore diseases.

O my God! guard my tongue from evil and my lips from speaking guile; and to such as curse me let my soul be dumb, yea, let my soul be unto all as the dust. Open my heart to your Torah, and let my soul pursue your commandments. If any design evil against me speedily make their counsel of none effect, and frustrate their designs. Do it for the sake of your name, do it for the sake of your right hand, do it for the sake of your holiness, do it for the sake of your Torah. In order that your beloved ones may be delivered, O save with your right hand, and answer me. Let the words of my mouth and the meditation of my heart be acceptable before you, O Lord, my Rock and my Redeemer. He who makes peace in his high places, may he make peace for us and for all Israel, and say ye, Amen.

May it be your will, O Lord our God and God of our fathers, that the temple be speedily rebuilt in our days, and grant our portion in your Torah. And there we will serve you with awe, as in the days of old, and as in ancient years. Then shall the offering of Judah and Jerusalem be pleasant unto the Lord, as in the days of old, and as in ancient years.

"Our Father, our King," is said after the Amidot of the Evening, Morning, and Conclusion Services. On Sabbath this prayer is said only after the Conclusion Service.

The Reader says the following verse, the Congregation repeating it—

Hear, O Israel: the Lord our God, the Lord is One.

The Reader and Congregation say the following three times—

Blessed be His name, whose glorious Kingdom is forever and ever.

The Reader and Congregation say the following seven times—

The Lord, he is God.

The Shofar is sounded.

ORDER OF COUNTING THE OMER
The Omer is counted from the second night of Passover until the night before Pentecost.

Lo, I am about to fulfil the affirmative precept of the counting of the Omer, as it is written in the Torah, And you shall count unto you from the morrow after the day of rest, from the day that you brought the Omer of the wave-offering, seven complete weeks they shall be; until the morrow of the seventh week shall you number fifty days.

Blessed are you, O Lord our God, King of the universe, who has sanctified us by your commandments, and has given us command concerning the counting of the Omer.

1. This is the first day of the Omer.
2. This is the second day of the Omer.
3. This is the third day of the Omer.
4. This is the fourth day of the Omer.
5. This is the fifth day of the Omer.
6. This is the sixth day of the Omer.
7. This is the seventh day, making one week of the Omer.
8. This is the eighth day, making one week and one day of the Omer.
9. This is the ninth day, making one week and two days of the Omer.
10. This is the tenth day, making one week and three days of the Omer.
11. This is the eleventh day, making one week and four days of the Omer.
12. This is the twelfth day, making one week and five days of the Omer.
13. This is the thirteenth day, making one week and six days of the Omer.
14. This is the fourteenth day, making two weeks of the Omer.
15. This is the fifteenth day, making two weeks and one day of the Omer.
16. This is the sixteenth day, making two weeks and two days of the Omer.
17. This is the seventeenth day, making two weeks and three days of the Omer.
18. This is the eighteenth day, making two weeks and four days of the Omer.
19. This is the nineteenth day, making two weeks and five days of the Omer.
20. This is the twentieth day, making two weeks and six days of the Omer.
21. This is the twenty-first, making three weeks of the Omer.
22. This is the twenty-second day, making three weeks and one day of the Omer.
23. This is the twenty-third day, making three weeks and two days of the Omer.
24. This is the twenty-fourth day, making three weeks and three days of the Omer.
25. This is the twenty-fifth day, making three weeks and four days of the Omer.
26. This is the twenty-sixth day, making three weeks and five days of the Omer.
27. This is the twenty-seventh day, making three weeks and six days of the Omer.
28. This is the twenty-eighth day, making four weeks of the Omer.
29. This is the twenty-ninth day, making four weeks and one day of the Omer.
30. This is the thirtieth day, making four weeks and two days of the Omer.
31. This is the thirty-first day, making four weeks and three days of the Omer.
32. This is the thirty-second day, making four weeks and four days of the Omer.
33. This is the thirty-third day, making four weeks and five days of the Omer.
34. This is the thirty-fourth day, making four weeks and six days of the Omer.
35. This is the thirty-fifth day, making five weeks of the Omer.
36. This is the thirty-sixth day, making five weeks and one day of the Omer.
37. This is the thirty-seventh day, making five weeks and two days of the Omer.
38. This is the thirty-eighth day, making five weeks and three days of the Omer.
39. This is the thirty-ninth day, making five weeks and four days of the Omer.

40. This is the fortieth day, making rive weeks and five days of the Omer.
41. This is the forty-first day, making five weeks and six days of the Omer.
42. This is the forty-second day, making six weeks of the Omer.
43. This is the forty-third day, making six weeks and one day of the Omer.
44. This is the forty-fourth day, making six weeks and two days of the Omer.
45. This is the forty-fifth day, making six weeks and three days of the Omer.
46. This is the forty-sixth day, making six weeks and four days of the Omer.
47. This is the forty-seventh day, making six weeks and five days of the Omer.
48. This is the forty-eighth day, making six weeks and six days of the Omer.
49. This is the forty-ninth day, making seven weeks of the Omer.

May the All-merciful restore the service of the temple to its place. May it be your will, O Lord our God and God of our fathers, that the temple be speedily rebuilt in our days, and grant our portion in your Torah. And there we will serve you with awe, as in the days of old, and as in ancient years.

Psalm lxvii.

We beseech you, release your captive nation by the mighty strength of your right hand. Accept the joyful chant of your people, lift us and purify us, O revered God. O you mighty One, guard as the apple of your eye them that meditate upon your unity. Bless them, purify them, have mercy upon them, ever vouchsafe your righteousness unto them. O powerful and holy Being, in your abounding goodness lead your congregation. Turn, you who are the only and exalted God, unto your people, who are mindful of your holiness. Accept our prayer and hearken unto our cry, you who know all secrets. Blessed be His name, whose glorious kingdom is forever and ever.

SERVICE FOR CHANUKAH
The Feast of Dedication lasts eight days. On the first evening a light is kindled, the number of lights being increased by one on each consecutive evening. The Chanukah lights should be kindled as soon as possible after nightfall.

On Friday the lights are kindled before the beginning of the Sabbath.

Before kindling the lights the following Blessings are said—

Blessed are you, O Lord our God, King of the universe, who has sanctified us by your commandments, and commanded us to kindle the light of Chanukah.

Blessed are you, O Lord our God, King of the universe, who wrought miracles for our fathers in days of old, at this season.

The following Blessing is said on the first evening only—

Blessed are you, O Lord our God, King of the universe, who has kept us in life, and has preserved us, and enabled us to reach this season.

After kindling the first light, the following is said—

We kindle these lights on account of the miracles, the deliverances and the wonders which you did work for our fathers, by means of your holy priests. During all the eight days of Chanukah these lights are sacred, neither is it permitted us to make any profane use of them; but we are only to look at them, in order that we may give thanks unto your name for your miracles, your deliverances and your wonders.

In the synagogue Psalm 30 is chanted.

In the home the following Hymn is chanted.

O Fortress, Rock of my salvation, unto you it is becoming to give praise: let my house of prayer be restored, and I will there offer you thanksgivings when you shall have prepared a slaughter of the blaspheming foe, I will complete with song and psalm the dedication of the altar.

Full sated was my soul with ills, my strength was spent with sorrow; they embittered my life by hardship during my subjection to the dominion of Egypt, but God with his great power brought forth the chosen race, while the host of Pharaoh and all his seed sank like a stone into the deep.

To his holy oracle he brought me, yet there also I found no peace, for the oppressor came and led me captive, because I had served strange gods: I had to quaff the wine of bewilderment; I nearly perished, when Babylon's end drew near; through Zerubbabel I was saved after seventy years.

The Agagite (Haman), the son of Hammedatha, sought to cut down the lofty fir tree (Mordecai); but his design became a snare to himself, and his pride was brought to an end. The head of the Benjamite you did exalt, but the enemy's name you must blot out: the many sons he had gotten you did hang upon the gallows.

The Grecians were gathered against me in the days of the Hasmoneans; they broke down the walls of my towers, and defiled all the oils; but from one of the last remaining flasks a miracle was wrought for your beloved, and their men of understanding appointed these eight days for song and praises.

SERVICE FOR PURIM

Before reading the Book of Esther the following Blessings are said—

Blessed are you, O Lord our God, King of the universe, who has sanctified us by your commandments, and has given us command concerning the reading of the Megillah.

Blessed are you, O Lord our God, King of the universe, who wrought miracles for our fathers in days of old, at this season.

Blessed are you, O Lord our God, King of the universe, who has kept us in life, and has preserved us, and enabled us to reach this season.

After reading the Book of Esther say—

Blessed are you, O Lord our God, King of the universe, who does plead our cause, judge our suit and avenge our wrong, who renders retribution to all that hate our soul, and on our behalf deals out punishment to our adversaries. Blessed are you, O Lord, who on behalf of your people Israel deals out punishment to all their adversaries, O God, the Savior.

The following paragraph is omitted after the Reading of the Book of Esther in the morning—

—Who brought the counsel of the heathen to naught, and made the devices of the crafty of none effect, when a wicked man, an arrogant offshoot of the seed of Amalek, rose up against us. Insolent in his riches, he dug himself a pit, and his own greatness laid him a snare. In his mind he thought to entrap, but was himself entrapped, he sought to destroy, but was speedily destroyed. Haman displayed the hatred of his fathers, and stirred up against the children the ancient enmity of the brothers (Esau and Jacob), remembering not the mercy of Saul, through whose compassion for Agag the enemy was born. The wicked plotted to cut off the just, and the unclean was caught in the hands of the pure. (Mordecai's) loving-kindness (to Esther) prevailed over the father's (Saul's) error, but the wicked (Haman) heaped sin upon the sins of his ancestor. In his heart he hid his cunning devices, and sold himself to do wickedness. He stretched forth his hand against God's saints; he gave his silver to cut off the remembrance of them. When Mordecai saw that wrath had gone forth, and that the decrees of Haman were issued in Shushan, he put on sackcloth and wrapped himself in mourning, ordained a fast and sat upon ashes. Who will rise up to atone for error, and obtain pardon for the sin rind iniquity of our fathers? A flower blossomed from the palm tree: lo! Hadassah arose to awaken the merit of those that slept in the grave. Her servants hastened to make Haman drink the wine of the poison of snakes. He rose by his riches, but fell in his wickedness; he made him a gallows, and was himself hanged thereon. All the inhabitants of the world opened their mouths, for the lot of Haman was turned to be our lot. When the righteous was delivered out of the hand of the wicked, and the enemy was put in his stead, the Jews ordained for themselves to celebrate Purim, and to rejoice thereon every year. You did regard the prayer of Mordecai and Esther: Haman and his sons you did hang upon the gallows.

The lily of Jacob rejoiced and was glad when Mordecai was seen in the purple. You have ever been Israel's salvation, and their hope in every generation, to make known that all who hope in you shall not be ashamed, neither shall any be confounded who put their trust in you. Accursed be Haman who sought to destroy me; blessed be Mordecai the Jew; accursed be Zeresh, the wife of him that terrified me; blessed be Esther my protectress, and may Harbonah also be remembered for good.

"But you are holy," etc., to "honorable." On Saturday evening begin "And let the pleasantness," etc. The Reader says Kaddish, omitting "May the prayers," etc. "It is our duty," etc. On Saturday evening say the Conclusion Service.

PRAYERS AND PIETY

The prayers in this book are fundamental elements of the life of pious Jews. Their piety fills their lives and endows them with transcendent meaning. The daily, weekly and annual routines of the observant Jew, as well as the rituals of the life cycle events—with the significances ascribed to them within the system of faith—form the core of Jewish religious life.

The piety Jews practice relates to rituals of the home, village and fellowship, especially those associated with prayer. Rabbinic Judaism expects Jews to practice rituals from morning until night. From the first stirring every dawn, the Jew begins the day with acts of religious significance.

Morning prayers are literally clothed in piety. A man puts on the *tallit* (prayer shawl) and *tefillin* (phylacteries) while reciting the blessings for them. Every pious male obtains and maintains these prized and essential objects of piety in accord with the prescriptions of the rabbis and scribes. He wears these objects to show compliance with the prescriptions of the verses of the Torah that he recites in the *shema* (Deut. 6:4-9, 11:13-21 and especially Num. 15:37-41). Each knot on the four fringes of the *tallit* garment is tied in accord with age-old tradition. The *tefillin* are crafted of select leather, made into cubical containers to hold the small parchments of biblical paragraphs written by trained scribes. The head-*tefillin* has to rest on the worshipper between the eyes on the forehead, neither too high on the head, nor too low on the face. The leather strap that holds it in place has to be tied in accordance with known custom. The wearer understands that the knot of leather that sits at the base of his skull represents the letter *yod*, the third letter of *Shaddai*, one of God's names.

On the leather box of the arm-*tefillin* is inscribed the letter *shin*. The wearer knows that the knot that holds it on his left biceps opposite his heart is a form of the letter *dalet*. Thus as he recites his prayers, the Jew is bound head and heart to God, *Shaddai*. He wears these appurtenances each weekday from the time he reached thirteen, the age of maturity, now commonly called the age of Bar Mitzvah. Obtaining a pair of tefillin from the scribe is the most significant overt sign of achieving adult membership in the rabbinic community.

The standard practice is to wear the *tallit* and *tefillin* during the morning prayers and then to remove them. In some communities in the past, to show extreme piety some few virtuoso rabbis wore them all day as they sat immersed in the study of Torah.

An ordinary Jew may recite prayers in a designated synagogue or study hall, in private, at home, or in any orderly place. For optimal piety he goes to a designated place to pray with a *minyan*, a prayer quorum of ten adult Jews.

Jewish piety centers on stability and repetition. On weekdays Jews gather for the morning, afternoon and evening prayers. Major elements of prayer are repeated with small variations at the three services. A person says the *shema* in the morning and evening services; the *amidah* (standing prayer of eighteen blessings) in the morning afternoon and evening services; the *alenu* (a sublime prayer proclaiming God king) to conclude all three. They add a morning Torah service to the public prayer on Monday and Thursday and on any festival or fast day. For this they read the first section of the seven of the Torah weekly portion that is going to be read during the Sabbath morning service at the end of the work week. This focuses attention on the coming Sabbath celebration and gives those gathered during the week an added opportunity to hear the inspiration of the words of Torah.

During the week a fourth service, the additional prayers, called *musaf*, is added to celebrate special days. On New moons, celebrants add several paragraphs to the regular services and read an appropriate passage from the Torah. They conclude the morning prayers with the recitation of the *amidah*–the standing prayer of eighteen blessings–of the additional service. Likewise on holidays, modifications are made in the regular prayers and the additional *musaf amidah* is appended.

Evening prayers consisted of the *shema*, *amidah* and *alenu*. A widespread custom is to recite the *shema* once more at bedtime. Many believe this protects the person who recites it from harm during the night.

In past times and in Orthodox Judaism today women are not assigned an egalitarian role in traditional rabbinic piety. In accord with the profile of Proverbs 31:10-31, they are assigned instead a life of valor. Piety for the woman in classical Judaism emphasizes more her personal character as wife, mother and homemaker, and less her participation in public rituals of prayer and the synagogue. In many Jewish cultures through the course of history, women were not required or expected to attend the synagogue. One rabbinic expression used to justify these choices is that, "The honor of the princess is in the interior (i.e., in the home, not the synagogue)."

For the Jewish woman, developing good character is elevated to a process of piety. Several meaningful prayers are reserved as acts of piety predominantly for women. Saying special chapters of *tehillim* (chapters from the book of Psalms) especially for the sick–is an act of piety more prevalent among women. Characteristically, lighting candles right before the onset of the Sabbath on Friday evening is a woman's act of piety on behalf of her entire household.

It is deemed a major act of piety to marry, raise children, and to maintain a pious family life. Thus the goal of the union of a man and woman is to create a Jewish pious home. Simple rites of piety marked the life cycle rites of passage in rabbinic tradition. The wedding ceremony creates the pious state of matrimony in a few symbolic stages. Bride and groom often fast and repent from wrongdoing on their wedding day, which some rabbis compared to Yom Kippur.

The writing of the *ketubah* formalizes the matrimony. This Aramaic legal document is given to the wife to protect her interests within the marriage. The writ is often read aloud by a dignified rabbi during the wedding ceremony. During the brief ceremony, the groom places the ring on the bride's finger and recited, "Behold you are sanctified to me in accord with the laws of Moses and Israel." The presiding rabbi or distinguished members of the family or community then recites the seven blessings that allude to the cosmic and mythic biblical accounts of the beginning and end of time, which sanctify the present moment of piety. The concluding blessing in a series of seven declares:

Blessed are You Lord our God King of the Universe who created joy and happiness, bride and groom, gladness, jubilation, cheer and delight, love, friendship, harmony and fellowship." It continued, "Lord our God soon may it be heard in the cities of Judah and the streets of Jerusalem the sounds of joy and happiness, bride and groom, exultation of grooms from their wedding canopy and of children from their joyous banquets." It concluded, "Blessed are you Lord our God who gladdens the groom with the bride."

The wedding is held under a canopy out-of-doors when possible or indoors. Thus it is imbued with the cosmic symbolism of the heavens and with a metaphor for the canopy of the new home. According to tradition, the Divine Presence comes down upon the canopy and angels of heaven cry out that it be God's will that the bride and groom rejoice with one another. After the ceremony, it is a common custom to break a glass, symbolizing both the fragility of the relationship and the sufferings of the Jewish people. The bride and groom then go briefly into a private room, to embody their intimacy. After the wedding feast, the couple continued to celebrate the marriage for one week with special blessings and customs at every festive dinner.

Part of the rabbinic way of life is devotion to children. This starts with the commandment that a father circumcise his son on the eighth day. This practice goes back to Abraham as the most ancient sign of the covenant between God and his chosen people. If the father cannot fulfill his role, he designated a professional *mohel* to carry out the rite. Most often the ceremony is occasion for a public celebration and an obligatory feast. All members of the community are expected to participate in the celebration. Members of the family and distinguished guests receive the honors of carrying and holding the infant before during and after the procedure. All the assembled guests bless the child that he might enter into a life of Torah, marriage and good deeds. The child's name is then announced in public for the first time.

There is no formal ritual to mark the birth of a daughter. However it became a common practice to name one's daughter in the synagogue after being called to the Torah on the Sabbath following the birth.

The motives and goals of piety within Judaism lead to several outcomes: Piety leads to a life of sanctification–*qedushah*–in accord with the *Halakhah*. It leads to a life of awe, love, and fear of God. It results in submission to a higher power engendering a sense of creatureliness. It enables the believer to insure entry into paradise in the "World to come" (i.e., the afterlife or heaven). Jews believe that piety aids in bringing about the messianic era. On the most material level, many believe that piety also results in well-being for the practitioner.

Jews believe that God wants constant contact with the believer, akin to an obsessive love affair, renewed frequently by expected daily affirmations. Constant devotion to the divine provides the perpetual training and conditioning for that relationship. Piety invigorates all the devotions of life, such as marriage, raising children, advancing one's vocation, and contributes to the well-being and wholeness of one's community.

BLESSINGS BEFORE MEALS

On washing the hands, previous to partaking of a meal, say—

Blessed are you, O Lord our God, King of the universe, who has sanctified us by your commandments, and has given us command concerning the washing of the hands.

The following Blessing is said over the bread—

Blessed are you, O Lord our God, King of the universe, who brings forth bread from the earth.

GRACE AFTER MEALS

On Sabbaths and Holy days, and on those days when Tachanun is not said, Psalm cxxvi. is said—

Psalm cxxvi.

A Song of Degrees.—When the Lord turned again the captivity of Zion, we were like unto them that dream. Then was our mouth filled with laughter, and our tongue with exultation: then said they among the nations, The Lord has done great things for them. The Lord has done great things for us; whereat we rejoiced. Bring back our captivity, O Lord, as the streams in the south. They that sow in tears shall reap in joy. Though he goes on his way weeping, bearing the store of seed, he shall come back with joy, bearing his sheaves. The following Introduction is customary if three or more Males, above the age of thirteen, have eaten at table together:

He who says Grace commences thus—

Let us say grace.

The others respond—

Blessed be the name of the Lord from this time forth and forever.

He who says Grace proceeds—

With the sanction of those present,

If there be present ten or more Males above the age of thirteen, the words "our God" are added—

We will bless (our God) him of whose bounty we have partaken.

The others respond—

Blessed be (our God) he of whose bounty we have partaken, and through whose goodness we live.

Persons present who have not partaken of the Meal, say the following—

Blessed be his name, yea, continually to be blessed forever and ever.

He who says Grace replies—

Blessed be (our God) he of whose bounty we have partaken, and through whose goodness we live. Blessed be he, and blessed be his name.

If less than three males above the age of thirteen be present, begin here—

Blessed are you, O Lord our God, King of the universe, who feeds the whole world with your goodness, with grace, with loving-kindness and tender mercy; you give food to all flesh, for your loving-kindness endures forever. Through your great goodness food has never failed us: O may it not fail us forever and ever for your great name's sake, since you nourish and sustain all beings and do good unto all, and provide food for all your creatures whom you have created. Blessed are you, O Lord, who gives food unto all.

We thank you, O Lord our God, because you did give as a heritage unto our fathers a desirable, good and ample land, and because you did bring us forth, O Lord our God, from the land of Egypt, and did deliver us from the house of bondage; as well as for your covenant which you have sealed in our flesh, your Torah which you have taught us, your statutes which you have made known unto us, the life, grace and loving-kindness which you have vouchsafed unto us, and for the food with which you do constantly feed and sustain us on every day, in every season, at every hour.

On Chanukah and Purim add, "We thank you also for the miracles," etc.

For all this, O Lord our God, we thank and bless you, blessed be your name by the mouth of all living continually and forever, even as it is written, And you shall eat and be satisfied, and you shall bless the Lord your God for the good land which he has given you. Blessed are you, O Lord, for the land and for the food.

Have mercy, O Lord our God, upon Israel your people, upon Jerusalem your city, upon Zion the abiding place of your glory, upon the kingdom of the house of David your anointed, and upon the great and holy house that was called by your name. O our God, our Father, feed us, nourish us, sustain, support and relieve us, and speedily O Lord our God, grant us relief from all our troubles. We beseech you, O Lord our God, let us not be in need either of the gifts of flesh and blood or of their loans, but only of your helping hand, which is full, open, holy and ample, so that we may not be ashamed nor confounded forever and ever.

On Sabbath say—

Be pleased, O Lord our God, to fortify us by your commandments, and especially by the commandment of the seventh day, this great and holy Sabbath, since this day is great and holy before you, that we may rest and repose thereon in love in accordance with the precept of your will. In your favor, O Lord our God, grant us such repose that there be no trouble, grief or lamenting on the day of our rest. Let us, O Lord our God, behold the consolation of Zion your city, and the rebuilding of Jerusalem your holy city, for you are the Lord of salvation and of consolation.

On New Moons and Festivals add—

Our God and God of our fathers! May our remembrance rise and come and be accepted before you, with the remembrance of our fathers, of Messiah the son of David your servant, of Jerusalem your holy city, and of all your people the house of Israel, bringing deliverance and well-being, grace, loving-kindness and mercy, life and peace on this day of

On New Moon say—
The New Moon.
On New Year—
Memorial.
On Sukkot—
The Feast of Sukkot.
On the Eighth Day of Solemn Assembly and on the Rejoicing of the Torah—
The Eighth Day Feast of Solemn Assembly.
On Passover—
The Feast of Unleavened Bread.
On Pentecost—
The Feast of Weeks.

Remember us, O Lord our God, thereon for our wellbeing; be mindful of us for blessing, and save us unto life: by your promise of salvation and mercy, spare us and be gracious unto us; have mercy upon us and save us; for our eyes are bent upon you, because you are a gracious and merciful God and King.

And rebuild Jerusalem the holy city speedily in out days. Blessed are you, O Lord, who in your compassion rebuilds Jerusalem. Amen.

Blessed are you, O Lord our God, King of the universe, O God, our Father, our King, our Mighty One, our Creator, our Redeemer, our Maker, our Holy One, the Holy One of Jacob, our Shepherd, the Shepherd of Israel, O King, who are kind and deal kindly with all, day by day you have dealt kindly, do deal kindly, and will deal kindly with us: you have bestowed, you do bestow, you will ever bestow benefits upon us, yielding us grace, loving-kindness, mercy and relief, deliverance and prosperity, blessing and salvation, consolation, sustenance and supports mercy, life, peace and all good: of no manner of good let us be in want.

The All-merciful shall reign over us forever and ever. The All-merciful shall be blessed in heaven and on earth. The All-merciful shall be praised throughout all generations, glorified amongst us to all eternity, and honored amongst us forever lasting. May the All-merciful grant us an honorable livelihood. May the All-merciful break the yoke from off our neck, and lead us upright to our land. May the All-merciful send a plentiful blessing upon this house, and upon this table at which we have eaten. May the All-merciful send us Elijah the prophet (let him be remembered for good), who shall give us good tidings, salvation and consolation.

The following has to be varied according to circumstances—

May the All-merciful bless my honored father, the master of this house, and my honored mother, the mistress of this house, them, their household, their seed and all that is theirs, us also and all that is ours, as our fathers Abraham, Isaac and Jacob were blessed each with his own comprehensive blessing; even thus may he bless all of us together with a perfect blessing, and let us say Amen.

Both on their and on our behalf may there be such advocacy on high as shall lead to enduring peace; and may we receive a blessing from the Lord, and righteousness from the God of our salvation; and may we find grace and good understanding in the sight of God and man.

On Sabbath—
May the All-merciful let us inherit the day which shall be wholly a Sabbath and rest in the life everlasting.
On New Moon—
May the All-merciful renew unto us this month for good and for blessing.
On Festivals—
May the All-merciful let us inherit the day which is altogether good.
On New Year—
May the All-merciful renew unto us this year for good and for blessing.
On the Intermediate Days of Sukkot—

May the All-merciful raise up for us the fallen Tabernacle of David.

May the All-merciful make us worthy of the days of the Messiah, and of the life of the world to come.

On Week-days—

Great salvation gives he to his king.

On Sabbaths, Festivals, and New Moons—

He is a tower of salvation to his king;

And shows loving-kindness to his anointed, to David and to his seed, forevermore. He who makes peace in his high places, may he make peace for us and for all Israel, and say ye, Amen.

O fear the Lord, you his holy ones; for there is no want to them that fear him. Young lions do lack and suffer hunger: but they that seek the Lord shall not want any good. O give thanks unto the Lord, for he is good: for his loving-kindness endures forever. You open your hand, and satisfy every living thing with favor. Blessed is the man that trusts in the Lord, and whose trust the Lord is. I have been young and now I am old; yet have I not seen the righteous forsaken, nor his seed begging for bread. The Lord will give strength unto his people; the Lord will bless his people with peace.

BLESSINGS ON VARIOUS OCCASIONS

Before drinking wine—

Blessed are you, O Lord our God, King of the universe, who creates the fruit of the vine.

Before partaking of food, other than bread, prepared from any of "the five species of grain" (wheat, barley, rye, oats and spelt)—

Blessed are you, O Lord our God, King of the universe, who creates various kinds of food.

After any food, excepting bread—

Blessed are you, O Lord our God, King of the universe,

After wine—

—for the vine and the fruit of the vine;

After partaking of grapes, figs, pomegranates, olives or dates—

—for the tree and the fruit of the tree;

After food prepared as above—

—for the sustenance and the nourishment;

After food prepared as above and wine—

—for the sustenance and the nourishment, the vine and the fruit of the vine;

—for the produce of the field; for the desirable, good and ample land which you vast pleased to give as a heritage unto our fathers, that they might eat of its fruits and be satisfied with its goodness. Have mercy, O Lord our God, upon Israel your people, upon Jerusalem your city, upon Zion the abiding place of your glory, upon your altar and your temple. Rebuild Jerusalem, the holy city, speedily in our days; lead us up thither and make us rejoice in its rebuilding. May we eat of the fruits of the land, and be satisfied with its goodness, and bless you for it in holiness and purity.

On Sabbath—
Be pleased to fortify us on this Sabbath day.
On New Moon—
Be mindful of us on this day of the New Moon.
On Festivals—
Make us rejoice
On Passover—
On this Feast of Unleavened Bread.
On Pentecost—
On this Feast of Weeks.
On Sukkot—
On this Feast of Sukkot.
On the Eighth Day of Solemn Assembly and on the Rejoicing of the Torah—
On this Eighth-day Feast of Solemn Assembly.
On New Year—
Be mindful of us for good on this Day of Memorial. For you, O Lord, are good and beneficent unto all; and we will give you thanks for the land,

After wine—

and for the fruit of the vine. Blessed are you, O Lord, for the land and for the fruit of the vine.

After fruit—

—and for the fruits. Blessed are you, O Lord, for the land and for the fruits.

After food prepared from any of "the five species of grain"—

—and for the sustenance. Blessed are you, O Lord, for the land and for the sustenance.

After food prepared as above and wine—

—for the sustenance and for the fruit of the vine. Blessed are you, O Lord, for the land, the sustenance and the fruit of the vine.

If wine and fruit are partaken of at the same time, begin the blessing thus—

—for the vine and the fruit of the vine, the tree and the fruit of the tree.

and conclude—

—for the land, the vine and the fruits. Blessed are you, O Lord, for the land, the vine and the fruits.

If food prepared from any of "the five species of grain," and Fruit are partaken of at the same time, begin—

—for the sustenance and the nourishment, the tree and the fruit of the tree.

and conclude—

—for the land, the sustenance and the fruits. Blessed are you, O Lord, for the land, the sustenance and the fruits.

If food prepared from any of "the five species of grain," Fruit and Wine are partaken of at the same time, begin—

—for the sustenance and the nourishment, for the vine and the fruit of the vine, for the tree and the fruit of the tree.

And conclude—

Blessed are you, O Lord, for the sustenance and the nourishment, for the vine and the fruit of the vine, for the tree and the fruit of the tree.

All the following Blessings begin with the words, "Blessed are you O Lord our God, King of the universe."

On eating fruit which grows on trees—
—who creates the fruit of the tree.
On eating fruit which grows on the Ground, Herbage, etc.—
—who creates the fruit of the earth.
On partaking of flesh, fish, eggs, cheese, etc., or drinking any liquor except wine—
—by whose word all things exist.
After partaking of any of the aliments referred to in the three preceding blessings—
—who creates many living beings with their wants, for all the means you have created with which to sustain the life of each of them. Blessed be he who is the life of all worlds.
On smelling fragrant woods or barks—
—who creates fragrant woods.
On smelling odorous plants—
—who creates odorous plants.
On smelling odorous fruits—
—who gives a goodly scent to fruits.
On smelling fragrant spices—
—who creates divers kinds of spices.
On smelling fragrant oils—

—who creates fragrant oil.
On witnessing lightning, or on seeing falling stars, lofty mountains, or great deserts—
—who has made the creation.
On hearing thunder—
—whose strength and might fill the world.
At the sight of the sea—
—who has made the great sea.
On seeing beautiful trees or animals—
—who has such as these in your world.
On seeing the rainbow—
—who remembers the covenant, are faithful to your covenant, and keeps your promise.
On seeing trees blossoming the first time in the Year—
—who has made your world lacking in naught, but has produced therein goodly creatures and goodly
trees with which to give delight unto the children of men.
On seeing a sage distinguished for his knowledge of the Torah—
—who has imparted of your wisdom to them that fear you.
On seeing wise men distinguished for other than sacred knowledge—
—who has given of your wisdom to flesh and blood.
On seeing a king and his court—
—who has given of your glory to flesh and blood.
On seeing strangely formed persons, such as giants or dwarfs—
—who varies the forms of your creatures.
On fixing a mezuzah—
—who has sanctified us by your commandments, and commanded us to affix the Mezuzah.
On tasting any fruit for the first time in the season; on entering into possession of a new house or land;
or on using new raiment for the first time—
—who has kept us in life and has preserved us, and has enabled us to reach this season.
On hearing good tidings—
—who are good, and dispenses good.
On hearing evil tidings—
—the true Judge.

The following is said on the appearance of the New Moon—

Blessed are you, O Lord our God, King of the universe, by whose word the heavens were created, and by
the breath of whose mouth all their host. You did assign them a statute and a season, that they should
not change their appointed charge. They are glad and rejoice to do the will of their Master, the truthful
Worker whose work is truth, who bade the moon renew itself, a crown of glory unto those that have
been borne by him from the womb, who in the time to come will themselves be renewed like it, to
honor their Creator for his glorious kingdom's sake. Blessed are you, O Lord, who renews the months.

PRAYERS BEFORE RETIRING TO REST AT NIGHT

Blessed are you, O Lord our God, King of the universe, who makes the bands of sleep to fall upon my eyes, and slumber upon my eyelids. May it be your will, O Lord my God and God of my fathers, to suffer me to lie down in peace and to let me rise up again in peace. Let not my thoughts trouble me, nor evil dreams, nor evil fancies, but let my rest be perfect before you. O lighten my eyes, lest I sleep the sleep of death, for it is you who gives light to the apple of the eye. Blessed are you, O Lord, who gives light to the whole world in your glory.

God, faithful King.

Hear, O Israel: the Lord our God, the Lord is One.

Blessed he His name, whose glorious kingdom is forever and ever.

And you shall love the Lord your God with all your heart, and with all your soul, and with all your might. And these words, which I command you this day, shall be upon your heart: and you shall teach them diligently unto your children, and shall talk of them when you sit in your house, and when you walk by the way, and when you lie down, and when you rise up. And you shall bind them for a sign upon your hand, and they shall be for frontlets between your eyes. And you shall write them upon the door-posts of your house, and upon your gates.

And let the pleasantness of the Lord our God be upon us: and establish you the work of our hands upon us; yea, the work of our hands establish you it.

Psalm xci.

He that dwells in the shelter of the Most High, abides under the shadow of the Almighty. I say of the Lord, He is my refuge and my fortress; my God in whom I trust.—For he shall deliver you from the snare of the fowler, and from the noisome pestilence. He shall cover you with his pinions, and under his wings shall you take refuge: his truth shall be a shield and a buckler. You shall not be afraid of the terror by night, nor of the arrow that flies by day; of the pestilence that walks in darkness, nor of the plague that ravages at noon day. A thousand may fall at your side, and ten thousand at your right hand; it shall not come nigh unto you. Only with your eyes shall you look on, and see the retribution of the wicked.—For you, O Lord, are my refuge.—You have made the Most High your dwelling place; there shall no evil befall you, neither shall any scourge come nigh your tent. For he shall give his angels charge over you, to keep you in all your ways. They shall bear you upon their hands, lest you strike your foot against a stone. You shall tread upon the lion and the adder: upon the young lion and the serpent shall you trample.— Because he has set his love upon me, therefore will I deliver him: I will set him on high, because he knows my name. When he calls upon me I will answer him; I will be with him in trouble: I will deliver him and honor him. With length of days will I satisfy him, and will let him see my salvation. Repeat the last verse.

Psalm iii.

Lord, how are my adversaries increased! Many are they that rise up against me. Many there are which say of my soul, There is no salvation for him in God. (Selah.) But you, O Lord, are a shield about me; my glory and the lifter up of my head. I cry unto the Lord with my voice, and he answers me from his holy mountain. (Selah.) I laid me down and slept; I have awaked, for the Lord sustains me. I will not be afraid of the ten thousands of people that have set themselves against me round about. Arise, O Lord; save me, O my God: for you have smitten all my enemies upon the cheek bone; you have broken the teeth of the wicked. Salvation belongs unto the Lord: your blessing be upon your people. (Selah.)

Cause us, O Lord our God, to lie down in peace, and raise us up, O our King, unto life. Spread over us the tabernacle of your peace; direct us right through your own good counsel; save us for your name's sake; be you a shield about us; remove from us every enemy, pestilence, sword, famine and sorrow; remove also the adversary from before us and from behind us. O shelter us beneath the shadow of your wings; for you, O God, are our Guardian and our Deliverer; yea, you, O God, are a gracious and merciful King; and guard our going out and our coming in unto life and unto peace from this time forth and forevermore.

Blessed be the Lord by day; blessed be the Lord by night; blessed be the Lord when we lie down; blessed be the Lord when we rise up. For in your hand are the souls of the living and the dead, as it is, said, In his hand is the soul of every living thing, and the spirit of all human flesh. Into your hand I commend my spirit; you have redeemed me, O Lord, God of truth. Our God who are in heaven, assert the unity of your name, and establish your kingdom continually, and reign over us forever and ever.

May our eyes behold, our hearts rejoice, and our souls be glad in your true salvation, when it shall be said unto Zion, your God reigns. The Lord reigns; the Lord has reigned; the Lord shall reign forever and ever: for the kingdom is yours, and to everlasting you will reign in glory; for we have no king but you.

The angel who has redeemed me from all evil bless the lads; and let my name be named on them, and the name of my fathers Abraham and Isaac; and let them grow into a multitude in the midst of the earth.—And he said, If you will diligently hearken to the voice of the Lord your God, and will do that which is right in his eyes, and will give ear to his commandments, and keep all his statutes, I will put. none of the diseases upon you, which I have put upon the Egyptians; for I am the Lord that heals you— And the Lord said unto the adversary, The Lord rebuke you, O adversary; yea, the Lord that has chosen Jerusalem rebuke you. Is not this a brand plucked out of the fire?—Behold the bed of Solomon: threescore mighty men are about it, of the mighty men of Israel: they all handle the sword, expert in war; every man has his sword upon his thigh, because of fear in the night.—The Lord bless you, and keep you: the Lord make his face to shine upon you, and he gracious unto you: the Lord turn his face unto you, and give you peace.

To be said three times—

Behold, he that guards Israel will neither slumber nor sleep.

To be said three times—

For your salvation I hope, O Lord. I hope, O Lord, for your salvation. O Lord, for your salvation I hope.

To be said three times—

In the name of the Lord, the God of Israel, may Michael be at my right hand; Gabriel at my left; before me, Uriel; behind me, Raphael; and above my head the divine presence of God.

Psalm cxxviii.

A Song of Degrees.—Happy is every one that fears the Lord, that walks in his ways. When you shall eat the labor of your hands, happy shall you be, and it shall be well with you. Your wife shall be as a fruitful vine, in the recesses of your house: your children like olive plants, round about your table. Behold thus shall the man be blessed that fears the Lord. May the Lord bless you out of Zion: may you see the good of Jerusalem all the days of your life. Yea, may you see your children's children. Peace be upon Israel.

To be said three times—

Stand in awe, and sin not: commune with your own heart upon your bed, and be still. (Selah.)

He is Lord of the universe, who reigned before any creature yet was formed:
At the time when all things were made by his desire, then was his name proclaimed King.
And after all things shall have had an end, he alone, the dreaded one, shall reign;
Who was, who is, and who will be in glory.
And he is One, and there is no second to compare to him, to consort with him:
Without beginning, without end; to him belong strength and dominion.
And he is my God—my Redeemer lives—and a rock in my travail in time of distress;
And he is my banner and my refuge, the portion of my cup on the day when I call.
Into his hand I commend my spirit, when I sleep and when I wake;
And with my spirit, my body also: the Lord is with me, and I will not fear.

MARRIAGE SERVICE

Blessed be he that comes in the name of the Lord; we bless you out of the house of the Lord.

O come, let us worship and bow down; let us knee before the Lord our Maker.

Serve the Lord with joy; come before him with exulting.

Psalm c.

He who is mighty, blessed and great above all beings, may he bless the bridegroom and the bride,

PRAYER OR ADDRESS

Blessed are you, O Lord our God, King of the universe, who creates the fruit of the vine.

Blessed are you, O Lord our God, King of the universe, who has sanctified us by your commandments, and has given us command concerning forbidden marriages; who has disallowed unto us those that are betrothed, but has sanctioned unto us such as are wedded to us by the rite of the canopy and the sacred covenant of wedlock. Blessed are you, O Lord, who sanctifies your people Israel by the rite of the canopy and the sacred covenant of wedlock.

The Bridegroom places the ring upon the forefinger of the right hand of the Bride, and says—

Behold, you are consecrated unto me by this ring, according to the Law of Moses and of Israel.

The Hebrew Marriage Contract is read by the Celebrant, after which the following Seven Benedictions are said—

Blessed are you, O Lord our God, King of the universe, who creates the fruit of the vine.

Blessed are you, O Lord our God, King of the universe, who has created all things to your glory.

Blessed are you, O Lord our God, King of the universe, Creator of man.

Blessed are you, O Lord our God, King of the universe, who has made man in your image, after your likeness, and has prepared unto him, out of his very self, a perpetual fabric. Blessed are you, O Lord, Creator of man.

May she who was barren (Zion) be exceeding glad and exult, when her children are gathered within her in joy. Blessed are you, O Lord, who makes Zion joyful through her children.

O make these loved companions greatly to rejoice, even as of old you did gladden your creature in the Garden of Eden. Blessed are you, O Lord, who makes bridegroom and bride to rejoice.

Blessed are you, O Lord our God, King of the universe, who has created joy and gladness, bridegroom and bride, mirth and exultation, pleasure and delight, love, brotherhood, peace and fellowship. Soon may there be heard in the cities of Judah, and in the streets of Jerusalem, the voice of joy and gladness, the voice of the bridegroom and the voice of the bride, the jubilant voice of bridegrooms from their canopies, and of youths from their feasts of song. Blessed are you, O Lord, who makes the bridegroom to rejoice with the bride.

A glass is broken by the bridegroom.

The Celebrant pronounces the benediction.

Psalm cl.

GRACE AFTER THE WEDDING FEAST
He who says Grace commences thus—

Banish, O Lord, both grief and wrath, and then the dumb shall exult in song. Guide us in the paths of righteousness. Regard the blessing of the children of Yeshurun.

With the sanction of those present we will bless our God, in whose abode is joy, and of whose bounty we have partaken.

The others respond—

Blessed be our God in whose abode is joy, and of whose bounty we have partaken, and through whose goodness we live.

He who says Grace repeats the last sentence, and continues the Form of Service.

At the conclusion of the Grace the Seven Benedictions are said.

SERVICE AT THE CONSECRATION OF A HOUSE

Psalm xxx.

Psalm xv.

A Psalm of David.—Lord, who shall abide in your tent? Who shall dwell in your holy mountain? He that walks blamelessly and works righteousness, and speaks truth in his heart. He that slanders not with his tongue, nor does evil to his fellow, nor brings reproach upon his neighbor. In whose eyes a reprobate is despised; but he honors them that fear the Lord. He that swears to his own hurt, and changes not. He that puts not out his money to usury, nor takes a bribe against the innocent. He that does these things shall never be moved.

Psalm ci. A Psalm of David.

I will sing of loving-kindness and justice: unto you, O Lord, will I sing praises. I will give heed to the way of integrity: O when will you come unto me? I will walk within my house in the integrity of my heart. I will set no base thing before my eyes: I hate licentious deeds; they shall not cleave unto me. A contrary heart shall depart from me: I will know no evil thing. Whoever secretly slanders his neighbor, him will I destroy: him that has a high look and a proud heart will I not suffer. My eyes shall be upon the faithful of the land that they may dwell with me: he that walks in the way of integrity, he shall minister unto me. He that works deceit shall not dwell within my house: he that speaks falsehood shall not abide before my eyes. Morning by morning will I destroy all the wicked of the land: to cut off all the workers of iniquity from the city of the Lord.

Psalms cxxi. (cxxvii, cxxviii, if appropriate).

Psalm cxix.

BETH

Wherewith shall a young man keep his way pure? By taking heed thereto according to your word. With my whole heart have I sought you: O let me not wander from your commandments. Your word have I treasured up within my heart, that I might not sin against you. Blessed are you, O Lord: teach me your statutes. With my lips have I declared all the judgments of your mouth. I have rejoiced in the way of your testimonies, as much as in all riches. I will meditate on your precepts, and look towards your paths. I will delight myself in your statutes: I will not forget your word.

RESH

Consider my affliction, and deliver me; for I do not forget your Torah. Plead you my cause, and redeem me: quicken me according to your promise. Salvation is far from the wicked; for they seek not your statutes. Great are your tender mercies, O Lord: quicken me according to your judgments. Many are my persecutors and my adversaries; yet have I not swerved from your testimonies. I beheld the treacherous dealers, and loathed them; because they observed not your word. See how I love your precepts: quicken me, O Lord, according to your loving-kindness. The sum of your word is truth: and every one of your righteous judgments endures forever.

KAPH

My soul pines for your salvation: I hope for your word. My eyes pine for your promise, while I say, When will you comfort me? For I am become like a wineskin in the smoke; yet do I not forget your statutes. How many are the days of your servant? When will you execute judgment on them that persecute me? The proud have dug pits for me, they who are not after your Torah. All your commandments are faithfulness: they persecute me with falsehood; help you me. They have almost made an end of me on earth; but I forsake not your precepts. Quicken me according to your loving-kindness; so shall I observe the testimony of your mouth.

HE

Teach me, O Lord, the way of your statutes; and I will keep it unto the end. Give me understanding. and I will keep your Torah; yea, I will observe it with my whole heart. Make me to tread the path of your commandments; for therein do I delight. Incline my heart unto your testimonies, and not to covetousness. Turn away my eyes from looking at vanity, and quicken me in your way. Confirm your word unto your servant, which leads unto the fear of you. Turn away my reproach whereof I am afraid; for your judgments are good. Behold, I long after your precepts; quicken me in your righteousness.

Sovereign of the universe! Look down from your holy habitation, and in mercy and favor accept the prayer and supplication of your children, who are assembled here to consecrate this dwelling, and to offer their thanksgiving unto you for all the loving-kindness and truth you have shown unto them. We beseech you, let not your loving-kindness depart, nor the covenant of your peace be removed from them. Shield this their abode that no evil befall it. May sickness and sorrow not come nigh unto it, nor the voice of lamentation be heard within its walls. Grant that the members of the household may dwell together in this their habitation in brotherhood and fellowship that they may love and fear you, and cleave unto you, and may meditate in your Torah, and be faithful to its precepts.

Vouchsafe your blessings unto the master of this I house. Bless, O Lord, his substance, and accept the work of his hands. Keep him far from sin and transgression. Let your grace be upon him, and establish you the work of his hands. May your loving-kindness be with her who looks well to the ways of her household, and may she be mindful that the woman who fears the Lord, she shall be praised. Bestow upon their sons and daughters the spirit of wisdom and understanding. Lead them in the path of your commandments, so that all who see them may acknowledge that they are an offspring blessed of the Lord, blessed with a knowledge of your Torah and with the fear of you. Preserve them from all evil; preserve their lives. May your gracious promise be realized in them, Blessed shall you be when you comes in, blessed when you go out. And even as we have been permitted to consecrate this house, so grant that we may together witness the dedication of your great and holy temple in Jerusalem, the city of our solemnities, speedily in our days. Amen.

SERVICE AT A CIRCUMCISION

Upon the arrival of the Child who is to be initiated into the Covenant of Abraham, those Present at the Ceremony rise and say—

Blessed be he that comes.

The Father of the Child says—

I am here ready to perform the affirmative precept to circumcise my son, even as the Creator, blessed be he, has commanded us, as it is written in the Torah, And he that is eight days old shall be circumcised among you, every male throughout your generations.

The Mohel takes the child, and, placing it upon a seat, says—

This is the throne of Elijah—may he be remembered for good!

For your salvation I have waited, O Lord. I have hoped, O Lord, for your salvation; and have done your commandments. I have hoped for your salvation, O Lord. I rejoice at your word, as one that finds great spoil. Great peace have they who love your Torah; and there is no stumbling for them. Happy is he whom you choose, and causes to approach that he may dwell in your courts.

Those present respond—

O let us be satisfied with the goodness of your house, your holy temple.

The Mohel places the Child upon the knees of the Godfather, and before performing the Circumcision says the following Blessing—

Blessed are you, O Lord our God, King of the universe, who has sanctified us by your commandments, and has given us command concerning the Circumcision.

Immediately after the Circumcision the Father says the following Blessing—

Blessed are you, O Lord our God, King of the universe, who has sanctified us by your commandments, and has commanded us to make our sons enter into the covenant of Abraham our father.

Those present respond—

Even as he has entered into the covenant, so may he enter into the Torah, the nuptial canopy, and into good deeds.

The Mohel continues—

Blessed are you, O Lord our God, King of the universe, who creates the fruit of the vine.

Blessed are you, O Lord our God, King of the universe, who from the womb did sanctify Isaac the well-beloved did set your statute in his flesh, and seal his offspring with the sign of the holy covenant. On this account, O living God our Portion and our Rock, give command to deliver from destruction the dearly beloved of our flesh, for the sake of the covenant you have set in our bodies. Blessed are you, O Lord, who makes the covenant.

Our God and God of our fathers, preserve this child to his father and to his mother, and let his name be called in Israel — the son of —. Let the father rejoice in him that came forth from his loins, and the mother be glad with the fruit of her womb; as it is written, Let your father and your mother rejoice, and let her that bore you be glad: and it is said, And I passed by you, and I saw you weltering in your blood, and I said unto you, In your blood live. Yea, I said onto you, In your blood live. And it is said, He has remembered his covenant forever, the word which he commanded to a thousand generations; (the covenant) which he made with Abraham, and his oath unto Isaac, and confirmed the same unto Jacob for a statute, to Israel for an everlasting covenant And it is said, And Abraham circumcised his son Isaac when he was eight days old, as God had commanded him. O give thanks unto the Lord; for he is good; for his loving-kindness endures forever. This little child — may he become great. Even as he has entered into the covenant, so may he enter into the Torah, the nuptial canopy, and into good deeds.

The Godfather drinks of the Wine; a few drops are given to the Infant, and the Cup of Blessing being Text to the Mother, she also partakes thereof.

GRACE AFTER THE MEAL FOLLOWING A CIRCUMCISION

He who says Grace begins thus—

Let us say grace.

The others respond—

Blessed be the name of the Lord from this time forth and forever.

He who says Grace repeats the last sentence, and continues—

We will give thanks unto your name in the midst of the Faithful: blessed are you of the Lord.

The last sentence is repeated by the company present—

With the sanction of the awful and revered God, who is a refuge in times of trouble, the God girt with strength, the Lord mighty on high, we will give thanks unto your name in the midst of the faithful: blessed are you of the Lord.

With the sanction of the holy Torah, pure and clear, which Moses the servant of the Lord commanded us to be a heritage, we will give thanks unto your name in the midst of the faithful: blessed are you of the Lord.

With the sanction of the priests and Levites I will call upon the God of the Hebrews, I will declare his glory in every region, I will bless the Lord. We will give thanks unto your name in the midst of the faithful: blessed are you of the Lord.

With the sanction of those present I will open my lips in song, yea, my bones shall declare, Blessed is he that comes in the name of the Lord. We will give thanks unto your name in the midst of the faithful: blessed are you of the Lord.

Then proceed, "We will bless," etc.

After "in the sight of God and man," the following is introduced—

May the All-merciful bless the father and mother of the child: may they be worthy to rear him, to initiate him in the precepts of the Torah, and to train him in wisdom: from this eighth day and henceforth may his blood be accepted, and may the Lord his God be with him.

May the All-merciful bless the godfather who has observed the covenant of Circumcision and rejoiced exceedingly to perform this deed of piety; may he requite him for his act with a double recompense, and ever exalt him more and more.

May the All-merciful bless the tender infant that has been circumcised on his eighth day; may his hands and heart be firm with God, and may he become worthy to appear before the Divine Presence three times in the year.

If the Mohel says Grace, one of the Company present says the following paragraph—

May the All-merciful bless him who has circumcised the flesh of the foreskin, duly fulfilling each part of the precept. The service would be invalid of one who is timid and fainthearted, or who failed to perform the three essentials of the ceremony.

May the All-merciful, regardful of the merit of them that are akin by the blood of the circumcision, send us his anointed walking in his integrity, to give good tidings and consolation to the people that is scattered and dispersed among the peoples.

May the All-merciful send us the righteous priest, who remains withdrawn in concealment until a throne, bright as the sun and radiant as the diamond, shall be prepared for him, the prophet who covered his face with his mantle and wrapped himself therein, with whom is God's covenant of life and of peace.

Continue, "May the All-merciful make us worthy," etc.

SERVICE FOR THE REDEMPTION OF THE FIRST-BORN

The first-born Child, if a male, must be redeemed on the thirty-first day of his birth. If, however, the Father be a Cohen or a Levite, or the Mother the daughter of a Cohen or a Levite, they are exempt from the duty of Redemption. Should the thirty-first day fall on a Sabbath or Holyday, the ceremony is postponed until the day following.

The Father, presenting his Child to the Cohen, makes the following declaration—

This my first-born son is the first-born of his mother, and the Holy One, blessed be he, has given command to redeem him, as it is said, And those that are to be redeemed of them from a month old shall you redeem, according to your estimation, for the money of five shekels, after the shekel of the sanctuary, the shekel being twenty gerahs; and it is said, Sanctify unto me all the first-born, whatsoever opens the womb among the children of Israel, both of man and of beast: it is mine.

The Father then places before the Cohen silver to the amount of five selaim or shekels (four dollars), and the Cohen asks—

Which would you rather, give me your first-born son, the first-born of his mother, or redeem him for five selaim, which you are bound to give according to the Torah?

The Father replies—

I desire rather to redeem my son, and here you have the value of his redemption, which I am bound to give according to the Torah.

The Cohen receives the redemption money, and returns the Child to his Father, whereupon the latter says the following Blessing—

Blessed are you, O Lord our God, King of the universe, who has sanctified us by your commandments, and given us command concerning the redemption of the son.

Blessed are you, O Lord our God, King of the universe, who has kept us in life, and has preserved us, and enabled us to reach this season.

The Cohen then takes the redemption money, and, holding it over the head of the Child, says—

This is instead of that, this in commutation for that, this in remission of that. May this child enter into life, into the Torah and the fear of Heaven. May it be God's will that even as he has been admitted to redemption, so may he enter into the Torah, the nuptial canopy, and into good deeds. Amen.

The Cohen places his hand upon the head of the Child, and pronounces the following Benediction—

God make you as Ephraim and Manasseh. The Lord bless you, and keep you: the Lord make his face to shine upon you, and be gracious unto you: the Lord turn his face unto you, and give you peace.

The Lord is your guardian: the Lord is your shade upon your right hand. For length of days, and years of life and peace shall they add to you. The Lord shall guard you from all evil; he shall guard your soul. Amen.

PRAYER TO BE SAID BY A SICK PERSON

Psalm xxiii.

A Psalm of David. The Lord is my shepherd: I shall not want. He makes me to lie down in green pastures: he leads me beside the still waters. He restores my soul: he guides me in the paths of righteousness for his name's sake. Yea, though I walk through the valley of the shadow of death, I will fear no evil; for you are with me: your rod and your staff, they comfort me. You prepare a table before me in the presence of my enemies; you have anointed my head with oil; my cup runs over. Surely happiness and loving-kindness will follow me all the days of my life; and I shall dwell in the house of the Lord for length of days.

Psalm ciii.

A Psalm of David. Bless the Lord, O my soul: and all that is within me bless his holy name. Bless the Lord, O my soul, and Forget not all his benefits: who forgives all your iniquity; who heals all your diseases: who redeems your life from the pit; who crowns you with loving-kindness and tender mercies: who satisfies your mouth with good things; so that your youth is renewed like the eagle's. The Lord executes righteous acts, and judgments for all that are oppressed. He made known his ways unto Moses, his doings unto the children of Israel. The Lord is merciful and gracious, slow to anger, and abounding in loving-kindness. He will not always contend; neither will he keep his anger forever. He has not dealt with us after our sins, nor requited us after our iniquities. For as the heaven is high above the earth, so mighty is his loving-kindness over them that fear him. As far as the east is from the west, so far has he removed our transgressions from us. Like as a father has mercy upon his children, so the Lord has mercy upon them that fear him. For he knows our frame; he remembers that we are dust. As for man, his days are as grass; as the flower of the field, so he flourishes. For the wind passes over it, and it is gone; and the place thereof shall know it no more. But the loving-kindness of the Lord is from everlasting to everlasting upon them that fear him, and his righteousness unto children's children, to such as keep his covenant, and to those that remember his precepts to do them. The Lord has established his throne in the heavens; and his kingdom rules over all. Bless the Lord, you his angels: you mighty in strength that fulfil his word, hearkening unto the voice of his word. Bless the Lord, all you his hosts; you ministers of his that do his will. Bless the Lord, all you his works, in all places of his dominion: bless the Lord, O my soul.

Psalm cxxxix.

For the Chief Musician. A Psalm of David. O Lord, you have searched me, and know me. You know my down-sitting and my uprising, you understand my thoughts afar off. You sift my path and my lying down, and are familiar with all my ways. For while there is not yet a word on my tongue, lo, you, O Lord, know it all. You have beset me behind and before, and laid your hand upon me. Such knowledge is too wonderful for me; it is too high, I cannot attain unto it. Whither can I go from your spirit? or whither can I flee from your presence? If I ascend into heaven, you are there: or if I make the grave my bed, behold you are there. If I take the wings of the morning, and dwell in the uttermost parts of the sea, even there shall your hand lead me, and your right hand shall hold me. If I say, Let deep darkness cover me, and the light about me be night; even the darkness darkens not from you, but the night is light as the day—the darkness is as the light. For you did form my reins: you did weave me together in my mother's womb. I will give thanks unto you, for that I am fearfully and wonderfully made: wonderful are your works and that my soul knows right well. My frame was not hidden from you, when I was made in secret, and curiously wrought in the depths of the earth. Your eyes did see my unshapen substance; and in your book the days, even all of them that were to be formed, were written, and for it also there was one among them. How precious unto me are your thoughts, O God! How great is the sum of them! If I would count them, they are more in number than the sand: when I awake, I am still with you. O that you would slay the wicked, O God: depart from me, you bloodthirsty men: they who mention you for treachery, your adversaries who take the name in vain. Do not I hate them, O Lord, that hate you? And do not I strive with those that rise up against you? I hate them with perfect hatred: they are become my enemies. Search me, O God, and know my heart: try me, and know my thoughts: and see if there be any way of sorrow in me, and lead me in the way everlasting

A prayer of the afflicted when he faints, and pours out his complaint before the Lord. Hear my prayer, O Lord, and let my cry come unto you. Hide not your face from me in the day of my distress: incline your ear unto me; in the day when I call answer me speedily. I beseech you, O Lord, Healer of all flesh, have mercy upon me, and support me in your grace upon my bed of sickness, for I am weak. Send me and all who are sick among your children relief and cure. Assuage my pain, and renew my youth as the eagle's. Vouchsafe wisdom unto the physician that he may cure my wound, and so that my health may spring forth speedily. Hear my prayer, prolong my life, let me complete my years in happiness, that I may be enabled to serve you and keep your statutes with a perfect heart. Give me understanding to know that this bitter trial has come upon me for my welfare, so that I may not despise your chastening nor weary of your reproof.

O God of forgiveness, who are gracious and merciful, slow to anger and abounding in loving-kindness, I confess unto you with a broken and contrite heart that I have sinned, and have done that which is evil in your sight. Behold, I repent me of my evil way, and return unto you with perfect repentance. Help me, O God of my salvation, that I may not again turn unto folly, but walk before you in truth and uprightness. Rejoice the soul of your servant, for unto you, O Lord, do I lift up my soul. Heal me, O Lord, and I shall be healed, save me, and I shall be saved, for you are my praise. Amen, and Amen!

CONFESSION ON A DEATH-BED

I acknowledge unto you, O Lord my God and God of my fathers, that both my cure and my death are in your hands. May it be your will to send me a perfect healing. Yet if my death be fully determined by you, I will in love accept it at your hand. O may my death be an atonement for all the sins, iniquities and transgressions of which I have been guilty against you, Vouchsafe unto me of the bounding happiness that is treasured up for the righteous. Make known to me the path of life: in your presence is fullness of joy; at your right hand are pleasures forevermore.

You who are the father of the fatherless and judge of the widow, protect my beloved kindred with whose soul my own is knit. Into your hand I commend my spirit; you have redeemed me, O Lord God of truth, Amen, and Amen!

When the end is approaching—

The Lord reigns; the Lord has reigned; the Lord shall reign forever and ever. (*To be said three times.*)

Blessed be His name, whose glorious kingdom is forever and ever. (*To be said three times.*)

The Lord he is God. (To be said seven times.)

Hear, O Israel: the Lord our God, the Lord is one.

THE BURIAL SERVICE

On those days on which Tachanun is not said, Psalm xvi. is read instead of the following—

The Rock, his work is perfect, for all his ways are judgment: a God of faithfulness and without iniquity, just and right is he. The Rock, perfect in every work, who can say unto him, What work you? He rules below and above; he kills and makes alive: he brings down to the grave, and brings up again. The Rock, perfect in every deed, who can say unto him, What do you? O you who speak and do, of your grace deal kindly with us, and for the sake of him who was bound like a lamb, O hearken and do. Just in all your ways are you, O perfect Rock, slow to anger and full of compassion. Spare and have pity upon parents and children, for yours, Lord, is forgiveness and compassion. Just are you, O Lord, in killing and in making alive, in whose hand is the charge of all spirits; far be it from you to blot out our remembrance: O let your eyes mercifully regard us for y, Lord, is compassion and forgiveness. If a man live a year or a thousand years, what profits it him? He shall be as though he had not been. Blessed be the true Judge, who kills and makes alive. Blessed be he, for his judgment is true, and his eye discerns all things, and he awards unto man his reckoning and his sentence, and all must render acknowledgment unto him. We know, O Lord, that your judgment is righteous: you are justified when you speak, and pure when you judge, and it is not for us to murmur at your method of judging; just are you, O Lord, and righteous are your judgments. O true and righteous judge! Blessed be the true judge, all whose judgments are righteous and true. The soul of every living thing is in your hand; your right hand is full of righteousness. Have mercy upon the remnant of the flock of your hand, and say unto the angel, Stay your hand. You are great in counsel and mighty in deed; your eyes are open upon all the ways of the children of men, to

233

give unto every one according to his ways, and according to the fruit of his doings. To declare that the Lord is upright; he is my Rock, and there is no unrighteousness in him. The Lord gave, and the Lord has taken away; blessed be the name of the Lord. And he, being merciful, forgives iniquity and destroys not: yea, many a time he turns his anger away, and does not stir up all his wrath.

Psalm xvi.

Michtam of David.—Guard me, O God, for in you do I take refuge. I say unto the Lord, You are my lord: I have no good beyond you. As for the saints that are in the earth, they are the noble ones in whom is all my delight. Their sorrows will be multiplied that have gotten unto themselves another God: their drink offerings of blood will I not pour out, nor take their names upon my lips. The Lord is the portion of my inheritance and of my cup: you maintain my lot. The lines are fallen unto me in pleasant places; yea, I have a delightsome heritage. I will bless the Lord, who has given me counsel: yea, my reins admonish me in the night seasons. I have set the Lord always before me: because he is at my right hand, I shall not be moved. Therefore my heart rejoices and my glory is glad: my flesh also will dwell in safety. For you will not abandon my soul to the grave: neither will you suffer your loving one to see the pit. You will make known to me the path of life: in your presence is fullness of joy; at your right hand are pleasures from evermore.

The coffin is borne from the Hall to the Burial Ground, Those who have not visited the Burial Ground for thirty days, say the following—

Blessed be the Lord our God, King of the universe, who formed you in judgment, who nourished and sustained you in judgment, who brought death on you in judgment, who knows the number of you all in judgment, and will hereafter restore you to life in judgment. Blessed are you. O Lord, who quickens the dead.

You, O Lord, are mighty forever, you quicken the dead, you are mighty to save. You sustain the living with loving-kindness, quicken the dead with great mercy, support the falling, heal the sick, loose the bound, and keep your faith to them that sleep in the dust. Who is like unto you, Lord of mighty acts, and who resembles you, O King, who kills and quickens, and causes salvation to spring forth? Yea, faithful are you to quicken the dead.

When the coffin is lowered into the Grave, the following is said, the sentence being varied according to the gender of the departed—

May he come to his place in peace.

May she come to her place in peace.

On quitting the Burial Ground it is customary to pluck some grass, and to say one of the following sentences—

And they of the city shall flourish like the grass of the earth.

He remembers that we are dust.

All those who have been present at the Interment wash their hands and say—

He will destroy death forever; and the Lord God will wipe away tears from off all faces; and the rebuke of his people shall he take away from off all the earth: for the Lord has spoken it.

They then return to the Hall, and say, "And let the pleasantness of the Lord our God be upon us," to "my salvation."

The following Kaddish is said by children after the Burial of their Parents. On those days on which Tachanun is not said the Kaddish, is substituted.

Mourners.—May his great name be magnified and sanctified in the world that is to be created anew, where he will quicken the dead, and raise them up into life eternal; will rebuild the city of Jerusalem, and establish his temple in the midst thereof; and will up, root all alien worship from the earth and restore the worship of the true God. O may the Holy One, blessed be he, reign in his sovereignty and glory during your life and during your days, and during the life of all the house of Israel, even speedily and at a near time, and say ye, Amen.

Cong. and Mourners.—Let his great name be blessed forever and to all eternity.

Mourners.—Blessed, praised and glorified, exalted, extolled and honored, magnified and lauded be the name of the Holy One, blessed be he; though he be high above all blessings and hymns, praises and consolations, which are uttered in the world; and say ye, Amen.

Cong.—Let the name of the Lord be blessed from this time forth and forevermore.

Mourners.—May there be abundant peace from heaven, and life for us and for all Israel; and say ye, Amen.

Cong.—My help is from the Lord, who made heaven and earth.

Mourners.—He who makes peace in his high places, may he make peace for us and for all Israeli and say ye, Amen.

PRAYER IN THE HOUSE OF MOURNING

After the ordinary Daily Service, the following Psalm (xlix.) is read in the House of the Mourner. On those days on which Tachanun is not said, Psalm xvi. is substituted for Psalm xlix.

Psalm xlix. For the Chief Musician. A Psalm of the Sons of Korah.

Hear this all you peoples; give ear, all you inhabitants of the world: both low and high, rich and poor together. My mouth shall speak wisdom; and the meditation of my heart shall be of understanding. I will incline my ear to a parable: I will open my dark saying to the lyre. Wherefore should I fear in the days of evil, when the iniquity of them that would supplant me compasses me about, even of them that trust in their wealth, and boast themselves in the multitude of their riches? None of them can by any means redeem his brother, nor give to God a ransom for him: (for the redemption of their soul is costly, and must be let alone forever:) that he should still live always, that he should not see the pit. For he will see that wise men die, the fool and the brutish together perish, and leave their wealth to others. Their inward thought is, that their houses shall continue forever, and their dwelling places to all generations; they call their lands after their own names. But man that is in glory abides not: he is like the beasts that perish. This is the way of them that are foolish, and of those who after them take pleasure in their speech. (Selah.) Like sheep they are laid in the grave; death shall be their shepherd: but the upright shall have dominion over them in the morning; and their form shall be for the grave to consume, that there be no habitation for it. But God will redeem my soul from the grasp of the grave: for he will receive me. (Selah.) Be not you afraid when a man becomes rich, when the glory of his house is increased; for at his death he shall carry nothing away; his glory shall not descend after him. Though while he lived he blessed his soul, and though men praise you that you do well unto yourself, he shall go to the generation of his fathers, who shall never see the light. Man that is in glory, but without understanding, is like the beasts that perish.

In addition to the above, other appropriate Psalms, such as Psalms xv; xc; xci; ciii; and xxxix, or such passages as Proverbs xxxi. 10-31, should be read in the House of Mourning.

Psalm xxxix.

For the Chief Musician, for Yeduthun. A Psalm of David.—I said, I will take heed to my ways, that I sin not with my tongue: I will keep my mouth with a bridle, while the wicked is before me. I was dumb, and kept silence, I held my peace, and had no comfort: and my sorrow was stirred. My heart was hot within me; while I was musing the fire kindled: then spoke I with my tongue: Lord, make me to know my end, and the measure of my days, what it is; let me know how fleeting I am. Behold, you have made my days as handbreadths; and my lifetime is as nothing before you: surely every man, though he stand firm, is but a breath. (Selah.) Surely as a mere semblance every man walks to and fro: surely they are disquieted for vanity: he heaps up riches and knows not who shall gather them. And now, Lord, what wait I for? My hope is in you. Deliver me from all my transgressions; make me not the reproach of the foolish. I was dumb, I opened not my mouth; because you did it. Remove your stroke away from me: I am consumed by the blow of your hand. When you with rebukes do chasten man for iniquity, you make his beauty to waste away like a moth: surely every man is a breath. (Selah.) Hear my prayer, O Lord, and give ear unto my cry; hold not your peace at my tears; for I am a stranger with you, a sojourner, as all my fathers were. O spare me, that I may again be glad, before I go hence, and be no more.

O Lord and King, who are full of compassion, in whose hand is the soul of every living thing and the breath of all flesh, who kills and makes alive, who brings down to the grave and brings up again, receive, we beseech you, in your great loving-kindness the soul of — who has been gathered unto his [her] people. Have mercy upon him [her]; pardon all his [her] transgressions, for there is not a righteous man upon earth, who does good and sins not. Remember unto him [her] the righteousness which he [she] wrought, and let his [her] reward be with him [her], and his [her] recompense before him [her]. O shelter his [her] soul in the shadow of your wings. Make known to him [her] the path of life: in your presence is fullness of joy; at your right hand are pleasures forevermore. Vouchsafe unto him [her] of the abounding happiness that is treasured up for the righteous, as it is written, Oh how great is your goodness, which you have laid up for them that fear you, which you have wrought for them that trust in you before the children of men!

O Lord, who heals the broken-hearted and binds up their wounds, grant your consolation unto the mourners: put into their hearts the fear and love of you, that they may serve you with a perfect heart, and let their latter end be peace. Amen.

Like one whom his mother comforts, so will I comfort you, and in Jerusalem shall you be comforted. Your sun shall no more go down, neither shall your moon withdraw itself: for the Lord shall be your everlasting light, and the days of your mourning shall be ended. He will destroy death forever; and the Lord God will wipe away tears from off all faces; and the rebuke of his people shall he take away from off all the earth: for the Lord has spoken it.

SERVICE AT THE SETTING OF A TOMBSTONE

Psalm i.

Happy is the man that walks not in the counsel of the wicked, nor stands in the way of sinners, nor sits in the seat of the scornful. But his delight is in the Torah of the Lord and in his law does he meditate day and night. And he shall be like a tree planted by the streams of water, that brings forth its fruit in its season, whose leaf also does not wither; and whatsoever he does shall prosper. The wicked are not so; but are like the chaff which the wind drives away. Therefore the wicked shall not stand in the judgment, nor sinners in the congregation of the righteous. For the Lord knows the way of the righteous, but the way of the wicked shall perish.

Psalm xv; xvi; xc.

As for man, his days are as grass; as the flower of the field, so he flourishes. For the wind passes over it, and it is gone; and the place thereof shall know it no more. But the loving-kindness of the Lord is from everlasting to everlasting upon them that fear him, and his righteousness unto children's children. Oh that they were wise, that they understood this, that they would consider their latter end. For at his death he shall carry nothing away; his glory shall not descend after him. Mark the innocent man, and behold the upright; for the latter end of that man is peace. The Lord sets free the soul of his servants; and none that take refuge in him shall be condemned. How precious is your loving-kindness, O God! and the children of men take refuge under the shadow of your wings. They sate themselves with the fatness of your house; and you give them to drink of the river of your pleasures. He shall enter into peace; they shall rest on their beds—each one that walks in his uprightness.

Psalm xci; "O Lord and King, who are full of compassion," etc.; Mourner's Kaddish.

MEMORIAL SERVICE FOR THE DEAD

On Holy Days, when the Memorial Service is held, and on the Anniversaries of the Death of Parents, the following is said—

Lord, what is man, that you regard him? Or the son of man, that you take account of him? Man is like to vanity; his days are as a shadow that passes away. In the morning he flourishes, and sprouts afresh; in the evening he is cut down, and withers. So teach us to number our days that we may get us a heart of wisdom. Mark the innocent man, and behold the upright: for the latter end of that man is peace. But God will redeem my soul from the grasp of the grave: for he will receive me. My flesh and my heart fails: but God is the strength of my heart and my portion forever. And the dust returns to the earth as it was, but the spirit returns unto God who gave it. I shall behold your face in righteousness; I shall be satisfied, when I awake, with your likeness.

May God remember the soul of my revered father [mother] who has gone to his [her] repose. May his [her] soul be bound up in the bond of life. May his [her] rest be glorious, with fullness of joy in your presence, and pleasures forevermore at your right hand.

Father of mercy, in whose hand are the souls of the living and the dead, may your consolation cheer us as we remember (on this holy day) our beloved and honored kinsfolk who have gone to their rest, our dear parents, the crown of our head and our glory, whose desire it was to train us in the good and righteous way, to teach us your statutes and commandments, and to instruct us to do justice and to love mercy. We beseech you, O Lord, grant us strength to be faithful to their charge while the breath of life is within us. And may their souls repose in the land of the living, beholding your glory and delighting in your goodness.

And now, O good and beneficent God, what shall we say, what shall we speak unto you? Our needs are many, our knowledge slender. Shame covers us as often as the remembrance of all your love for us rises within our minds. O turn this day in loving-kindness and tender mercy to the prayers of your servants who pour out their souls before you. May your loving-kindness not depart from us. Give us our needful sustenance, and let us not be in want of the gifts of flesh and blood. Remove from us care and distress and fear, shame and contempt. Let your grace be with us, that we may rear our children to keep your commandments and to fulfil your will all the days of their life. O God, take us not hence in the midst of our days. Let us complete in peace the number of our years. Verily we know that our strength is frail, and that you have made our days as handbreadths. Help us, O God of our salvation, to bear ourselves faithfully and blamelessly during the years of our pilgrimage. And when our end draws nigh and we depart this world, be you with us, and may our souls be bound up in the bond of life with the souls of our parents and of the righteous who are ever with you. Amen, and Amen.

NIGHT PRAYER FOR YOUNG CHILDREN

Blessed are you, O Lord our God, King of the universe, who makes the bands of sleep to fall upon my eyes, and slumber upon my eyelids.

May it be your will, O Lord my God and God of my fathers, to suffer me to lie down in peace, and to let me rise up again in peace.

Hear, O Israel: the Lord our God, the Lord is One. Blessed be His name, whose glorious kingdom is forever and ever.

And you shall love the Lord your God with all your heart, and with all your soul, and with all your might.

And these words which I command you this day shall be upon your heart: and you shall teach them diligently unto your children, and you shall talk of them when you sit in your house, and when you walk by the way, and when you lie down, and when you rise up. And you shall bind them for a sign upon your hand, and they shall be for frontlets between your eyes. And you shall write them upon the doorposts of your house and upon your gates.

Blessed be the Lord by day; blessed be the Lord by night. Blessed be the Lord when we lie down; blessed be the Lord when we rise up.

Behold, he that guards Israel will neither slumber nor sleep.

Into your hand I commend my spirit: you have redeemed me, O Lord God of truth.

For your salvation I hope, O Lord.

THE MOURNER'S KADDISH

Mourner

Yis-gad-dal v'yis-kad-dash sh'meh rab-bo, b'ol-mo di-v'ro kir'-u-seh v'yam-lich mal-chu-seh, b'cha-ye-chon u-v'yo-me-chon u-v'cha-yeh d'chol bes yis-ro-el, ba-a-go-lo u-viz-man ko-riv, v'im-ru O-men

Cong. and Mourner

Y'heh sh'meh rab-bo m'vo-rach, l'o-lam ul'-ol-meh ol-ma-yo

Mourner

Yis-bo-rach, v'yish-tab-bach, v'yis-po-ar, v'yis-ro-mam, v'yis-nas-seh, v'yis-had-dor, v'yis-al-leh, v'yis-hal-lol, sh'meh d'kud'-sho, b'rich hu. L'e-lo min kol bir-cho-so, v'shi-ro-so, tush-b'cho-so, v'ne-ch'-mo-so, di-a-mi-ron b'ol-mo, v'im-ru O-men

Y'heh sh'lo-mo rab-bo min sh'ma-yo v'cha-yim, o-le-nu v'al kol yis-ro-el, v'im-ru O-men

O-seh sho-lom bim'-ro-mov, hu ya-a-seh, sho-lom, o-le-nu v'al kol yis-ro-el, v'imru O-men.

RITES OF PASSAGE

While piety and devotion fills all facets of the life of the rabbinic Jew, it is most moving at times of personal passage such as coming of age, passing away or marrying. Selections that follow illustrate several aspects of the pious life.

Creating a household in Israel enables the transmission of the pious culture. No moment more encapsulates that than the dedication of a new house. The rules and Psalms designated for the occasion place the acquisition of material into the context of the spiritual and historical destiny of all Israel.

Visitation of the sick is another example of an act of pure communal devotion that normally would be a subjective encounter undertaken out of the goodness of one's heart. As the texts below show, Judaism distills an objective phenomenology from this pious act and concretizes a set of rules and procedures for the visitation.

The devoted care for the remains of the dead is strongly emphasized within Judaism. The texts below spell out the exacting ways that piety must be invoked in the sacred activity of purification of the body prior to burial. Though piety and devotion are again objectified, this heightens the feelings of involvement in the period of grief that a community undergoes when one of its members passes away.

Remembrance of departed relatives is not a core value in the formal expression of the Judaic systems of religious devotion. Nevertheless, the unveiling of the stone at a relative's gravesite takes on both devotional and ritual significance in the customs outlined in the texts that are cited below. The recitation of the Kaddish prayer at this occasion evinces how a doxological praise of G-d can be taken into a specific context as a prayer of mourning and thus transformed entirely in the minds of the pious who recite it.

Finally, the wedding ceremony shows how cultural rituals can intermix. The new status of the couple who marry reflects a complex combination of material issues, social changes and spiritual dimensions. The ceremony includes the reading of an Aramaic legal document, the recitation of Hebrew blessings and symbolic gestures that meld together the concrete and the imagined in a transition to a newly sanctioned condition for bride and groom within the pious community of Israel.

The rules and texts are drawn from Rabbi Hyman Goldin's, *Hamadrikh: The Rabbi's Guide. A Manual of Jewish Religious Rituals, Ceremonials and Customs (Hebrew Publishing Co., 1939).*

Rules for a Bar Mitzvah

1. On the day a male youth enters his fourteenth year, that is, he is thirteen years and one day old, he becomes *Bar Mitzvah* (i. e., subject to punishment) *(Abot V, 21)*, and is for the first time called up to pronounce a benediction over the Torah. According the opinion of Rabbenu Asher, this rule of law, that a youth of thirteen becomes subject to punishment, was handed down by Moses on Sinai *(Teshubat Rabbenu Asher,* rule 17; *Rashi* ad Abot V, 21)

2. After the Bar Mitzvah has pronounced the second benediction over the Torah, the father pronounces a benediction, without mentioning the name of God or His kingship, thus: "Blessed is He who has released me from the responsibility of this one" *(Orah Hayyim CCXXV, 2, gloss)*

For, before his son has become Bar Mitzvah, the father was held responsible for the actions of his son *(Beer Heteb* ad Orah Hayyim 1. c., note 4).

3. It is the duty of every father to prepare a feast on the day his son becomes Bar Mitzvah (Beer *Heteb* 1. c.).

Special Prayer for a Bar Mitzvah

May He who blessed our ancestors Abraham, Isaac and Jacob, bless this youth who was called up today in honor of God and in honor of the Torah, and to give thanks for all the good that God has done for him. As a reward for this, may the Holy One, blessed be He keep him and grant him life. May He incline his hear to be perfect with Him, to study His Torah, to walk in His ways, to observe His commandments, statutes and judgments. May he be successful and prosperous in all his ways, and may he find grace and mercy in the eye of God and man. May his parents deserve to raise him up to the study of the Torah, to the nuptial canopy and to good deeds. Let us say, AMEN.

Dedication of a House

1. If one builds or buys a house, even if he previously possessed another house, he must pronounce the benediction, "Who has granted us life," etc. *(Berakhot* 54a, 59b; *Maim. Berakhot X,* 1; *Orah Hayyim* CCXXIII, 3).

2. The benediction should be pronounced at the time the purchase is made or upon the completion of the building, although he had not yet made use of the same, as the benediction is pronounced on account of his joy of acquiring the house *(Orah Hayyim* 1. c. 4).

3. It is the custom to prepare a feast and be joyful at celebrating the dedication of a house, and to give charity to the poor. This custom is based on Midrashic dictum *(Tanhuma, Bereshit):* "The Holy One, blessed be He, blessed and sanctified the Sabbath upon completing the world, like a human being who builds a house and makes a feast."

4. The owner of the house should recite these chapters from the Psalms:

PSALM XV.

A Psalm of David:

Lord, who shall sojourn in Your tabernacle? Who shall dwell upon Your holy mountain? —He that walks uprightly, and works righteousness, and speaks truth in his heart. That has no slander upon his tongue, Nor does evil to his fellow, Nor takes up a reproach against his neighbor;

In whose eyes a vile person is despised, but he honors them that fear the Lord;

He that swears to his own hurt, and changes not; He that puts not out his money on interest,

Nor takes a bribe against the innocent.

He that does these things shall never be moved.

PSALM CI.

A Psalm of David:

I will sing of mercy and justice;

Unto Thee, 0 Lord, will I sing praises.

I will give heed unto the way of integrity;

Oh when will you come unto me? I will walk within my house in the integrity of my heart. I will set no base thing before my eyes;

I hate the doing of things crooked;

It shall not cleave unto me;

I will know no evil thing. Who slanders his neighbor in secret, him will I destroy;

Who is haughty of eye and proud of heart, him will I not suffer. My eyes are upon the faithful of the land, that they may dwell with me;

He that walks in the way of integrity, he shall minister unto me. He that works deceit shall not dwell within my house;

He that speaks falsehood shall not be established before my eyes.

Morning by morning will I destroy all the wicked of the land;

To cut off all the workers of iniquity from the city of the Lord.

PSALM *CXXI.*

A Song of Ascents:

I will lift up my eyes unto the mountains:

From wheree shall my help come? My help comes from the Lord, Who made heaven and earth. He will not suffer your foot to be moved;

He that keeps you will not slumber. Behold, He that keeps Israel does neither slumber nor sleep. The Lord is your keeper;

The Lord is your shade upon your right hand. The sun shall not smite you by day, Nor the moon by night. The Lord shall keep you from all evil;

He shall keep your soul. The Lord shall guard your going out and your coming in, From this time forth and forever.

PSALM *XXX.*

A Psalm; a Song at the dedication of the House; of David:

I will extol Thee, 0 Lord, for You has raised me up, And has not suffered my enemies to rejoice over me.

0 Lord my God, I cried unto Thee, and You did heal me;

0 Lord, You brought up my soul from the nether-world;

You did keep me alive, that I should not go down to the pit.

Sing praise unto the Lord, 0 ye His godly ones, and give thanks to His holy name. For His anger is but for a moment, His favor is for a life time;

Weeping may tarry for the night, But joy comes in the morning. Now I had said in my security:

'I shall never be moved.' You has established in Your favor, 0 Lord, my mountain as a stronghold — You did hide Your face; I was affrighted. Unto Thee, 0 Lord, did I call, and unto the Lord I made supplication: 'What profit is there in my blood, when I go down to the pit? Shall the dust praise Thee? Shall it declare Your truth? Hear, 0 Lord, and be gracious unto me;

Lord, be You my helper.' You did turn for me my mourning into dancing;

'You did loose my sackcloth, and gird me with gladness;

So that my glory may sing praise to Thee, and not be silent;

0 Lord my God, I will give thanks unto Thee forever.

Laws for Visiting the Sick

1. It is the duty of every man to visit a person who has fallen sick *(Baba Mesia,* 30b; *Maim. Abel* XIV, 1; *Yoreh Deah* CCCXXXV, 1).

2. The near of kin and friends who are accustomed to visit the sick person's home often, should visit him as soon as they are informed of his sickness. Acquaintances, who were not frequent visitors of his

house, should not call immediately, but should wait until at least three days have elapsed, in order not to spoil his chance of recovery by casting upon him the designation of an invalid. If, however, one is stricken ill suddenly, even acquaintances should visit him immediately (*Yerushalmi Peak* III, 17d; *Maim. Abel* XIV, 5; *Yoreh Deah* CCCXXXV, 1).

3. He who visits the sick frequently is praiseworthy, providing he does not become troublesome to the invalid *(Nedarim 39b; Maim. 1. c., 4; Yoreh Deah 1. c., 2).*

4. The essential feature in the religious duty of visiting the sick is to pay attention to the needs of the invalid, to see what is necessary to be done for his benefit, and to give him the pleasure of one's company; also to consider his condition and to pray for mercy on his behalf. If one visits the sick, but fails to pray for mercy, he does not fulfill his religious duty *(Yoreh Deah 1. c., 4, gloss; Kitzur Shulhan Arukh CXCIII, 3).*

5. When the visitor prays for mercy, he should include the invalid he visits amongst all the sick of Israel, and say thus: "May the Omnipresent have mercy upon you and send you a perfect cure among all the sick of Israel." On the Sabbath and Festivals, he should add: "This is Sabbath (Festival), we are forbidden to complain, but a cure is near, because His mercy is abundant; celebrate the day of rest in peace" *(Shabbat 12b; Maim. Shabbat XXIV, 2).*

6. They who visit the sick should speak with him with judgment and tact; they should speak in such manner so as neither to encourage him with false hopes, nor to depress him by words of despair *(Kitzur Shulhan Arukh CXCIII, 5).*

7. One should visit neither a person suffering from abdominal troubles so as not to put him to disgrace, nor one who is troubled with his eye-sight, nor one who suffers with headaches. A person who is very ill and to whom conversation is difficult should not be visited personally *(Nedarim 48a; Maim. Abel* XIV, 5; *Yoreh Deah* CCCXXXV, 8), but one should call at the door of the house to make inquiries regarding his condition, and to ascertain if he is in need of anything; he should pay heed to his distress and pray for mercy on his behalf *(Yoreh Deah 1. c.).*

8. If a sick person desires to confirm his last will by means of symbolical ceremony of transferring possession *(kinyan),* it may be done even on the Sabbath *(Baba Batra* 156b; *Hoshen ha-Mishpat* CCLIV, 1). If he desires to send for his next of kin, a non-Jew may be hired and sent for them even on the Sabbath *(Orah Hayyim CCCVI, 9).*

9. If a member of the family of the invalid dies, the latter should not be informed thereof so that it may not worry him. If however he does hear about it he should not be told to tear a rent in his garments, so that his distress be not increased *(Yoreh Deah CCCXXXVII).*

10. Immediately upon coining in to visit the sick, one should recite:

And the Lord will take away from you all sickness: and He will put none of the evil diseases of Egypt which you knowest, upon you, but He will lay them upon all them that hate you.

And He said: "If you will diligently hearken to the voice of the Lord your god, and will do that which is right in His eyes, and will give ear to His commandments, and keep all His statutes, I will put none of the diseases upon you, which I have put upon the Egyptians; for I am the Lord that heals you."

Peace, peace to him that is far off and to him that is near, saith the Lord that creates the fruit of the lips; and I will heal him.

Upon going out, one should say:

May the Omnipresent have mercy upon you and send you a perfect cure among all the sick of Israel.

On the Sabbath and Festivals, one should add:

This is Sabbath (Festival), we are forbidden to complain, but a cure is near, because His mercy is abundant; celebrate the day of rest in peace.

Laws of Purification (Taharah) and Shrouds

1. The rite of washing the corpse before burial should not be commenced before the shrouds are ready *(Derekh ha-Hayyim)*

2. It is the custom to make the shrouds of fine white linen, but they must not be too costly (Moed Katan 27b; *Maim. Abel* IV, 1; *Yoreh Deah* CCCLII, 1, 2).

3. Neither a hem nor a knot of any sort may be made while sewing the shrouds, or when dressing the dead *(Minhage Yeshurun* CCX; *Hokhmat Adam).*

4. The shrouds should consist of no less than three garments:
The shirt, the breeches, and the over garment with the girdle. White stockings should be put on the legs of the corpse and a white cap on his head *(Sefer ha-Hayyim).*

5. A dead male should be wrapped in a *tallith* with fringes, and) one of the fringes should be rendered unfit for religious use, to indicate that the dead are exempt from fulfilling the Law. The better procedure, however, is, that instead of rendering one fringe unfit, to put one fringe in the corner pocket of the *tallith* when the body is already in the grave. If the deceased leaves a costly *tallith* in which he prayed during his lifetime, it is not proper to wrap him in an inferior *tallith,* for a person is anxious to be buried in the *tallith* in which he prayed during his lifetime *(Yoreh Deah* CCCLI, 2; *Hokhmat Adam; Kitzur Shulhan Arukh* CXCVII, 1).

6. The body of a dead female must be attended to only by females. In the place of the *tallith,* an additional over garment is placed on her shoulders *(Semahot* XII; *Yoreh Deah* CCCLII, 3; *Derekh ha-Hayyim).*

7. When beginning the washing of the body, respect must be shown to the dead as though he were alive. No idle conversation should be indulged in in the presence of the dead, but it is permissible to speak of the necessary preparations for the funeral. The body must not be moved from place to place by a single person, but it must be performed by two or more persons, to prevent the corpse's legs and hands from being suspended *(Derekh ha-Hayyim; Sefer ha-Hayyim).*

8. Those engaged in attending the dead, shall say the following prayer before commencing their duties *(Ma'abar Yabbok).*

0 God of kindness and mercy, whose ways are merciful and truthful, You has commanded us to practice righteousness and truth with the dead and engage in properly burying them, as it is written *(Deut.* XXI, 23): "But you shall surely bury him." May it therefore, be Your will, 0 Lord our God, to give us fortitude and strength to properly perform our undertaking of this holy task of cleaning and washing the body. and putting on the shroud, and burying the deceased. 0 keep us You from any harm or fault, that we fail not in the work of our hand, and grant that the verse be fulfilled regarding us: "He who observes the commandments shall never know aught of evil." May our merit, in the performance of this work of loving-kindness, prolong our lives in happiness, and may the mercy of God rest on us forever.

9. Purification of the body: The entire body, including the head, should be washed with warm water. The fingers and toes, and well as all other parts of the body, should be thoroughly cleansed the hair of the dead should be combed *(Yoreh Deah* CCCLII, 4 *Hokhmat Adam).*

10. The corpse must be entirely enveloped in a white sheet while being cleansed, and the body should be washed, while half covered, by holding up the ends of the sheet. The washing must be started from the head, and then downward to the feet *(Sefer ha-Hayyim).*

11. Care should be taken not to place the body with its face downward, as that is a degrading position, but it should be inclined, first on one side and then on the other *(Yoreh Deah* CCCLII, 4: *Kitzur Shulhan Arukh* CXCVII, 2).

12. After the body has been thoroughly cleansed, it is placed in a standing position on the ground or upon straw, and nine *kabbim* of water should be poured over the head so that it runs down over the entire body. This last operation constitutes the real purification (*taharah*) (Kitzur Shulhan Arukh CXCVII, 2). While the water is poured over the corpse, the mouth should be covered by hand or otherwise, to prevent the water from running into it. The body is then thoroughly dried *(Derekh ha-Hayyim).*

When pouring the water on the corpse, the following is recited:

And I will pour upon you pure water, and ye shall be cleansed; from all your uncleanness and abomination will I purify you.

13. Concerning the measure of nine *kabbim* there is a diversity of opinion. To comply with the law, it is therefore best to take about twenty-four quarts of water. It is not necessary that the water be poured out of one vessel, as the contents of two or even three vessels may be combined to make up the required quantity. It is, however, necessary to commence pouring out the contents of the second vessel before the first is finished, and from the third before the second is finished. Even when pouring the water out of one vessel, the flow must not be interrupted. Four vessels cannot be combined to be counted as one, even if the water is poured out from all four simultaneously (Magen *Abraham* ad *Orah Hayyim* DCVI, note 9; *Kitzur Shulhan Arukh* CXCVII, 3).

14. Then an egg is beaten with a little wine (the beating should be done in the shell of the egg), and the head of the dead washed therewith *(Yoreh Deah* CCCLII, 4, gloss; *Kitzur Shulhan Arukh* 1. c.. 4).

15. Care should be taken not to allow the fingers of the dead man's hands to remain closed *(Kitzur Shulhan Arukh* 1. c., 5).

16. After having been cleansed, the corpse should not be allowed to remain in the place where the rites of purification had taken place, but it must be placed inside the house towards the door *(Kitzur Shulhan Arukh* 1. c., 6; *Ma'abar Yabok)*

17. The board upon which the corpse was washed must not be turned over *(Kitzur Shulhan Arukh* 1. c.).

18. One must not kiss his dead children, because it is dangerous *(Kitzur Shulhan Arukh* 1. c., 7).

19. If one falls and dies instantly from wounds from which blood issued forth, and there is apprehension that the blood that sustains life was absorbed in his clothes, his body should not be ritually cleansed; he should be interred with his garments and shoes, but above the garments he should be wrapped in a sheet which is called *sobeb*. It is customary to dig up the earth at the spot where he fell, and if blood happens to be there, all that earth upon which blood was found should be buried with him. Only the garments which he wore when he fell are to be interred, but it there were blood-stains on other garments which he did not wear at the time, or if he was placed upon pillows and sheets while the blood was flowing, all these need not be buried with him, but they must be thoroughly washed until no trace of blood remains, and the water should be poured into his grave. If, however, the one who fell and died did not bleed at all, his garments must be removed, and his body must be cleansed and dressed in shrouds, as is done in the case of all other dead persons *(Beer Heteb* ad *Yoreh Deah* CCCLXIV, note 7; *Hokhmat Adam* CLVII, 10; *Kitzur Shulhan Arukh* CXCVII, 9).

20. If blood has flown from the injured body and his clothes were removed, and thereafter he recovered and lived for a few days and then died, he must be cleansed and dressed in shrouds. Even if his body is stained with the blood which issued forth from him, he should be cleansed, for the blood lost during his life-time is not to be regarded; we are only concerned with the blood which one loses while dying, for it is likely that this was the blood that sustains life, or it is possible that the blood sustaining life has become mixed therewith *(Beer Heteb l.c.; Hokhmat Adam* 1. c.; *Kitzur Shulhan Arukh* 1. c., 10).

21. The body of a person that was drowned should be stripped of its clothes, and be treated as required by law in the case of ordinary death. In some communities it is the custom to bury drowned

persons in the clothes in which they are found; such custom should be observed without interference *(Beer Heteb* 1. c.; *Hokhmat Adam* 1. c.; *Kitzur Shulhan Arukh* 1. c., 9).

22. If a woman dies while giving birth, the laws applying to a slain person apply also to her, and if it is known that she hail lost much blood, she must not be cleansed. If the blood had already ceased flowing and then she died, she should be treated as required by law in the case of all other dead persons. In many communities it is customary to cleanse the body of any woman that dies at childbirth; and there are also many other customs prevailing in such cases; such customs should be observed without interference *(Beer Heteb* 1. c.; *Kitzur Shulhan Arukh* 1. c., 11).

23. It is forbidden to derive any benefit from either the dead body or the shrouds, whether it be of a Jew or a non-Jew. Likewise ornamental objects which are attached to the corpse, as for instance a wig tied to, or woven into the hair, or artificial teeth, must be interred with the body, and no one is permitted to derive any benefit therefrom. Such ornamental objects that are not attached to the body, one is permitted to use. In any event, use may be made of articles which are not reckoned as a part of the body, such as jewelry and clothes *(Sanhedrin* 47b—48a; *Erukhin* 47b; *Maim. Abel* XIV, 11; *Yoreh Deah* CCCXLIX, 1, 2).

Dedication of a Tombstone

1. It is an ancient custom in Israel to set up a tombstone in honor of the departed at the head of the grave. Our patriarch Jacob set up a monument on the grave of his wife Rachel, as it is written *(Gen.* XXXV, 20): "And Jacob set up a pillar upon her grave; the same is the pillar of Rachel's grave unto this day." The tombstone is set up so that one should know where to pray, and also that the dead be not forgotten.

This custom is mentioned many times in the Talmud. In the days of the Talmud it had already been the established custom to engrave inscriptions on tombstones, as is evidenced by the expression *(Horayot* 13b): "Others would also include the one who reads the inscriptions on the graves" (vide *Shekalim* II, 5, 7; *Maim. Abel* IV, 4).

2. It is the custom in some localities not to put up a tombstone until twelve months after death, because a tombstone bears marks of distinction and within the twelve months the deceased has anxiety. Another reason for the above custom is, that tombstones are put up so that the dead may not be forgotten, and as a rule the dead is not forgotten until after twelve months *(Berakhot* 58b). But there are other localities where people are not particular in this regard *(Kitzur Shulhan Arukh* CXCIX, 17).

3. It is customary to cover the tombstone with a veil on the day of the unveiling, and before the service is begun for one of the mourners to unveil the stone.

4. Those who have not seen any graves during the preceding thirty days, should recite the prayer on page 125.

ORDER OF SERVICE

PSALM I.

Happy is the man that has not walked in the counsel of the wicked, Nor stood in the way of sinners, Nor sat in the seat of the scornful,
But his delight is in the Torah of the Lord;
And in His law does he meditate day and night.

And he shall be like a tree planted by streams of water,
That brings forth its fruit in its season, and whose leaf does not wither;
And in whatsoever he does he shall prosper.

Not so the wicked;

But they are like the chaff which the wind drives away.

Therefore the wicked shall not stand in the judgment, nor sinners in the congregation of the righteous.
For the Lord regards the way of the righteous;
But the way of the wicked shall perish.

As for man, his days are as grass; as the flower of the field, so he flourishes.

For the wind passes over it, and it is gone; and the place thereof knows it no more.

But the mercy of the Lord is from everlasting to everlasting upon them that fear Him, and His
   righteousness unto children's children.

Oh that they were wise, that they understood this, that they consider their latter end!

For at a man's death he shall carry nothing away; his glory shall not descend after him.

Mark the perfect man, and behold the upright; for the end of that man is peace. The Lord redeems the
soul of His servants; and none of them that take refuge in Him shall be desolate. How precious is Your
loving-kindness, 0 God! and the children of men take refuge under the shadow of Your wings. They sate
themselves with the fatness of Your house; and You give them to drink of the river of Your pleasures. He
shall enter into peace; they shall rest on their beds—each one that walks in his uprightness.

For a woman the following selected verses from Proverbs XXXI are read:
A woman of valor who can find? For her price is far above rubies. The heart of her husband does safely
trust in her,
And he has no lack of gain. She does him good and not evil, all the days of her life. She stretches out her
hand to the poor;
Yea, she reaches forth her hand to the needy. Her husband is known in the gates, when he sits among
the elders of the land. Strength and dignity are her clothing, and she laughs at the time to come. She
opens her mouth with wisdom;
And the Torah of kindness is on her tongue.

She looks well to the ways of her household, and eats not the bread of idleness.

Her children rise up, and call her blessed;
Her husband also, and he praises her:
"Many daughters have done valiantly, but you excel them all."

Grace is deceitful, and beauty is vain;
But a woman that fears the Lord, she shall be praised.

Give her of the fruit of her hands;
And let her works praise her in the gates.

PSALM XV.
Lord, who shall sojourn in Your tabernacle? Who shall dwell upon Your holy mountain?
He that walks uprightly, and works righteousness, and speaks truth in his heart;

That has no slander upon his tongue,
Nor does evil to his fellow,
Nor takes up a reproach against his neighbor;
In whose eyes a vile person is despised, but he honors them that fear the Lord;
He that swears to his own hurt, and changes not;
He that puts not out his money on interest, nor takes a bribe against the innocent.

He that does these things shall never be moved.

The Rabbi delivers a sermon after which the following is said.

PSALM *XXIII*

The Lord is my shepherd; I shall not want.
He makes me to lie down in green pastures;
He leads me beside the still waters.
He restores my soul;
He guides me in straight paths for His name's sake.
Yea, though I walk through the valley of the shadow of death,
I will fear no evil
For You art with me;
Your rod and Your staff, they comfort me.
You prepares a table before me in the presence of my enemies; You has anointed my head with oil; my
    cup runs over.
Surely goodness and mercy shall follow me all the days of my life;
And I shall dwell in the house of the Lord forever.

MEMORIAL PRAYER FOR MALE

0 God, full of compassion. You who dwells on high, grant perfect rest beneath the sheltering wings of
Your presence, among the holy and pure who shine as the brightness of the firmament, unto the soul of
..., son of ... who has gone unto eternity, and in whose memory charity is offered by .... May his repose
be in paradise. May the Lord of mercy, bring him under the cover of His wings, and let his soul be bound
up in the bond of eternal life. May the Lord be his possession, and may his repose be peace. Amen.

FOR FEMALE

0 God, full of compassion, You who dwells on high, grant perfect rest beneath the sheltering wings of
Your presence, among the holy and pure who shine as the brightness of the firmament, unto the soul of
. . . , daughter of . . . . , who has gone unto eternity, and in whose memory charity is offered by ..... May
her repose be in paradise. May the Lord of mercy, bring her under the cover of His wings, and let her
soul be bound up in the bond of eternal life. May the Lord be her possession, and may her repose be
peace. Amen.

ADORATION

It is our duty to render praise unto the Lord of all existing things, and to adore Him, the Creator of
the world, since He has not assigned unto us a portion as He has unto all other nations and families of
the earth.

For we bow the head and bend the knee before the King of kings, the Holy One, blessed be He.

Who spread out the heavens and established the earth, whose seat of glory is in the heavens above, and
whose abode of might is in the loftiest heights. He is our God, there is none else. In truth, He is our King,
there is none beside Him; as it is written in His Torah: "Know this day, and lay it in your heart, that the
Lord, He is God in heaven above and upon the earth beneath."

0 God, may the time not be distant when the glory of Your might be perceived throughout the
world, when abominations will be removed from the earth, and idolatry be no more; when the world
will be perfected under the kingdom of the Almighty, and all mortals will call upon Your name; when all
the wicked of the earth will turn unto Thee. May all the inhabitants of the earth know that to Thee alone
every knee must bend and every tongue give homage. Let them bow before Thee, 0 Lord our God, and

let them give honor to Your glorious name. May they all acknowledge Your kingdom, and do You reign over them. Yea, the kingdom is yours, and to all eternity You will reign in glory; as it is written in Your Torah: "The Lord will reign for ever and ever." And it is said again: "And the Lord will be king over all the earth. On that day the Lord shall be one and His name shall be one."

ORPHAN'S KADDISH

Extolled and hallowed be the name of God throughout the world which He has created. May His kingdom be established in your life-time, and in the life-time of the whole house of Israel, speedily and without delay; and say ye, Amen.
(Congregation and repeated by the orphan.)

May His omnipotent name be praised for ever and ever throughout the world.

May the name of the Holy One be praised, glorified, extolled, magnified, honored, and most excellently adored, in words far surpassing all homage, hymns, praises and eulogies that can be expressed in the world; and say ye, Amen.

May abundance of peace and happy life be bestowed upon us and upon all Israel; and say ye, Amen.

May He, who establishes peace in His high heavens, grant through His mercy peace to us and to all Israel; and say ye, Amen.

Order of the Wedding Ceremony

It is the custom that, when the bride is a virgin, the Rabbi and the bridegroom visit the bride, before the performance of the hupah ceremony. The bridegroom covers the bride's head and face with a veil, while the Rabbi pronounces the following blessing:

Our sister, be you the mother of thousands
of myriads. God make you as Sarah, Rebekah, Rachel and Leah.
May the Lord bless you and keep you. May the Lord let His countenance shine upon
you, and be gracious unto you. May the Lord lift up His countenance upon
you, and give you peace.

The Ketubah (marriage contract) is now written as required by law. The witnesses attesting to the Ketubah must not be related either to the bridegroom or to the bride. Thereafter it is necessary to make a Kinyan (the legal formality of symbolic delivery, the Rabbi handing over a kerchief to the bridegroom), and inform the bridegroom that in doing this he obligates himself to fulfill all the terms and conditions embodied in the Ketubah and to pay the additional sum mentioned therein.

Entrance march: The Rabbi takes his place under the Hupah, facing the entrance.

The bridegroom is led by his father and mother, or their representatives, to the hupah. The Rabbi, upon seeing the groom enter, says:

Barukh haba (may he who comes be blessed).

Under the hupah, the bridegroom is placed facing the Rabbi's right (eastward, if possible), and the Rabbi either recites or chants:

He who is supremely mighty;
He who is supremely praised;
He who is supremely great;
May He bless this bridegroom and bride.

Now the bride is led by her parents, or their representatives, to the hupah. The Rabbi, upon seeing the bride enter, says:

Berukhah habaah (may she who comes be blessed). Then the Rabbi either chants or recites the following:

Mighty is our God.
Auspicious signs, and good fortune. Praiseworthy is the bridegroom. Praiseworthy and handsome is the bride.

In some localities, it is customary to march with the bride around the bridegroom seven times; while in others, they march around three times. Now the bride is placed at the right of the bridegroom, facing the Rabbi's left.

An address may be delivered by the Rabbi at this point.

BETROTHAL BENEDICTIONS

The Rabbi fills a goblet with wine, and recites the following two benedictions over it:

Blessed are you, O Lord our God, King of the universe, who has created the fruit of the vine.

Blessed are you, O Lord our God, King of the universe, who has sanctified us with Your commandments, and has commanded us concerning forbidden connections, and has forbidden us those who are merely betrothed, but has allowed to us those lawfully married to us through *hupah* and betrothal. Blessed are you, O Lord, who sanctifies Your people Israel through *hupah* and betrothal.

The bridegroom and the bride are given to taste from the goblet of wine.

RABBI TO GROOM:

N. N. *(naming the groom):* do you of your own free will and consent, take . . . *(naming the bride)* to be your wife; and do you promise to love, honor and cherish her throughout life? If so, answer YES.

RABBI TO BRIDE:

N. N. *(naming the bride):* do you of your own free will and consent, take . . . *(naming the groom)* to be your husband, and do you promise to love, honor and cherish him throughout life? If so, answer YES.
The Rabbi then appoints two witnesses, who must not be related to either the groom or the bride, to witness the betrothal.

RABBI TO GROOM:

You will now betroth the bride, in the presence of these two witnesses, by placing this ring upon the forefinger of her right hand, and say to her in Hebrew:
HARE AT MEKUDESHET LI BETABAAT ZU, KEDAT MOSHE VEYISRAEL.
Behold, you art betrothed to me with this ring, in accordance with the Law of Moses and Israel.

After this the ketubah (nuptial agreement) is read.

FORM OF KETUBAH

On the (first) day of the week, the . . . day of the month . . ., in the year five thousand, six hundred and . . . since the creation of the world, the era according
to which we are accustomed to reckon here in the city of (name of city, state and country), how (name of bridegroom), son of (name of father), surnamed (family name), said to this virgin ("Widow", or

"Divorcee", as the case may be and so on throughout) (name of bride), daughter of (name of father), surnamed (family name): "Be you my wife according to the law of Moses and Israel, and I will cherish, honor, support and maintain you in accordance with the custom of Jewish husbands who cherish, honor, support and maintain their wives in truth. And I herewith make for you the settlement of virgins, two hundred silver zuzim, which belongs to you, according to the law of Moses and Israel; and (I will also give you) your food, clothing and necessaries, and live with you as husband and wife according to universal custom." And Miss (name of bride), this virgin, consented and became his wife. The wedding outfit that she brought unto him from her father's house, in silver, gold, valuables, wearing apparel, house furniture, and bedclothes, all this (name of bridegroom), the said bridegroom, accepted in the sum of one hundred silver pieces, and (name of bridegroom), the bridegroom consented to increase this amount from his own property with the sum of one hundred silver pieces, making in all two hundred silver pieces. And thus said (name of bridegroom), the bridegroom: "The responsibility of this marriage contract, of this wedding outfit, and of this additional sum, I take upon myself and my heirs after me, so that they shall be paid from the best pan of my property and possession that I have beneath the whole heaven, that which I now possess or may hereafter acquire. All my property, real and personal, even the mantle on my shoulders, shall be mortgaged to secure the payment of this marriage contract, of the wedding outfit, and of the addition made thereto, during my lifetime and after my death, from the present day and forever." (Name of bridegroom), the bridegroom, has taken upon himself the responsibility of this marriage contract, of the wedding outfit and the addition made thereto, according to the restrictive usages of all marriage contracts and the additions thereto made for the daughters of Israel, in accordance with the institution of our sages of blessed memory. It is not to be regarded as a mere forfeiture without consideration or as a mere formula of a document. We have followed the-legal formality of symbolical delivery (*kinyan*) between (name of bridegroom), the son of . . ., the bridegroom and (name of bride), the daughter of . . ., this virgin, and we have used a garment legally fit for the purpose, to strengthen all that is stated above,

AND EVERYTHING IS VALID AND CONFIRMED.

Attested to .... (Witness)

Attested to .... (Witness)

A second goblet of wine is now filled, over which the Rabbi recites or chants the following seven marriage benedictions:

Blessed are you, O Lord our God, King of the universe, who has created the fruit of the vine.

Blessed are you, O Lord our God, King of the universe, who has created all things to Your glory.

Blessed are you, O Lord our God, King of the universe who has created man.

Blessed are you, O Lord our God, King of the universe, who has made man in Your image, after Your likeness, and out of his very self, You has prepared unto him a perpetual fabric. Blessed are you, O Lord. who has created man. May she who is childless (Zion) be exceedingly glad and rejoice when her children shall be reunited in her midst in joy. Blessed are you, O Lord, who gladdens Zion through (restoring) her children.

May You gladden the beloved friends (the newly married couple), as You did gladden Your creature (Adam) in the Garden of Eden in time of yore. Blessed are you, O Lord our God, who gladdens the bridegroom and the bride.

Blessed are you, O Lord our God, King of the universe, who has created joy and gladness, bridegroom and bride, rejoicing, song, pleasure and delight, love and brotherhood, peace and fellowship. Soon may there be heard in the cities of Judah, and in the streets of Jerusalem, the voice of joy and gladness, the voice of the bridegroom and the voice of the bride, the jubilant voice of bridegrooms from their nuptial canopies, and of youths from their feasts of song. Blessed are you, O Lord, who gladdens the bridegroom and the bride.

The bridegroom and the bride are given to taste from the goblet of wine.

A glass is now broken by the bridegroom, and those present proclaim: *"Mazal tov"* (good fortune). The guests wash their hands for the repast, and upon breaking bread say:
Blessed are you, O Lord our God, King of the universe, who causes the earth to yield bread.

Before Grace after the meal, the Rabbi recites or chants the following blessing:
May He who blessed our ancestors Abraham, Isaac and Jacob, bless the bridegroom and the bride and henceforth prosper their ways upon which they walk. May they always find grace and favor in the eyes of those who meet them. May they deserve to build a famous and a praiseworthy house in Israel. May peace reign in their home, and may contentment and happiness be in their hearts all the days of their lives. May He bless with all good the best man and the bride's maid, and all those that are assembled here, and prolong their lives in happiness. May He send blessing and prosperity upon all the work of their hands, as well as upon all Israel, their brethren; and let us say, Amen.

Printed in Great Britain
by Amazon

38020416R00145